Footprints
in the Sands of
Time

Footprints in the Sands of Time

HANK OPDENDRIES

Print information available on the last page.

Rev. date: 04/08/2015

To order additional copies of this book, contact:
Xlibris
1-888-795-4274
www.Xlibris.com
Orders@Xlibris.com
701157

CONTENTS

PREFACE

WE LIVE IN a careless world like in the days of Noah, and many feel that the end is near. Now we have entered a period of excessive air pollution, floods, earthquakes, and warming of the polar ice caps. Strangely enough it was more than thirty below last night, and I began to wonder what happened to the warming trend, although the weather is becoming more extreme in many places and heavy snowstorms are creating havoc in places where there was hardly any snow before. The writer is a person with no education outside the elementary schools as they taught it in prewar Holland. A few years of evening schools and a great deal of self-education have completed my education. Yet I dared to set the impressions of one's lifetime on paper for the betterment or punishment of the reader. I hope you can handle it!

The best years of our lives were wasted on wartimes and later during the immigration period. I believe that we were put in these situations because all that happens is under God's guiding control.

Much of our efforts were directed to raising our families and, last but not least, to building and maintaining of schools and churches.

These memoirs cover the lives of ordinary people and the way they were living in the twentieth century. Life was simple and uncomplicated but by no means easy especially during the hungry thirties.

It started with the horse-and-buggy days when everything moved by foot-and-hoof locomotion. Humankind made giant steps after that time—from horse and buggy to bicycle to automobile, from that to air travel and airplanes, and eventually to nuclear devices and bombs. All these inventions are hovering over us and making us believe we no longer need a savior. Needless to say, these inconveniences have created a difficult time for our teenagers, since they are bombarded with programs that are not God's nature.

It scares me to look at the lessons God has taught me and the judgment He will eventually reign down. It won't be long before a leader like Adolf Hitler will come on the scene again and lead an unresponsive world to total destruction.

HANK OPDENDRIES

Dedication: I dedicate this to my loving wife of sixty-three years. She has stuck by me through it all, and I wouldn't be here without her.

Acknowledgements: Thanks to Carolyn Wordstar and her husband for doing some editing; to my brother, Adolf, and his granddaughter, Cherie, who copied the pictures of this book with great enthusiasm; and to my daughter, Irene Manning, and my granddaughter, Alexandria Manning, for helping to get my story and my message out there for people to read and remember.

CHAPTER 1

WISHFUL JOURNEY

I T IS 1995, November 3, and cold outside, so I have decided to
start my memoirs after I had the heartbreaking experience of
losing a complete document due to a power failure! Our very beginnings
were in a little town in the Netherlands, a place close to the German
border. This town of my birth was nestled between two woodland hills.
Snug as a bug in a rug!

We used to call these hills "the Mountains," and we were very proud
of the imposing structures. They were our own private little worlds, and
we felt safe and secure in the presence of those sand dunes and heater
fields.

It was not much more than sand dunes—but we did not realize this
then. We revered those "Mountains" as only small-time buggers can
do because our life was so uncomplicated. Life in my childhood was so
simple that people would come out in droves when a new contraption
called an automobile made its way through the dusty gravel roads.
Mothers would warn their children to stay behind the safety of their
collective skirts, and the farmers would watch with anxious eyes for the
welfare of their cows and horses. You could never know what would
happen when those machines made their way under hacking, coughing,
and thundering explosions when the old-time engines backfired.

Some farms were still around, close to the center of town, and it was
quite common to see some schoolchildren with a herd of cattle right on
Main Street. All traffic had to come to a standstill as the mooing and
bellowing crowds made their way to their home or pasture.

My brothers would bring the milk cows to the pasture in the
morning and haul them home at night—a distance of about one

kilometer—and they would feel very privileged that they allowed them to do this important assignment. It also turned them into little capitalists. The owner of the cows paid them two pennies a week, and that set them apart from the lower-class neighborhood kids. They were men of substance, and the other children would be jealous of my privileged bigger brothers.

The ruling powers of the day had named this town the Pearl of the Province, trying to attract an ever-increasing tourist publicity, although not much tourism was there at that point in time. Everything moved by foot or bicycle.

Many people worked from eight in the morning until six in the evening, five days in a week, and four hours on Saturdays. All this for about two or three guilders a week—and people were glad to have work. This was in the early thirties, and the crisis years were just around the corner. Nobody in his right mind would walk or ride a bicycle more than what was strictly necessary in those days. An effort like that was just too tiresome unless you had pressing business. Fortunately, it did not occur all that often.

We were in the horse and horse-buggy days after all. The pace of life was slow and sure. Saturday afternoon was for relaxation or for puttering around with the rabbits and the pigeons. Rabbits were the milk cows of the poor men, and pigeons were for the more-enterprising folks. Many pigeon milkers, as they called them, would spend all their free time in their pigeon houses built into the roof of the home—more often than not! They treated those little birds like members of the family, and their owners would spend more time with the birds than with their wives.

Buses or trains sent these homing pigeons all the way to Belgium or even further. It was here that the expert could show off his knowledge and expertise. It was a matter of great pride to see your pigeon come in as number one—just by instinct and strength of muscle and feather. Many of these men would speculate their hard-earned money on the expertise of those little birds.

Our parents did not approve of this kind of sport. Our Saturdays were spent in preparation for Sunday. Sunday was set aside for the service of the Lord. It was a day of rest and worship. The devoted believers of those days would not even ride a bicycle on a Sunday unless there was an emergency, and even then it had to be a serious event!

The generation of this day looks down on those early Christians. "They were so simpleminded, you know!"

I wonder at times, is Sunday celebrated better in these days of fast-moving cars and miniskirt women? Oops! I had to throw that in.

Occasionally we would go for a walk in our Creator's handiwork: the forest with the ageless pine trees that spread their branches reaching for heaven, like shriveled old men, bent over and vulnerable in their sand-blasted resting places.

On our travels we would be passing the so-called folks' gardens winding their way up into the heather fields on the far horizon. A purple blanket of heather, which was a feast for our eyes, would welcome us and place us in a completely different world.

This would happen on those days that my parents could do so. They were just too tired most of the time.

The country to the west was as ageless as the sea and just as enduring. The hills on that side were slowly undulating to a horizon that was lost many days of the year in misty, cloudy skies. Low-hanging clouds appeared to hug the tree-filled skyline of mostly pine and poplars with a sprinkling of birch and other deciduous trees.

Suddenly, the sun would break through and create a completely different landscape. Sun and shade would be playing over that beautiful blanket of purple heather that wound its way up the sloping hillside. Further up, it would be mellowed by the sobering abundance of so-called gin trees to lose itself into the variation of the more-subdued color facets of every shape and hue. Then the gin trees, as lonely centennials in their prickly ugliness, were just as ageless as the sheepfold, complete with shepherd and sheepdog, adding to the wholesome picture of undisturbed peace and quiet.

It is hard to understand that those sheep could find enough to eat in that sparse environment of bunt grass and woody heather plant. Nevertheless, these hardy animals seemed to do good enough on this diet of grass and heather. Heather plants may be hard to swallow, but they are beautiful to look at when they are in full bloom. The little purple buds around a crown of lilac stems set into the rust-colored background of the hardy plant make for a wonderwork of color and harmony.

All this formed a panorama that is far beyond anything that human hands can create. The Creator's hand has thrown this abundance all over His creation in an almost callous way. He has all that beauty in the palm of His hand and much to spare. We have seen this many times, and never more so than in the present time of TV and deep-sea diving.

Even the deep sea is full of color of unknown dimension in places that no ordinary human has ever been or will ever be! Schools of fish of unbelievable beauty and variation of color swirl back and forth over and under all things. Everything is in unison of movement that is amazing and wonderful.

The most ardent researcher cannot explain this play of movement in unknown dimensions set out against a background setting of swaying plant growth in a watery world in a mixture of blue and turquoise color. All this makes you wonder when you look at the pictures of the deep-sea divers of the modern age.

However, this was in the far future at the time when we were little children. Nobody could foresee the present explosion of knowledge that is so evident and common today. The country to the east lost itself in the heather and peat lands where the ordinary working man dug the light-colored peat briquettes and dried them into four-by-eight squares called turf. This was the heating material that would be warming the poor man twice—first, when he poured out his sweat to dig the stuff in the hot and humid summer days and, later, in the cold winter weather conditions when he sat with his family huddled around the potbellied stove with a cup of chocolate milk, if he were that fortunate.

We will hear more of that east country later! I wanted to show you the setting and the surroundings of . . .

CHAPTER 2

MY HOMETOWN!

I T IS IN this little town where our story begins.
Dad was a quiet little man with an unpredictable wisdom
that was as hard to fathom as a quiet mountain lake that has great
depths and unknown riches. The common folk wisdom describes this
so nicely with the saying, "Quiet waters have often great depths!" (Still
waters run deep) That was how my dad was.

Our mother explained to us in one of her colorful stories that her
brothers were teasing her with that giant of a man in leather boots and
corduroy pants. The Goliath of the high country, they would call him.
This was in the time before they were married in the days of wine and
roses, before the thorns and ten children made inroads into their happy
ignorance.

Dad proved them all wrong. He was a giant of a man in his own
right. He was his own man whom money or favor could not buy. He
was the leader of a labor union that was the underdog in their battle
with high finance.

The management offered him an easier lifestyle when the going
was tough and many were unemployed. He refused! He wanted to be
one with the other union members. A deal like that would have put a
distance between him and his fellow workers. He did not want that! The
great Goliath stood his ground. They could not buy him at any price.

It reminds us a little bit of Moses in Egypt when the Israelites fell
on hard times (just a little, mind you!). Dad was a man of high morals
and way ahead of his time.

For instance, our father did not allow us to make fun of anyone
who was different in any shape or form, whether it was by religious

conviction or merely handicapped by shape or birth. It is a fact that we knew every person was different.

Some were Catholic, some were Reformed, and others were from different denominations of every shape and color. All this made no difference to our parents. They believed all to be serving the same Lord unless they showed that they were faking a faith life that was not theirs because they practiced the wrong way of living.

It was this kind of thinking that shaped our neighborhood relations, and more importantly, it shaped our outlook on life. We are from a gypsy offspring, according to some unconfirmed story. This may or may not be true. Nevertheless, it would explain our great love for music and our emotional approach to many situations in life and also our somewhat reckless nature!

Whatever the case, my father was a king among men, as he has proven time and again in his later life.

People have named my mother "a mother in Israel"—and rightly so! She had a most endearing quality that seemed to reach out to others no matter what the circumstances or personalities are, the invisible quality of touching the heart when others are lost or uncaring.

It happened once that an older man went to the hospital to comfort Mother when she was sick. He came back from that visit and said in amazement, "I went over there to bring comfort to her and came back from that visit being comforted!"

That was our mother all right. Always giving!

She came out of a large family. They told us that her grandparents were not all that church-minded. The family fell on hard times, and there was no one around to help them in their time of need. This changed when a Gereformeerde minister gave the growing family living quarters and the means to make a living. It was this minister who changed their lives, and they became Christians.

It was not so much the preaching of that minister that changed their lives but this man's action when the family was in need. His action was the better sermon and was giving the better witness by far. All the members in that family became members of the invisible church of the Living Savior. His actions gave quite a testimony to the humane attitude of that humble minister in days long ago.

A sister of my mother got married to our neighbor who was living across the road from us. (You will read more about this man and his family later.) This woman died at a young age after she had three children with this man.

Mom's parents raised the third son in that family under the influence of my mother's brothers. It put a lasting impression on this young man's approach to life, and afterward, he was always attracted or drawn to my mother and her children.

The brothers of my mother were more inclined to reach for a higher education, except my uncle Hank, who was a bicycle repairman, and one other uncle who turned out to be the black sheep of the family, as it appeared to be then.

This man was a happy-go-lucky kind of guy, since his life was a big game of change—whatever might have been the case! He could have been the best of them all. Uncle Gerritjan was his name, and he moved to Canada in the early twenties. He came back to Holland with the liberation armies that liberated Holland during the war.

The army brass had promoted him to a higher rank on several occasions, but he would promptly get in trouble and be demoted again. He felt more at home with his bosom buddies. It was a character trend in our family as far as I can remember.

Let us return to my mother. She would sing psalms most of the day with great abandon and a joyful spirit of which nothing was make-believe. It came straight from the heart. It was a joy to behold and hear her sing songs of a lighter genre. She would sing with complete abandon, giving it the full treatment, and the words she did not know or had forgotten she invented with sometimes hilarious results.

She had some kind of eye sickness when we were children. Help was hard to come by, and medicine was relatively simple in those days, not nearly as far advanced as in today's world. The doctor gave her some medicine and told our mother to keep her eyes covered for several days. The result was that she went around the house with her eyes covered with an old but clean diaper, a leftover from one of her children, singing at the top of her voice. It was then that the doctor came around the corner of the house for a house call.

He looked at the singing woman in amazement and said, "Truly, here is a woman singing in the night!"

We will hear more about her adventures later. We have to go on to a more-important matter, which is the historical occasion of my birth. Dad and Mom were married shortly after the First World War, the war that was to end all wars! My grandfather from Mother's side was still living then, and Mom was taking care of him in his old age. Children came along effortlessly in quick succession.

I should say that a little differently. Childbirth is never easy, and most certainly not in those days when the children were delivered at home with the help of a midwife and well-willing neighbors. It was in those moments that the women were at their best and had some of their most glorious moments.

Several neighbor women and the midwife would be in full control of the house and its surrounding area. Even the doctor had to take a backseat to some older midwives. Those women would be flouncing through the house like broad-beamed ships sailing over troubled waters. Ankle-high skirts were swishing and apron strings were flying in an age-old rhythm of birth and renewal.

Everything was under control, since the midwife was around to dictate the operation and its different aspects, like an experienced conductor of a well-rehearsed practice of harmony and sound. The doctor was contacted at the last moment and only in cases of complications that surpassed the knowledge of the well-experienced midwives.

The husband would be traveling back and forth through the kitchen in his own little purgatory—if luck were with him! Most of the time, he was not tolerated at the premises at all. He was wandering outside in a self-imposed desert land with eyes as big as saucers burdened with the pangs of guilt under the accusing stares of the surrounding women. He was the culprit who had started all this misery, and he deserved a lot of punishment for his evil deed. He was a lonesome man in no-man's land. The poor man would be allowed back in the house after the first cries of a wellborn baby, and there would be rejoicing in the whole neighborhood if mother and child were in good health.

It was in this kind of environment that it was my turn to enter this vale of tears, way back in 1924, but I forget much of it. It has been said that the midwife slapped my mother when she first laid eyes on me because I was so ugly, but that is not very likely. On the contrary, I was actually a delightful little fellow for the eyes of the beholder, blond hair and blue eyes, a beautiful sight for sore eyes! Even so, I was the one who was slapped on my pearly little bottom!

Times were good yet in that year, and my parents had decided to build their own new house (heavily mortgaged!), but it was a good move as was proven later. My memories go back to that little house, slightly off the center of town but still within a half mile from school and church.

Our house was in two sections. There was the main building with a kitchen and a living room and three bedrooms and a second story with two rooms. The main section was for hay and straw. A straw-cutting machine had been hoisted up to that part of the ceiling. It was a heavy piece of machinery that must have taken tremendous efforts to get it up there. It had blades that would make the former inventor of the guillotine jealous beyond compare.

Then there was the front part that was rebuilt into a bedroom in later days. A smaller building had been added to the back of the house. It had a ceiling for hay upstairs and a lower section for our herd of cattle. And that was a herd of one calf and one cow. That herd has, in later days, swollen to the inconceivable number of one cow, one heifer, and one calf.

A billy goat was included in later days to the sum total of animals. That goat became my prized possession!

Our kitchen was sandwiched between the two buildings. It had a stove that would be smoking when the wind came from the northwest because of a downdraft.

My dad came to the ingenious solution to that problem with the help of my uncle. They put a fool on top of the chimney. It was called a fool because it would turn with the changing of the wind, just like a person who can't decide. It also sounded like a fool at the best of times—"always squeaking and complaining!"

I almost forgot the most important part of our home—the toilet! It has seen a lot of heavy weather over the years. Thunder and lightning and everything else between! Two grown-ups and ten children were regular worshippers in that place of torture and delight.

That was during the war years and also right after the war. There was only room for one on that three-by-four-foot board with an eight-inch hole in the middle resting on a square pit with an odor trap to control the fumes, a combination of today's toilet and the old-time outhouse.

I can clearly remember how I used to lower half of my body through that hole until only my head and my knees were above the board. The rest hung in the lower section like a bat in a belfry. Flies would be buzzing around in the hot summer days and make a humming and droning noise without equal in all the worlds. Even so, I was in glory land uninterruptedly dreaming of my childhood dreams, if none of the others were in need!

I realize that all this doesn't sound fresh, but it was part of my childhood and could not be that bad because all ten children are still alive to this very day, seventy years later.

Our mother ruled the roost with little money and a lot of imagination. Dad came into his glory when we were all gathered around the dinner table. He could not reach all ten children by hand and would have to resort to a bamboo fishing rod to correct the children who were in transgression. Not that this would come to pass all that often, but we had moments when we lost our saintly halos, and the fishing rod was handy to create order in a situation like that.

Across from us was an old farmhouse with untold mysteries, and it was very fascinating for the small fry's that were we—snot noses—and much abused by our older brothers and sisters. This house was one of the oldest houses in town. I mean that house was really old! The main house had a straw roof, a roof that settled over the low-slung building like a mother hen over her brood of little chicks.

That describes fairly closely the functional character of that rustic farm building. The roof sloped down low to the ground on the side walls that reached not higher than six feet at the highest point. The livestock were kept under the same roof as the family who lived there, well established in a lifestyle that went back in tradition to the very hazy days of the early Saxons who were living in the lowlands even before the birth of our Lord Jesus.

A row of little windows and almost as many small doors added to the rustic atmosphere of the whole building. It also added to the useful function of unloading the manure that the farm animals produced so diligently throughout the winter season.

Cattle were in the stalls behind those little doors. A wide alley in the middle of the barn made separation complete between boys and girls, cows and bull—most useful!

This alley had the illustrious name of threshing floor. The grain was threshed there in the cold winter months. It was quite often that the farmer came threshing straight out of bed, right in his long johns. He was dressed in his long johns might be a better expression. He never would have threshed much grain in his long johns because there was only room for one in there! The pigs had an abode in the front of the barn, living their short and noisy life with great optimism—completely unwarranted! The whole setup made for a warm and cozy lifestyle, and it was not nearly as smelly as you would think. Houses like that still are found in the countryside of Holland, Germany, and many other European countries.

Hay was stacked on a low ceiling above the cows on both sides of the alley and on the larger ceiling higher up above the threshing floor. This hay was brought in through two beautiful big barn doors on the end of the floor. They were at least twelve feet high and had an imposing curve, large enough to let a high hay load pass through under the high ceiling. Those doors made the buildings look even more beautiful. The doors were a work of art in many farm buildings, adding even more to the rustic countryside appearance of those farms. Wrought iron letters beside the farm doors announced the year in which the farm was built. There were two numbers to the left, the others to the right anchored in the brick walls with ornamental curls of black iron forced in the smithies of the nearby blacksmith shop.

It was easy to walk from the animal section of the house to the living quarters. An old oak door with another artfully wrought iron handle gave entrance to the kitchen. One would enter that room and was replaced in another age of rest and beauty.

The kitchen was half hidden in a fascinating semidarkness that made everything look mysterious and forbidding. Several old reed-covered chairs stood in a haphazard way around a heavy oak table in front of a beautiful open fireplace. Those fireplaces had blue delft tiles along the back surface. Tiles that were worth a fortune, many of them having a Bible picture burned on the surface—Adam and Eve—or any other type of Bible story most fascinating for us as children! I would never get enough of the picture of the twelve spies coming out of Canaan with sticks loaded with grapes on their heavy-muscled arms and shoulders.

Santa Claus was supposed to have come through some of these fireplaces according to an age-old story that had its origin in the Low Countries (you will hear about that later). The fireplace was important not only for the fire but also as a place to smoke the meat and the famous Dutch Farmer sausage. Whole sides of bacon and row upon row of sausages hung in the upper structure—smoked to an unbelievable delicacy, as time and smoke had their way with these farmer delicacies.

The sleeping place for some folks was along the side of the kitchen—a kind of cubbyhole that was about five feet deep, five feet wide, and six feet high. Nice ornamental doors in front were shutting off the hostile world, often hiding some heavy romancing. Many wedding nights were consummated behind those doors. Joyful but also sad moments were experienced in those bedsteads, as they were called. Reed-covered chairs were placed on a clay-covered floor, and on the whitewashed wall was the grandest of all grandfather clocks! Ticking away time into eternity, sometimes that was reassuring and sometimes aggravating. Ticktock, ticktock, going on and on. This clock was more than one hundred years old; it had been counting away many a lifetime from birth to death.

The face of that clock was a painting in its own right consisting of a landscape with cows, horses, and sheep and an old farmhouse surrounded by trees in the background, and above the trees was a picture of the moon going through the cycle of a new moon, half-moon, and full moon. All in its own time and place.

Much copper work was in and around this wholesome picture of time and rhythmic movement powered by two heavy copper weights, polished and spotless by the enduring efforts of Auntie Riek and her robust three daughters. This was not the end of it. Those weights had to be pulled up every evening at the exact moment in time, a ritual that repeated itself night after night for as long as there was a living being in the house to pull those weights.

Old eight-by-eight oak beams supported the ceiling, smoke colored and strong. These remnants of days past were carrying the winter load of hay stored there throughout the fall and most of the winter. Springtime would lighten the burden for a time of relapse. Then the cycle would start again.

The walls had been whitewashed so often that the old clock was bedded down snugly in layer over layer of whitewash in a time-honored resting place. The front of the house was of really old brickwork. Time and elements had honed these bricks into a real work of art, always pleasing to the eye. This front was overshadowed with a row of beautiful old chestnut trees. These trees would be casting a shade on the building, ever mysterious with a promise and warning of well-hidden secrets, present and past, forbidding and enticing! This impression was even more pronounced by blinds, little doors beside the windows. These could be closed to shut out the sunshine or the night.

Heart-formed openings in the doors sent out a warming welcome when the evening was stormy and wet.

We looked at this house first thing in the morning and the last thing at night, ending the day when the sun set over the incomparable trees surrounding the house or when the moon ruled over the night.

"If cloud and rain did not obscure her serene majesty."

Our own house was an anticlimax; since it was new and untried, it held no secrets yet and no romance to speak of. My first memories are a very vague collection of how I stood at the top of the stairs looking down at my brothers, fearful and a little proud that I had risen to such heights.

My grandfather from Mother's side died when I was only two years old, and my memories of that time are vague and very distant. Mom and Dad were walking through the house with sad faces, and Mother was crying most of the time. Grandfather was lying in the front room, still and not moving. Strange men came in the living room later with a long wooden box and put grandpa in. Strange and very scary that was.

Death seems to have a language of its own, and even a little boy could understand that Grandpa would leave forever. The other grandparents had passed away many years before. None of them got much older than sixty years of age.

This was an age that was normal for the former generation. We often missed our grandparents in later years! Other children had their grandparents and could show of their presents, bragging about them, while we were standing empty-handed—until I thought I had found the solution. Down the street lived an old lady who was always sick and in bed. I went to the old lady and asked her if she would be my grandma. That would remedy the situation and the lack of presents! I would be in for the good times, or so I thought in my children's imagination. But alas! I bet on the wrong horse (or the wrong lady to be more to the point!). The old lady did not have much money and had to share the little she had with the folks that looked after her. No presents! Easter was also a mixed blessing in my mother's country, a mixture of old pagan tradition and Christian faith. Folk tradition was a leftover from the Old Saxon and German forefathers.

The strange part is that many Nazi leaders of later days were following many of the same customs for all the wrong reasons. They had their bonfires and dances around the May Day tree, closely linked to the old Teutonic customs that followed pagan rites and spirit worship based on satanic believes. Many of our district people would work together to build an Easter fire of great dimensions. All kinds of burning materials were brought together from all over the country. Brush and shrubbery were saved for months ahead of the great day.

Old tables and old chairs, bedsteads, and any material that would burn were dragged to the Easter fire by the young and old. Nothing was safe for the greedy hands of the little folks—they would drag your mother-in-law to the fire if she were any good for that purpose.

It has happened that a little white-haired Dutch boy got carried away by the spirit of the moment taking their wooden shoes and throwing those in the blazing inferno. This was risky business, for swift punishment was sure to follow.

I remember a time that a regular war erupted between some neighbors when one neighbor stole some kindling wood from our Easter fire. All primitive instincts erupted in a blaze of indignity. Fathers and sons and even some daughters exploded in a righteous wrath about this affront to neighborly conduct. The passions of wrath flared higher than the flames of the Easter fire and died just as quickly.

It was a glorious moment when a tiny flame was started on the bottom of the pile. The smoke and tongues of fire erupted throughout the kindling wood to swell to a great bonfire. We boys stood around that fire like old pagan priests, taken up in the heat of the moment in more ways than one. The joy would reach a new high when our parents helped us to roast potatoes, apples, and chestnuts in the fire.

Most folks would stay around until late at night when the fire had died down to glowing embers and the little kids were chewing on burned potatoes with grains of sand. But it was fun! By the way, this custom is followed to this very day! Then there was the custom of hard-boiled eggs hidden in all kinds of hiding places. The children had a whale of a time to crawl over and under any object that might be hiding some eggs.

There was another custom that involved little swans on sticks. You would see children toting sticks with many branches and a little swan on every branch. I hate to say it, but we had no branches and no sticks to carry around. We had little of anything. Dad and Mom had not that kind of money. We were also left out on another custom.

Many children carried a network stocking around their ruddy little necks. These stockings were often filled to the brim with little chocolate eggs, sugar eggs, peanuts, oranges, and much more.

The grandchildren of the folks across the road had stockings that were so long and had so much stuff in it that they tripped over it when they ran too fast. Sugar eggs were as big as your fist and chocolate eggs that were even bigger. Small eggs, big eggs, white eggs, colored eggs, eggs, eggs, and more eggs: it was like the horn of abundance.

And here we were—the poor folks of the neighborhood, running around with holy stockings (the ones with holes in them!) with a few peanuts and one or two oranges. It was remarkable that we were so content; it was the way of the world, and we did not know any better than it had to be that way. It would not enter our mind to ask for any of those things, not from those children and not from anyone else—it was good the way it was. We were happy and content. Our parents showed us the real meaning of Easter, and that was far more important than any amount of sweets and candies. We learned the real meaning of Easter and of the values in life. We still missed out on these material things.

We had the same luck with our Sint-Nicolaas (the Dutch Santa Claus). Our neighbors across the road were Catholics. They always gave very expensive presents to their children, from Sint-Nicolaas, while we had to be satisfied with a few peppermints, some peanuts, and very small gifts—a very unsatisfactory situation. Life would be much more pleasant if we became Catholic and had their Santa Claus—that would improve our lives considerably. Then we would have paradise on earth. Even so!

The Catholic Church was very scary on the other hand. They would have a procession around the church occasionally. These events were always very colorful—the church band playing sacred music, the priest dressed rich and colorful in long dresses, and the altar boys, also in long dresses, carrying Mother Mary around the church in the company of other many-colored symbols. But the most imposing and fearful Image in that procession was the Lamb of God, "a pure white lamb" carried on a platform under a beautiful purple canopy. Many somber people followed behind in this solemn procession.

Some priests were swinging gold and silver incense vessels filling the air with an ever-persistent aroma. That alone was an experience in itself. All this was in honor of the Christ Child. The Lamb of God!

Everything made a sobering impression, the aroma of incense, and the somber and reverent people, mixed with the subdued music and the colorful priest. It all made an overpowering impression on my little child's imagination.

This really was God!

Our neighbors across the road had three large pictures on the wall, and those pictures would fill me with great fear. Jesus was shown there with bleeding hands reaching out to everyone looking up to Him. This really was God! Mother Mary was there also looking down at you with a great bleeding heart in the middle of her chest and several other saints, more or less graphic.

I was in such childhood awe and wonder that I would enter those rooms under no condition. The children of that household went in and out, without any reserve, and I marveled at that. I wonder sometimes, could it be that we as parents force our children too close to the awesome majesty of God without teaching them about a GOD who is infinite, that He is the ruler of us all, also in the small things of life? Somehow, we seem to lose the greatness of our Lord because we become too familiar with His awesome majesty. We lose sight of the fact that God is not the next-door neighbor, but He saved us at great sacrifice. I would like to mention again the priest and those boys!—we never got used to those dresses. It just was not fitting for boys to be dressed like that.

"I had forgotten that I had a dress on myself when I was smaller." It was the dress code of those early days for the little ones in diapers. We got a little higher on the ladder of life when we progressed to pants-wearing boys. These pants were an art form in itself with flaps on the back and on the front. These flaps could be lowered or raised, as the occasion demanded. Either way, to do a big one or a small one sure is neat, eh? It was interesting that a person who was not well liked was called a flap-peeing person.

We climbed higher on the ladder of the establishment as we progressed to short pants and knee-high stockings. We became little men then.

That was a proud moment when I walked to school in the hand of my mother. A little boy with white hair dressed in a blouse with a marine collar and knee-high socks. Just the right setting for a lover boy like me!

The women had a dress code also. Their head covering was often of an unsurpassed beauty that was seldom equaled by any hat maker. This headgear had to be spotless with white pleat coverings, complementing women in a way that I have never seen since then. The headdress was not complete if it was not accentuated by gold earrings and head irons and other fineries as well. The higher the status, the more finery! The old dress form was accompanied by a long dress that reached to just above the shoes.

An eye-pleasing picture in young women and old! Purses were obsolete because the long dresses had slits on each side. And any woman, worth her mettle, had a kind of apron under her garment—an apron with many pockets. These aprons were real treasure coves; almost anything could pop up out of there, and often did. Handkerchiefs, safety pins, candy, lose change, ends of string, etc. In there was an almost endless supply of odds and ends.

An old *Oma* was living with her sons and daughter (a young couple blessed with many children). It was a rainy day, and the children were playing hide-and-seek in the kitchen area. Everyone was found after much searching, except the smallest one. He could not be found no matter where they went until suddenly the little boy came peeping out of the side slot of Oma's dress.

The little tyke said in a choked voice, "You never would have found me if Oma had not blown a smelly wind!"

The old lady had eaten a little too much rich food, and that brought on the disaster for the little buccaneer. Old folks had a saying: "The last one that told that story is in the graveyard."

The story is highly suspected of exaggeration.

Only the farm people wore this dress code, and every country had a different dress code. Not only that! Every district had its own dress code and often its own language. Some people living less than four kilometers apart had their own distinctive language and customs. There was no one bold enough to date a woman in another district. Men would fight with knives with anyone bold enough to approach one of their women.

There were taverns in the 1800s that had their own special way of doing things. Rough-looking characters would be associating in these bizarre places. One rough individual would run the show, as it often happens. He would plant a knife in the table, and the unwary stranger who did not know the custom and was so unfortunate that he would look at the knife in the table would be challenged to a knife fight. It is hard to understand, but it happened. We had outlived that kind of behavior and became more civilized. (That is what we like to think anyway.)

We were almost as good as the folks living in Amsterdam and Rotterdam in the west of Holland. But not quite! Wooden shoes were also very common among us. Those shoes were an institution in themselves. Warm in the winter and cool in the summer. A little straw could be added if it was really cold, but that was not done all that often.

Those instruments of subtle torture might have given me calluses in later days when I had difficulty walking. I had calluses under the ball of my feet as a result of these wooden culprits. Even so, they were of use even after they had worn out. You could make a boat out of them; put a little stick in the middle for a mast and tie on some cloth and—voila!—you had a sailboat.

Wooden shoes were awful handy in a soccer match. The play of the ball was usually spirited by clean play, but things could get out of hand sometimes. Then the cry would sound, "First, the man and then the ball!"

Then all the primitive instincts would break lose.

"Blood on the goal post!" would be the cry in the really rough neighborhoods, but our parents would not allow us to play in that kind of neighborhood, and they were right in that.

A neighborhood gang went on the warpath one day. They hammered four-inch nails in the front of their wooden shoes and were all set for business. But the opposing party showed great insight and vacated the premises. It is not a pleasant feeling when your rear end is stuck to a wooden shoe by means of a four-inch nail.

Not that I was in much danger. I was too much of a coward.

We were not involved in fights that often, but we had other means to settle our accounts. One could take off his wooden shoes and hammer away at the opposing party. But that too was more for the rowdy types. Our parents did not approve of that kind of conduct.

I was a coward and, therefore, contacted one of my bigger friends and hid behind him in time of need. I repeat—I was a coward, but a live coward, or else I would not be sitting here to tell you about it.

In our town, we had a guy who was quite a character. Crazy Dieksy was his name. But he was far from crazy. His thought process was a little different from an ordinary person. That was all. He was in good company! Albert Einstein was like that too, although to my regret, I must say, "Dieksy was no Einstein."

On the other hand, Dieksy was wild about soccer. This was proven again when Dieksy was sitting at the sidelines while his team was losing a very important game. He was not allowed to play because one player had donated a regulation soccer ball. The possession of a ball like that was very unusual in the deep depression of the middle thirties.

Only players with leather shoes were allowed to play with this treasure of a ball. Dieksy had only wooden shoes, so he had to sit out this game—the powers that were had dictated this. But his team was losing and losing in a big way—until finally Dieksy could stand it no longer. He demanded the loan of another player's leather shoes and entered the game with vigorous abandon. He got so involved that he lost all rhyme and reason. He went after the ball and kicked the ball through the goal post, including the goalkeeper and half the opposing team. The other half got out of there fast!

The game was over, and the opposing team had lost by default! Hurray for Dieksy? Not really. There are rules and regulations, and this behavior was well outside expected behavior. But a lot was forgiven because Dieksy had a special place in the sentiment of everyone that knew him!

All this shows a little of our feelings to the number-one pastime of our youth! Soccer and bicycle racing were the real deal in those days! Our neighbors on the farm had several boys, and they were all soccer players. Hank and Hans, especially, were our heroes. The role models for our budding soccer talents.

We asked Hank once, in a very confidential moment, to tell us the secret of a successful soccer player. He gathered us around in a tight circle and, in a conspirator tone of voice, told us his great secret:

"Take a little piece of brown rye bread," he said, "make it about one inch thick, two inches long, and two inches wide."

His freckled face, with red hair and stubble beard, could never have been more serious and solemn.

"Take that little piece of bread and dry it for three days where no sun can reach it. Then carry it in your pockets at all times! Don't"—and his big finger waved at us—"ever leave home without that little piece of bread!"

The net result of it was that we had a piece of bread in our pockets always, to the desperation of our mothers.

I can clearly remember that Hank was working at a wooden wheel that he was cutting with the help of a knife. This wooden wheel was handmade to drive the butter churn with an electric motor. This was a giant step forward in the line of progress.

All butter churning had to be done by hand in those days, and the condition had to be just right. No butter was made if it was not. It was the age-old tradition that no woman "who had the time of the month" could hope to make butter or can food for that matter.

Making this wheel to drive the churn was real progress, and we, as little boys, were speechless with admiration for the expertise of Hank the dragon slayer. There were many nails in this wheel, and Hank pointed from one nail after the other to explain the different positions of the players in a soccer team. It is on that butter-churn wheel that we learned the elementaries of the soccer game—the meaning off penalties and offside, out ball and corner ball, and much more. Hank's family was the proud owners of a radio, and that brought his expertise and knowledge to ever-new dimensions.

He was the number-one source of all there was to know about the game of soccer. He could quote the greatest experts of the hallowed soccer game.

A sports announcer got so excited one day that he screamed at the top of his voice, "Look at the quivering of the thighs and the shivering of the stomach!"

That became a catchword and the slogan of soccer teams for years to come.

We tried to make our stomach shiver and our thighs quiver, but you can't make anything shiver if it is not there to start with. Hank and Hans were well equipped for that kind of exercise, and we loved them even more for that reason. Our soccer matches had very humble beginnings. We never had the money to buy a decent soccer ball, so we looked for a substitute.

(It is with great caution and a humble and forgiving spirit, great imagination, and great trepidation, a strong stomach, and a warm heart that I caution you to look at the rest of the story.)

We had to look for a substitute, drawing on the great wisdom of our forefathers. We went to the butcher shop on slaughter day and begged the man for a pig's bladder. We would get one free on our lucky days, and the fun could begin. We walked as conquering heroes to the field of battle with our treasure, pumped air in the bladder with the help of a bicycle pump, shivering with expectation, and the game could start before long.

The bladder was wet and heavy at first, and little slivers of fat and meat had a nasty habit of slapping one in the face, but that improved by the minute until the ball became so dry that it started leaking out of little holes and the game had an untimely end. But it was all in a day's work, and the bladder would be good for an hour or so until the game had a deflated end, period! The next game had to wait for the next slaughter day.

You might have some difficulty believing this story. Even so, this is how it happened time and again. We were a happy bunch of boys as long as the game lasted. This is indeed a sobering thought for the spoiled generation of this day!

Almost anyone has those days that everything seems right with the world. We had one of those days. The sun was shining, and one of the better "to-do" boys had received a real soccer ball—very unusual! The older boys in the neighborhood had graciously decided to play a game with the little fry that were we, the would-be victims.

Our heroes, Hans and Hank, joined also in the joyful throng. We, the little guys, were deliriously happy—but not quite. There was work to be done!

I had no idea that I was the supreme dummy when they put me in the goal and another little fellow in the other goal. Presto! The game was on, and it was a fairly good game in the beginning. Then the mood changed, and the cry went up: "First, the man and then the ball!"

That's when the game got really interesting. Those big guys were charging each other with wooden shoes that were as big as tugboats.

I thought that my end had come when a bunch of those jokers came barreling through the goal like the steers of Bashan. The little guy on the other side of the field did not do all that much better. He was ground into the dust even more than I was. Even so, the big guys praised us to the high heavens, and they had us really convinced that we were almost ready for the big league!

The ball and we were kicked from pillar to post, and we returned home from the field of honor covered with lumps and bruises. But that was later! The game had to be played on the road, and not the mill yard. That place would have been better by far, but out of bounds because the miller had a big mean dog with the grandiose name of Prince. This dog would bite any ball to shreds the moment he could get hold of it. The animal was chained to the doghouse, but the chain was long enough to make the situation very risky indeed. Nor were there any volunteers to take the ball away from the dog. Not in that situation.

It was in this fashion that a number of blond-haired and half-crazy Dutchmen with wild eyes and fearsome expressions were chasing an empty space of pig leather filled with nothing but air. All good things must come to an end, also this day of days. Maybe just as well.

We went home conquering heroes, wounded and wearied, but a day of reckoning was coming. We would be there to participate. We would have a good sleep, lick our wounds, and come back for more. Such was the nature of the beast!

My dad made a big mistake on a certain day. He knitted a pair of knee-high socks for me with the colors of our opposing soccer club! You could not blame Dad all that much because he was not all that wise in the ways of the world. But I absolutely refused to wear the socks with those offensive colors.

Our favorite team had white and green colors, and the other team red and black. I would rather die than wear the red and black colors. Period!

It was at that moment that my dad showed great insight and gave the socks to a less tenderhearted person. My reputation was saved from a disastrous and inglorious ending.

It was a very joyful day when our favorite team got a new goalie. The man was a German by birth, but we did not hold that against him. He was awfully talented. He could twist himself in the most impossible forms and positions. We called him the Snake-man, and the Snake-man was our hope and glory.

He was a promise of better days to come. It's a good thing we could not see in the future—into the difficult times ahead of us. You will meet the Snake-man again not too much later!

We had reason for joy and optimism because the near future was looking a lot better. Now we had the combination of soccer talents of the fearsome trio of the Snake-man and his inhuman endeavor between the pipes. The heavyset neighbor boy Hank was playing the back position before the Snake-man. Last but not least was the incomparable Uncle Hans in the offensive. He fooled the opposing team with dazzling speed and surprising moves into a magic show of unexpected feats that gave our team a victory after a disheartening string of losses.

Our favored team did not have the money for dressing rooms, and the players of both teams had to dress up in the bushes behind the soccer field. A group of mild-mannered civilians would disappear in the bushes to come back moments later like the snake. Regular fighting machines! Frothing at the mouth and ready for action, and the action was not long in waiting. Huge mountains of flesh were weaving back and forth over the green turf, like waves in the ocean, weaving a tapestry of movement and collar in a dazzling display of knowledge and skillful cunning.

That's how it looked to us, but what did we know of the ways of the world of grown-up folks? Soccer was strictly a men's game in those days. Women were hardly tolerated!

Although, some brazen ladies would have a sneak preview of things to come. They were peeking behind the bushes when the men were changing. They were not very high-class ladies. This was not acceptable behavior.

Soccer was almost a religion for many people. It happened that a Catholic priest came to a soccer match so that he could give a benediction to his favored team.

We will leave the soccer champions for a while and go to another fascinating place. This was the bicycle shop of our beloved uncle Hank. My uncle, the bicycle repairman, was named after me—I think.

His repair shop was one of the favorite places to meet people. This had a lot to do with his personality. Always in a good mood and upbeat, he had the knack to handle the young ones. It was in this place, of all places, where I almost met disaster. A truck of the steam-cleaning factory would come to his place once a week. This truck came from another place to pick up clothes that had to be dry-cleaned for the prospective customers, and it was my uncle's job to line up the customers. He would go from house to house to pick up the materials.

It was that truck that was so fascinating to my nephew and me. Only the doctor and the lawyer and perhaps the mayor of the town had a car in these days. The trucks that our town could muster could be counted on the fingers of one hand.

It was quite an occasion when this steam-cleaning truck came into town, and a little boy like me felt really privileged that I could participate in this glorious moment.

One time when I was about four years old, my nephew and I snuggled up to the truck in great awe, and we dared each other, really fearfully, to touch this wonder of wonders.

Familiarity creates contempt! My nephew dared me to hang on to the back of that truck and hang on until it started moving. Disaster struck right then and there. I could not let go! This little boy (me) was dragged over the sharp basalt gravel for more than half a block, with my knees dragging through the gravel. My father and uncle watched, in great horror, as I was dragged away behind that truck so that I almost certainly would do great harm to my knees.

The men started waving in desperation in the hopes that the driver might see something was wrong. But the driver drove on in blissful ignorance—just dreaming along. Every child must have one or more guardian angels beyond any doubt. Mine was standing a little ways down the road in the form of a middle-aged lady. She noticed the desperate gestures of the men and waved the truck to a standstill.

My knees were a bloody pulp by then, and my parents had to pick out little pieces of basalt and gravel for a long time to come. The bone was showing, but no serious damage had been done that a little vinegar could not fix up. Was I lucky or not? I like to think that I was blessed! It could have been so much different.

Uncle Hank was also the proud owner of an air gun, and he would invite all the able men from far and wide to participate in a competition of sharpshooting with the air gun. A target was set up, and the competition could begin. The gun had little pointed plugs with a feathery end. These plugs could be pulled out of the target to be used over and over again. It was interesting to see the different sharpshooters at work in these competitions, which were usually held close to New Year.

There was the chewing type who could not shoot straight unless they had a chew of tobacco. A great big lump would be fighting the battle of the bulge behind his gray and often unshaven cheek. Men had a fairly good aim if they could move the bulge over far enough to make room for the rifle. You could watch the hunchbacks with burdened shoulders leaning into the prospective target. This seemed to help in some unexplained way.

Some shot with both eyes open, and some with both eyes closed. It stands for reason that the later character would be all by himself, while the others waited outside for the duration. Then came the day when the second girl in Uncle Hank's family came to the conviction that life could not go on unless she had a potshot at Uncle Hank's elusive target. This had to be done in Uncle Hank's dimly lit repair shop, and that made it even worse.

This was something unheard of. Girls did not shoot guns. That was men's work.

She was different in more ways than one. She did not give up but wheedled and whined until she broke down the defenses of Uncle Hank. But alas! She was better at whining than shooting! She was also cross-eyed. And so it happened that this scrawny little girl shot the air gun of Uncle Hank in the bicycle repair shop of Uncle Hank, and all the dwellers of that building flew outside for the safety of their miserable lives. The cowards! The girl shot, and the plug disappeared never to be seen again.

Thus is the story of Hanna, the second girl in Uncle Hank's family. She told this story herself about fifty years after that fateful moment in the bicycle shop of dear uncle Hank! Such were the days of our childhood.

One day followed the other like a string of pearls. Some days better than others, but always exciting and full of activities as one learning process followed the other through sunny and through rainy days, winter and summer, spring and harvest. I loved to go through nature from one wonderworld to the next.

I would watch the dew-drenched meadows at dawn when every blade of grass had its own dewdrop sparkling in the morning sun and creating untold variations of jewels in our Maker's crown. I used to dream that every drop of dew was a jewel that belonged to me and no one else. I would watch the many-colored spectrums as the sun and shifting meadow blanket would create a new rainbow on every blade of grass.

At other times I would lie belly down beside a creek with a little waterfall not far away from where we lived. The misty spray of the falling water would form much a variation of light and color in ever-changing patterns bouncing and swirling around and over a number of rocks in the bottom of that creek. Little insects would clamber up the reed stalks, hardy plants that wrestled, and won a place in this ever-changing wonderland of swirling water and shifting sand. Little sticklebacks would stand in the shadow of plant and rock, fins moving in constant motion. Standing still and not moving backward or forward until a shadow fell in that little paradise. Then the little fish would shoot away, faster than anything you have ever seen. Not a ripple would be left in its resting place, and everything would return as if nothing had been there before. I was reminded of this children's song that we learned at school in first grade.

> In a peaceful quiet valley,
> Near a murmuring waterfall,
> Little flowers there are blooming
> Water drops fall on them all.
> Even on the smallest flower.
> Just let me be such a little one.
> High above up on the mountain,
> Giant trees grow everywhere.
> Thunderstorms are ruling there.
> Mighty trees will then be falling,
> Ending their superior calling.
> Just let me be a little one.
> Then I will choose by my desiring
> The lowly place, the waterfall.
> Just to be a humble being.
> Live with the smallest of them all.
> Just a tender little flower.
> Praise to my Lord will be my calling
> Let me be a little one.

I could see this so clearly in my childhood imagination. Let others be with the high and the mighty. I would prefer to be small and humble and do my own thing in my own small way. Others can have the big stuff.

I still feel that way! There was another song that left a deep impression on me. It went as follows:

Do you know how many stars are twinkling high in heaven's firmament?
Do you know how many bugs are dancing round the place where you just went?
On those thousands upon thousands rest the eye of God above.
He arranged it all with love and not one escapes His eye.

I thought that this was a marvelous thing. The Almighty Creator, high above, in the highest heavens, looking down on everything below. Even the lowly mosquito is included in that loving care. Everything that moves is under His constant supervision, even the little bug that we squash under our feet without a thought.

It was mind-boggling! There were many fascinating things in our little world, things that are missed by the grown-up people. Grown-ups live a lot further away from the ant-size world of the level of the little people.

We would see the bulbous eye of a grasshopper or a pie-size bug. Light would reflect in many variations and in every conceivable color. It was as if those bug eyes were swiveling on a little stem, going in every direction and seeing everything without resting.

A grasshopper will scrape the lower part of her raspy leg against the shield of her upper body and make the screeching noise that fills the summer night. It is hard to remember a summer night without the sound of crickets and the droning sound of the insects filling the night air, with a thousand variations in a lullaby that soothes the feelings and secret fears of a play-worn little human who has so much growing up to do and so little time to do it in.

I spent many happy moments just lying there on my belly on the grass in front of an anthill, fascinated by the constant and orderly movements of these industrious creatures. I have seen ants pulling weights that were several times bigger than their own body structures over obstructions that must have been like mountains in their own little world. Nothing is impossible when they have set their mind on moving an object. Others would join the effort if the strength of one was not enough to the task at hand. These ants would move anything they had set their mind to whether it took one or two or a dozen all working in unison until the job was done.

Would it ever be nice if we as human beings could work like that together? But we are way too smart for that—or are we?

Did you ever watch a little ladybug, so exquisitely made? We would watch this little creature when it crawled from underneath a chestnut leaf, a bright red little bug with pitch-black trimmings and pinhead with dots all over its little body.

We had a song about this little being:

> Little humble ladybug;
> Fly for us to heaven.
> Father and mother are dead.
> Bring them all our love.
> Father and mother are dead.

I have never known the true meaning of this little song, but it did speak to our childhood imagination telling the story of a little orphan who had lost its parents. An orphan lonesome and hungry in an uncaring world, she was reaching out to this little red-and-black messenger, an ambassador for the heavenly beings far away in heaven and closer than we were to this little bug on that chestnut leave.

Then there was the much larger May bug, giant in proportion to the first one. We could prod it to life out of a lethargic existence. It would pump its wings up and down and make ready for flight while we were counting off the seconds going until takeoff. The whole procedure could be upset with the simple flip of a little stick that would flip the creature on its back, and it would lie there harmless as Samson without hair. It would starve to death if someone did not turn him over.

Many in this modern world have forgotten God. They are beetles in their own right, powerful and strong. Nevertheless, He that is in the heavens will laugh and turn these beetles on their backsides, leaving them to die, if they do not repent and turn back to the *Word of God*, to the center of our being. *His name is Jesus!*

Sometimes we would go to a quiet pool in walking distance from our home. Salamanders would be lurking in the shadow of the green-turquoise water. It would be a glorious day if you could snatch one of those giant salamanders out of that shadowy water. We called them giant salamanders, but they were only about six inches from head to tail.

The male would have beautiful colors that could match anything in that smelly pond. We used to think that they were the males because these animals would follow another species of the same make but with a more subdued, almost drab color. We did not know all that much about the male/female relationship, but our neighbor Hank had told us that it was the basic rule: the fish up front is always the female when two fish follow each other. The one that follows is the male. His stubby gnarly finger was wagging back and forth in front of our startled faces once again, and we had to bow for his superior knowledge.

Hank was an expert on soccer. It stands for reason that he would be an expert on fish too. It was as simple as that. We were convinced of that. It was a strange affair that no fish seemed to follow Hank. He did not seem to be following any other fish either. Hank did not seem to be an expert in that kind of endeavor. He lived and died as a bachelor in later days.

Life of a growing little boy has many variations and often goes from one extreme to the other. One day on the mountaintop and down in the valley on the next. There came a time that the wisdom of our grown-up neighbors was of no avail. They had no answer for the ultimate mystery of death.

Our neighbor on the eastside had been sick for a long time. Mom would not let us play in the hallway between the houses for a long time. The whole side east of the house was barred from loud noises. Mother was very strict about that. It was the unwritten code of the neighborhood. Everyone cared for the other person especially when sickness was involved!

Then came the day when everything became very quiet. The wooden covers were up in front of the windows and the windows in back of the house were covered with white coverings. The people next door were in mourning. We were to confront the majesty of death and the grim reaper, twice, in quick succession!

Mom told us that the neighbor had passed away. We should go to the widow and tell her that we were truly sorry for the loss of her husband. So that's what we did.

The woman was very touched by this tactful gesture, and she asked us if we would like to see the body. She brought us to the front room to a simple wooden coffin. The sight of it shook us with the force of a sledgehammer. The man had been sick for a long time and had passed away three days ago. It is a well-known fact that the hair of a person will keep growing for days after the dying of a person. This had happened in this case so that the result was really gruesome. The man had hair on his face a quarter of an inch long, and the overall picture was so shocking that I could not forget for a long time the awesome reality, and finality, of death.

I understood then and there that life and death cannot be separated and that dying was by no means the end of all things. The old and ageless wisdom had the following quotation: "That man, or woman, has passed out of time!"

This is a very interesting statement well worth thinking about. Passing out of time would suggest that the departed is in a realm where time is no more—biblical really!

I would like to think that Adam and Eve and the last man to live are at the same level as far as eternity affects us. I believe that anyone who dies as a believer in the saving grace of Jesus will be with Him immediately.

There was a boy living about half a block away from us. He was one of the most favored and most spoiled of the children in the neighborhoods. The farmers seemed to prefer him to most of us. He was the one who got permission to sit next to our neighbor on the farm wagon—something we wanted to do ourselves in the worst manner! He even got to hold the reins of the horses sometimes—something that would have put any one of us in seventh heaven! He could do all the little chores, while we were looking on—just hankering to do the same thing.

The farmer even gave him the nickname Patty vou, von Simsy. A name with a very musical sound, we liked to listen to the sound of it. Sounding like a mixture of French, German, and Dutch, it was very romantic. This boy could do no wrong with the rest of the grown-ups! (Maybe the grown-ups knew something that we did not.)

This boy became sickly and had to stay in bed for longer and longer periods until we were told that he had passed away. He was only eleven, just my age at the time.

This boy was born on Christmas Day, and in the Catholic Church that was considered very special. The church provided a beautiful casket, pure white inside, with candles all around it.

We all went out to see him. It was almost as if an angel was lying there in perfect peace. It was the nicest thing we had ever seen. Much nicer than anything we were accustomed to. Altogether an unearthly scene! There was this beautiful coffin with golden trimmings with the little boy in pure white—right in the middle of the mediocre surroundings of that humble, poor labor man's house.

That's how we learned to respect and fear the majesty of death at a very young age. This impression was so intensive that I never forgot those scenes and adjusted my life accordingly. The funerals in those days were very impressive and of a morbid beauty.

A caller would come past every neighbor's door to announce the date of the burial ceremony. This man was in total black uniform, with a high hat that had a long black fringe trailing down to his coat sleeves, and the rest of his coat was covered with ornaments all in somber black. His voice was low and subdued as he informed the neighbors of the passing away of a loved one.

The hearse was total black, with black fringes, set off with black bells all around the shining coach. Two, four, or even six horses pulled the hearse, all black but ordinary workhorses, doubling as coach horses.

The reins were set off with black fringes, and every horse had a black plume on his headset. The horses' heads nodded with every footstep in time with the procession. Solemn and somber but sure, oh so sure, going forward to their last destination.

They always returned empty. Always! Forgive me for showing those scenes in detail, but this had a very great part in our lives also.

We were living in a mid-sized home with a cabled roof, attached to another building, our barn that housed our livestock. The story would not be complete if I did not tell you about our farm operation, if one can call this humble setup "a farm operation."

We had a cow and a calf, all under the same roof as where we lived. Our dad was very proud of his little herd, and we had to go throughout the country to pick up potato peels for dad's herd!

Many people from all over town were sympathetic to Dad and Mom. After all, they had a large and fast-growing family. Some people would have the opinion that my parents should know better, but it seems that my parents lived by their understanding of the Bible in much the same way as the Catholics.

"Many children are a blessing of the Lord."

The old ones have a saying: "It's faster to get a dozen kids than a thousand guilders!"

It all depends on where your values are. Some people want the money, and some want the children! Only eternity will disclose which are better and greater riches! I have my own viewpoint on that matter. My parents had ten children and followed through on their commitment with all their ability working more than twelve hours each day.

They also had a few animals to supplement the income in respect to milk and butter. We had one cow, and this animal was our pride and joy. It had its stall in the back section of our dwelling place producing milk and butter and one tiny calf once a year—if we were lucky!

My older brother had to look after her, doing the milking and cleaning the gully behind the cow, for after all it is an established fact that a cow will produce more than milk, in case you did not know this.

All things went on an even keel. The cow did what she was supposed to do day after day and year after year. Life was as it should be.

Then disaster struck. The cow had been eating a potato, and one became stuck in the cow's throat. She swelled up like a toad in no time flat. Someone went to the veterinarian at once but almost too late. The cow swelled up to at least two times her normal size. It was a scary sight, and we started moving stuff out of the way because the animal could fall over any moment and burst wide open, spilling all her insides over our humble abode. This would be a disaster in more ways than one, for then there would be no more room for Derk and Geertje and their ten children. We would be on the outside looking into a horrible mess of blood and bones mixed with grass and grain and potato peelings.

That is what we thought anyway. The vet came in at the last moment. He tried for several minutes to reach the offending object but no luck. A long flexible steel tube was the last resort, and he shoved the potato down in the cow's gullet into the rumen (stomach)—that's what he thought—and suddenly the cow coughed and blew the offending fruit of evil out into the blue yonder. The doctor was utterly amazed. It seems that he had broken off a little of the potato enough to give the cow a little air and room to move the thing out of her throat.

It sounded like a big tire going flat with all the air escaping in a horrible smelling stream of polluted air. The stink was beyond compare!

Smell or stink, we could not care less. The cow was alive, and that's what counted. Our milk supply was saved at the sounding of the bell and the producing of the smell.

Dad and our older brother could keep milking and cleaning after the cow, and we could go through the neighborhood for potato peelings. Things were back to normal. Now comes the story of the bees, and that's no beeswax.

Our farm was also the proud owner of a colony of bees. Every bee colony has one queen, and the whole life cycle of the colony rotates around the queen bee . . . just as in my family.

A colony has workers, nursing bees, soldiers, architects, and much more to regulate the bee collection, very much like a human society. All goes well until problems arise if the colony gets more than one queen. Almost half the colony will follow the new queen.

"The bees would be swarming" was the expression the common folk used when that happened.

And one day a swarm like that came flying past our home. My mother was running outside like a woman possessed, and the kitchen maid was just as wild. They had flipped a lid. At least that's what it looked like to the harpies in the neighborhood.

They, Mom and the maid, were throwing water in the air, hammering pots and pans together, and my older brothers were waving coats and jackets, blankets, and all kinds of housewares. One was even running around with a piece of underwear.

The people around were almost convinced that our family had finally cracked up. Two wild-looking women and a half-dozen kids jumping around like Indians in a war dance—that was the way it looked, but it was not all as bad as that.

A swarm of bees was flying over, and Mom was trying to bring it down using the age-proven manner of duplicating a thunderstorm and rain. They did a good job of thundering and raining. The swarm of bees settled down a little further, and a beekeeper out of the neighborhood helped Mom to get the bees in the hive. We had another swarm of bees, thanks to the thunder and rain of Mom and the maid.

Bring the swarm of bees down and the possession of the bees is yours. This was the unwritten rule. Getting the queen bee is the name of the game! Everything will come together if you have the queen bee.

I ought to know—I married one! Hee-hee! You are supposed to laugh now. That was a joke! Got it? Queen bee!

Mom and Dad had a whole row of beehives some three hundred yards from our house. I came walking past there on a nice and warm sunny day. It was hot, and I became suddenly convinced that life could not go on properly if I did not hit those beehives with a rake.

One of those handy instruments happened to fall into my hands at just the right moment. The bees were doing whatever they do best—making honey. I did my thing and followed my noble intent. I hit one beehive with a resounding whack, and that was almost the last whack I did in all my life if it had not been for the fast action of my uncle who was just at our place.

The bees came after me in great numbers and would have stung me to death if it had not been for my uncle who covered me with his coat. Mother treated me with vinegar and scolding, and I was left as a very disillusioned boy—bees are not very friendly!

September has always been a very important month in my life. This was the month that I got slapped for the first time. My older brother went to school that day and said to the teacher, "I got another brother today. It was a good thing that my mom was home or else I would have had to face it all alone!"

September was also the first month that I went to school. My free life was over, and I had to learn to be quiet and humble, also to have clean hands and fingernails that were not in mourning—you know, nails with nice black edges! Clean ears and a clean nose became a deciding factor in my life. I was not happy. I felt like a bear in a cage. I would much rather be outside than inside of that school—looking from the outside in.

Let someone else do the learning—I would do the yearning for the wide open spaces and faraway places. And yet it was in the first grade that the values were formed. These had a deciding influence on my life. Those values followed me all my life. But it did not start all that smooth. The teacher ordered me to come to the front one day to do some writing on the blackboard. But I flatly refused to go there. I hated to be the focus of attention even then. It is still that way!

The teacher was well-endowed with the necessities of life, and her great bulk put a lot of pressure on little old me. Her upper structure with the two moon-shaped objects hung over me like the sword of Damocles. She put a real scare in me, but I was more afraid of the fact that I had to go up front—all by my lonesome self. I fought like a man possessed.

I think that the teacher had the wrong approach, but she was pressed for time. She had forty kids in her class . . . Anyway . . . she tried to drag me to the front, but there was no way that she could handle me; I was hanging on in desperation, fighting tooth and nail. It took the teacher and three other boys to drag me to the front, screaming like a stuck steer. The rest of the class watched the battle in great amazement and then in silence. Most of them were very impressed with the fight I put up in total disobedience to the schoolteacher. They did not understand that it was a fight of desperation on my part.

I was finally subdued by the superiority of numbers. The pressure of human flesh put an end to this heroic struggle.

It was a broken little boy who stood in all his naked feelings in front of a class of some forty children. It brought to the surface those trends that have followed me in later life. I have always hated to be the center of attention or of public display.

But an amazing fact showed up when I was about fourteen when I joined a drama club and played for crowds of a thousand many times. A crowd of three thousand at one time, an amazing accomplishment of character discipline, if you consider the absolute fear, and even panic, of that first day in school. And then there was the second trend that has followed me all along! The ability to take charge against overwhelming odds when there was no outlook anywhere.

What follows is a statement of fact and hardly self-glorification! I have grown old enough not to look for brownie points . . . I don't need them!

Authority has always been sacred to me. I believe that God ordains the forces that are and should be obeyed, unless their morals are wrong. To follow and obey has been a sacred trust to me, more than 90 percent of the time.

The other 10 percent was to show my ability to lead when no others came forward. The school life was not at all kind to me. On the contrary, we were given a twelve-by-fourteen-inch board with slate in it. A person could write on that slate with a kind of pencil of the same material. The writing could be washed away with a smelly sponge that was kept in a sponge box. This sponge box became very smelly too after some time. In my case to say the least, I was too indifferent to take proper care of that little box, while most of the girls kept their box smelling like the rose of Sharon.

This was only part of the problem. On that board of slate we had to draw slanted lines—nice and even! My whole life has never been even, and those lines on that board were a perfect example of my lack of expertise. Those little lines of mine were wandering all over the board like withered old men. There was no rhyme or reason to any of my creations.

In front of me sat a little girl with a beautiful ribbon in her hair. I adored that girl from a distance, and I adored even more the lines that she could produce on the slate board and elsewhere. Most of the other girls were almost as good, but the girl with the hair ribbon had them all beaten to smithereens. I think that I am still in love with that girl and her lines, even now after seventy-three years. One calls that nostalgia.

It is a funny thing, but I went to a hypnotist a number of years ago. I wanted to know why I was so insecure at times. She put me under hypnosis, and to my amassment I started crying. The hypnotist asked me why I was crying, and I told her in a wavering voice that I could not make straight lines. Believe it or not! The lack of straight lines still bothered me after seventy years of living with my beloved Johanna who had no ribbon in her hair. Strange but true!

The Bible lessons and psalms that we learned had the greatest impact on me. Many songs that we learned in first grade have followed me all my life! I can quote them in my mother tongue, even now, after sixty-five years living in a strange country not speaking my mother tongue. I could quote them in good times, but more in the bad times when my whole life was turned upside down.

I can still quote almost by heart Psalm 131:

> Lord my heart is not proud, nor mine eyes haughty. Nor do I involve myself in great matters. Nor in things too difficult for me.
> Surely I have composed my soul, and I quieted it like a weaned child, resting against its mother. My soul is like a weaned child within me.
> O Israel, hope in the Lord, from this time forth and forever!

The infinite peace and quiet that reaches and flows out of that chapter, like a soothing song, have done just what that song said. It has quieted my soul again and again, day after day, and year after year.

Psalm 81 was another key in my life.

Hear o people, and I will admonish you. O Israel, if you would listen to me! Oh that my people would listen to me. Open your mouth and I will feed you. But my people did not listen to my voice, and Israel did not obey me. Oh that my people would listen to me, That Israel would walk in my ways. I would feed you the finest wheat, and with honey from the rock, I would satisfy you!

This is among the most beautiful languages in the Bible. It comes at you like a lullaby and surrounds you like a song. Singing—soothing—and you can hear the Lord, pleading with His people. "Please listen to Me! And I will feed you with honey from the rock! Please give Me your love and ask, ask, just ask anything, and I will give it to you."

Did you ever hear greater love than the one that's calling to you out of these passages? I confess that I love Him. I tried to love Him from day to day and to serve Him from year to year. I did not ask for riches, and He gave me abundance. He gave me all things, and nothing that's good for me was withheld from me.

I have a wife and children with all their love and grandchildren and great-grandchildren.

Trials and misfortunes—yes—but He was always there! I had a completely full life. Another familiar Bible passage, Psalm 103:

As for a man, his days are like grass, as a flower in the field, so he flourishes. When the wind passeth over it, it is no more.

This also was very familiar to me! Five times I have been confronted by death. I had to face untold danger time and again, and through it all I learned to understand the lessons of my childhood.

"The end of the road is Jesus. And all between is Jesus!"

I remember the psalms and, even more important, the Bible lessons of the early years. I have walked with Adam and Eve in paradise and pictured how he named the animals after their nature one by one! I followed the creation of Adam and Eve and their fall in sin. Their sin and self-will and how God gave humankind a second chance with the promise of the Savior.

I did see it, and I believed. I followed Cain and Abel and the first violence, Abel's dying. And then there was Enoch, "the man who walked with God." He did not see death because of that.

On and on, through the Old Testament, from Abram to Jacob . . .

Jacob was a guy I did not like all that much. I would sooner have gone fishing with Esau. But Jacob believed and Esau did not! And that's what saving grace is all about! I walked with the Jews in the desert through the burning sand, with dangerous enemies all around.

I watched the Ammonites and the Moabites when they were lying behind the sand dunes ready to pounce on the Israelites in an unguarded moment when the Israelites would be vulnerable. They did not seem to see the presence of the Lord who was leading the people. I watched that stupid donkey of Balaam—you know, the one who refused to walk when he saw the angel in front of him. This stupid donkey was smarter than the prophet who was riding on his back. I remember that I was thinking that this donkey was most likely a girl because girls are smarter than boys when something like that happens.

Just think about it—this prophet was not as smart as the donkey, but he was smart enough to talk the Israelites into sinning with the Moabites when they were drinking and merrymaking, and the whole kit and caboodle was in one mix-up.

I did not understand how the women related to all this. They were just girls, only a little bigger than schoolgirls, and I had absolutely no interest in those squealing little creatures with their swinging skirts and knitted stockings.

This little donkey was smarter than all the rest as far as I could see, I think.

It is funny how a little child can see through the issues. I was well aware of the fact that the disobedience of the people of God was the issue at stake.

Then I suffered with Saul and wondered about David. I watched Agag and the evil Jezebel, the battle of Ilyga, and the trip of Elysa and the leper, Naaman of Syria. I watched Daniel, Shadrach, Meshach, and Abednego in the burning fire, and Esther and Mordecai, Esther and the evil Haman.

I went on and on right through the Old Testament, past Jonah and the fish, through the prophets and the Kings—good and evil one after the other. But it all was in the hand of God.

Then came the birth of Christ! I walked with Mary and Joseph through an unwelcoming Nazareth and wonder of wonders have seen the Savior become one of us, only even much poorer in fulfilling the prophecies of the prophet Isaiah 53. Then I sat with Jesus on the hillside—this was behind our neighbor, in the meadow behind the barn. I could see it clear as day—the people on the hillside when Jesus took mercy on them because they were so hungry and He gave them food to eat. I had that all figured out how that was. The hungry people were sitting on the meadow at the neighbor's farm. This meadow was sloping uphill with some oak trees in the background. That was the place where the people were sitting all over the place on the hillside.

They were tired and hungry, but they did not want to leave because this Man was so nice, and His deep brown eyes had a depth to it that far surpassed anything that they ever witnessed. Many of them were poor with no hope of a better future in this grim world of enemy soldiers and hard-hearted priest who made life even harder with grim warnings of punishment if they did not live according to their law. There was so little love, and the whole temple worship seemed to evolve around money and more money.

The hunchback of the bush country was sitting to the side away from the crowd because he was dressed in nothing but rags—that is all he could afford. He was clean but did not really belong here. Nevertheless, he wanted to be there. He wanted to see with his own eyes and then—wonder of wonders—this Man with his kind eyes came to him personally. He talked to him as if he was a real person.

This Man hand touched him and healed the sores on his face and his hands and feet. Nobody had touched him in years, but this Man did.

He talked about a New Kingdom that would be a kingdom of love with answers to many unanswered questions and with solutions to many problems.

One woman in the neighborhood who had many children was there too. The smallest ones were hanging on her skirts, and one of them had a snotty nose. She did not see any of this, but He did. And He talked to her and then He sat under the elm tree, which was the tree with so many branches. The shadow of the tree was falling over His face, and He was telling them about the shepherd and the little sheep that went astray. How He went after it and brought it back.

I never could comprehend the suffering of Jesus, and I don't think anyone can. Not in Gethsemane and not on the cross of shame! But I joyfully embraced the glad tidings of his resurrection, and again and again, right through the New Testament, including the last revelation and the last AMEN! I believe and hope to see Him one day soon! This is the end of my testimonial.

The following pages will show you how I walked, and often stumbled, following the *Master*. The playground of the school before the war was very adventurous and often mysterious, vibrant, undulating, and interacting with life forces of hundreds of kids. Every child had his or her own interpretation of how the game should be played. Sounds familiar? It is—"in the schoolyard and in life." Life on the playground was carried on within its own cycles with rules that nobody laid down, and everybody obeyed. There was a time for soccer and a time for— snap the whip! A time to play marbles and a time to catch the robber! Ever changing and always inventive!

It was a bad day indeed when the teachers and the sports directors invaded the playground and started dictating the activities. The creative force has been smothered and often disappeared altogether. It is a well-known fact that young children can do some very creative drawing until the school system forces them in the one-on-one mode. Everything is valued in numbers and facts from that moment on, and the creative mind is subdued or disappears completely. This is what happened on the playground in later days.

Some people may think that we had an inferior system in respect to our playground activities. Nothing is further from the truth. One would do well to remember that the generations of those days brought forth the jet plane and the atomic bomb (nothing to be proud of but impressive nevertheless!).

I said this . . . just to prove a point. There was a time to play marbles. We would be playing hide-and-seek one day, and suddenly, everyone had marbles, a game that brought out the colorful characteristics of the children like no other game I know. You had boys who had trouble adding and doing fractions in school, but the same boy came to school with a handful of marbles in the morning, and the guy would go home with many times the amount in the evening. One of those boys came to school with a board that had slots in it as wide as a barn door. Everyone was throwing marbles at that board and aiming for those slots for a fast win, yet almost no one succeeded. It looked so easy and was so deceptive. This boy had the mark of a shrewd salesman. I have seen the same system at work in almost all-gambling machines, but the boy in the playground came up with it first. Almost sixty years ago!

I have known a person who started with a whole bag of marbles. She kept counting her riches over and over again and lost a few every time she was counting until she ended with next to nothing. I have seen that in real life also, many times over! Marbles were also a game that boys and girls could play together, a fact that was a no-no at all other times. It would develop something like this.

The girls had the boys running in circles most of the time. I have seen the women play with the marbles of life, many times with much the same result. Boys play with boys, and girls with girls! That was the unwritten rule of those days. Then suddenly on no special day and for no special reason at all, the boys would play with the girls the games of catch the robber.

The boys went after the girls first and made short work of it. They rounded up the girls in no time. Then the girls went after the boys, but the boys run too fast and were hard to get. Never mind!

The girls picked one boy at a time, running in relays in groups of about ten, taking turns, and they ran the victim into the ground, literally into the ground—the poor sucker did not have a chance! I have seen the women do the same thing in real life, many times, with many variations. Fascinating—is it not?

Life is really one big playground, but the marbles are for keeps! Real life is just an extension from the playground in many ways! Soccer was always fascinating on the playground especially with the addition of the wooden shoes. Usually fairly mild, but a heated debate could flare up at any moment, and the shoes would come off. They were used as weapons of war, and it became important—what was harder, the wooden shoes or the wooden heads? Two players would miss the ball occasionally, and the wood wear would clash head-on, and one or both covers would come off the shoes. That would be the end of the game for the victims, but not the end of the wooden shoe.

Dad or a favored uncle would drive a small nail in the bottom of the shoe, wrap a wire over the cap, and fasten it on the other side with another nail, and the musical sound of clop-clop would become clip-clop, clip-clop, etc.! All this did not round off my education. There was more to it than that as you will see in the next little heartrending story. We had boys' club one evening, and we were standing with a group of boys during recess.

A guy by the name of Getty was also present. Normally, he would not associate with small fry like us, but this evening was different. He had a mission, and I was soon to find out what that was!

My humble person was just a stick in the mud in his opinion. But I was good enough for a practical joke. Only I did not know that!—dear me!—I was soon to find out what his plans for my humble person were.

I was a gullible person at the best of times, and I was going to prove it again—boy, oh boy was I ever! Getty kind of snuggled up to me and said to the other guys, "Don't you guys think that Hank is old enough to smoke? He is every bit as good as anybody! I don't see any reason that he does not smoke!" "Absolutely not!" said all the other guys in touching unity.

I was trying to back out of the joyful throng, but they had me hemmed in pretty good. There was no one to help among the grinning faces all around me. Hank was a very lonesome boy at that convention.

"My mom and dad don't want me to smoke" is what I came up with as a last resort, and this was true enough.

The illustrious company was starting to crowd me in the corner ever more. "Well," said Getty, quite helpful and understanding, "you can always make a start with chewing tobacco. That's not as good as smoking but will do for a beginner. You got to start small! Isn't that right, boys?"

And the chorus chimed in quite dutifully, "That's right, Getty!"

And Getty, who was all heart just then, handed me his tobacco pouch with some heavy black Negro chewing tobacco. So I was forced to take a little chunk of the stuff very reluctantly. You got to keep in mind that this was very heavy chewing tobacco, and here I was, a beginner, like David tackling Goliath.

"That's not a chew," said Getty. "That's not even the beginning of a chew!" And so with his ardent help and encouragement, little Henry dug in a little further and ended with about one-third of that package under the expert advice of my counselors. About the size of a chicken egg!

The bell sounded just then, and we were called inside for the after-recess program.

(There must have been about thirty or forty boys in that class and no one was on my side.)

The program started, and I did not feel good at all. I was solid enough, but it seemed that the whole room was on the move, including the whole convention of would-be saints: the teacher, the boys, including Moses, who was carrying the Ten Commandments in a picture on the classroom wall. Wow, what a nightmare!

"What am I going to do with the spittle?" I said to Getty.

"Swallow it!" was the answer. "That's what I am doing!" Henry swallowed obediently as he was told.

This made things a lot worse, as was to be expected. The rest of the boys were watching the proceedings with hawk eyes. This was something nobody wanted to miss, and all around the room were boys with grins and sly faces.

"What am I going to do with the chew?" I said to Getty.

"Swallow it!"

"That's what I am doing!"

"Swallow it!" said good old Getty.

And so I swallowed, and that was almost the end of me. The room caved in on me, and some boys had to carry me outside where the fresh air woke me up to some degree.

Getty and the boys had a whale of a time of course. And I had proven, again, that old Henry was a really naive and stupid little boy who needed a lot of protection from sources unknown! Life was tough in those days not only for me but for the rest of my brothers also. This was especially so during the weekends when our dad had a change to work on our well-being.

A great cleanup would be in progress just before Sunday mostly on the physical end of our endeavors. Cleanness was next to godliness! Such was the opinion of our parents—and we had to go along come what may!

We had to be the unwilling participants in this adventure. Saturday was wash day in our household. We all had to go in the tub—that is, Dad put a sink tub in the living room, and we had to go in the tub, one after the other, while Dad did the wash job. This was not done in a wishy-washy way either. We were scrubbed down with a fairly heavy hard bristle brush that really dug into the dirt and in the skin, and it left an interesting burning sensation all over your system.

It was no picnic, I can tell you that. It was no use to cry when you got soap in your eyes for then a swipe around the ears might follow to stabilize the situation.

The job was followed by a haircut, about once a month, and there was nothing wishy-washy about that either. Hair cutting was done by hand. Dad did not have the money for an electric machine—the trouble being that the thing that he used was way too dull half the time. The cutting became a hair-pulling contest with Dad on one end and us—the victims—on the other end.

Contest—by the hair, that is! Our hair was cut in bangs. Completely bald with a little tuft of hair up front—that's the best the artistic qualities of our dad would allow.

One of us ran off to bed one evening with the hair cutter hanging from the back of his head. He was in opposition and was not going to take it any longer. Life is hazardous with a haircut like that! I was to find that out the hard and painful way.

I was on my way home one day, and I decided that I should try how far I could walk backward without looking up. I went a wonderful long way. I might have gone all the way to Canada if the grocer's horse had not stopped me in a painful manner. The grocer's horse happened to be a really mean little pony, and he bit me right in the back of my head. I have been watching my back ever since! Living with a baldhead and Tuffy is very precarious!

Our mother must have had the makings of an old-time saint when I think of the trials and tribulations that she had to endure with a host of children, eight boys and two girls. It was on a nice, sunny, hot summer Saturday afternoon that she dressed the children in their Sunday best clothes: short pants and spotless white shirts. Clothes had to be spotless in small-time Holland. It was the earmark and the crowning glory of any well-meaning housewife.

Several elements worked together to turn the afternoon into a complete disaster.

The road repairmen had repaired the road in front of our house. That was good! But the hot sun had turned the tar of the road surface into a gooey mixture of glorious play material for us as children. That was not so good.

We had a whale of a time, and our pure white shirts turned into coats of many colors. The tar stuck to our clothes, and the debris of the road hung on to the tar in very satisfying patterns. We had tar in our ears and our noses and mostly in our hair. It was awe-inspiring.

One of my younger brothers had the habit of twirling his hair with his pointing finger. He had little pigtails of tar and hair standing on top of his head like the cedars of Lebanon.

He was grinning from ear to ear, a perfectly happy little Dutch boy. The rest of the clan was not looking any better until Mom got hold of us. She turned the smiling faces into crying ones with one mighty swipe of the flat of her hand.

Our heads were soaked in butter and vinegar, and we were rolled in old blankets and kicked into bed, while Mom and Dad looked at the ruins of a perfect Saturday summer afternoon. It stands for reason that ten growing children could get into a lot of mischief, but the bigger boys created the greatest upheavals. I was the third boy in the family, and my place was near the top of the totem pole.

The relation with my older brother was lukewarm at the best of time, and the hostilities broke out one day in a very unusual manner. Our mother had set out the dinner table for twelve people. The plates were set out around a big pot full of porridge with the spoons neatly arranged in front of each prospective guest at the table. It was then that the hostilities broke out between my brother and me.

It should be mentioned that I have always been a sloppy dresser, and this day was no exception, since my oversize shoes were not laced up as they should have been.

This was a small matter in the heat of battle, and I hauled out to give my brother a solid kick in the unmentionables. He jumped sideways, and my shoe flew of right through a three-by-six window and in the middle of the pot full of porridge.

The soup and the glass flew all over the place, mostly in the plates around the table so that everything was spoiled beyond redemption in front of Mom's unbelieving eyes. She took one look, piled up the plates, and put the pot away. Then she went to the cupboard and cut up a few loaves of bread to feed the hungry crowd.

Dad would take care of the punishment when he came home, but this was the most surprising thing of all: he could not hide his laughter and send us to bed without food.

That was all—we could not believe it. Small blessings do come our way at the most unexpected moments. Something similar happened around that time, but this time the hostilities appeared in reversed order. My older brother was about eighteen months older than I was. He still is!

He was also a grade higher in school. One grade is an awful distance when you are between eight and ten years old; it is like living on another planet, but I did not understand that properly. I did not have the proper sense of proportions.

I wanted to go with my brother and his friend on a short field trip to the forest. This was unthinkable—but I kept wheedling and whining until I got the higher authorities involved in the form of my mother. She told George in no uncertain terms that it was his duty to take his little brother along. It stands for reason that we did a lot of haggling after that so that we finally struck the deal that my brother could throw a little potato against my head.

This may be worth the privilege of going with George and his friend into the wide blue yonder, and so I took my stand in the appointed place waiting for the little potato to come flying against my skull.

Several things went wrong with the setup.

The potato was not all that little. It was huge and became bigger as it came near my defenseless head. My name was not Custer, and I did not make a last stand. I ducked the flying missile so that it sailed right through the neighbor's window.

We had forgotten that we were in front of the window, and Dad had to pay for another broken window. You might have the impression that we did not get along all that well, but nothing is further from the truth. We had a good relationship and shared a lot of livestock.

We had several rabbits in a number of pens behind the house. We cut grass together, and we would see to it that the rabbit pens were clean and dry.

The physical needs of these animals were not forgotten. We took the females to the males so that we might get more rabbits and more rabbits and more rabbits, etc. We would watch in fascination when one old lady with a male rabbit tied a little string to the tail of the female rabbit to make room for the struggling male animal.

It never entered our mind to lay a connection between the action of the animals and men and women around us. It would take many more years before we realized the true actions between a man and woman in love.

We were well in our teenage years before we discovered the facts of life, and we could not believe that Dad and Mom would do a thing like that!

I was fourteen before I learned about the birds and the bees, and I was so angry and disappointed that I killed the bees on that same day.

I can always tell you a different story if you don't believe this one. We will try your patience with another story of those unforgettable moments of our childhood.

It was somewhere around that time that the conferences came into our town. This was a group of people who were working the trapeze in death-defying acts of daring and courage—that's the way it looked to us.

There was one man with one leg. He had lost the other one in a miscue in another performance. That's what the story was as it was told among us. He was swinging around on that trapeze some forty or fifty feet in the air. It made a person dizzy just watching the impossible feats of these daring people. We were awestruck and would have traded places with him if we had the courage, but none of us was nearly that brave.

We went home and rigged up a ladder of about twelve feet. Three or four boys held the ladder in an upright position, and one of us climbed to the top, doing his best to copy the acts of our hero on the flying trapeze. Our house doctor happened to drive by at that very moment and watched the performance with great interest.

Then he went to my mother and said, "I'll be home, Geertje, in case my services are needed."

He shook his head and went his way, meditating on the daring acts of the sons of Derk and Geertje.

My mother had a story that this doctor wanted to buy our little sister when she was born. The doctor and his wife had no children, so he wanted to help Dad and Mom and give the child a good home. It seems like an unlikely story, but our mother was quite adamant that he had said this. It is more likely that the doctor had said something like that in jest and that Mom had taken him seriously.

There is little doubt that he liked my father and mother a little more, which is the case usually. He knew very well that my parents had to struggle to make ends meet, but I have no recollection that he helped us in any financial way, not then or at any other time. My dad was a man with good insight and wanted his kids at home and around the house where he could keep track of them, and so our yard became one large playground. We turned the place upside down and dug holes in the sandy soil to the point that it was not safe anymore.

Especially to Adolf, who was a giant among men. We called him for dinner one day, but he did not show up. One of us had seen him digging away until his white-colored tuffy disappeared below ground level. Only shovels full of sand and the reflections of the shovel were seen. He dug a hole that was so deep he could not get out without help. Not the first and the last time . . .

Our beloved Getty had advanced my education with giant strides, but something happened before that in the fourth grade that was even more important in the shaping of my character.

It was in the fourth grade that we had a teacher from Friesian descent. This man did not think that he was fulfilling his calling if he did not get every student to stand in front of the class. This person would have to sing a song to the best of his or her ability. Every day two or three children would go to the front of the class to bring a heartrending message in song. Some forty children would sit there listening with bored expressions on their lovely faces. Except me! I was not bored. I was scared stiff, and I had sleepless nights when the fateful day came closer.

The day of my first appearance in public!

There was no getting away from it, and the day came that I had to go to the front of forty-some children. The horrible day of my first appearance in the first grade came back in full force, but I made up my mind that it would be a stellar performance, and that it was!

Most children would sing a song of lighter genre, but I decided that I was going to sing a psalm. I opened my mouth, and a high squeaky sound burst forth out of my inner being. I was so nervous that my voice brought forth the most impossible thrillers of nervousness. It sounded like a dog with his tail caught in between the door. It was awful, and the whole room full of children laughed that the tears ran over their collective cheeks. The ribbon girl laughed the hardest of all, and that really hurt.

After that heartrending audition of that psalm, I returned to my place as a broken man. Deep down inside I was crying my eyes out, but nobody could see this, and that was good. My misery was great enough as it was. It really hurt, and the laughter of the ribbon girl was the worst of all. She really did me harm.

The teacher tried several times to get me to sing again, but all to no avail. I had met my waterloo, and there was no power on earth that was going to get me to perform again in front of that class and—what was even worse, in front of my beloved ribbon girl!

It was several years later that I could overcome my fear of that song session in front of the class. A good friend gave me advice in that respect.

"Go to the front of the class," he said. "When you are there, you have to close your eyes, and then you will have to sing our national anthem as loud as you can. Don't stop for nothing but holler as loud as you can."

The result was that I went up front while shivering in my wooden shoes and gave a rendition of our national anthem such as never was heard before. I was howling so loud that the steers of Bashan would have been cross-eyed from jealousy.

I had overcome and was as proud as a peacock. Even the ribbon girl was impressed, but that did not impress me all that much anymore because the fires of my love for her had all but died down to nothing. There was hardly a spark of life left in my former enchantment with that pesky little girl of yore.

This happened a little while before my rendition of the national anthem. It was on a day that our teacher had an urge to lead us into the unknown dimensions of chemistry.

The teacher had a little machine that would create a fairly severe electric shock if he turned a little handle on that little gizmo. This machine had two handles, and if you held these handles, you would get a severe shock of electric voltage, something like an electric fence for cattle control. The teacher told the whole class to join hands. One end of the line would hold one handle of that machine. The very end of the line of hand-holding victims would hold the other handle of the machine, and the shock would travel right through the hand-holding congregation. It worked like a charm with one exception.

My beloved ribbon-girl was sitting in front of me, and I had to hold hands with her if the project was to succeed. I put my sweaty little hands in the soft, sweet-smelling hands of my idol. The teacher turned the handle of the machine, and the shock traveled right through my sweaty little hand over to the soft, sweet hands of the ribbon girl.

I got a shock, and she got a shock, with the result that something broke in my inner being. My infatuation (obsession) with the ribbon girl was ended. The magic chain was broken, and I was a free man again. I could smell the roses again rediscovering the joys of the beetle and the grasshopper in company with a host of other little creatures that dwell in the lower realms of the Dutch lowlands. I rediscovered the beauty of the starry heavens on a cloudless summer night. I was a renewed person!

CHAPTER 3

THE WAR YEARS

L IFE WENT ON like that during most of my childhood, but there were rumors of war in the air. The Germans were getting restless under the godless leadership of the dictator Adolf Hitler and his evil companions.

Times were tough where the rich had abundance and the poor got poorer as time wound its way through the fateful days of the hungry thirties. It was Hitler who seemed to have found a way out of the deadlock of unemployment and near-hunger conditions.

He forced the rich people of Germany to choose for the glittering system of the Nazis out of fear for the rising might (power) of the Communist in Great Russia.

This, combined with the bitter feelings over a hard and unfeeling peace contract negotiated in Versailles after the First World War and the feeling of betrayal by the home front that still rankled in the minds of many former soldiers in Germany, had forced the masses into the arms of a hypnotic agitator by the name of Hitler. The demonic insight of Hitler and his thugs set forces in motion that were to destroy millions of people. All this within about ten years, but even so he created much employment at the first years of his reign. He showed also great insight in some other areas so that many in Germany were taken in by the dream of a Thousand-Year Reich. Holland, on the contrary, was ruled by a Christian coalition of most Protestant parties, and the Catholic under the leadership of an antirevolutionary leader by the name of Colyn.

He was hailed as a great statesman. The sad part was that he ruled under the motto "Protect the guilder and keep up its value." The result was that shiploads of potatoes and other food stuff were thrown in the sea just to keep up the price, and many people went hungry in a country that was flowing with milk and honey.

Holland was a country that had not seen war in more than a hundred years. All this may sound a little bitter, but that is just what it is.

Here was a Christian leader with all the resorts to help a country chained in the bondage of unemployment, and he passed laws to protect the rich and punish the poor.

I will give an example.

I came home one day on my father's bicycle. It had the proper license in the form of a little copper plate. Even the bicycles were taxed in these days!

There was one little oversight on my part. This plate had a little hole in it so that only my dad was allowed to ride this precious machine.

I was stopped by a policeman (who was a member of our church), and I got a ticket for 2.50 euros. This was a small fortune in those days. Our mother gave me the money and told me that I had to tell this Samaritan that he had a stone where others had a heart.

In the meantime, Holland was going on in its own slow and unsuspecting pace. The big neighbor to the east was getting ready to pounce on a world that was tired of war and unwilling to face facts. Then came the day that the Dutch army held a field practice in our neighborhood. The Dutch army of that day was totally obsolete. Holland had not seen war in more than a hundred years, so it really was no wonder that they were so ill prepared for what was coming.

But the Dutch had a secret weapon, and that was that the future enemy might die laughing when they saw our armament. Most of the armies were still going with horse and wagon, another section was going by bicycles, and then there was the cream of the crop: the motorcycles.

The motorcycles might be dating back to the First World War; it was most interesting that you could see the valve springs operating outside the motor block. I never could understand how they managed to keep the dirt out of the engine with a setup like that. It would be completely unacceptable in this day and age. They were a good machine, from what I hear from the experts, and we leave it at that.

Here came the Dutch cavalry! A bunch of Dutch citizens dressed up as soldiers in the caterpillar-green uniforms with bandage-type legs covering dating back to the First World War. The Dutch were too thrifty to set in their ways to make any amount of change in their outdated army, and here they were thundering up the driveway of our neighbor's farm.

We did not know whether we should laugh or cry. It looked ridiculous and glorious—all at the same time. Most of these boys had white hair and should have been home where they belonged. The cavalry was put up on farms in the neighborhood, and a detachment found a place with our neighbors across the road. That made for some very interesting situations.

One of the horses kicked a wall section completely out of the side of the barn. This raised a few eyebrows, you could count on that, but this was the army after all, and nobody talks back to the army—not if you know what is good for you.

The army was made out of the good and the bad, like all armies over the world, and a good deal of girl chasing was the result. But you have to close an eye at times like these, was the opinion. "Boys will be boys," you know. Still, it can be a dangerous mix as some found out nine months later.

It was a strange mix that landed in our front yard like a bunch of proverbial locusts. Some of those boys came out of the city, while others came out of the country from the farms and little holdings.

"They could swear like a trooper" is a saying that is well deserved. These boys could swear! They would have won the war if it had been fought by word of mouth. It was so bad that Dad and Mom told us to stay away from these rough characters.

No good would come out of it, but this was one time that we did not listen. We went anyway. It was too tempting. We had our education behind the barn, so to speak. The big cannons were an interesting thing to look at. These pieces of artillery were good enough armaments, as was proven not all that much later when the going really got rough!

It has always been a mystery to me that those cannons had an inscription: "God is with us."

The German soldier had much the same inscription on his belt buckle. Here we go killing, in His name, and both sides have some people in their ranks who pray for deliverance and victory, and everyone thinks that the right is on their side. They pray, and the killing goes on in the meantime . . . unabated and unhindered. A mystery for many, that is sure.

All this might make you think that the Dutch soldier was lacking in courage, but nothing is further from the truth! The Dutch soldier was every bit as good as the next, bar none. But they were highly individual, which was part of the trouble. These guys were hard to discipline, and that was one of the greatest drawbacks. But these hard-to-handle fellows turned out to be some of the best soldiers after the whole shebang exploded. We were standing there watching when one of those guys was cleaning his saber. He could not even get it out of the scabbard! He had to hammer it out! It had not been out of the scabbard for ages by the look of things. The clodhopper foamed and grumbled while he was kicking the thing all over the neighborhood.

"I better get this thing out and cleaned," he said. "The sergeant will take me apart piece by piece if I don't!"

This boy put up a tremendous fight when war broke out, and there were lots more like him. Those guys could never be drilled like the German soldier. They just were not built that way—not until war forced the reality on them and then they performed above the call of duty most of the time!

But all this was some little way off at that time, and we lived on in blissful ignorance. War was for other nations . . . We would have peace in our times. So we thought!

I will have to tell you a little about the history of Holland to explain the mind-set of the Dutch army. It is a well-known fact that most big cities in the world had their origin close to great waters, along the oceans, mostly downstream from the great rivers that originated in the mountains of mid-Europe. London in England at the Thames, and Rotterdam and Amsterdam at the end of the Maas, and the Rhine, Antwerp, and Paris are all on great rivers.

There were no roads in the middle ages most of the time, and the roads would be hard to travel on when the seasons were bad. Boats and barges could travel in most weather conditions.

The Romans had built roads at often great expense, at great cost. That was not all! These roads had to be maintained at great expense to the Roman Empire. It was easier and faster to follow the waterways moving heavy loads of merchandise from one district to the other. The cities on the mouth of the rivers were used as distribution centers, and smaller centers developed further inland as a spin-off effect of all this activity. These were in turn supported by the activities of the other commodities, like farming, hunting, forestry, and much more.

Belgium, France, and Holland have also great harbors. This was even more important. Most goods for the inland of Europe had to come through the great harbors of Amsterdam, Rotterdam, Antwerp, and some harbors in France and Spain.

It is important to remember that Amsterdam, Rotterdam, and Antwerp have harbors at the North Sea. The goods coming through Antwerp had to cross mountain ranges to the east before they could reach the inland states of greater Germany.

Bishops of the Roman Church ruled many of these states, some places like Munster and Keulen and many more inland, like the countries of France, Belgium, Holland, and Germany, etc. The country east of the great Dutch harbors is practically level and easygoing compared to the harbors further south. These harbors have mountain ranges to the east, making traveling difficult. It stands for reason that the route through the Dutch harbors was preferred for that reason. This put the Dutch merchants on the controlling end of all goods going inland. These men were on the controlling end of the feeding trough!

This is one of the reasons that the Low Countries were rich in many ways. The Dutch became sharp businessmen that made them the envy of many other countries.

This information might be a little boring, but I would like to go into the history of Holland a little further.

Karl V became one of the greatest rulers in the fourteenth century. He was not only a conqueror but also a wise ruler who built a mighty empire and united most of Western Europe. This man loved the Low Countries, and he spent much time in those regions.

All this changed when he died, and Philip II, king of Spain, became ruler of the better part of Europe. He made William of Orange, who was a Catholic at that time, overseer (*stadhouder*) of North and South Holland.

The king of Spain started to persecute the Protestant population of Holland, and William of Orange threw in his lot with the suffering Dutch population. He was assassinated by instigation of the Catholic priest. The Dutch have never forgotten this sacrifice of the House of Orange, and that is one of the main differences between Holland and England regarding the kingship.

The Dutch got in a wide-open war with Spain in a war that lasted eighty years and brought Spain to the verge of bankruptcy. Holland was invaded by four countries (around 1700s). England and France had formed an unholy alliance, and two Catholic states, Munster and Keulen, had jumped in to share the spoils of the stone-rich Republic of Holland.

There was only one savior next to God at that time, and the Dutch population turned to one of the sons of Orange who fought all their enemies to a standstill. This prince of Orange became king of England in later days, and he led the English into a period of freedom from Catholic oppression. It is remarkable that the Dutch worked out the differences between Catholic and Protestant, while the Irish are still fighting the old battle under the banner of the Orangemen and Catholics.

Let's leave the battles of old-time Holland and return back to the ferocious men in green—the Dutch army!

There was also a mock air attack scheduled one evening. The whole town came out to watch the event. The expectations were really high, but the whole show did not turn out to a hill of beans. One airplane was flying over and dropped a couple of dozen balloons. These were supposed to be bombs. A pile of wood was put on fire, and that was the air attack. At that point, the fire brigade came flying around the corner with a lot of racket and little conviction. Even so, you had to admit the firefighters looked firm and courageous in their hopscotch uniforms. Their heroic appearance was the end of the show for the day.

The Dutch army was indeed naive and ill prepared for the things to come. So were the government and the Dutch overall! A detachment of gunners was in a shelter, facing the river close to the bridge. These guys would be written off if an attack was launched against the bridge. Such was the folks' wisdom of that day. The thought of this made me shiver. Those poor courageous guys! Bottled up like that!

The enemy came in the back door when the attack came—and the pillbox was empty. Was there betrayal? Nobody knows for sure, but that we were sold out in places is an established fact!

The other gunners' nest was right across a villa, where a family lived with several grown-up girls. These girls were caught up in the spirit of the moment and made it a practice to go on a swing right across these young fellows. These guys grew ever more excited the higher the swing went. The girls on the swing left little to the imagination, and the language of the young soldiers even less. These girls had a way of advertising themselves, there is little doubt about that. Not very upbuilding if one takes in consideration that the girls were from very a good upbringing. Even so! We all do foolish things at one time or another, and everyone is entitled to his or her own mistakes.

Still how unprepared we were! And so we lived on in blissful ignorance. Bad things always happen to other people. This is often the mentality of most folks, and here there was no exception. The Dutch had made good money in the first war, and many thought that it would go the same way this time. Let the other people fight and we look on, and we might make some money besides. That seemed like a good policy.

My friend's name was Dick, and we had been friends for some time while the friendship was still growing as time went by. Other guys were taken up in this close circle as time passed by, and we had a lot of fun together. But the fun was a little doubtful on the night that I had to babysit. Dad and Mom were entitled to a supplement ration in the latter part of the hungry thirties. The supplement was for families who were partly unemployed. Usually canned meat, good to eat, but it looked kind of gruesome. The top layer of the can of meat was filled with about an inch of some quivering substance that looked a lot like yellow, only more transparent.

One fellow claimed that part of this was made of frog legs, and that turned a few people off, and they quit eating this food. But it was really nutritious, and we were only too happy to eat the stuff. We also got some cans of hamburger with that—a kind of Spam! This stuff was really delicious when it was fried. But for the moment we were more interested in the margarine that came with this supplement—that evening anyway! The margarine butter came included with this supplement—usually in packets of twelve, one kilo each. My uncle had made a breadboard for Mom, which was a regular piece of art. It was about ten inches long and eight inches wide, and it had a nice handle on it.

One brilliant brain among us put two and two together (the board and the butter, that is!) He suggested a competition about which person could smash the butter and flatten it the most in one fell swoop. It turned out to be a very interesting competition indeed.

There was my friend Dick, who was always trying to be a little more debonair and sophisticated than the rest. He had a very dignified swing, you had to admit that! But not nearly as effective as the swing of lanky easygoing Albert, who had a much longer reach. He also had a much better coordination of head and hand. Albert did all right! But just not good enough! My brother George had a much more coordinated and vicious approach. He flattened the butter in one fell swoop so that half the table was covered!

But what about me, you may ask? I failed miserably. I was never any good in sports and totally incompetent at butter swapping. I just did not have what it takes in a demolition exercise. We had to scrape the butter back together and try to form reasonable little packs again before Mom and Dad came back home. The wrapping paper was of a good quality, lucky enough.

Crazy? I guess it was at that. We had some growing up to do yet!

Our mother was very strict when it concerned food. "Never throw away food! Someday you might lick your fingers for it!" she said.

These words were very prophetic because we did exactly that, not all that much later.

She was also a forerunner of Colonel Sanders, who called his product finger-licking good.

Do not misunderstand what I just wrote. In my opinion, the wasting of food has always been a great sin. It turns me off and makes me sad when I see good food wasted in the restaurants when sometimes as much as half a meal is thrown away because we can't eat it all. This is not good stewardship according to me! I wish something could be done about it!

Dick and I had not been friends all that long yet, but he was to become one person that has been very close to me, all those years gone by. He knows things about me that nobody else does. It is a little like the story of David and Jonathan, the manner in which we met and became friends.

Dick is a year younger than I am, and he was in a lower grade in school, and that's an awful long way when you are of that age. And, of course, I could not associate with a person that young. This was completely unacceptable. But the years fall away when you grow older—that's the way it seems anyway.

We were chumming around a little at times, but nothing all that serious, when on an ill-fated day, he made a remark to me that did not come over that nice. He called me a few names, and that did not sit well at all. This was kind of damaging to my dignity, to my way of thinking. I told him in no uncertain terms what I thought of him, and we were involved in a good fistfight before you could say "Boo!"

This was not all that serious at that point, but the onlookers got involved, and according to the custom, one boy acting as referee would go between the two fighters. One of us had to hold up his hand and dare the other party to knock it off. We should have knocked his lights out instead—but were too stupid just then.

The strategy worked like a charm. Neither of us wanted to be declared a coward, and so the fight was on, and stayed on! We had to walk about one mile to get home, and we fought every inch of the way. The referees made sure of that. How stupid can you get?

One pause in the hostilities came as a blessing in disguise in the unlikely form of our new minister and his wife. The couple was out for a walk and almost bumped into us at that unsavory moment. We had a warning just in time so that we could hide behind some bushes along the roadside. It was most interesting that the two fighters were joined for the purpose that the two enemies could resume the tit-for-tat after the minister was out of sight.

And we fought all right. It was ferocious. None of the spectators gave us an argument about anything from that time on after that battle of the Royals—Dick and me, that is!

This is the only favor that came my way from that minister in all the times I have known him. More about that later!

Our status among our classmates had grown considerably after that! It is interesting that all my life events have developed along much the same pattern.

I was real shy most of the time, with no desire to share the limelight at any cost! But suddenly, when the need arose, the urge came over me to take control and take a situation in hand when nobody else had the will or the insight to do so! We believe that we might have been of service when the occasion arose. At least, that's what I like to believe.

Dick came over the next morning to apologize. He was sporting a beauty of a blue eye and many bruises, and I was in no better shape.

"I lost a lot of sleep last night," and he looked sheepish when he said that. "My conscience has bothered me because I have hurt you so much!"

Well, he was one up on me at that one—my conscience did not bother at all! But this was a mighty big gesture on his part, and that's the way we got so close later.

"But I gave you more than I got!" he said as a parting shot.

Then he asked me very earnestly if I would ask my mother if we could become friends. That was the beginning of a friendship that lasted a lifetime. My father was a quiet little man. He never said all that much, but what he said was well worth listening to.

His brother, Marten, would come over sometimes, and they would sit together, with the uncle smoking away on his old pipe as if laying a smoke screen. This uncle was a very heavy smoker, and they would sit together for a couple of hours, hardly saying anything. Then Uncle Martin would leave, and they would know everything about each other after this quiet conference. Strange but a true story nevertheless!

This uncle fell off the roof of a building some years later and broke his neck. This was awful hard to handle for Dad because he was so close to that man. Dad felt even worse because my uncle had been betrayed not that many years ago in a very dirty way, and he went broke later.

A widow with nine children was left behind in very difficult position.

Uncle Martin used to be in a very successful partnership in our hometown, when he was approached by an individual from another town some ten miles away from us. This man had a sawmill for sale. There was a good market for lumber, the man said, and many people were waiting to buy lumber from his mill. My uncle, who had a large family, was taken in by his sweet talk. He did some checking in the background but was as good as sold to the deal right from the start. The man mentioned quite casually that he was an elder in the church of Uncle's denomination, and that convinced Uncle. After all, an elder of the church could be trusted—am I right or not?

The mill was bought, and my uncle could sell all the lumber he could saw and even more. But he could buy no trees. All the trees had been bought up by the former owner, and next to nothing was left in the whole country. He went broke in no time flat. Guess what? The people around there helped the family in any way possible. That those people were mostly Red Socialist and never set foot in the church was a mere coincidence. They were only Samaritans, you know!

One question, who was the greater witness? The Christians had the calling, but the Red Socialist lived it. This is not the only time that I have seen this kind of behavior. Some people can evangelize like you would not believe. But don't deal with them!

Our family has been on the same receiving end of that treatment, while the world stood back shaking their heads, so to speak. There was something else that happened around that time that had a great influence on my life. It was another example of Dad's quiet wisdom.

There were not many holidays before the war, not for the ordinary working man anyway. We had the church holidays, like Christmas and Easter and Pentecost, also Ascension Day, and that was it. Dad would go with us on a bicycle ride on those days. This one day, he took us for a ride to a coffeehouse that included a play garden with a live donkey. It was a stubborn little animal, but you could not blame that poor animal all that much.

I would have been stubborn too if I had to carry a bunch of screaming children on my back all day long with not-too-gentle treatment that was easy to see. One red-freckled buffoon out of our hometown had taken charge of the animal. Nobody else had a chance to have a ride. Dad got quite upset at one point and told the guy in no uncertain terms what he was going to do if the other little ones did not get a turn for a ride also. That was good for the other kids, but we still did not go for a ride.

Oh well, there were many other things to do, and it was not the end of the world. There was something going on that was way more interesting. Dad was sitting at a side table with a bottle of beer. This was very unusual. Dad was not a drinking person at all. This was the first time that we had seen him behind a bottle of beer. Mom would be very upset if she had seen Dad with a bottle of beer in front of him. We asked Dad for the reason for his unusual behavior.

"It is like this—" he said, "it is no sin if you drink a bottle of liquor in moderation, if you don't overdo it. The Lord has given us many things. And many things can be used or abused. Beer is one of them. Always drink in moderation. I know that your mother is afraid of liquor, and that is the reason that I never drink it while she is around."

She has a good reason to be afraid! Her grandfather was one of the richest people in his district. He lost it all because he could not leave the liquor alone. He drank too much. He had one of the biggest farms in the country, and her grandmother was allowed to wear the silver scissors on a silver chain around her middle. This was a sign of great distinction. They lost it all in one lifetime.

"Be careful in the future," Dad was saying while he took a sip of his beer. "You have drink abuse in your bloodstream. Handle the stuff with care. Your mother was so poor in her childhood that she went to school on two left wooden shoes. Both the right shoes were broken, and they did not have the money to buy new ones. Drink in moderation, or not at all. Remember the history of your forefathers!"

We have never forgotten those words even until this very day. Liquor was never used in my childhood years and very seldom in my adult years. I have never bought the stuff because I never wanted to give the wrong example for my children when they were growing up. We have never made a big issue out of it either. Dad gave us sound advice on that day long ago. Many things are good in themselves if they are not abused.

CHAPTER 4

WAR!

LIFE WENT ON at a fairly slow pace, and my life was filled with all kinds of activities, some more important than others, but it was never boring. Holland was a good country to live in, a country of abundance, but the riches were loaded up in the wrong places.

"Fat will float on the top!" refers to an old saying, and proven time and again! Holland had many colonies, and that was part of the reason that life was so good for the upper class. East India, as it was called before the war, country of mystery, country of romance. The country of a thousand islands, as it was called before the war. The country has suffered and benefitted from the Dutch. The inhabitants of that fair land have been taken advantage of often and their women abused repeatedly. Their men have had to work at rock-bottom wages in often poor conditions, not only there but also all over the world to our eternal shame, although this was counterbalanced with the fact that the Dutch also brought much that is good to this fair and humble land.

The little man in India was often abused, but the common man in Holland did not make out all that much better. They were being used and abused. I could write a book on that alone. Child labor was quite common in those days. My aunt had to watch the cows from four in the morning until late sundown in the summertime. She was eleven years old then; schooling had to wait for a more convenient time!

My parents had to work like that more often than not, but nobody complained all that much. The next generation made up for that, and they did not need much practice.

I have seen children working in the beets from sunup to sundown right here in sunny Alberta. That was in the beginning of the immigrant days. Nobody wanted to notice their plight. They did not seem that unhappy either, come to think of it, making good citizens in later days! Against the law, of course, but it was done!

Holland was a stone-rich country. That's how the Germans called it later when they robbed Peter and Paul in an unprecedented manner. For them it was a good enough reason to invade the country anyway!

Our family was not all that unhappy. Mom and Dad carried a heavy burden, but we were too young to notice. We did learn to appreciate the small things in life. Many people never went any further from home than a bicycle could carry them. That's how they lived. They were happy and content. Our present day is different. Your car can bring you out of sight and sound in a matter of minutes.

We never had a radio before we went to Canada. Our main source of information was the newspaper and the rumor mill. The newspaper of that day brought news in a responsible manner, while the rumor mill was very emotional and independent. The prewar days were hardly paradise. But we did have many good things in our life. Evenings were to sit together and have a good time, be *gezellig*, sociable, especially in our family.

Uncle Jan, who was an uncle from Dad's side of the family, was the owner of a small farm, just a little bigger than my dad's holdings. We, as boys, were just a little bit jealous of that uncle. His place seemed just a little bit nicer than Dad's place, and it had a few more animals to its credit. But Uncle Jan was not a happy person.

I remember best the discussion they had about Germany and Hitler, the upstart Austrian corporal! Uncle Jan did not think that Hitler was all that bad. He had put many people to work and had done many other good things. The working conditions in Germany had improved a great deal, and many good things were happening in Germany.

Dad, on the other hand, had some second thoughts. He had a lot of concern about the rumors that the Jews were being persecuted in Germany. He had some undefined misgivings about a man that could treat other human beings in that manner, but there was no way that he could convince Uncle Jan. He believed in Hitler and continued to do so throughout the war. Never did he come to understand the evil intent of the Nazi system. Many more individuals were taken in by the hypnotism of the glittering Nazi system, especially in Great Germany. Only the outcast sounded the alarm.

Reverend Mueller was one of them.

"First, they came and got the Jew," he said. "I did not say anything. Then they came and got the Communist, and I said nothing. They came and got the gypsy, and I said nothing. Then they came for me, and there was nobody left to say anything!"

It is well always to test the spirits and see whether they are of God. We can only do that on the hand of the Bible. How I wish that more people would be aware of that in this day and age! Getting back to the prewar days . . . It is not hard to understand the attitude of the people of that day. Conditions were so bad that a farmer took his little pigs to the market and nobody was buying, not even one! He went home very downhearted that evening and found double the amount of pigs in the back of his wagon, an unwanted gift from another farmer unloading his pigs on someone else rather than taking them back home, where he had more pigs to feed. And life went on within its own slow rhythm that put people to sleep as in a lullaby.

A friend walked up to me at that time and told me that there had been a lot of shooting going on at the border. It had something to do with smugglers. This was a little disturbing for the peace-loving Dutchmen but soon forgotten.

The real story was different. The border guards had a shootout with some Germans, while some Dutch uniforms and other military hardware were secreted across the border. The Germans were well informed about the Dutch army and were going to make good use of it! Dad must have had a bit of suspicion because they had witnessed the first war from a distance. They had a deep down fear of the future.

We, as young guys, lived on with no idea of what could come. Although ever more rumors started swirling around, we went to bed quite unconcerned on the night of May 10. It had been a warm and cozy day, and all may be well with the world. Looks are deceiving! It would be the last peaceful night in a long, long time! A dark night of violence and terror was just about to enter our cozy little world!

We were knocked out of bed at five o'clock in the morning as an awful lot of concerned people were filling the streets. The sound of many airplanes was heard throughout the night. People had a good reason to be concerned, for this was a very unusual sound in the peaceful skies over the lowlands.

These were no Dutch airplanes, that was a sure thing. The whole Dutch air force could not bring that many planes together at the best of time.

Faraway thunder reverberated through the night. Only, this was no thunder, as we soon were to find out. Most of our neighbors had one opinion or another.

But our friend Hans said, "These must be the Germans. Boy, oh boy, are they going to find out a thing or two before they know what hits them. The Dutch have a mighty army, and we will beat the tar out of them. The English and the French have promised to help us, and we are going to show that corporal from Germany what real fighting is all about!"

He hitched up his pants and spit a time or two, gesturing with mighty arm strokes. Hans had the Germans all but beaten, and he started to build the courage of all spectators. My dad was not so sure that it would go as easy as all that, but he did not say all that much. He went home and quietly started packing some highly needed supplies in case the need arose.

Radio Holland announced that Germany had invaded Holland and admonished the population to be calm because the army had everything well in hand. The bubble had burst. We woke up out of a fool's paradise and were to enter the real world. The New Reich had a crash course of new knowledge in terror and suppression all lined up, especially for us! We figured that our boys would give a good account of themselves. Hitler has made his first big mistake, was the general opinion. Our boys are going to beat them to pulp. We are going to drown them in the waterline.

This was followed by the message: "The English are landing on the coast, and the Belgian and French troops are coming in from the south. The Germans' dead are lying three feet thick in front of our lines!"

The rumor mill was going full tilt, and we all thought that the enemy would be in for a hard fight. All were convinced that the Germans would be beaten to a pulp. We had it all figured out pretty good, but there was one serious mistake in our calculations: the Germans did not know this yet, and it would take us five years to convince them!

I mentioned the bridge to the west that would be one of the first battle lines and then you would see something. Well! The enemy came from the south and bypassed the bridge altogether. This was just one of many surprises in store for the bewildered population.

The ultramodern tank traps on the bridge, pride of our engineers? They were never even tested! A blacksmith in town was forced by gunpoint to cut away the heavy steel bars cemented in the bridge deck. The rest just was bulldozed away. That was that! The main force of enemy troops went through to the south of us! The first detachment of troops came through our town at ten o'clock in the morning.

Our beloved Snake-man, the man of many wonders and our beloved goalkeeper in days of yore, this lovely man sat on the first motorcycle with a sidecar. He was called back about a year earlier, like so many German citizens, and here he was—the conquering hero—liberating our country just like so many others who had worked in Holland years before. They came back to repay the hospitality of our countrymen.

The Snake-man died not many days later in a battle before the Ysel River. My cousin talked to him on the first day of the invasion, and he was friendly enough—small wonder! It was the same story time and again. People who had worked in Holland in former years came back to show the shortcuts and the best way to kill our boys.

Our soldiers were shot at from the rooftops, often by people who were sympathetic to the Nazis, willing to sell out their country for a handful of silver.

It happened that our boys found sawdust, instead of dynamite, in places where it was needed most. Officers ordered their men to fight in places that were unimportant. These men found death, many times, in situations that were impossible to hold and had no bearing or importance to the defense of our land. Betrayals like that happened in every war, but it sure hurt when it happened to us. But why be surprised? It was just one of the first lessons in the German mentality.

Their beloved leader, Adolf the Hun, was quoted as saying, "Everyone will believe a lie, if it is repeated often enough!"

These leaders clearly had no morals of any kind! Some enemy storm troops stayed long enough to buy some things for their wives and girlfriends. These jokers were very impressed with the quality and quantity of the Dutch articles in the stores. There was stuff that they had not seen in years, and they bought all they could carry—not much for a soldier at war, but they would be back. Often, very, very, often!

Why should they not? The money that they used was as worthless as the paper it was written on! The stuff was as useless as the black souls of the army leaders who conquered us in such deceitful manners. They were only the forerunners of the locust who settled down not that much later for the wholesale rape of the Dutch countryside.

The trains came and came, over and again, for months on end, rolling east, plundering our country of produce withheld from those that were poor and hungry not that much earlier. May 10 was a beautiful spring day. Spring had just conquered winter. Greens and flowers were bursting out all over, proclaiming a festival of joy and new life, a feast dedicated to the honor and glory of the Great Creator, He who is Creator of all that is living and beautiful.

The sun was sparkling in untold dewdrops, sparkling, just like just the many jewels in the crown of its Maker. Birds were bursting out in song, carrying stick and twig for the nest of future young ones. The skylark reached out for heaven because earth was not big enough to hold her reaction to the birth of the newborn day, and in the meantime, the proclaimed masters of the earth, the stewards and caretakers, had put in motion forces and powers of unsurpassed terror and destruction.

Death was on the march, and it will not be denied. A grim silence had fallen over the countryside as we watched the Snake-man and his cohorts move along a shortcut, orchestrated by the ever-so-helpful Snake-man.

Faces, camouflaged with dark colors, have entered day. This is no make-believe! This is the real thing! The set faces of the grim-looking soldiers promise swift retribution for anyone who dares to oppose. It gave me the coldest feeling I had ever experienced in all my life. It was almost as if death itself was passing in front of our eyes. And that is what it was that was coming our way right in front of us.

It was a very good thing that no civilians were foolish enough to come shooting. The enemy would have shot innocent people without any hesitation. That lesson was well learned in Belgium and France in the First World War. It was there that many civilians were shot by these same invaders.

German honor demands that only people in uniform have a license to kill legally. How crazy can you get?

I was wandering around with a lump in my throat and ice in my stomach. We realized, full well, that here was the ultimate terror. It would take something bigger than us to turn back the spawn of hell that had descended on us! A strange kind of mood had set in. There was this terror on one side, and on the other side was some pleasure in the unexpected holiday. The ever-present boy-meets-girl syndrome was reaching out for better things even now on this grim day.

Many folks got dressed up and mixed the horror of this day with more life-centered ideas. They had dressed up in their better clothes to watch the proceedings of the glorious conquerors, not realizing that the German propaganda, ever watchful, made full use of the display of the throng of spectators. They showed the home front how glad the brother's nation of German descent welcomed the conquering heroes.

Opposition to the invading army was almost nonexistent until they hid in the great rivers to the west of us. The Germans had to cross the rivers, and it was there that they met stiff opposition. Very heavy fighting broke out at the Grebbe Line. It was there also that the Snake-man died, and many of his weapon brothers with him.

Do you remember the guy I mentioned before? The one who had the saber rusted in his scabbard? This guy fought like a man possessed, as he well might have been. It was not a playground for him anymore, and he fought long and determined against superior numbers and better-equipped men in front of him. We lost track of him later, but it is very likely that he became a member of the Resistance later. He would not give up either, like so many others who were fighting next to him in that war with the Germans.

The story goes that there was a gun crew manning the big antiaircraft cannon. They were fighting on with unbelievable results. They never paid much attention on how to handle a gun when they were in training. It took the whole crew together to figure out how to handle the big cannon. But they made it work, with old-fashioned ingenuity, with excellent results. It is a well-known fact that the Dutch antiaircraft cannon was one of the best in the armies of that day.

Very heavy fighting broke out along the great rivers at Amsterdam and Rotterdam. The enemy tried to cross the river at one of the main bridges. This bridge had a very high crown, and the Dutch marines shot everything crossing the high point of the bridge with great results.

The Germans tried to cross the river in rubber boats that were heavily laden with equipment. The Dutch marines jumped in the river with their knife between their teeth, and next thing you knew, no more Germans. The marines slit the bottom of the boats, and the whole kit and caboodle went to the bottom! The German army never did take those rivers. No matter what they did, their boats became waterlogged, and so did the invader's.

The Germans favored weapons were the parachute troops. These troops were thrown off in great numbers behind the Dutch lines, often assisted by Dutch traitors, who were giving a helping hand in many situations. The Germans were piled three feet high in front of the Great Afsluitdijk, a dam separating the North and the South Seas. That's what the rumor was saying.

The dike, as it was called, was the pride of the Dutch nation. It had been put in place as a divider between the North and the South Seas during the hungry thirties when times were hard and many folks went hungry. The beginning of the dike was heavily fortified with reinforced bunkers, and it was in front of these bunkers that many Germans lost their lives.

Hitler could have bombed the dike easy enough and flooded the whole center of Holland, but that did not fit in with his master plan. He would have lost a lot of good farmland so badly needed for the future war effort. The people really did not matter; it was the land that was important. He had way better methods to force the Low Countries to surrender. Land was important. Humans were not.

He sent up his airplanes and bombarded the heart and soul out of Rotterdam and out of the nation, with the ultimatum that more cities would follow if the Dutch did not surrender. The Dutch generals counted the cost and decided to surrender. The message of the capitulation was falling on us like a clap of thunder. It was an action that shocked us to the core.

The capitulation was unbelievable news for us, but the departure of the queen was far more damaging. We felt like we had lost the mother of the nation. Holland without her was like a beehive without the queen, and much more damaging.

We found out later that the queen and the government escaped to England to form a legal government in exile, and it was a wise move after all.

We were standing on the mill yard in heated discussion when we heard the bad news. We felt betrayed and sold out. How could they do this to us? There was so much left to fight for, and here we were left all alone. Our leaders left us to fight the battle without resources and without weapons of any kind.

Hitler got the country, but he did not get the queen, and he did not get the government. Neither did he get the navy of Holland or her ships and merchant vessels—ships he needed so badly for the upcoming invasion of England. The Dutch sank most of their biggest ships in the mouth of the North Sea Canal, and they took off with the rest of the navy.

The Germans had also dropped paratroopers in the palace gardens to capture the queen. They came too late there also.

What is more important, he did not conquer our hearts. Darkness ruled our living from that point on.

"The enemy is starting to turn on the screw!" our friend Hans was saying.

An expression that was new to us, but it was a saying that was going to be used often from that point on. All windows had to be covered with blankets to keep the light from shining in the streets, and the night got darker and darker. Order followed order by the German war command. No more meetings of more than three people anytime. Heavy penalties would fall on the disobedient. Curfew was set at eight o'clock. Nobody was allowed in the streets after eight o'clock. Anyone hiding weapons of any kind would be shot. Anyone helping Allied soldiers would be shot. Anyone helping or hiding a Jew would be shot. The list went on and on.

The humble Dutch became joke bearers, and all life went underground. Dutch people had not known war or suppression in more than one hundred years, and they had become law-abiding people at that time. This was a habit that was hard to break. But we were learning fast. It did not take long before the Germans ordered that all lead and copper should be brought in. The enemy needed copper and lead to make ammunition for the war effort, and the population started grumbling but obeyed. We were used to obedience before the war. Then all radios had to be brought in. This was hurting the pocketbook, and folks grumbled a little louder. They brought in a few old radios but kept the good ones.

We needed them too badly. We had to listen to the BBC, something that was also strictly forbidden. People hid the radios and started listening in hiding places but oh so carefully. Traitors and Nazi sympathizers were lurking all over, and nobody trusted anybody anymore. The screw was slowly tightened ever more, and the Dutch were slow to react, true to their nature.

The prisoners of war were ordered back into captivity less than a year after they had been set free by a seemingly generous German war commander.

Then the thing happened that woke many of us up to the reality of our condition. The Jews were ordered to wear a yellow star proclaiming to the entire the world that the Jews were proclaimed to be the outcast of society. The scum of all nations! That's the impression that the Nazi butchers wanted to impress on the entire world, and in this they succeeded only too well in the minds of many people. Excuses could be found left and right. The Jews had betrayed this one. The Jews had sold poor stuff to someone else. They were leeches, not to be trusted. Too many reasons to count, on and on!

The strategy of the enemy was to set the Jews apart. That was the reason for the yellow star. Often they succeeded, but not always. Many churchgoing people started to see the writing on the wall. Our leaders sounded warnings about the German intent. I will never forget how these unfortunate people were scuffling through the streets of our hometown, hugging close to the buildings, almost as if they were trying to hide in the brickwork. I believe that they would gladly have done just that if they only could do so. Their entire livelihood was taken away from them, and this was only the beginning.

If anyone had told us on May 10, when the war started, what was to happen, we would not have believed it.

The younger of the two Jewish families who lived close to us came over then and said, "It might not be all that bad for the men, but the women will be forced to go to the hayloft often when the Germans take over!"

A trip to the hayloft would have been paradise compared to what was in store for them. Little did we know what was waiting for them soon in the future!

I have never seen the man again. They went into hiding from thereon, until one day the Germans ordered the Dutch police to escort the Jews to the train. They were to be put to work in a place of unknown destiny.

The shame of it all was the fact that some Dutch police lent a helping hand, and I am a little surprised about that to this very day. Most of us had heard rumors by then about death camps, and these men must have heard it too.

"Their hairs are black, the noses bent, disappears the Jew in concentration camp!"

This was a song that was well known in those days. The instinct of the common folk sensed with their heart what highborn people were denying as much as four years later. The song pointed to the distinct Jewish features that gave them away at every turn of the road. Most of them disappeared without a trace as time went by, and we were standing by, helpless, and slowly the facts started filtering through. We started hearing about SS troops using vans with exhaust welded into the rear to blow the fumes into the closed area, poisoning Jews, as so many cattle.

The treatment of humans became worse than that of animals. Death camps were set up later for the only purpose of killing the Jews. They were only more efficient. Those camps were regular death factories where people were burned in great ovens and turned into ashes in an assembly line of morbid efficiency.

CHAPTER 5

MIDNIGHT

THE JEWS WERE not without help, not entirely—especially in Holland. A handful was saved from destruction, often at great cost to some well-meaning Dutchmen. It also prompted the rise and organization of some cells of the underground movement. I can testify to that myself, as you will see later in this story.

Even so! Not all the Jews were prepared to accept help, and that was part of the problem. Some of them were offered a hiding place and received many warnings. The Germans could not be trusted! Many were told that they were not going to work camps in East Germany or Poland, but that they were in danger of losing their lives. But most of those unfortunates were not prepared to take the risk of disobeying the new master race. The Germans set up Jewish committees under Jewish overseers who helped to register and organize the shipment of Jews. All the time, the Jews misunderstood the true intentions of the Germans. They still believed that the Jewish population was relocated for work somewhere else.

"It might not be so bad," they were telling themselves. "The children might be better off if we obey. A little work is not going to hurt anybody."

On and on went the excuses and arguments. Do not judge us too harshly (neither judge them). Human nature seeks the way of least resistance in moments like that. And many of the Jews went . . . never to be seen again.

I was fifteen years old then and can testify that this is true. My father and mother were not able to do much of anything, even if they had been approached, but I am sure that they would have found a way . . . somehow . . . somewhere. Mom and Dad had ten children then and were hard-pressed to keep body and soul together.

Many stories have been told about the Jews and their disappearance. I won't go into that here. You can look that up in other books, but it should be mentioned that the Jews are still the apple of God's eye—nobody can touch them and escape punishment. My parents thought so, and I completely agree with them.

Everything was getting in short supply. The trains kept rumbling past our hometown—direction Germany . . . day after day and month after month . . . and the Dutch countryside was bled to starvation.

We were on rations for everything—another weapon in the hands of the enemy. He could hold back the rations and starve you to surrender. The Germans used this fact of life to our detriment. My cards were held back when I was forced to work in the enemy country at a later date.

And the war went on, while the German army seemed invincible. The glorious Thousand-Year Reich was *sighen* (fighting). Their arrogance drove them to the point that they invaded Russia. They were convinced that victory was eminent and that the rest of the world would fall into their hands like an overripe apple. We were happy to take note of their overconfidence.

"This is the last step!" we were saying. "Russia will swallow them alive in the same way it swallowed Napoleon some hundred years ago!"

And our humble company gained new confidence and became more determined to fight on with each passing day. But the fighting intensified and grew more vicious as day followed day and night followed night.

The nights became more important. Meetings were held and actions were carried out at an increasing pitch as time went on, and the night became more important than the day. The resistance and underground movements were ultrasecret in the first years.

Ordinary people like me were not invited to the party. It was mostly for a select group of people, and what did we do? We went fishing! That is what we did. The bicycles had still some form of tires, and we pedaled long distances to catch some fish. We did this partly to supplement the food supply.

On the other hand, we did this for relaxation. We went to a fast-flowing river about five kilometers past the next town. We would sit there—alone with our thoughts, spending a day in complete relaxation in an imaginary land filled with peace and dreams of days long gone by or yet to come.

You sat in a hiding place of head-high reeds, surrounded by the pungent aroma of water plants and calamus roots. The birds would be singing all around, and the water would be nibbling at the shore. The panorama at your feet would take on the dimensions of another world. You were floating away in timeless fashion, cherishing the present moment with no fears for tomorrow.

A dog barking in the distance was the only sound, and occasionally a rooster in the distance was crowing . . . He was proclaiming independence day in the chicken world. A duck would be diving underwater, once every so often, recovering a little tidbit that's only important to the lowly duck.

There we would sit, hour after hour, watching the pen of a chicken feather that served as a bobber on the end of the line. It was a tricky operation, and you had to watch every second, or a well-educated fish would nibble the bait off the hook, putting the sucker on your end of the line.

These were hours of complete relaxation and peace. In this way our day was spent at peace and atonement with all creation. Bait was very important! Someone told us that he had put together bait that was so effective that he had to crawl behind a tree to bait the hook. The fish would come up the shore to get at the bait if he did it any other way. I'll gladly tell you another story if you do not believe that one!

Another guy went out fishing and ran out of bait. The passions were high, and the need of this unbearable moment was beyond description. He looked around in desperation, and what did he see? . . . A dead cat! He cut the head off the cat and mixed it with some even more unappetizing substance, making fish food of an unbelievable delicacy. He caught more fish that day than he did on any other day of his miserable fishermen's existence.

The stories were many, but the fish were few. The fish stories were of great variety, and the fish would grow little by little until all the wagons of our hometown could not have carried all the imaginary fish. I can honestly say that I never met a wagon with fish, unless it was the three-wheeler bicycle of the fish peddler.

Our neighbor went fishing one day, with no luck at all, but he found many bushes loaded with saskatoon berries, ripe and ready. Saskatoons were always better than no fish, and he ate his fill on the saskatoons. They were good!

There was absolutely no doubt about that fact of life. But he ran into problems, according to his account of the scenario of events that followed shortly afterward. He was so overloaded that he got the runs. He could relieve himself easily enough but had no toilet paper, so he used the next best thing. The bag around the sandwiches would have to do. But alas! He miscalculated on two accounts . . .

His sandwiches had been prepared in a pack that had served as a salt bag. The salt bag and the fact that he had piles (hemorrhoids) were a bad combination!

"I jumped clear over the saskatoon bushes!" he recalled, as he told us the story in later days somewhat downhearted and shamefaced.

I can handle a big story as good as the next guy, but this one takes the cake and is a little hard to swallow. I have heard many fish stories over the years and enjoyed most of them. They are fun to listen to and gave us a little diversion in times when everything looked dark and dreary.

Some young people of our church had a competition at that time—the Christian Reform Churches against the Reformed. At stake was the number of fish each church would wrangle on shore.

Would you know it? The competition was won by the Reformed with the overpowering number of one measly fingerling. A fingerling is a fish about a finger long.

The Reformed people were hard to live with after that overwhelming victory. They sure made us aware of it . . . repeatedly.

The competition was set up in the spinning factory where I worked in a support service to the main job of spinning cotton on spools. The refined product could be used by the weavers in the textile factories. Our job was to remove the full spools and to replace them with empty ones. The empty spools were stored in boxes along the walls, and it was absolutely forbidden to drop any empty spools in the hallways without picking them up right away.

Several other young guys and I went to the boxes to pick up some empty spools, and boys being boys, one boy said, "Any one of you dare me to throw this bunch of spools on the floor?"

Well, this was no contest. Two or three guys challenged him right away, right then and there. Down went the spools: right where they should not be. I wish the guy had stayed that brave in the following moments. The manager of the factory came by that spot in the next few minutes and took up the challenge then and there. This man was an old German officer who had fought in the First World War.

This man was no one to fool around with anytime and most certainly not at a time when we were so vulnerable. The man was a naturalized German, to make matters even worse. He would stand still occasionally during the surveys of the factory. He would wipe with his hand over his eyes as if he was trying to get rid of something.

The story was that he was reliving some scenes of the trench war of the years 1914–1918. It was to his credit that he had no use for Hitler and his crooks—none whatsoever—because he ordered a handful of high Nazi officials right out of the factory. He claimed that they were spying out factory secrets, and he would not put up with that—no matter who they were. It had to be this man of all people who ran into that pile of rubbish on the factory floor. He had his foreman line up our crew in front of him and demanded that the man responsible for the mess should step forward and declare himself.

All to no avail—the man who was so brave before was not brave enough to come forward now. Then the German said, "I want anyone who witnessed the act to tell me at once. I am giving you five minutes starting now."

Nobody was willing to do that either. There were only a few who had seen the guy's handiwork, and no one wanted to tell on a buddy. After that, the manager threw us all out of the factory.

We were with a crew of eight, and all of us would have to report for work in Germany . . . so much for that. It was with a heavy heart and dragging footsteps that I went home to face my parents.

My father was the union leader of the Christian Labor Association. He climbed right on his warhorse after I had told him the bad news.

My father huffed and puffed and said to me, "You go and see that manager in his office first thing in the morning. Tell him it's our own business whether you want to report for work in Germany. He better not have the heart to report on us, or he is going to hear a lot more about this. As for wanting you to tell on someone else, he has got enough foremen around to watch what's going on. It's not our duty to inform on anyone . . . period!"

A scared but very determined eighteen-year-old girded his loins the next day to do battle with the giant of the spinning factory.

One other boy (a fellow sufferer) caught up to me just before I entered the factory grounds. His dad had sent him on much the same mission.

"Will you do the talking?" he said to me. "I get mad in no time and fly off the handle, doing more harm than good."

I was not all that enthusiastic but did agree to the added responsibility. We were directed to the main office as we entered the factory grounds, and the man agreed to see us, almost at once, strangely enough. He was the head of a thousand-man operation and had a lot of other things on his mind. But he met with us, and I delivered my speech, shivering in my boots . . . wooden shoes. The meeting was short and not very sweet. He assured me that we would have to report to work in Germany ourselves, and I told him that this was none of his business. So he told me to get out, and that is just what we did. My partner Bill did not say a word all the while, and I had to lead the attack—all by my lonesome self.

We left the place, with the clerks sitting there, flabbergasted at this unusual spectacle. The other guys went back to the factory and asked if they could come back to work. Anything was better than going to work in Germany.

All were accepted to come back, without any problems, all the boys, excluding Bill and me, that is. His conversion had not lasted that long. It so happened that the manager and the foreman had cornered Bill's sister, who worked in another department. They had tried to force information out of her about the whole unsavory affair. This did not sit well with our friend Bill, and he went after the manager hammer and tongs.

"Pick on the guys involved and not on my sister!" he told the headman. "This is men's business—you keep my sister out of this!"

Well, to make a long story short, the manager turned absolutely livid and told Bill that he would get the police to throw him out on the street.

Bill replied, "You just try and throw me out yourself, if you think you are man enough!"

Poor old Bill ended on the cobblestones, but good. The whole situation was very unpleasant, to put it mildly. For Bill, but more so for the management, they had a lot of face to lose, as the Chinaman would say.

I was left as the odd man out by this turn of events. We had received a message that I was to attend this meeting also. To that message, Dad replied that it was not convenient just then; I had lost enough time already and had just picked up a job in the neighborhood for that particular day. I had to do some threshing for a widow, and Dad wanted me to fulfill that commitment before doing anything else. That kind of rebellion would have been totally unacceptable in normal times, but times were not normal times anymore, and we had to learn to assert ourselves.

We would have to do this even more as time passed by. The head manager and the foreman were waiting for me the next day. They put the pressure on again, and I refused to inform on my friends.

"You have a foreman to look after this kind of business, let him keep an eye on it," I told them. "They get paid for that! You will get nothing out of me!"

The result was that I could come back next day. I could even come back the same day if I wanted to. But the mighty men refused to let Bill back in. That in turn did not sit right with me. So I told them that I would not return unless Bill was hired also. It seemed to me that there was a gleam of appreciation in the old boy's eyes when he replied that Bill could come back the following week.

Bill had a notice from the unemployment office that he had to report for work in Germany less than two months later. Coincidence? you might ask. Bill ended in one of the heaviest bombed areas in Germany—Hanover, to be exact.

The old man tied into me again several days later when we were horsing around in the bathroom.

"You again!" he hollered after he swung open the doors to be a witness to that unsavory scene of us boys lazing around with the smoke of cigarettes hanging in the room.

The whole crew flew out of there as if somebody had shot a load of a bug shot in their rear ends. The old man and I met again at another time after that. Someone had thrown a handful of sandwiches loaded with butter and other goodies in the trash can. He did not think kindly about that at all.

"Many people are going hungry," he said, "and you throw the food away like trash, like so much junk!"

The old man was almost crying when he said that, and I believe that he was absolutely sincere. You had to respect him for that. It's the little thing that sticks with you over the years.

Life went on in an almost normal routine, if such a thing is possible in a war-torn country. There were always little boys sitting at the front gate of the factory. It was quite an honor for them to be associated with young men that were a lifetime older than they were.

One little guy piped up and said to us one day, "I am going to have a little baby brother!"

We joined in on the act and asked him very seriously, "How do you know that you are going to have a little brother and not a sister?"

He sniffled a little contemptuously and wrinkled his face when he replied, hunching his shoulders, like the little folks do. "Last year my mother was in bed and we got a baby sister, and now my father is in bed!"

He looked at us with a lot of pity that we did not even know this simple fact of life. That's how we learned the facts of life at the tender age of fifteen years old.

Life went on, and the war intensified on all fronts, with the German troops battling before the gates of Leningrad with dubious results. Ever more men were sent to the killing grounds in the east to face an uncertain future and death very likely.

Italy lost all heart for fighting so that Germany had to stretch their manpower over greater territory as time went on. Germany needed workers to fill the place of the battling soldiers so that many men were conscripted in an unwilling labor force. The logical conclusion was that our town did not escape the high-handed methods of the enemy either.

The bell tolled for me one day, still unexpected. I had to report to the unemployment office for a medical. We were now in the position that the Jews had been only a short time ago. Would we disobey straight out? Or was it better to report and hope for the best? Dad and Mom had to feed ten children, and it was impossible to feed more mouths if we were to lose our ration cards beside that. The underground was top secret, and unknown to most of us, so the options were limited or none.

I had no choice and reported for the medical—a most degrading experience, as I remember it. We had to parade naked in front of some kind of horse doctor, who was assisted by a fairly good-looking woman.

Thus, my humble person made his entrance into the real world. The doctor and his nurse had a good look at me and burst out laughing, and that really hurt. I know that I am not that good looking but then again, it is not as bad as all that either. The doctor was not mellowed by the entertainment, not even a little bit, and he declared me fit for work in Hitler land.

My friend Dick and I had attended an evening school for the last two years, under the able but somewhat shady guidance of a former East India officer. We worshipped that man who had a rough character but had seen his share of the world. He was a top-notch teacher who had time to spare to throw in several jokes that would make a dock worker blush. Nevertheless, we had to take the bad with the good, and walking out was out of the question, for that would mean the end of our education, and that would never do!

My friend Dick had convinced me that I needed more education. My personality had the necessities for boss material, according to his infinite wisdom. I needed this education badly as a first step into the hallowed halls of boss men. So much for that . . . I became educated, I think, to get back to the instructor. He told me to stay behind after class when he heard that I had to report for work in Germany. He told me in deep secrecy that he could find ways to support me if I refused to go to Germany. Sorry to say, but I missed the real implication of what he was trying to say. Too bad that I did not understand what he had in mind. I might have ended in the ranks of the underground movement if I had accepted the offer. Mom and Dad had a big family, and I could not take the risk of putting additional weight on their shoulders.

The instructor asked Dick, almost half a year later, about my whereabouts and started cussing and swearing when Dick told him that I had escaped out of German paradise.

"I knew it!" he said. "That guy had that in the back of his mind all along!"

Maybe he had seen something that I did not, but we just reacted to the events as they burst upon us, driven by a faith in God's providence, then and always.

The matter of working in Germany would have been an interesting experience if it had been for a different cause. As it was, a very glum group of young men boarded the train. We felt like traitors to the good cause, ready to give service to the enemy.

Things started going wrong, almost from the very beginning. We were promised that we would be put to work in a border town so that we could go home every weekend. Instead we ended in a transfer barrack with an insecure outlook and sad feelings.

This barrack was something else. Men and women of all nationalities were mixed in one big melting pot. Several fast women were dancing on the tables that evening, leaving little to the imagination. The toilets were so dirty that we did not dare to do what comes naturally. Danger of sickness seemed to be all over the place. It was most certainly not what our parents had in mind when they gave us a first-rate education.

Whatever that may be!

We were in the boat in more ways than one and had to row as best as we could. We were put on a train for an unknown destination, after a morning spent in total frustration, running from one office to the other. The fast click, click of the Dutch railroad system, was replaced with a much slower click, clack, since the German rail section was a lot longer than the Dutch. We were in enemy country.

I can't say that I was really homesick, since I am one of those people who can leave everything behind the moment the home place disappears behind the horizon.

The train walls were covered with slogans, reminding us that we were in a country at war. "Careful in conversation, the enemy listens" was one of the most prominent. "Fighting first and then traveling" was another favored one, and many more that have disappeared in the midst of time.

We were all but ignored by the German travelers on the train. They treated us like some foreign species, and that was fine with us. We did not like them either, and we could play that game with just as much effect.

We ended in the city of Munster, a city on the northern tip of the Ruhr district. This district was the heart of the German war effort with its enormous steel mills and factories. All factories were geared to the weapon production of Hitler's hungry armies, and it was in one little corner of that bees' nest that we found a—resting?—place.

It never has been clear to me what we were supposed to do there—we never did any work that amounted to anything, and our usefulness was next to nil. It might have been just an exercise in bureaucratic stupidity, a move to strip the home country of fighting men. Nevertheless, I do know that the contractor was charging big money for every person in his employ, and that might have been the only reason that we were there, for all I know or care.

A large old baking oven was our home for the next four months. The place was surrounded with a high barbwire fence so that nobody could get in or out, except through the main gate. We were allowed to go out occasionally on a night pass. Getting away without a pass was out of the question, and you could not go very far without papers anyway. Police would start searching right away if a person was reported missing.

Concentration camp or death would be the result most often if you were found at large. Options were limited indeed. The ring oven was an interesting place. It was a very large structure with a high chimney in the center. A good-size tunnel ran all along the outside wall, and little holes were brought on in the roof every hundred feet or so.

Bricks were loaded in one section, and burning coals were dropped through the holes in the ceiling for a certain length of time until the clay was fired into solid bricks. The new clay bricks had been started in the next section and were fired in turn, while the first room was cooling off and bricks were unloaded in the room before that. Bricks were made in a continuous operation in that manner. We did none of that—strangely enough. We had to pack lumber repeatedly. Little come in and little went out, also in a continuous operation.

Then came the day we had to reinforce a section of the tunnel with heavy timber, for no reason at all, the way it looked to us anyway. These strange orders came through one day, and we asked the man in charge what this was all about.

"We reinforce the tunnel," he said in typical Prussian overblown manner, while he was standing there with protruding stomach and spread legs, hands on his hips, and a face full of wrinkles. "We reinforce the tunnel to keep the roof from caving in if the chimney falls on top of the tunnel when bombs fall around the factory."

None of us were looking for that anytime after—something that stands for reason.

These were the inconsistencies of things and events in that unreal place. It was really no wonder that it was that way. The man in charge was a nut! A SS man who was mentally incompetent and not fit for active duty, you really had to be off the beam to be discharged out of former sergeant Hitler's armies.

The mighty German intellect had put him in charge of a forced labor camp, and we happened to be the beneficiaries of the Great German logic. And so we were wandering in that Great German wonderland as an anticlimax to the happy wanderers. The mornings were still very cold in that time of the year, and that was something that none of us had counted on. Nobody was too warmly dressed.

One fellow was walking around in sandals all day long, with the result that he had very cold feet.

"I wish I had shit myself to death in the high chair," he grumbled, looking at us with bloodshot eyes. His wispy, thin hair was sticking out of his old black fisher cap, and he continued. "I would rather that a big bear would come and eat me!"

These expressions were not upbuilding and certainly not the kind of language that Mother Geertje would approve of, but we were caught, and there was no way out the way it seemed at that time.

We had two men in our group who were declared as an example for all of us by virtue of the wily SS trooper. These two guys were walking all the long day with several boards on their shoulder, never standing still, from morning till evening. They were really working overtime, and our German guards were really impressed by that outpouring of hard-core labor. They were the best among the best! The poor German suckers never caught onto the fact that these two men were carrying the same boards from one place to the next. Those men never did any real work, but they were good at what they did. Nothing! There is no doubt about that.

One of my friends from the hometown had quite a background in poaching. He and his brother got caught one day when they were still in the Old Country. There was never any love lost between the game warden and those two fellows, and they were mighty upset that they had been caught. A knife fight erupted before this deal was settled. Those lovelies carved each other so bad that the people who were coming on the scene a little later had to roll the whole company in heavy wool blankets. They were almost freezing to death because of blood loss. This was before the time of blood transfusion.

Such was the company that we were blessed with in those days of no wine and no roses. George was the man's name, and poaching was his game. George, the poacher, had to fulfill his calling no matter what the circumstances, and poaching he did. He fell right back into his evil ways, only this was wartime, and that, what was bad before, turned out to be good now. It hurt the enemy in a small way, and it helped our food supply.

He asked me to help him in his enterprise, but the risk was not worth the gain, and I politely, but firmly, denied.

I was shaken awake one morning, bright and early, when I could go home for a weekend. It was my indestructible friend George. He had a bloody rabbit head dangling on the end of a piece of wire. His face split almost in half because he was laughing so hard. It seems that the second boss had found the rabbit in one of George's snares, and he had cut off the rabbit and left the head as a friendly reminder. The second boss was a Communist and did not get along with the SS joker at all. He turned out to be a partner in crime, much to the enjoyment of our friend George.

Luck turned against our friend in a matter of a few weeks. He caught the hunting dog of the SS man in one of his snares, and all furies descended on us in a matter of hours. The man of evil called the police, and we had to line up in front of the barracks, facing a very wrathful SS man. The procedure was much the same as in the Old Country when I was facing the old manager. We were threatened with the direst consequences if the culprit did not come forward. Nobody did because nobody knew anything, except George and me. Even so, most of us were close to crying! You can take my word for that.

The SS joker turned on me suddenly and said, "You know more about this *op den Driesss*. We will give you three days to come up with the guilty one. You will go to concentration camp if you do not show us the guilty one!"

He must have thought that I was the most likely one to break down because I was the smallest and least impressive one in the whole group of suspect sinners. Old George must have lost a little bit of sleep in the next few days. I know I did.

I was scared stiff and did not sleep much at all. It was a tempting situation. Nevertheless, I would not tell on a buddy under any circumstances. I choose to worry and suffer through the following days.

We never heard any more about it. The local police were handling the case, and that might have made the difference. The SS or the green police would not have given in like that. George became my friend and protector after that episode, but that did not stop him from pulling a practical joke on my humble person.

"Let's give Hank a ride for the money," he said to the other fellows.

And so he walked up to me in the morning and said, "I never thought that you would stab me in the back like that. We are supposed to be friends, and then you pull something like that!"

I did not know what he was talking about and just shrugged it off and thought no more about it. But he came back, repeatedly, with the same words. No wonder that I started worrying and became plump scared after some time.

Then he came over, close to quitting time, and said, "Get your knife ready. Blood will be flowing tonight!"

He had a couple of other guys with him, and they all looked as serious as undertakers. What was I to do? It was a completely bewildered little Dutchman who went to the barracks at quitting time. Then my courageous half took over, and I picked out the biggest knife that I could find and started sharpening it. I still did not know what was wrong but decided that if there had to be a fight, blood had to flow.

The blood of someone else would have to flow, and not only my blood. George and followers came trundling along in due time, and we went to the far corner of the yard. Time had come to settle our differences. Custer was going to make his last stand. A good group of spectators had lined up on the sidelines, and all things were set for the final showdown. We walked the last few paces as a couple of warriors, ready to die.

Old George pretty near keeled over, laughing, when we got there, and he said, "Hank, my friend, I got to hand it to you. I did not think you would show up—you got spunk!"

He put his arms around my shoulder and took me along for a couple of beers. He thought that it was a great joke. I did not agree with that at all! Neither was I happy at all! I would have worried a lot less even without spunk.

The Great War lord Adolf Hitler had his birthday . . . sometime in April. We all had to line up in front of the main barrack and had to listen to one of those long-winded speeches that the Nazis were so good at.

Hans and I stood in the back row and foolishly turned our backs on the proceedings as the Swastika flag was raised. This was an act of great stupidity on our part. It was one of the greatest insults to the Germans who were ruling the day with saber and gun. Nobody noticed us, and that was good indeed. I would not have been sitting here if anyone had reported us at that sacred German ceremony.

The Lord sent his angels again to protect me from my own foolishness. Our benefactors handed us a bottle of Voesel, a cheap kind of gin with the kick of a gypsy horse. The Great German nation was generous to us for all the wrong reasons, generous to men who should not have been there in the first place.

I just mentioned the name of Hans, who was a good buddy of mine. He was close because I never made fun of him due to the upbringing of my parents. Others would tease him very often. This happened mostly in good nature, but not always. Hans was a little different. Hans and the SS guy had much in common, with the exception that Hans had X legs and the SS had O legs. Hans was mellow and good-hearted, also a little simple. This could not be said of the SS guy. Oh, come to think of it, Hans had no shiny boots either.

Back to the story!

Hans asked me if I would trade with him—my Voesel for a bread ration, and I agreed without thinking over the consequences. I never suspected that Hans would dig into that gin with a ferocious appetite. He became so drunk that he could not walk or see straight anymore. He managed to get on his bunk and sat there singing at the top of his voice.

It got so bad that one other man said, "We should try and get that shirt from his back—it's of excellent quality, and it would be a pity if he wrecked that material."

So we tried to get it away from him, but he was of a way different opinion. He was going to stick with that shirt to the bitter end. Nobody . . . but nobody . . . was going to talk him out of it! That was that!

Then all of a sudden, he jumped up and hollered, "I am short of breath, I need air, I need freedom!" and he tore the shirt to shreds right off his back.

We tried to get him to go to the toilet after that. It seemed likely that we would have to clean him and his bed before long. He wanted nothing of that either.

But he changed his mind again and hollered, "I need to take a shit. I got a chunk in my rear end as heavy as ten thousand kilos. This is the first bomb that I am going to throw on German soil!"

Nobody knew where he got that silly talk, but it sounded awful funny at the time, and we laughed our heads off while we carried him to the outdoor toilet. His legs were sticking out in front of him, like two underdeveloped turkey legs.

The same Hans asked me one day to trade bunks with him. He was sleeping on the top bunk but did not feel all that safe anymore. Ever more planes were coming over at night, and the antiaircraft guns around the camp were getting more active as time went by. The shreds of those shells were flying in every direction, not up only but also sideways and down to the ground more often than not. It sounded at times as if there was a heavy thunderstorm in progress, a complete hailstorm battering away at the top of the barracks. Nobody was sure what was going to happen next, and we had to be prepared for the worst. I felt sorry for Hans, and we traded bunks so that Hans would have a little more protection on top of him in time of danger.

He was not the bravest of men at that. He asked me one night to come with him to the bathroom. I had told him some ghost stories the night before, and he was scared that the spooks would get him that same night. My behavior was not all that Christian at times, but times were unusual, and I gave in to some bad manners.

My prayers were said before every meal. I was more faithful in that respect. Something that was not always that easy because my meat would be disappearing from my plate, and a man had to pray with one eye open or have a lot of faith and little meat. The other guys had a lot of fun at my expense but would return the meat later—but not always, and that was not pleasant because we got meat very sparingly.

One guy was saying that we should have a pair of binoculars and a bicycle along with the soup. You need the binoculars to find the meat and the bicycle to drive from one piece to the other, was his opinion on that subject.

The war was starting to go sour, mostly in Russia. The German army had come to a complete standstill before Stalingrad. After that every forced laborer was forced to donate a day of free labor. This was supposed to be a gesture of sympathy to the German soldiers, who were having such a hard time before the gates of Stalingrad. But that was not all! We were ordered to appear in a great assembly hall.

We were on the end of one of those long-winded speeches again. This time it was a speech about the great sacrifices that the German soldiers were making for the rest of the free world. Those rallies were really impressive. Loud march music started the proceedings, and row upon row of colorful flags were lining the stage where the brass-ornamented big shots were lined up under a more-than-life-size portrait of "Lord Adolf the Lionhearted."

The youth of Germany had been taken in by this farce. And it also influenced us up to a point, but not enough to make us join forces with the enemy against the great villain from the east: Russia. Each of us had to enter a big roomful of army colonels and captains and whatever else the army had in store. After that show of force, we were asked, one by one, to join the German army, all by our lonely selves.

They let me go easy enough. I was not that impressive looking—a scrawny fellow, to say the least—and my claim that I was antimilitaristic got me off the hook.

But not for everyone! One fellow was forced to join the Waffen-SS. He had been working in Germany on a contract just before the war, and he had broken that contract. He met a roomful of very wrathful men, and a whole bundle of papers were thrown in front of him with the choice of joining the army or going to concentration camp. He chose to sign and was forced to join the SS core.

The nitwit of an SS man who was our camp director was discharged from the army but was still crazy about army life. He tried every trick in the book to get those ignorant Dutchmen to march and sing.

Singing and marching were some of the most interesting features of the German army, and they were good at it. Like them or hate them, this was the main attraction that made the army so interesting for the youth of Germany. "Innocent kids who had never learned to look past the glitter and fool's gold of the superficial Nazi system."

Then one day everything was falling into place. The Dutchmen agreed to march and sing—not nearly equal to the army—that would be asking a little too much. But Rome was not built in one day; you never know what might happen. The beginning was there.

The SS joker was about five foot seven with the beginning of a potbelly, but that was a small matter! It was overshadowed by his beautiful shiny boots. But then again the boots could not disguise the O form of his spindly legs, and that was pitiful. The man had an oversize Adam's apple that was bobbing up and down like a yo-yo on a string, and he had a tick under his right eye. The tick would go up as the apple went down and vice versa. The apple-tick worked overtime as he was marching proudly along in front of this group of depleted Dutchmen, and wonder of wonders, those crazy Dutchmen were marching along, singing at the top of their voices, "We are too lazy for working."

"Poopsack is leading us on. All in wooden clogs are walking. Poopsack in leather shoes up front." These men were singing in Dutch, but apple-tick did not understand that inferior language. Even so! That was small matter. His troop was singing and marching!

Little did he know that the song they were singing was the team song of the Red Socialist when they were marching through Amsterdam following their leader, who was named Poopsack. The song was born out of the somewhat rough humor of some free people of days gone by when there was still freedom of expression.

PS: Poopsack was not a nice expression.

We must have looked like the happy wanderers as we went up and down the hills and dales of the German countryside, but we were anything but happy and wanted to go home desperately, and we wanted the Germans to do the same. It would have been comical if we had been in a better mood, but life was getting distinctly unhealthy. The Allied planes had thrown out many leaflets over the countryside with the warning that the bombing would be intensified more in the near future.

Even so! This fact did not scare me all that much. There was something else that bothered me a lot more. We had to stay in Germany for two months at a time from that time on, and the once-every-weekend trip home was canceled. That was a lot harder to handle. We were now to stay in Germany for two months at a time.

Heavy punishment would follow for our buddies if we did not return after this, our last weekend. These men would be held indefinitely, and thus we were honor bound to return from this two-week break at home.

The enemy followed the same system with us as that they had done with the Jews not all that long ago.

"Do as we have ordered, or the ones left behind will suffer the consequences."

Some boys asked me to take some letters along, over the border, and mail them in Holland. It was an unnecessary risk, but I did it anyway. I cut some slices of bread right through the middle, lengthwise, and sandwiched the letters between the two halves. That's how I smuggled them across the border without difficulty, but with a pounding heart. The border guard was very interested in a wrestling manual that I carried in my suitcase. He started asking questions about the wrestling sport and forgot to look through my suitcase. I was saved from great danger again. The whole thing was silly and not necessary, since I would have been treated as a spy if they had caught me with those letters.

My brother and his two friends were caught with some letters and beaten too within an inch of their lives with a rubber truncheon. They had welts on their bodies that were more than three inches wide. The whole game was not worth the candle. They were still lucky.

Worse things were happening nearly every day. The restrictions that followed shortly after my return were prohibitive. They really burned me up, and I started looking for a way out of that mess.

The Allied airplanes started to throw out pamphlets with the warning that the bombing was going to intensify. All forced labor was advised to get out of the Ruhr district just as soon as possible. Something that was easier said than done! It was even well the cancellation of our two-week stay at home bothered me more than the bombing. I was too stupid to be scared at that time, and I decided to do something about this. The Lord would provide in this also as I was soon to find out, for then I met Sam! He was a newcomer out of Holland, well acquainted with the border region northeast of my hometown. He had sold dry goods on both sides of the border and was still in possession of a border pass.

Sam was one of those men who seemed to have absolutely no fear of consequences: acting before thinking, impulsive, and somewhat undependable. This sounds bad? Well, he was not that bad a guy, but this was the nature of the beast.

I did not like him that much at first sight but changed my mind later. He had a mighty heavy grudge against the black-shirt police who had picked him up. He was very determined to have the evil deed undone—Sam was a man with a mission, and that was to get home and back at the black-shirt hooligans. He started talking about escape from the very moment that he entered our barracks. His audience did not share his convictions at first, but that improved as time went by. Meetings were held and plans were made until even the date was set, and it seemed likely that friend Sam was really serious. This had to be the turning point, and the audience started dwindling until only Sam and I were left.

Secrecy was the code word from that point on. Sam was so secret that he was gone one morning, and even I did not know of his intentions.

It was a kind of betrayal according to my code of conduct. He could have given me some information on his plans, but then again it was war, and nobody knew much about the other person. It was much safer that way. Anyway, Sam was gone, and there was little that I could do about that. I settled down and started to make other plans, but we were really surprised when a very disappointed Sam was ushered back into camp that very evening. He had tried to make it across the border with the border pass that was still in his possession.

Our not-so-beloved hero, the SS man, was no clutch either. He phoned the border right after the first alarm when Sam was reported missing. Dear old Sam ran right into an enthusiastic welcoming commission with Willy, who was one of the most feared border guards heading the parade. You know what? Willy let him go with a severe warning. He took his border pass and told him to get back to where he came from, under an escort, of course. They would beat him to death if he ever showed up again.

He would end in concentration camp if there was anything left to go. No idle threat indeed! Willy was just the man to do it. He was the very man who had beaten my brother and his friends not all that long ago. So much for that! Munster had received its heaviest bombing yet, and we were ordered to go to the rescue. A horse and wagon were commandeered for half a dozen men and their guards. We were on our way to the hapless city of Munster.

Not to the rescue: that would have been too much of a good thing. No, there was a way more selfish reason for this mission. The camp commandant lived there, and he wanted his furniture rescued. Hang the need of the local citizen. The furniture of the commandant was more important. I have to say we did a good job of rescuing and managed to break several pieces by accident.

The Hitler youth had complete control over all operations in the city limits, and nobody . . . but nobody . . . dared to disobey the orders of those ten- and eleven-year-old boys. Neither did we! There were signs all over.

"Anyone caught plundering will be shot on sight!" and many more threats like that.

The display of ruthless power made us shiver, and we could not get out of there fast enough. Old Russian women were clearing rubble in the streets, bent down to do a man's job, with little protection except a pair of hip wader boots. Some women were as old as my mother, and I felt very sorry for them. Others were young and good-looking, but no matter, the treatment was the same for young and old. This was women's lib to perfection.

We were caught in another air warning when we were still in the city. Everyone headed for the bomb shelters except the ignorant Dutchmen. Our friends would not hurt us? We were above the law. How wrong can you be! Education came in a hurry when a German policeman ordered us to clear the street.

We had to go through the streets frequented by the oldest trade. Prostitutes were wheeling their scant possessions on little cars, trying to reach a relative save shelter that could turn into a death trap at any given moment. The whole thing was extremely sad. War like that does not make any distinction between citizens and soldiers, women or children. Everything is welcome to the ever-hungry war god's appetite.

Women and children have been known to jump in the water, burning while still alive. They were covered with phosphorus, trying to quench the flames in the water, but they started burning again the moment they surfaced above water. I have not had to witness this, but others did and survived to tell about it. Nothing can justify that kind of war. The German had sown the wind and was reaping the storm. The ghost of Rotterdam, London, Warsaw, and many other cities was crying for retribution and would not be denied! But did we have to make war on women and children?

Our company traveled along and arrived safely back to the barracks, and Sam found a message waiting that he could pick up a package from home in the SS office. He was not looking forward to that because he had not seen the man after his little trip to border land, and he asked me to come along as a morale builder.

The code of honor among friends demanded that I come along, but I was not rejoicing at the prospect either. The possibilities of a general love-in were remote indeed.

Our friend, the SSR dug right in, as was to be expected the moment we entered the room.

"Well, Sam," he said, "how did you enjoy the pleasure ride with the German army? You should know better than to try and get away from the long arm of the German army! What do you say, op den Dries?" and he looked at me with eyes that tried to look fearsome.

I agreed with him wholeheartedly, praising the mighty and great works of the invincible German army core. I practically fell over my verbal feet to make a good impression on the man.

You just wait, I was thinking in the back of my mind.

He was making fun of us while we were already planning for another kick at the cat. I would have given almost anything to have seen his face, only weeks later, when we were gone again. This time for good!

The camp commandant allowed one free Sunday every other week. We could do as we pleased: stay in bed all day if we wanted to or visit friends outside camp, even a trip to Munster or anywhere else within reason. We could not go far at the best of times, since we had no weekend papers. It was fairly safe to let us out on those terms. This is exactly what we needed! It worked in our favor in a strange kind of way. It was the day before the long weekend, and Sam and I made sure that we were working close to the main boss.

I walked up to Sam and said, "Let's go to our friends on the other side of Munster tomorrow. It looks like a nice day, and we can have a little party together."

Germans are always in favor of a good time, and this man was no exception. He listened with a big grin on his face and threw in a few ribald remarks—better left unmentioned. The man took the bait, just the way we planned it, and the alarm went off, much delayed, the next day. It gave us most of the day to disappear, without any Willies looking for us at the border. Sam and I crawled over the barbed wire fence in the middle of the night and started our reckless journey all alone and unnoticed by friend or foe. We bypassed the local railway station and walked to the Munster City *bahnhof* (station). The main station in Munster was a better place to disappear, since most personnel in the local station were only too familiar.

The time of decision came when we were only some little ways from the Munster railway station. Each was busy with his own thoughts and fears.

"Shall we go or turn back?" put one of us into words.

I prayed to the Lord for strength and guidance at that difficult moment and was very much comforted. A knowledge and a surety took hold of me, and I felt serene at that difficult moment.

I looked at Sam and said, "I prayed to my Lord and am assured that everything will be well no matter what happens!"

"I did the same," said my friend. "I think that we should go on!"

A strange encounter indeed! There were the two of us—Protestant and Catholic—in the dark of night at the outskirts of Munster. Very different in temperament, but yet so close, praying to the same Lord and Savior. I believe to this very day that Sam was put on my way so that the way was opened for escape for the two of us—Sam with his knowledge of the country, while I was a little more level-headed with a little more insight when planning was called for.

I never doubted for a moment that Jesus sent His help in more ways than one when the occasion arose. You will see proof of that as we go on our way! The Munster railway station of that day was of huge proportions. Steel girdles along the roof reached as far as the eye could see. The locomotive smoke of many generations had put layer upon layer of soot on the steel rooflines. Many glass sections of the roof had been broken and shattered with the passing of time. Some might have been the result of bombings, but that was quite limited then. This would change not all that much later, as history has recorded. Many rail lines beside each other entered and left the station at all directions. The station was connected to most the major centers of wartime Germany. Trains went by in the thousands during the two months that we were in the forced labor camp along that railroad, giving testimony to the hyperactivity of the German war effort. The hustle and bustle in the railroad station was ideal for our purposes. We bought tickets and boarded the train unnoticed with Holland as destination.

Things were going very nicely this far, and the train ride was remarkably uneventful right up to the border station. It was not until we left the train that I got the scare of my life. Sam was walking in front of me as we were walking into a whole line of soldiers, all lined up in front of us, in full battle dress. It was a really grim-looking lot that had their guns leveled at us, ready to take us in. That's exactly what it looked like at first sight. These soldiers must have been leaving on some kind of assignment, but it did not look good for us in the first few moments.

Sam, who was a really cool cucumber, hardly hesitated but shoved his hat on the back of his head and walked right past the welcoming committee. If he could do it, I could do it too. I followed right in his footsteps. My pants were not completely dry after we had survived that ordeal! We turned our back on the main border crossing where the border guard Willy resided as the proverbial spider in his web.

We went to a little railroad station instead, on the other side of the tracks, and bought tickets for a little railroad that went right back into Germany. This was a little branch line that served mostly the small settlements along the way. This train seemed to stop anywhere where there were more than a half-dozen houses.

Willy and friends were looking for people who went over the border. Nobody bothered us because we were going into Germany. We did not even try to cross the border at that point. The beauty of that branch line was the fact that it headed inland for a little while and then curved right back to cross the Dutch border an hour or so later.

Four men boarded the train in a stretch when there were no other people in our compartment. I know that all this sounds unbelievable, but it happened just as I will describe it. All the four men had a hat on. This was very unusual and looked kind of odd to me. If there had been one or two, I might not have noticed it, but four men and all with a hat on? It was almost ridiculous.

One man came running up to Sam the minute he laid eyes on him.

"Man," he said, "of all the guys I had to meet, it had to be you!"

We asked them what they were up to, and they took off their headgear. Every one of them was as bald as a billiard ball. They had just been released from the Osnabruck concentration camp and tried an escape at the first opportunity. This was a joyous reunion for those guys, a fact that could not be denied. Still, it increased the danger manyfold! We were starting to look like a Sunday class on the way to a picnic. One of those guys was a nervous type, and that made matters even worse. He kept jabbering away about being caught and what would happen, etc.

This guy stuck out like a sore thumb. He was more than six feet tall and acting like a baby. There was no help to it; we had to shut him up one way or the other. The result was that we took him into a corner and told him that we would take him on the platform and throw him off the train if he did not shut up. This helped a lot. He was more scared of us than anything or anyone else. There were no other people on that train, not in that compartment anyway, so we escaped undue attention, luckily enough, and that was good under the circumstances. We could have been in big trouble.

There was a little settlement about one hour walk from the Dutch border. That is where we got off the train. It is an amazing thing that nobody asked us for our tickets—something that is normal procedure on all trains.

The idea was to contact some of Sam's friends, men who helped other escapees before. It was our hope that they would be willing to help us. Our bad luck was the fact that all those people were in church around that time. A beer parlor close by the church seemed to be the only place where we might escape attention, and that's where we spent the next little while, while Sam made his way to church to try and contact these folks. He was Catholic too and knew the men we needed. He was the most likely candidate for this job. It is a pleasure for me to tell about these helpful people whom we met only a short while later. They were willing to help us without a moment's hesitation. Their wives set up an excellent meal before anything else.

These people hated Hitler almost as much as we did and were very willing to risk their freedom and much more to help us to get across the border. "Something that should not be taken lightly." They had little to gain and everything to lose. What is even more striking is the fact that the war was by no means lost for Germany at that point in time. Those men and women helped us out of sheer compassion and solid conviction in the virtues of their religious beliefs.

It was decided to split the escape parties into three groups. One young German would take two of the other boys under his care. The other young German would try and take the other two across, and Sam and I would make our way to a point close to the border, hiding there until the young Germans would return to pick us up.

It seemed a lot better to do it that way because six of us and the two Germans would make a big enough crowd that nobody could ignore, even if they wanted to. It would have been an awful tempting catch for any border guard with a good chance for promotion.

Sam and I were the last to leave for an uncertain future. We went into hiding in a ditch, a little ways away from the Duane Station. Our hiding place was far from comfortable, but we were still free, and that was worth a little discomfort.

The rain was coming down steady at a fairly heavy rate during the time that we were in that ditch for hours, the way it felt, and our nerves were strained to the breaking point. Still, nobody came back for us. Something had to be done. Neither one of us felt much like talking.

My clothing got heavier as it soaked up the rain. I had put on two sets of underwear, a coat, an overcoat, and an extra pair of socks in my pocket, plus all the stuff I could carry. Our suitcases had been left in camp to prevent early detection. The result was that I was a very heavy little Dutchman by the time I had soaked up a couple of hours of rain.

Sam was in a little better position, since he had left most of his stuff with the family that we just left. He could pick it up later because he lived just across the border. Friend Sam was not prepared to wait any longer.

"Let's go," he said. "Something must have gone wrong. Waiting much longer will only make it worse!"

This seemed a little radical to me, but he was in the driver seat at that stage of the game. I was afraid that our German friends would end up looking for us all over the country when we were not there after they returned to pick us up. Sam could be a little selfish at times. He was looking after his own hide first, an attitude I had noticed before, and would again before it was all over and we parted company for good. Sam knew the country. I had little to say in the matter. He had done me a lot of good, so I went along somewhat reluctantly.

We took a roundabout way and bypassed the border guard station. This meant another half hour or so in the driving rain through heavy bush country. But we made it and returned to the main asphalt road. We walked there for about a half hour when I heard a whisper of tires behind us.

"It's over," I said to my pal. "The police are coming!"

The situation looked very grim indeed, but Sam was not ready to give up yet.

"Put your hand in your pocket when he asks for papers and then hit him."

That's all the time we had, and the man was upon us. His rifle was hanging from his shoulder, the barrel down to keep out the rain.

"Well, you guys," he said, "what are you up to? Taking yourself on a Sunday walk?" He was laughing when he said this.

"We are visiting relatives!" Sam said.

"Well, have yourself a good time," the policeman said and continued on his way, shaking with laughter.

God's providence had used a kindhearted German to keep us from harm and imprisonment. My guardian angel must have worked overtime that day and the next—humanly speaking. A lot more was going to happen before I got home.

I really do not know what would have happened if the man had acted differently. We would not have had much of a chance. Then again, who knows? We were awfully keyed up and would have done strange things in a moment of desperation. Neither one of us had much to say after this encounter. This had been a little too close for comfort.

One thing was certain! We had to get off that road in a hurry. The chance of running into another patrol was just too great. A choice had to be made. The only way out was to take a chance and go to the next farm and ask for directions to the Dutch border.

Our choice could not have been much better. An old man lived in the next farm. We could see that he was another Catholic by the crucifix hanging over the fireplace. He gave us a bowl of soup before asking any questions. He must have seen already what was going on. Then he told us that he had been a prisoner in England in the First World War. He was well aware of our difficulties and only too willing to help us get away. Here we were yet again with another generous deed of the ordinary German farmer—a deed that will stay with me until my dying day.

The old man pointed to two little red houses in the far distance.

"That's Holland," he said. "Just walk through my pasture and walk in the direction of those two houses. Walk to my cows if you see any soldiers coming."

He looked at us with a little grin on his scraggy face and said, "You know what a soldier looks like? A man with a gun, you know."

We assured him that we knew all about soldiers.

"Just walk up to my cows and look them over closely, patting them just as if you are interested in buying. Then come back here, and we try again tonight."

His precautions were not needed after all as we walked through the meadow in the direction of the little red houses. A high railroad dike was in front of us, about eight feet high, a barrier that we would have to cross unseen. Anybody could see us for miles around against the evening sky if we just walked over that railroad dike.

Border guards were sure to be around because the old man had told us so. We practically rolled over that railroad to land in a muddy ditch on the other side. And so we were all muddy again. What else is new?

The Dutch border was about one mile away at that point, and we followed a little winding road that must have been used by farmers as a pathway from pasture to pasture. It was at that point that we noticed a border guard about five hundred meters to the left of us. Turning back was out of the question, and going on was almost certain capture. Good advice was hard to come by on that lonesome stretch of a cow path. What should we do? Going on seemed to be the better way, and we went forward with fear and trembling. I'll never know what happened. Maybe the man was blinded, like the Assyrians in Elisha's days, or he might have been too cold and too miserable to bother. Then again, he could have had pity on us. I don't know! We just walked straight ahead, and nothing happened.

We had reached Holland, our beloved country.

Disillusion was our first experience on native soil. An absolute anticlimax! We entered the farm in front of us and asked if we could rest for a moment. The man who answered the door told us in no uncertain terms that he did not want us around. It was much too dangerous, and he could lose his farm and all his possessions. I wondered what would have happened to the folks on the other side of the border under the same circumstances. So much for the Dutch hospitality!

"What way did you come?" he asked before we left.

We pointed to the little path that we had followed.

"Man," he said, "there was a border guard at the left of you about five hundred meters away."

"We have seen that," we told him.

"There was another one to the right of you." We had never seen that one. My Lord had sent His angels again and let us through dangers unknown but very real.

I was allowed to change into a new pair of socks. Then we were ushered out of the door politely but very insistently. The journey was all but over for my friend and partner Sam. We reached a farmhouse not all that much further, and the folks in that place were easier to talk to. They were acquainted with Sam somehow, and again I noticed that strange willingness of Sam to send someone else in danger to protect his own hide.

He told me, more than he asked me, to go to his parents about twenty minutes' bicycle ride away and tell them that we had managed to escape that very day. There were half a dozen people on that farm, and any one of them would have been more able to make that trip. I could hardly do that trip in the shape that I was in after a heavy day that we just went through.

Sam himself did not want to go for fear of meeting his black-shirt friends again. That was understandable, but there was no reason that this could not have waited until the next morning. I went. What else could I do? I owed Sam for the help he gave me during the trip and mostly for the last little while. On the other hand, he might not have been this far without my help either. I went reluctantly to his parents in the town of Coevorden. His parents lived just over the bridge as you come into Coevorden. It turned out that these folks were very sympathetic and very considerate for my well-being and overjoyed to have their son back from Hitler land.

We made the return trip after they had fed me an excellent meal. They made sure to ride in front of me so that they could warn me if anything went wrong on the way down there. This gave me a good feeling, and I appreciated their consideration. You may believe that I was dead tired when I got back to the place where Sam was, and I fell asleep in a matter of minutes after my return to that farm. Sam brought me to the train early next morning.

It must have been around five o'clock that morning when Sam and I had a very emotional farewell, for it was hard to say farewell to this man with a mixture of good and bad. We had traveled a long and dangerous road together—from Munster all the way through enemy country, through many dangers, and made it safe this far. I owe him and wished him well.

The road ahead was far from over, and I had to continue that road by my lonesome self. But not really! It was God's hand leading me the rest of the way in a special way. This was really the same railroad track that had brought us out of Germany but going in a westerly direction to the center of Holland. It was one of those midsummer mornings when the day is coming forth out of a night of darkness out of the midst of the night, a day when everything seemed right with the world, but everything was not right, far from it. There was a war on, and I was surrounded by enemies. I had become a hunted man, and I would be in hiding from that day on until the end of the war, almost two years later.

I had planned to transfer to a train going south in the next station, but my God decided differently. I fell asleep within minutes of boarding the train, and the train carried me to the middle of Holland, dead to the world and directed into unforeseen territory. I woke when the train came to a standstill, about fifty kilometers west of my hometown, and not fifty kilometers east, as I had planned. You can imagine my amazement when I woke in the Zwolle train station in the center of Holland, and not in Almelo, a city that is to the east of my hometown. My plans were upset again, and I headed for the exit to find a hiding place.

The conductor told me that I had to make a transfer to another train. He insisted in paying me the money that I had overpaid at the beginning of the journey. Much to my dismay! He held up the whole line in front of that ticket office and attracted way too much attention to my way of thinking. I wanted to get out of there. That's all! Go to a quiet corner and wait for the train going east, back to my hometown.

I was a lonesome boy indeed in a city full of people and no place to go. It was with a sigh of relief that I boarded the train going east, finally, without any more holdups. It was still early morning when the train pulled into the station of my birthplace, and I had a feeling that everyone was watching me. The omnipresence of the German army 'n' might be reaching out from every direction to pull me back into captivity.

My brother George and his friend were the first people that I met when the train arrived in my hometown. They had to leave with this train to go back to work in Germany in one border town. They were absolutely speechless and wanted to know where I came from and why I was not in Munster as I was supposed to be. Both of them wanted to go right back with me and go underwater—a term used for people hiding from the Germans. I asked them to hold off for a little while until I had found a place to hide. It might be a little too much for Mom and Dad to have two people in hiding in that short order. They were hard to persuade and had their minds made up that they wanted to come with me! They kept arguing, and I felt very ill at ease. The feeling persisted that half the police force was on the lookout for me. It was at that point that my brother asked me how I got back home. He told me that the Germans had surrounded the city to the east of us and that they were searching every house and every moving vehicle in that city, including the trains. I would have walked right into their arms if I had come in from the east, as I had intended.

I had abundant proof again that the Lord protected me in every step of the way. My smaller brother Gerrit was at the railroad station with a bicycle, and he insisted that I would ride on the back of his bicycle. Would you know it? Some policemen told us to stop before we had gone much further—do you think I was scared? No comment!

I covered the rest of the way home as if going on wings, extremely happy, but afraid that Mom and Dad would be angry with me for showing up like that.

"I could not have been more wrong."

My father was just getting ready to leave for the factory where he worked as a weaver of textile goods. And our mother was doing what she always was doing, making ready for a new day with new problems in an ever-changing way.

"I had a feeling that something was going on with you yesterday. I had it in my heart to pray for you all day long!" These were the first words of my mother.

She had known . . . somehow. I asked my father not to be angry, for they had so many mouths to feed already. All they did was hug me . . . repeatedly. Neither of them was ashamed of their tears, and I was not free of tears either. The fact that my mother prayed for me without any knowledge of my danger is an undisputed fact. Only the ones that know the secret relationship with the Lord can testify to those things. My parents were true children of their Heavenly Father.

More was to come yet!

The door opened, and the father of my friend Hans came in. We had never seen the man before, but he came anyway. He had seen me when I left the train and had followed me with the hope that I would carry news from his son Hans. This was a shocking experience and just one of many reminders that the world around us is ever watchful.

Nothing is secret for long, and it would be wise to move on as quickly as possible, but all avenues to a safe hiding place were closed. So it seemed. The German police could be coming to take me in at any moment, and the future seemed bleak indeed. That this man was at our doorstep so quick was a reminder that caution was well advised.

We were in luck. Or to put it in a better way, the Lord had seen our need before it was at our door. He sent a messenger in a scrubby middle-aged man on wooden shoes with a beard of two days or more, hollow-eyed and dressed in warm down clothes. This was an unlikely angel if I have ever seen one, but that is just what he turned out to be. I could assure him that all was well with Hans when I left him.

The man was a bricklayer, and he had worked for a farmer in a little place east of us. He went to see this farmer straightaway, and the farmer agreed to take me in for room and board and twenty-five guilders a month. It was much more than I ever had hoped for, an answer to a prayer that I had not even prayed yet, and a godsend for my family.

CHAPTER 6

RESISTANCE

"FROM MUNSTER TO the hamlet of Haarle."
A trip that began early Sunday in the German city of Munster ended Monday afternoon in the flatlands of a one-horse town in Holland. It was a long way to travel in a short period, but here I was in Haarle between twelve and one o'clock in the afternoon.

Everyone was asleep when I got there; it was the custom in the farm country—early to rise and a nap in the afternoon, hard at work and hard at play.

It was a beautiful summer day, and I stretched out in the grass to enjoy the quiet of the countryside. There was hardly a sound, maybe a dog barking in the distance. The birds were singing in the trees ever so nice and peaceful, while one scrawny little bird was having a tug-of-war with a fair-sized worm oh so reluctant to leave the safety of Mother Earth. The worm did not seem to agree with the bird's plan for his or her immediate future. It's hard to tell with a worm if it's a he or a she, and it does not matter anyway—the result is the same.

A rooster was crowing trying to wake the neighborhood with little effect. He might be the rooster, but the chicken had to lay the egg." It is still that way.

Quiet reigned supreme, except for a few doves cooing away on top of the farm building. The leaves of the trees were shivering through the efforts of a lazy wind. The whole nature seemed to act like a haven of rest and peace. A peace surrounded this quiet farmyard. The devil of war had stolen it from all other civilizations.

My tired nerves were soaking in the peace and quiet of this surrounding. A great feeling of peace settled over my whole being. From the storm into the quiet . . . blessings were unsurpassed by anything I had known for months.

This is going to be a boring place, I thought while I was getting the rest that I desperately needed.

That is how it looked like, but I could not have been more wrong as I was soon to find out. Quiet waters have great depths (still waters run deep) is a saying that applies very well to life in the sedate farmer's country life. Life is experienced much more intensive in close communities like these—love and hate, bitterness and compassion, jealousy and greediness. The whole range of human emotions runs the gauntlet of human behavior in an intensive pattern well established in age-old settings.

I was to spend some of the most exciting days of my youth in that quiet little settlement. You never would have thought so when you looked at the graceful lines of these Sacsish farm buildings.

Those farm homes must be some of the most romantic structures ever created, as I have explained in a previous chapter. The livestock and the farm folk share the same building through most of the winter, but the stables are whitewashed during the summer so that hardly a speck of dirt can be found. These places are so clean that you can almost eat from the floor . . . during the summer anyway.

A warm and cloudless sky hovered over this idyllic picture with the exception of a dark cloud bank that was building up in the west. It was a reminder that nothing is ever perfect in this earthly abode. The ever-changing objects in the distance were shivering in an ever-changing kaleidoscope of colors and hues floating aboveground in a mixture of reality and misconceptions. Even the chickens had quit their unending bickering and had given in to the all-prevailing heat syndrome.

I could hardly see myself fitting into this picture of rest and seeming boredom. The waiting was almost over, and I was soon to find my place in the realm of things. The old farmer appeared followed by his wife and two daughters, none of them ready to face the realities of life. Not by the looks of them anyway! The old farmer, by the name of Jan, was the blustering type, overpowering and forceful. Yet he had a heart of gold but managed to hide this fact most of the time really well.

They did take me in with great risk to themselves. Jan was something like the rough chestnut, rough outside and mellow in the core. He was known like that in the whole district. His wife, who walked in Jan's shadow most of the time, was the motherly type—one of those people who do the job before them without fuss or complaint, somewhat subdued in manners. Yet those types are the prevailing powers in the scene of daily life!

The two daughters will be introduced later—a date usually too soon! Young John was out with the milk wagon and would not be back for some time. The family checked me out like a newly acquired possession, and some approval was hinting, especially from the women's quarter.

Then they put me to work without any further ado. We went straight to the field, digging potatoes.

The youngest daughter made it a point to work in my neighborhood most of the time. She would be my downfall later, like a twentieth-century Delilah. She was not a bad looker and got her point across. A closer relationship would be much desired. This served to make my outlook on life a little brighter. Follow-up work would have to be done in one form or another.

My real job started the next day when we brought out the milk wagon for the daily pickup of milk from the farmers. We had to pick up the ten-gallon cans of milk that the farmers set at the roadside and bring those to the factory. I got a milk wagon with a gypsy palomino horse, a little horse, slightly crippled; this happened at the time that she had a foal at a younger age. That little horse was all heart, and I grew quite attached to the little critter.

It is hard to describe the accelerating feeling that a horse provides when they pull the wagon, with no other sound than the clip-clop of the horse's hooves on the sandy ground. No other sound is heard, and the feeling of power and companionship is ultimate to horse and driver at the same time.

The whole settlement was aware of the new help that worked at old Jan's farm. Everyone, including the Catholic priest! Everyone was involved when the word was passed around at the local Catholic Church. I was now one of them and under the protection of the church, in a manner of speaking. They told me to jump off the wagon and go in hiding at any moment that there was danger or even a hint of danger. Never mind the horse and wagon, just get out. Such was to be my life from that point on. The first passing farmer would take care of the horse and wagon and take it to a safe place.

Everyone was in on this, and almost all of them were Catholics. The whole community was just like one big family with all the virtues and vices involved. There was only one Protestant farmer in the whole district, and he was good in his calling. He was handled with good-natured respect for that reason. He was counted as one of the community. My parents had taught me to respect all people with other forms of worship. Here I learned to love those people with all the good and the bad involved.

We had to pick up the milk at the farms and bring it to the factory over a hard service road, a trip of about two hours, one way. The drivers would wait sometimes for each other at the main road. A get-together was held on the last wagon when they were in the mood for trading gossip and telling jokes—not always that clean but in an acceptable code of ethics. The front horse would bring the whole train of wagons to the factory, without fail, every time.

One of the drivers was not all that bright, but he loved to sit in on these story sessions, most of the time without understanding what the jokes were all about. One of the men would tell a joke, and everyone would have a good laugh, everyone . . . except this boy. Then almost at the end of the trip, he would start laughing his head off, and we looked at him without understanding what brought that on, but it was just a delayed reaction to the joke of half an hour ago. He would enjoy the joke all over again. I think that the simple folks have often a much nicer time than the so-called normal folks. Things are uncomplicated for them, and they worry much less.

We were in the harvest time before long, and every person had to go out to the field to bring in the harvest. Old Jan told his daughter and me to get a load full of rye bundles. Any farmer can tell you that it is a real art to load rye bundles, but I did not know beans about it.

The youngest girl, Marie, told me that she knew all about loading the grain bundles, and we did not have a worry in the world. We were in good hands. Her grandma had shown her exactly how to stash the bundles on the wagon in the right manner.

The load had to be built out when we got above the wagon boards, and that is where the expert shines at its brightest. I was loading bundles with the pitchfork, and Marie was stashing them in the right manner.

She would call to me every so often, "How am I doing?"

I would do my job and would say, "Pull in a little on the left, you are over a little."

This would be repeated for the left and the right all along until we had a load as skinny as a beanpole. The whole thing was shaking back and forth like a drunken sailor. But Marie and I went home with great pride. We had a beautiful high load of bundles!

Marie sat on top of the load. She looked much like Cleopatra in her glory days. The whole family was lined up in front of the house when we were ready to turn in the driveway. They looked on in great horror, but we thought that they were speechless with admiration. But alas! The glory parade would come to an untimely end, for the front wheel went through a puddle in the road, and disaster overtook us. Cleopatra came down with the whole kit and caboodle—an untimely end to the victory parade.

The farmer went absolutely berserk. "That Hank is so stupid to make that mistake is one thing—he doesn't know any better—but you should have known."

Those were words of bitter disappointment. Cleopatra was sent into the house crying her lovely eyes out.

The farmer sent me away to do a job where I would do less harm. The rest of the family reloaded the grain that had fallen off the wagon, grumbling about the loss of seed that had spilled out of the overripe ears of rye. The lost grain could have brought good money on the black market. Too bad!

All the grain had to be turned into the German authorities. Only about 10 percent was returned to the struggling farmers. This was a fact that was heavily detested by the overall farm population.

Farmer John was determined to do something about this, and Little John and I were called out of bed early every morning to help him thresh a layer of grain before going on the milk haul. Old Jan never bothered dressing for the occasion. He jumped into the fray, threshing only in his long johns—I mean, he was dressed in his long johns. His underwear had only room for one and would not hold any amount of grain to speak of.

This threshing by hand was an interesting procedure. A layer of grain was spread out on the floor about three bundles deep. We would beat the tar out of the bundles, hitting the grain with alternating strokes of heavy wooden flays. This was tricky business, for your timing had to be perfect or someone else would hit your stick with a bone-jarring crash.

This crash would travel all through your arms right into your head, setting your teeth shattering. All this put me in a vulnerable position, since my head needed protection and my teeth were getting loose, so I learned to keep perfect timing. Life was hard indeed for a city slicker like me, and a person had to be on constant alert against the danger that surrounds you from every direction. But life has its own compensations. A little sweet is often mixed in the bitter moments of your life.

This happened when my friend Dick and his girlfriend came over on a Sunday to visit his wayward friend and to correct my erring ways. It must have been a pleasant outing for him and his girl. He was still a free man in good company, while I was a fugitive on the run from Hitler the Lionhearted, but this was going to change drastically in the following moments.

It turned out to be a beautiful revenge for the harm he had done me in years gone by. We had our meals and coffee in the front of a pig barn. No farmer would open the front room for normal living under no circumstances. These rooms were the holiest of holiest in the farmer's world. The rooms had beautiful furniture but were never used. They were kept in immaculate shape, and the women spent hours to keep it that way.

This sanctuary had the illustrious name of *"pronkkamer"* (showroom), and with good reason—this was its only function—just to show off! We did not even sit in the kitchen in the summer months. Even that was too good for us.

We had the unsurpassed blessing that we had our abode in front of the pig barn. There was a wall between the two rooms, of course, but that did not keep out the flies. There were so many flies on the whitewashed wall that the walls were more black than white.

My friend Dick was always finicky about his food, and this was going to be his waterloo. Dick and his girlfriend were invited for a cup of coffee and a bite to eat. Neither Dick nor his girlfriend could talk themselves out of it.

He got a cup of coffee in front of him and had a fly in the coffee in no time flat. The first fly was joined by a second fly in no time, and Dick sat there, looking at the two insects, rowing away in his cup.

He could not bring himself to drink until the farmer said to him, "Your coffee is getting cold. Drink it that so we can pour you another one!"

Dick pointed at his coffee and said, "There is a fly in the coffee."

"Is that all?" replied the farmer, and he scooped it with his finger through Dick's coffee!

My friend turned green and rushed out of the door after drinking the stuff. I found him back behind the haystack, throwing up all he had in his system. I did feel sorry for him, a little bit! But I laughed so hard that I was bawling. It is natural that he never came for a second visit.

The farm community was made up of all kinds of characters, and you had some dillies among them. There was a farmer in the neighborhood; this person was awfully stingy. He had a large family, but he for sure did not spoil any of them. The man was so stingy that he sold all the cutlery when the black market prices were high. It stands for reason that his wife became desperate and did not know how to serve food for her large brood of children. Nevertheless, the farmer opened the way for untold opportunities. He had the wife serve mashed potatoes. All day, every day, seven days a week . . . he told her to dump the mash on the middle of the table, make a hole in the middle, and pour some gravy in the hole. Nobody needed cutlery in that manner of eating.

This woman cried a lot. I wonder why!

Nobody escaped the scrutiny of his or her fellow men in a closed community like this, but it was no big deal either. Not to us anyway. On the contrary, we had our own problems to deal with. There were so many flies in the cookhouse that it went too far for Marie. She begged her father to do something about that, but even so she was very secretive about the procedure, and for a good reason.

The old man was very reluctant at first, but Marie talked him into it. She made sure that I was around on that fateful day as she was stacking little bundles of straw in the cookhouse. Some great tempests of activity burst loose up on our weary heads. The table and all the chairs were cleared out of the house, and she invited me inside with her dad and the mean old dog of the family. The farmer invited the other ones in also, but there were no takers, and he locked the doors as tight as Noah's ark. Then he set the little bundles of straw on fire, running around the room like a man possessed. Marie and I were running in front of him, and the German shepherd joined the fray and bit my rear end to make

HANK OPDENDRIES

it more interesting. The dog was acting according to its nature, and you could not blame that animal for that, but my nature and rear end were closed in the confines of that cookhouse.

It was not funny.

The idea was to burn the flies off the wall. The intentions were good, but it was all to no avail; twice as many came on the funeral only days later. Nothing good came my way ever from anything German, not even from a German shepherd dog. Life was interesting indeed, but we were still in a war-torn country. And the effects were all around us every day. Everything was in short supply, and the danger increased by the day as the war was being fought with ever-increasing intensity. We were made aware of that from day to day. Things got even more hectic on the day that we were on our way traveling to the milk factory. I was following the main highway when I got a lot closer involved.

The date was September 18, 1943. I was on my usual milk run, and my little horse was having a hard time pulling the wagon up the railroad dike. Then I heard the sound of heavy trucks coming from the other side of the dike. I could see nothing but thought it might be wise to vacate the premises. It could mean only one thing. The Germans were the only ones in those days who had fuel to run a vehicle. The better part of discretion told me to get out of there, fast. So I slipped off the back of the wagon and landed in a cluster of willows right in front of a culvert that ran under the road. The opening was covered with willows and high grass, and I really went underground that time, just in time too.

A truck full of Germans stopped on the road and started searching the wagon and the surrounding area. They left when they did not find anything. I in turn thought that it would be a good idea to get out of there also and leave the wagon for the honest finder, just like the farmer had instructed me to do. The next farmer passing by would take care of the horse and wagon. I headed home to the farm, taking a shortcut through the fields. Some farmers told me that the Germans were searching for Allied flyers. An airplane had been shot down not long ago. The town of Haarle was completely surrounded. This complicated matters, and I thought that the best thing was to stay out of sight until young John got home from the factory. He would likely know more about the situation. I came home in the late afternoon and found an excited farmer.

"I got something now that is too dangerous to tell you," he said. He grumbled around for a while, and then he said, "A strange man came walking in the yard . . . He was holding a little rubber bag . . . No one can understand that man . . . Do you know any English?"

I did, in fact. My friend Dick had talked me into going with him to learn English about two years ago, and I had picked up more than I realized. So I looked at the man who was dressed in a blue flyer uniform. It was hard to tell anything. He seemed like a queer bird to me, since he had removed all markings and stripes that could give away his identity. I walked up to him and started talking to him in broken school English.

He was awful secretive at first but loosened up somewhat after he realized that he had to trust somebody sometime. It seemed that they had been shot down over Dutch territory, and he had been walking for three days, living from the produce of the field. He had also some chocolate bars that seemed to have a special meaning, but I could not find out what.

The farmer and his wife were the first people he had contacted in the last three days, and he was very touched by the kindness of the farmer and his wife. They had given him milk and bread and a place to rest. The options for the farmer were very little, and there was always the possibility that the man was a German in disguise. The consequences would be deadly if that was the case. It is hard to believe how quickly something unusual attracts the attention of the most unlikely people. The mailman entered the farm yard just when the farm family was trying to decide about the course of action. He warned old John that the German soldiers were in town less than a mile away from where we were then.

To make matters worse, a neighbor came over and suggested that we turn him into the police.

"The Germans will shoot everybody in the neighborhood and burn our houses down if he is found!" he whined.

It was a grim situation, and I asked the farmer if I could go away with the man and try to reach England.

Jan got very angry at my suggestion and said, "The Germans will beat you to a pulp if they catch you and trace you back here, and the place will still be burned down!"

He did not want to turn him in, and he did not want to keep him.

It would have been easier if we could have contacted the underground, but this organization was still very secretive at that moment in time. There was no help there either. The farmer decided that Bob could stay overnight in a chicken coop way back in the field. He was putting him, and his family, in deadly danger.

We brought Bob to a chicken coop in the field and made him as comfortable as possible, assuring him that we would be back for him in the morning. The women also bandaged the blisters he had on his feet—blisters as big as a guilder (the size of a quarter).

The man was still there the next morning and was willing to trust us apparently. He did not have much choice, with his feet the shape they were in. The most logical action would be to get him civil clothes and turn him loose, but he wanted no part of that. He claimed that the Germans would shoot him as a spy if he was caught out of uniform.

This made everything even more difficult, and I asked the farmer again to let me go home, say good-byes to my parents, and let me go with the man to England.

Old Jan got even angrier that time, and I had to promise on my word of honor that I would stay on the farm when they went to church. He would lock me up if I did not make that promise. Not only that but he also put the watchdog in front of the door so that we could not leave even if we wanted to, for that was a mean old dog, with only one person that this beast would listen to, and that was old Jan.

I spent three hours with the flyer, as Bob recalled later. He really opened up at that point. He showed me some maps of Western Europe, printed on silk, with most German troop locations. He had several thousand German marks and as many francs for use in France and Belgium, also some Dutch money. He had some kind of candies to keep him awake and some chocolate to feed him in time of need.

He belonged to the RAAF and was a radio operator on a Lancaster airline. He explained that he would like to reach Belgium and go to the Pyrenees Mountains from there, crossing into Spain and from there to England. The farmer's wife had already suggested that we bring him to a canal that night.

This canal was going from north to south and would give him a bearing on the direction on which way to go. So we devised a plan as best as we could between the two of us. It would be impossible to walk that distance with those blisters on his feet, so I suggested that he should do the impossible—walk to the city of Zutphen, a town about forty kilometers south from the farm, bypassing the city of Deventer, since that city had heavy troop formations. He was to walk in the local railway station, hand over ten guilders, and ask for a ticket to Tilburg, a city that was close to the Belgium border.

I then taught him to say *"Enkele reis* Tilburg" (one way Tilburg).

He repeated that over and again until he knew it by heart and could repeat it flawlessly in Dutch. He could still say it when I met up with him again in 1986, right here in Canada!

Everything went as planned. We brought him to the canal that night. He walked to Zutphen and repeated the words "Enkele reis Tilburg," boarded a train, and traveled in full uniform on a public railway right through the center of wartime Holland. He even had a German soldier sitting next to him with his rifle between his knees. The soldier never had any suspicion, and neither did several other Germans that he met at one point or another. Not one member of the German armies had any idea that an enemy soldier would travel on a public railway in British uniform.

He ended back in England right around Christmas.

That he had much more help stands for reason, but you can read all that in a book he wrote, *Path to Freedom.*

It was not such a bad solution if you think about it. Bob would have ended in a prisoner of war camp if he had been caught, but no one else would have been in danger up (after?) to the point that he reached Belgium. He contacted the underground movement in a monastery by the name of Abbey Pastel. Life turned back to normal for us after this episode, as normal as you can expect in a war-torn country.

Soap had become a thing of the past, and it was harder to keep clean. We even had a run-in with lice in the latter part of the war, but that was no problem yet. The pesky little fleas became ever more of a problem. These little rascals can jump seven or eight feet and have room to spare. They also can make a very fast getaway. I have experienced that many times. I believe that they had their breeding ground in the reed-covered roof, but they sure did not despise a little warm hollow in the hidden places of human bodies.

I learned that the most effective way to catch them was to roll them over the skin of your body. They would break their ruddy little legs, and you could crack them between your nails of your fingers with a satisfying crunch. I learned to perfect that technique when I sat on the milk wagon delivering milk to the factory. The only trouble was that they—the fleas, that is—were worse than the Germans. One would be killed, and a dozen or more took their place.

The stygian darkness was another major problem at night. The whole countryside had to be blackened out so that no light was shining anywhere. No one that has not lived in the Low Countries can imagine the total darkness on some nights. A person cannot see a hand before the eyes, and that is absolutely true. This was even worse in the war when no lights were allowed anywhere, but every cloud has a silver lining even so, and we learned to feel our way through the darkest night.

Everything became possible if we were in the right company, and that company was never far away. There were always some ladies of the night who wanted to do a little experimenting as long as it stayed within acceptable limits.

So it was on one of those dark nights that we were stumbling over a little country road, boys and girls, feeling our way through the darkness. We figured if we could not see the Germans, the Germans would not see us, and we made a late night of it.

I was stumbling along with my favored girl, stealing a kiss off and on. It was at the height of passion that I heard something clicking on the other side of her. This was strange, so I did a little feeling to the other side of the girl and found another lover making time from the other side. This complicated matters a little, and it was the first and only time that I was sharing a girl with another party.

This was the end of our relationship, I may add. It was disastrous for my macho image. Women are an uncertain possession! Here today and gone tomorrow.

Life went on in this manner, and I learned to adapt myself to the most unusual circumstances. I became one with the community and learned to deal with man and beast. A case in point was the farm animals. The farmers would treat their animals in much the same way as their children, spoiling them sometimes and correcting them when necessary. This was a lifestyle that could lead to strange results at times.

Jan was involved, at times, with the breaking of unwilling horses. Jan and his sons would try their hand when other farmers had a horse that refused to pull. A licking would help sometimes, but not often. That would happen only as a last resort. Some other horse might be hitched to the rebel, and the striker would be pulled around the yard until he was willing to go by himself—that did not work all that often either. Another farmer hitched the horse to the wagon and built a fire under the horse, but the horse was not crazy either. He walked ahead until the fire was under the wagon and went back to what he was doing before—nothing!

Then they got a horse that would not be cured no matter what they did. Old John was sitting on the wagon when he happened to look at the cookhouse where turnips were brought to a boil for pig feed, and his eyes lit up suddenly. He walked to the cooking pot and fished a boiling turnip out of there with a pair of thongs. He walked to the wagon and told young John to hold on tight and shoved the hot turnip under the tail of the horse. The horse clamped down on the turnip in fear and exasperation. Then it took off as if a nest of hornets were after him. The horse was cured and never gave any trouble again.

I thought that this was cruel, but you could not deny that a useless horse had been turned into a productive animal. Not a practice that would pass by animal lovers, is it?

Something else happened as an example of the often unpredictable and colorful nature of these down-to-earth people. One cow was in heat and had to be served by a bull to be any good as a milk cow nine months down the road. Hardly any farmers had a bull of their own in that part of the country, but the farmer had a bull that was ready to be shipped. This was a young animal and not all that tall. He really could not do a grown man's job, since the cow was almost a foot taller, but the farmer decided that they were going to do a mission impossible.

He had his son dig a hole of a foot deep and placed the cow with the rear legs in the hole. Nature could take its course from that point on. The bull jumped fearlessly and was somewhat on the same level, and everything started to look promising until the moment that the cow jumped out of the hole, and the little bull was thrown over backward— an untimely end to a budding romance.

I never found out if this endeavor was successful because I was gone before the results were known, but I do remember that the farmer lifted his hat, scratched behind his ears, and remarked,

"We don't want to do that too often or we will wreck the little rascal."

I enjoyed these things immensely, but danger was always present, and problems arose at the most unexpected moments.

An old school buddy of the farmer stopped in one day. This was strange because the man had left the country to go and work in Germany many years ago. Why would this man show up just at this time after that many years? Fear of betrayal was underlying all our actions, and this was no exception. The old beggar was made welcome nevertheless, and he sat at the table like one of us.

The man asked, "Are these your children?"

"Ja," the farmer replied, "except the young man over there," and he pointed to me. "That is a boy from down south. He has studied for a priest but had a nervous breakdown and is here to recover."

It was a nice story, but it put me in great difficulties. It was time to say the evening prayers, and the whole family went on their knees to say the customary "Hail Marys" and "Our Fathers." This usually lasted about a half hour. I deeply respected their devotions but did my devotions in my own way.

This evening was going to be different. The farmer waved at me desperately. I had to go on my knees with the rest of them in order to fool the old visitor. There was nothing left but to listen, and I sank down in a very uncomfortable position. The old beggar was watching me like a hawk. I did not know the prayers but grumbled along to fit in with the rest, hoping to fool the unwelcome guest. I sat in a very cramped position with a chair crowding me in the back so that I was afraid to move and I had a very uncomfortable prayer session.

"How did you do?" the farmer asked when it was all over.

"Not all that good," I told him. "I was in a very cramped position."

A wide grin split his face, and he replied, "That's good, Hank. That makes for a really good confession."

The old peddler was not a very high-standing man at that. He asked me that evening if I wanted some condoms to make out with the women. It is hard to say what he was up to, but my parents had brought me up differently, and I stayed away from this degrading behavior. I mentioned that I would tell the farmer if he kept after me, and we have never seen him again, and that was just fine with us.

It is not so much that we were innocent of the facts of life, far from that. We had seen the German soldiers standing in line waiting their turn with the really professional ladies of the night in the lesser streets of the city of Munster.

The dock workers of Amsterdam and Rotterdam in the forced labor camp had given us an education that was second to none. Even so! There was something in our upbringing that kept us from sliding to a much lower level. The example of our parents was a mighty strong force in that respect.

I can't say that I was sorry when the old peddler left a short time later. We did not have time for that because the community threshing machine came to the farm. This machine was going from farm to farm under the supervision of a government inspector, a man who had to make sure that all the grain was turned over to the authorities.

Some tricky negotiations were in order, and old farmer John was just the man to do this. The inspector got invited in for coffee halfway down the proceedings. He could also get something a little stronger. It was a matter of your hand washes my hand and we both get clean. Although Farmer Jan was not very clean in body and soul, but that was beside the point at that critical moment of time. There was work to be done and money to be made. An amount of grain could be held back in the time that the man was gone.

This was an arrangement that would work with some inspectors—but not with this one. He had his own coffee and intended to stay with the machine come hell or high water. The guy was young and awfully stubborn. He was absolutely incorruptible. He was a German hireling to perfection well-trained in the ways of German conduct.

Old Jan and this man got in a fight that was unbelievable. We thought for a while that they would come to blows. Even so! Jan made enough distraction that his sons could steal part of his own grain back from the government. Old Jan kept screaming like a man possessed for his dear life, and for as much grain as possible. He was heaping abuse on the man, his present and past generation, and the ones to come.

The farmer told the man that his name would be remembered for use after the war. He even got the dog involved, and that was enough to scare the most lionhearted. But all to no avail! The farmer's portion of grain remained pitifully small, and the inspector departed with the solemn vow that he was going to return with more help. Farmer Jan was in big trouble because the inspector told him that he would be back to check out the farm for black market produce.

HANK OPDENDRIES

It should be noted that old Jan was a great sinner. He had stashed away a lot of stuff that should have been reported. All farmers were involved in this more or less, but old Jan was bad.

"A little pig here and a little calf there, produce, produce everywhere!"—just like Old MacDonald's children's song.

We who were young, John and I, had to hide stuff that evening all over the countryside. My little palomino horse was working overtime. It was as if the little critter could understand the importance of these moments. I have never seen her work like that, that evening. She was doing the work of two others. This might sound funny. It's true nevertheless!

We had to hide stuff in hedges and bushes, in culverts and in old sheds, all over where a place would stay dry. It turned out to be a very long day indeed, and it was a couple of very tired and unhappy young men who hit the sack in the late evening. We had to thresh all day long, and now we had to carry those heavy sacks all over the green acres and stubble fields.

"There is nothing that will get me out of bed again," said my partner in crime after it was all finished.

Famous last words! We bedded down in flea country, and I had the uncomfortable feeling that the day was not yet done, and sure enough, we woke up when we were still in our first sleep. Some thundering sound rumbled by over the roof of the farm. It sounded like a freight train passing over the house, followed by a thundering explosion, and later by several more. Neither John nor I had much to say about the matter. We had been thrown out of bed while half asleep.

So much for the accuracy of John's predictions and the promise of uninterrupted blissful sleep. It sounded like the whole farm building was collapsing around our ears, while the dust of generations was swirling around the building and the acrid smell of explosives was hanging over the whole neighborhood. Dark, billowing clouds drowned out the relative light of a tempered moon landscape.

Fires were burning not far away, and voices of consternation and fear could be heard in many places. A damaged bomber had dropped her load over the defenseless countryside. She must have ejected her bomb load trying to gain an altitude after some bad damage on her trip to a German city. Things like that happened often in those days.

"That's the way it's got to go!" someone said not long before that, and that sounds nice until you come on the receiving end of a bomb load, and then you learn to think a little differently.

One murder can never cancel a previous murder, and one bombardment cannot cancel the former one. It's a vicious circle that has no end.

"He who pulls the sword will be devoured by the sword." This is what the Master said when he was on earth. "If someone asks you to go one mile, go also the second." "Return good for evil," etc.

Did the Jews have the better way after all? The Jews were driven in concentration camps and slaughtered like sheep, just like their native Son so long ago. He had the perfect army on call, yet He chose another way—the way of sacrifice. He could overcome death to a life that will last forever, opening that way for you and me, if we only believe.

We have fought two large wars and many smaller ones to protect our rights. And the net gain is a world that is moving further away from God, a world that is indulging in self-gratification and self-glorification. Humans are willing to go to all sorts of violence to protect that way of life.

Will I do it differently if I had to do it all again? I really don't know. Will future generations see the great tribulation that the Bible talks about? Will we have to walk the way of total submission? The way of the first Christian church? The blood of the martyr is often called the seed of the church. Is that the better way?

Let's go back to the story. The unloaded bombs must have been of very heavy caliber indeed—the so-called air mines. These bombs have explosions with much air displacement. No houses were hit, but seven heifers were killed in one pasture. One cookhouse was moved about seven inches from the foundation—most remarkable if you consider that this was a brick building. All the furniture in the house was blown all over creation, and the doorknobs were pulled out of the doors.

And the greatest miracle of all was a Mother Mary image under a glass dome. It was sitting on the mantelpiece, unhindered and undamaged, in the middle of all this destruction. There was little that we could do. Everything might be under control as much as this could be under the circumstances, and we left that place of desolation to try and get some sleep.

John and I ran into the dead heifers on our way home. We stopped for a moment and then went further to tell the men in the neighborhood about the dead heifers. Was that ever a great mistake! We should have kept our mouths shut, for they made fun of us right away. We could have cut some meat off the dead animals before someone else got at them. A cut in fresh meat would not have shown, and the animals would go to the emergency slaughterhouse anyway.

We were reminded again about our place in life! Many endearing words came our way: babes in the wood, look in the world, peep in the world, and more disheartening words like that. John and I felt like worms ready to be squashed into an unsightly puddle of misery. Little did we know that the big boys were reacting to their own fears and unloaded their frustration on the first ones they met, and that was John and me.

Two disappointed and chastened sinners went home to check on the possible damage on the rest of the place. Our own farm had only a little damage to the roof, and life went on as before after a little repair here and there. The days were getting shorter and the evenings longer. Winter was close, and the days turned colder and wet. We had to walk most of the time beside our wagons on our milk hauls to the factory, partly to save the horses and, on the other hand, to keep warm through unwanted exercise.

These moist, wet days could be mighty chilling, and the trips on foot started to affect my performance. The trundling trips on wooden clogs produced some mighty painful calluses right under the balls of my feet. The wooden shoes became instruments of torture, and this got worse by the day. Bitter is life indeed when you are a little boy who is lost in a war that he did not want trundling along in unforgiving footwear while being tortured by fleas and all kinds of unknown species including some wild-eyed women. There was nothing for it but to grin and bear it. I got plenty of practice in grinning and bearing as time went by. But there were also some bright spots, other things in our lives that made our lot easier to bear. The evenings made up for a lot of grief and suffering.

One bright spot was the evening that we went walking with a group of young folks of the neighborhood. It had snowed all day, and six inches of snow covered the ground. One boy had a wooden leg, and he was drilling neat little holes in the snow with every move he made. We were moving along at a fairly good clip, with some enterprising girls in tow. The boy with the wooden leg was hanging on for dear life to a solid-built farm dame.

He had a tough time of it, since his wooden leg kept sliding sideways in every step he made. It did not seem that his acts of desperation were always that genuine, if you ask me, but that was beside the point. We struggled on, and the joyful throng ended in a straw stack of the stingy farmer who had sold all his wife's cutlery. The stack of dry straw did not seem all that solid, but that was overlooked in the heat of battle.

We climbed that mountain and settled down for an entertaining interlude. I was in deep conversation with my favored girl. We locked eyeballs, and the light reflections of the silvery moon in her eyes were fascinating beyond compare. I could not get enough of it. The boy with the wooden leg tried to get a point across to his well-formed companion, while some others had a wrestling match going on in the dim background. It was a night full of promise and suspension until the interlude was cut short.

The whole straw stack fell apart, and all the contents scattered all over creation, boys and girls included, so that we had to move onto other more stable endeavors. We did regret the wrecked haystack. Most of us had enough farmer's pride and decency to stay away from other farmers' property, but it happened in one of those forlorn moments that can't be called back. The deed was done, and there was no honorable way to make the amends without getting in more trouble. So we tried to make up for it by doing some work for the man later.

The boy with the wooden leg was a very likeable person. His disability did not bother him at all, and he had a beautiful disposition to carry him through the flat spots. He had one leg that had stopped growing when he was about one year old, leaving him with the foot of a child, just below the knee. He showed me once because he was not a bit inhibited about his misfortune. He really cut a big figure when he participated in a play later.

The family had asked me to write this play when I mentioned my experiences in an unguarded moment. So I went to work with enthusiasm and unwarranted optimism.

The first play was a comical act—very inexperienced writing—but hilarious like you won't believe. It was about a farmer lying in bed, recovering from an illness. He was somewhat delirious through the effect of a fever. His wife was sitting next to him, stuffing goose feathers in a pillow. There was also a pot of honey sitting on a chair beside the bed—don't ask me why! It just was there.

I forgot to mention that the man was bald-headed. "A dried cow's bladder painted in flesh colors created that effect."

The man started fighting in his delirious state and fell headfirst in the pot with honey. His wife tried to help him, but that made matters only worse, and they started to struggle together right into the pail with goose feathers. Two people covered with honey and goose feathers were the result of this little wrestling match. It was ridiculous and out of this world, and the audience laughed until they cried.

Everyone had a whale of a time, with coffee and refreshments after the play, and a call for another play to be held around Christmas.

Of course, the Germans would have had an even better time if they had raided that little convention of careless sinners. A serious theme was requested for the next play. The audience thought that it would be nice that a person would die on stage. A priest would have to do the last rites, and the man would have to be carried off, accompanied by the sound off church bells. A small choir would have to sing the requiem—a Catholic funeral song—and that would be the end of the play.

It was along those lines that I wrote another masterpiece, with Cleopatra at my elbow to give expert advice on her background education of the sacred rites involved in matters of this nature. The play was ready on schedule, beginning December, and the whole neighborhood showed up to have an evening of entertainment.

Our fame had spread far and wide, and many more people wanted to participate. A wagon bed had been brought in the barn with a lot of hard work and goodwill, and the stage was set for a command performance. And some performance it turned out to be. The stage had one serious flaw, and that was that the floor was made out of wooden slats with slits of about one and a half inches apart. This turned out to be the Achilles' heel of the whole performance.

Our priest—who was none other than the guy with the wooden leg—kept dropping out of sight every time he stepped on one of the cracks in the floor. The colorful tablecloth that served as his priestly raiment would ride up to his mousy, priestly head. Only the cloth and the skullcap he was wearing could be seen for a space of time until he managed to pull his leg out of the crack to be back on even ground.

The patient did a good job of dying, and the priest did OK to that point in time, but he dropped out of sight just before the critical moment. The church bells were passing all expectations. They were the nicest bells I ever heard.

We had taken a scarf off the big bomb that had fallen in the neighborhood not that long ago, about two feet in length and one foot wide. This was hung on a piece of rope. Young John had the impressive task of hammering away on that with a four-pound hammer. The rest of the play was not all that bad either, but the critics said that the first play was a lot better. The whole plot was a little too sad, and they had enough to worry about without another reminder of life's futility.

Fickle is the public, and hard to please.

Many stayed behind for a cup of coffee and exchange of the latest gossip. A good time was had by most of the folks in spite of the harm we had done to their refined tastes.

Now we come to the sad ending of my adventures with these colorful and good-hearted folks. My stay with the folks in Haarle was coming to an abrupt end, not all that long down the road. But several things happened before I left. The company of young folks around the district had accepted me as one of them, and that was very unusual because dating was very restrictive in those closed communities.

No one from outside the settlement was allowed to date a native girl. This was strictly enforced! Whole battles were fought about the possession of local girls. It has happened that outside boys have been thrown in the canal, beat up, or even carved up with knives. One group of defenders used a very sophisticated piece of equipment—a two-and-a-half-cent copper piece—the size of a quarter. It was sharpened to a razor-blade edge. This was held between thumb and finger, and many intruders had the back of their Sunday coat cut in two halves, all in protection of the honor of the local girls! Then came the one day in the year that the women had total control dictated by age-old laws—the men had to obey them in everything the women demanded for one full day during the fall season, and this made for impossible situations. Old Jan told us that a bunch of girls had chased him throughout the house and into the barn when he was young. These girls intended to strip him naked.

This was serious business, and the women had their minds set on doing just that, and nothing less! They cornered him behind the cows, in a corner of the barn. He was so desperate that he jumped in the trench filled with cow manure, and he started throwing the green manure all over kingdoms come just to save his miserable skin! He might have acted like a real man, but deep down he was a brazen coward. It was not nearly that bad on the day that we celebrated that feast, but bad enough. We were chased through the barn while pails full of water poured over us, from the ceiling and from the haystack and any other place you can think of. We were pushed in the pigpen, the bull pen, the playpen, and every other pen, real or imagined.

The girls who were not all that good-looking had a hay day because we had to kiss on command, like it or not. Punishment was swift and without mercy if we dared to disobey. The women were in complete control until evening when the festivities reached the boiling point. At that time the boys were expected to slap hands. One would hold up his hand, and the challenging boy would slap the outstretched hand with all his might.

The winner had first choice of the girls, and it stands for reason that the biggest guys got the pick of the crop. Not a very nice arrangement because I ended with a scrawny little girl, since I was so small and scrawny myself. It was an age-old custom, and not all that bad, if you think it through. Many girls, or many boys, got a date with the unlikeliest partners, with some good results sometimes!

My waterloo was nearby on the day that another guy came on the farm. This unworthy person was also on the run from the Germans, so he said. He was a seedy-looking character who did not make a very favorable impression on any of us, not on me and not on any of the girls either, but it was some more low-cost labor for the farmer. He was appointed to drive the second run to the factory.

We picked milk in separate wagons in the sand roads where the pulling was heavy and loaded the cans on one wagon when we reached the hard surface road, continuing to the factory together. It was in this way that he was taken up in the select group of fellow sufferers. All farmers of the milk run were allotted a share of butter in proportion of their herd. Our job was to deliver this butter to each farmer on our return trip with the empty milk cans. The butter was kept in a cardboard box on the front of the wagon box, in full view of anyone passing by, and nothing was ever missing. It was that kind of trust prevailing under the milk haulers. The new man was accepted in this routine with no questions asked, and this became my waterloo.

It had a disastrous result for my trusting personality. It is hard to believe, but two kilos of butter were missing on the end of my run! I never made a connection then or even after, but I had to face the music, and the farmer was very unreasonable. He told me that I had to replace the butter out of my own pocket—twenty-five guilders for each kilo of butter. Hank was out of two months of wages! Farmer Jan was very upset with me and not nice at all. Life carried on in the old way after that in spite of this disappointment.

Even so! The shine was taken out of things, and I did my work faithfully, but it was different from before.

Then the new guy hit a new low. He informed on me that I was having a relationship with the farmer's youngest daughter. He had tried his luck with both girls, and neither was interested, so he told the farmer's wife what was going on. This was only partly true, but I was guilty enough that the farmer's wife called me over and advised me to leave the farm that same day before she told her husband. Both girls were crying their lovely eyes out, and young John was not at all happy either. Nevertheless, the facts were there, and Hank had to leave. The new man had destroyed my reputation in less than a month.

Old Jan had come to like me, it seems. It was as if I gave him a slap in the face when I told him that I was leaving. He got roaring mad and told me that he was going to hold back the wages that he owed me and fifty pounds of grain, food that I had bought in the meantime. The loss of the grain hurt the most!

I had worked for nothing. I came with nothing, and I left with nothing! Still I am thankful to that family. The money was not important, but their hospitality was! I visited that farm after the war and was welcomed very warmly. I heard the real story then. The new man had taken off with a whole box full of butter not all that much later, and Jan had to replace every pound of it out of his own pocket. This cost him more than two thousand guilders—black market prices. I was cleared from all the blame, except my involvement with the girls, and that was not mentioned again!

The family also showed me a scroll of honor that they had received from the Allied high command for the help that they had extended to Bob in September 1943. My name was not mentioned, but that was rectified later by Bob himself. I could not help but think by myself, *You could have mentioned my part in that drama.*

Old Jan told me that they had more guys later, even a Jewish woman, but never an airman again. That was too dangerous. The old scoundrel and I met again later—once, and that was not that nice.

You will hear about that a little later, but he is high on the list of people that I have respected over the years, a family that I owe a lot of thanks, although he never gave me my money back. But money is always a necessary evil and not a means to an end!

And now, thanks to Jan and his family who helped a boy in need when he had nowhere to go! I walked home after the breakup with the family that had looked so well after me for about half a year. It should be said that the appearance of the double-crossing fellow might have been a blessing in disguise. I could have ended up marrying a local beauty in that neighborhood and have been forced into the Catholic faith with all the consequences. And so the wayward little Dutchman with a shaded past walked through the beautiful surroundings of my hometown woodland. It was on an early January day, and the air was cold and brittle. The scenery around me held the promise of renewed life, but my heart felt heavy. I surely had made a mess of my life. The future looked bleak. My beloved Cleopatra would be in someone else's arms before long, and not only that—I was a man with an insecure future with nothing to look forward to.

I had no work, and the prospects of any form of security in days to come were very dim. It was doubtful that my parents would be overjoyed with the homecoming of the wayward wanderer, and I sure did not expect a joyful welcome home from my family, but that did not turn out all that bad. Dad and Mom had seen so much trouble in the last little while that my arrival did not make all that much difference anymore.

Nobody had inquired after my whereabouts—no secret police, no SS, or anyone else for that matter. My older brother had stayed home from work in Germany also, and that brought no repercussions either. I moved right back with the crowd as if I had never been away. But caution was advised, and we had a reminder around that time that all things were possible and even likely to happen. Our neighbor had died, and I felt that I should walk in the funeral procession to the nearby graveyard. This was the next day after my return from my former hiding place. The procession went through the heart of town, and it was right in the center of town that a column of German soldiers came marching in our direction, and my heart went cold with fear. This could well be the end of the trail for me. I started looking for a way out, but then the army sergeant called a halt to the marching column, and the soldiers stood at attention as the hearse passed by.

The German army had a certain amount of class, and that showed up in this moment. A column of SS troops would have acted way differently under the same circumstances. Caution was advised, and I could not afford to take many chances like that.

This was made abundantly clear within the next few days. My older brother and his friends had gone for a hiding place in another small settlement nearby around Denham. This was the place where the Lancaster of Bob and his friends had come down—the two boys had seen the burning plane of Bob and his buddies not all that long ago.

It was on this day that the boys were traveling to their hiding places in the best of spirits, when they were stopped by the so-called black-shirt police—Dutchmen who had gone into the service of the enemy, betraying their own countrymen. These two men were father and son.

My brother was lucky to have a weekend pass that was still valid. He was allowed to go back home, but his friend was taken to a concentration camp in Ommen, a concentration camp near the town of Ommen. He was shipped from there to a camp in Amersfoord. This camp was far worse than the one in Ommen, and he was forced in the TOD troops of the German army. The TOD troops were in uniform but had no weapons.

He ended in Russia eventually. They had no weapons of any kind and should not have been treated like ordinary soldiers, but somebody had forgotten to mention that to the Russians. They shot everyone in sight.

The front would fluctuate back and forth, so that this man's troop had to run for their lives more than once. The German soldiers grabbed all available travel machinery, even bicycles and horses, in a situation like that, and the TOD troops were left behind to fend for their own lives as best as they could.

The Germans would push the front back on a later date, and the TOD troops would find their buddies dead with a neck shot.

Much more happened, of course, but this much is enough for the present. My brother was allowed to go back home, dove right under again, and went to work braiding straw. He was to stay this time to the end of the war, but I had the impression sometimes that these narrow escapes did not teach him anything. He was as careless as ever before. We will never know the suffering and worrying my father and mother did to keep body and soul together.

The guiding and protecting hand of our God over us was unearthly—out of this world might be the best way to describe His dealings with His people. Enterprising Dutch dealers had found a way to sell straw mats and braided straw shopping bags—like suitcases—to the German population. These products were really nice to look at and even beautiful at times, very useful for hauling groceries, etc.

What was even more amazing was the fact that there was room available in the much-needed train space of the German Wehrmacht. The trains had to be used to the utmost for the war effort, and here was room provided for our produce repeatedly, contraband articles that were manufactured by people who were under cover, hiding from the German authorities.

I marvel at that even now after all those years. It just did not make any sense, and the hand of God was truly at work. Even the greatest skeptic cannot deny this fact. Here we were with four grown-ups all underwater, and then there was Dad also braiding straw. He was too old for forced labor, but that would also change in the next half year.

That would make five of the twelve people in our household living on borrowed time. Truly amazing! My friend Dick approached me right away to come back with him braiding straw in some little shed only a few houses away. The danger of walking the street was minimal that way, although danger was ever present. We could never leave the house without looking in every direction for police SS or soldiers. The fear gnawed in our stomachs day and night. We were never free of pain—nerves.

Any member of the German army could shoot us on sight—no questions asked. A soldier would get a decoration instead of a reprimand. Even so! The three of us were quite content, strangely enough. We worked in a shed with a person named Albert, a married man, as our host. Albert was hiding from the Germans also, just like the rest of us. More than 90 percent of all men remaining in Holland were in hiding in fact. The rest had been put to work in Germany or in the war effort.

There were also a few men who were involved in the food production, and they had a special permit that allowed them a certain amount of freedom to go from place to place. My oldest brother had a permit like that, but he was also in the underground movement.

We had to be ever so careful, for behind the shed lived a man with the meaningful name of "Miaow the Cat." This man was suspected to be collaborating with the enemy. The difficulty was that he could see us moving in and out of that little shed, and he could report us to the authorities at any given moment. He might have, but that could never be proven. "He was dead by then." He came to an untimely end. Miaow was snooping around in the heather-covered fields east of us.

This was mostly bush country also, and the underground had dropping zones in that district where the Allies would drop weapons after curfew. This man, "Miaow the Cat," who was not trusted at the best of times, was found in that area when a dropping was expected. The Cat seemed to have been caught up in the deadly game of cat and mouse between the underground and the secret police, the gestapo. The opposing parties were playing with lives like children with marbles. The Cat might be an informer, and his presence could not be explained any other way.

We will never know what really happened, but the story goes that the underground members asked the Cat, "What are you doing here in the middle of the night during curfew, when all citizens have to be inside by order of the Germans?"

The Cat must have been scared by then, as he answered, "Just looking around."

The underground was not willing to take chances and told him, "You better say your prayers—you have done your last snooping around."

Miaow was found the next day, a block from where we lived, beside his bicycle, with a bullet through his head. This must be impossible to understand presently, but I will try to explain the background. The underground was involved in the dropping areas. They, who were the underground, ran a vast network of illegal activities at that time because the many people in hiding needed ration cards. That's where the knock plough (raiding parties) of the underground came in.

The underground raided many offices that had a supply of ration cards. This included town offices for registrations of people in hiding and at times even prisons, to free underground members who would be shot to death without trial and in deep secrecy by the SS and gestapo. These activities required weapons, and the weapons had to come out in dropping areas in the forest of Holland. One of these areas was in our bush country. One traitor, like the Cat, could lead to the death of many freedom fighters. The death of the Cat was just a trade-off in lives.

Do I agree with these practices? I don't know. But I would not have pulled the trigger at any cost! Life was cheap in those days of violence, but the men had a soul to lose, and it is quite a responsibility to send someone into eternity. I was never put in that position, and thank the Lord that this is so.

I should add that we were receiving ration cards from the underground also, and that is what kept us alive. Life would have been impossible without these ration cards, and we could not have gone on with our straw-braiding business without those lifesavers. The difficulty was that the straw braiding was insecure at the best of times. Sometimes the sales were good, and at other times it came to a complete standstill, but we had enough money to make ends meet, very close to starvation most of the time.

There was also the fact that our money could not buy anything. No sugar, no milk, no flower for bread, or anything else for that matter. We got to the point that we would beg for a helping of rye porridge. The rye grains could be years old and had mouse droppings in them more often than not. Hard to believe but true!

We could not even get salt anymore in later days, and that is the greatest punishment of all. A person can put up with much, but life is without meaning when the salt is missing. We had to live close to starvation with hunger pangs gnawing on our insides, like worms eating your stomach, but we did not die from hunger. That would be an overstatement.

Still we were hungry enough that we slept till noon every day to spare a meal a day. Then came the day that Dad asked me to come and work with them. He told me that my loyalties should be with my uncle Bert, who was our contact with the underground. He also supplied us with ration cards for food and the odd cigarette.

The chance did not make me all that happy, but I could see the point and changed working places. This was maybe for the better, but I could not see this at the time. Anyway, that is how I got involved with Uncle Bert. He was quite a character with many emotional ups and downs. The story that we come from the gypsies becomes almost believable when I think back to the antics of my uncle Bert. He had curly black hair and fearsome brown eyes, and those eyes could shoot fire at times when he was angry or emotional, and that was quite often. Our uncle had only one arm, but that did not stop him from throwing his weight around at the most unlikely places. One of these places was the underground. He is one unsung hero of those dangerous days during the war. It was not unusual to see him enter our workplace, and he would start complaining about cold fingers on his right arm. This was ridiculous, for he had no right arm. We did not understand that his nerve ends gave him the feeling of cold fingers, and that would make him appear even more eccentric.

The story goes that a couple of young fellows wanted to stop him when he wanted to visit his girlfriend. These fearless warriors figured that a one-armed man could be pushed around at will. They came out swinging but got persuaded to a different vision after they were thrown over a high thorny hedge by the locomotion of the one-arm bandit. Uncle had a very strong faith and was not afraid to witness to his convictions at any time or any place. It was this faith that helped him to keep his actions under control most of the time. This made him a very likeable person. He would come flying around the corner every so often with eyes as big as saucers and holler, "The nest is laying under the tree again!" and this meant, freely translated, "The shipment of produce was held up again." Uncle's moods would bounce up and down in tune with the shipment of our braiding materials. All this became very unsettling at times. Rumors were flying around in those days, like bees around a beehive when there is thunder in progress. It actually happened that a person would announce a raid by the German troops just to see how long it would take before the rumor got back to him. Then the guy ran like mad to get in hiding because it returned so often to him that he started believing it himself.

This might sound exaggerated a little, but it is a fact that there were rumors almost every week that a raid by the German troops would be on such and such day. Some came from the underground, and some were just pure speculations, and we did not know what to believe. Even so! The rumors were true very often, and then on a certain day there was another raid in progress. The German troops had surrounded our town and shut it up tied so that no one could get in our out. All men went underground in every conceivable hiding place. Some made it and some did not.

The Germans were at one place on the highway when a young man tried to outrun them on a bicycle just on the other side of a railroad dike. He would have made it, but it was unfortunate that his head was showing just above the railroad dike. A German took aim and shot him right through his head. Period!

Someone told us how this happened, and the cold shivers went up my spine. This was pure unadulterated violence and a display of force that left nothing to the imagination. The Germans would stop at nothing if it would help to win the war.

These happenings prompted me to build a hiding place of mine from timber that brother Adolf had stolen from the German troops. I don't know how, but he did it. He had more guts than brains, I think! We built the hiding place underground, beside the barn, about three feet down, and we planted a flowerbed on top of the place. Not a bad place after all, but it had one flaw—it was the entrance underneath a rabbit pen, inside the barn. It was so constructed that it was almost impossible to find. The floor of the rabbit pen could be lifted and give entrance to the hiding place. Like I said, there was one flaw in the construction. The air supply was the weak link in the setup, just a little hole behind the pen.

My brother George and I crawled in this hole when another raid was announced, well prepared with a handful of tobacco leaves to tide us over until everything would be safe again. We had a good time for a little while, and then the air supply came in short demand. It got so bad that we could not even light a match anymore.

Smoking became impossible while ever more oxygen was used, and we became jollier and jollier, laughing about the silliest things until the point that we lost consciousness. This must have happened by God's providence, for just at that time the German troops walked over our hiding place and tamped the bud of their guns on the ground above our heads.

A neighbor who witnessed the actions of the soldiers almost fainted, since she knew that we were in there. She thought for sure that we would be hauled out of there before her eyes. I had built another hiding place upstairs also, behind a false wall. The results may have been different if we had been in there. Betrayal was always a possibility, and a neighboring lady who was not completely normal might have betrayed us. She was always complaining that we, as healthy boys, stayed home and her husband was away because he had reported to the Germans. We will never know and did not try to find out either!

It's possible of course that the soldiers knew we were in there. But they chose to leave us there. Not all Germans were bad. The adventure of my friend Dick's brother was an example. He was hiding behind a rye field. The rye was quite high already, and he decided to come out to have a look around. He had been in there for most of the day.

So he crawled to the edge of the field on hands and knees. He was rounding the corner just at the time that a soldier came from the other side. He looked at the man, like a scared rabbit, and the man looked at him. Both turned around, and each went his way, but not in peace. That would have to wait for a while. Not many people were collaborating with the enemy. Many people were forced into labor for the enemy. For example, the dairymen and farmers were forced into hauling lumber for the enemy, something they hated. It would happen that they would leave a certain location with a load full of trees. My brother Adolf and friends would be waiting for them along the road full of expectations and goodwill for the prospect of stealing some firewood. The drivers seemed deaf and dumb. They never noticed that Adolf and friends stole trees from the wagons, and the unwary drivers drove on. These goodly men were looking at everything but forgot all about the load of trees behind them.

One of these drivers was a cousin of ours, about five feet six inches tall, very well built, but he had a disability, and that was the fact that he had a harelip. This was a disability that set him apart from the rest of humanity. Not that this bothered him, for he had a sunny disposition and was one of the happiest men I have known. He was also one of the dumbest of the drivers. He never noticed anything, and the little fry had a heyday when he arrived on the scene. He lost more trees than anyone else, but he slept on.

He was also the guy who drove through the center of town with a load of trees, including a shipment of weapons for the underground underneath a load of trees. Completely unconcerned by the looks of things, he was whistling a happy tone as he drove by some German soldiers who were strolling over the sidewalk along the road. Losing a few trees was chickenfeed compared to the trips he made for the underground.

Not much harm was done in the stealing of a few trees, but every little thing was gained. I got wooden poles to build a hiding place out of that deal. It is funny that we taught the kids to steal and had to break them off the habit after the war. That was damaging in more ways than one. Adolf's forages helped to solve the heat problem. Another problem was the electricity.

Curfew was at eight. Any person who remained outside after that time was considered to be dangerous for the defenseless German army. But that was just the time our day really started! We were underwater with five people in our household, and many friends used to come over to visit, so it was always a full house. Only the lighting was a problem.

The electricity was forbidden in any normal household. A seal was put on all electricity meters, but that only stopped some households. Some folks drilled a hair-fine hole through the top of the meter and set a very little pin in the winding little disc that turned and counted the kilowatt meters of power being used.

Another friend of us who was also born with the name, Albert, had a very eccentric father. This was a man of great imagination and not that humble. He drilled a hole in the meter and set a knitting needle in there, the size of a four-inch nail. He could have hung the national flag on there and it would have shown less, and the family lived happily ever after.

We were not that demanding. Dad and Mom had ten children to look after, so we did nothing that might attract undue attention. I connected an alternator to the rear wheel of a bicycle and put the cycle on a hoist—and, presto, there was light if someone would pedal the bike without going anywhere.

It was usual to have six or more young men sitting around the wooden table in our home. The windows were covered with black-out paper to keep the light from shining out, but even that was done in a haphazard way, and the cracks were showing in several places. Some boys sat on worn down wooden chairs and others on a sofa, which was nothing but an old table with the legs cut off. We had some kind of brew made out of burned rye kernels supposed to be coffee but in reality was nothing but a hot water brew with some undefined substance in it. The real coffee had not been around for years.

All the men were smoking self-grown tobacco. This stuff was as green as grass in our household. We used to grow that stuff in a little plot behind the house.

I never had the patience to wait for it to cure but would rip of a few leafs and throw them in the oven of the wood-burning stove. The stuff would crumble in your hand after drying and was ready to be rolled in a piece of newspaper. The stuff had the kick of a mule on a normal day but would be so potent in the early morning that it felt as if somebody hit you with a sledgehammer. We would be wheezing like an old locomotive coming up steam. Our eyes would pop open with a bang, and we were ready for another day.

This was the kind of stuff we that would enliven our evenings, and our parents would find their way through the billowing clouds, happy as clams and worried sickly most of the time. Those evenings were unbelievably pleasant with a lot of conversations—some serious and some plain silly, but never boring. I have met people who remembered those evenings as much as fifty years later.

We would have to visit our friends in other evenings, after curfew of course, and never without danger. The night could be dark as pitch, and we would feel our way through along the hedges and fences. The tingling sensation of danger was always present, and an unknown object or little bush could scare the living daylights out of the unwary seeker. A figure jumped out of a hedge on the night that I was on my way to my friend Dick. It turned out to be my friend who was smooching away with his girlfriend in an untimely fashion. They laughed until they cried when I almost fainted, but I did not appreciate that sense of humor at all. I almost had a heart attack then.

Life went on in that fashion, and we went from house to house night after night. The father of Albert was also on the house-visiting list. This man was dealing and wheeling in dogs. Little dogs, big dogs, any kind of dogs—but no hot dogs; they had not been invented yet—often purebred dogs, but not always. It looked at times as if he lived more for the dogs than for the family.

And so it happened when his wife was expecting a baby, and the doctor had to come out to assist the mother-to-be. The doctor, who was also a lover of dogs, followed Albert's dad to the dog kennel. A very valuable dog was getting little ones and could not be left alone. The woman was having a baby with the men spending most of the time in the dog pen!

This is Albert's story, and not my invention. It could well be true, for some strange things happened in that household. They had a large

HANK OPDENDRIES

family, and the same man went to visit his brother-in-law when he saw a little boy walking in the distance.

"Who is that you have walking over there half a mile away?" he asked.

"Well," the man said, "that's one of your kids!"

He was flabbergasted and said. "I never had missed that one yet!"

He was a strange man with a strange family but fun to go to.

We were on our way to that family in the dark of night, feeling our way along a hedge less than half a mile away from the German patrol when an airplane came droning over. This was not that unusual, but what followed was the plane dropped a magnesium flare and turned the night into day! We were caught like rabbits in a light beam. A German detachment of soldiers had their headquarters in a school building less than half a kilometer away. We got caught in that torrent of light, and the chance of capture was more than likely; but nothing happened, and we disappeared back in the dark when the flare was burned out.

I give you to think what we felt like just then. We went on from one crisis to the next, and the pressure became almost unbearable as time went by. The worms squirming in the pit of our stomach became a real torture as the days went by, but we had our lighter moments to ensure that we would not lose our sanity.

Albert's family had clandestine pigs in a little shed behind the house. They were kept there for future reference. But the animals got so noisy that they had to be butchered before someone else did it for them. Their pets would end in the German cooking pot when that happened. It was decided to turn them into sausages—into so-called bread sausages.

This would have worked nicely with the exception that the mixture had to be stuffed in linen cloth bags. There was none of that around anymore so that the linen bags were substituted with paper bags. The result was that the stuff started expanding and busted wide open, with the result that the contents had to be eaten on short notice. So the whole family ate until they all ended with the runs—diarrhea. This called for emergency measures, and fresh troops had to be brought in before everything was wasted.

That was where I came in—I had to play a part in the drama that was unfolding in horrid detail! We had not had a good meal in months, and I dug right into the feast until I could hardly walk anymore. It was at that point that Albert asked me to play a game of checkers with him. This was to be in the luxury room, as it was called.

Everything in that house was topsy-turvy, and even a doorknob was missing in the door between the kitchen and the luxury room, so I had to make a detour through the hallway before the game could begin. We were well into it when the door opened and the hall door opened, and a German came walking in with his gun leveled at us.

My whole life flashed in front of me when I looked in the boor of that ugly weapon. The ultimate power is gathered in that little hole, and it is hard to believe that your end can come out of that little hole. Eternity in the form of a rifle was looking us right in our face.

"Don't you guys have to work?" he said. "Identification papers, right now!"

I was looking for a way out and said, "My identification is in my coat in the porch," and started walking simultaneously.

Albert had seen me go and said much the same thing. He jumped right over my head in the porch where I was putting my wooden shoes on, and both of us started running for our lives. Another guy came walking in the doorway when we ran out and ran right along with us without asking questions—a sign of the times.

We'll never know what was up with that German. Nevertheless, he seemed to get caught in front of the door without a doorknob and was slowed enough that he lost us.

It could also be that he really was not interested about bringing us in. Albert's dad in turn had seen us leave, and he jumped out of the front window, and that is the end of that story. This is the only time in my life that I outran Albert and his friend, who was a head taller than me. Our home was an interesting place, and so was the home of Albert and his family. Nothing was quite normal in that place.

Albert's dad and his neighbor were both involved as dealers in purebred dogs. The brother of my friend Dick was also included in that illustrious company. They had their best days if they could sell a dog with a flaw to one of that company. This was not that they wanted to be crooked but just a battle of witticisms and a matter of principle, and it was very fitting that they used their wit in all areas of life.

And so it happened that they had a beautiful purebred dog that they would like to have bred to a dog from the same genre. However, the fee was a problem, and it would cost a fortune to get the right male. They looked around and found a male dog that would serve the occasion. This dog belonged to a woman who did not want that dog to be used for that purpose under any circumstances. Good advice was hard to come by, but eventually Albert was told to play with the dog in heat and sent over for a little talk with the women in question. And would you know it? The male dog slipped out of the house the same time as Albert did. The dog did his job at no cost to anyone.

It reminds a person of the story of Jacob and the peeled sticks in the water drinking troughs in the story of Jacob and Laban. But let's get back to the war . . . Shenanigans like these made life a little more bearable but did not make life a bed of roses.

Ever more men were put to work in Germany or in the different activities that the German forced on the defenseless population of war-torn Holland.

The English broadcast station of the BBC became a lifeline for our embattled senses. There were not many radios around then, and we had to depend on the hearsay of the fortunate people with a radio. We were allowed in the neighbor's house occasionally, if we were lucky, to listen to the clandestine radio, and this was a great privilege, since this operation was ultrasecret. Penalties for listening were severe, and traitors could be anywhere. Still, it was the lifeline of the downtrodden, and the news was getting better. The English BBC was talking ever more about the second front—a front that was to break down the western front along the west coast of Europe.

Most of us realized that this would not be a mean task, since the Atlantic Wall was a masterpiece of engineering, and it would take a tremendous effort to break through that barrier. This good news gave us more courage, but the living conditions were getting worse by the day, and it started to look like nobody would escape capture if this war went on much longer.

It is a good thing that life has its compensations, and love came back in my life, and that had also some dire consequences for my well-being. The main street of our town was the boy-meet-girl place par excellence. We would walk that street from east to west, from one end of town to the other. The courting instincts were so strong that we walked that stretch of road every Saturday and Sunday evening even though we were underwater and the whole German army was after us. We walked that stretch of road just to meet a member of the other sex—a strong testimony to the eternal attraction between the two sexes.

Even the German Wehrmacht would walk that stretch of road—with little success, I may add—although many German boys did not like this war any more than we did.

I was in love with a girl who was really out of my class. She was a girl of the fast lane, and I was very shy at the best of times. This girl was moving in a circle of smooth-moving, fast-talking boys with a way different lifestyle than we had. This made me a Lilliputian in the land of giants.

My courage never got up to the point that I dared to ask this girl for a date. My friends Dick and Adolf were getting really worried about my outlook on life, so they set out to remedy the situation. They told me that I had to take the bull by the horns—walk up to the girl and ask her for a date. But it still took them the better part of the evening to bring me around to their superior insight in matters of the heart. I was persuaded by a torrent of love advice from the two experts and agreed to meet the challenge. I would walk up to the girl and pop the question.

The girl in question came walking in our direction. She was right in the middle of a row of girls, about four on each side.

"Now is the time!" Dick and Adolf yelled and pushed me in the line of girls.

It is hard to believe, but I was desperate and was silly enough to ask the girl, "Can I have a date with you tonight?"

She looked at me and said, "I don't think so!"

The whole group of girls burst out laughing, but the girls did not laugh nearly as much as Dick and Adolf. They were crawling over the sidewalk in uncontrollable mirth—some friends! It was as simple as that. The actions of my friends and the snide remark of a snip of a girl had turned me into a quivering mash of shame, mixed with anger and frustration. One fact was established: Old Henry was no lover of renown.

I have to explain that we had two friends with the name of Albert. One was of my age, and he was the one who abided in the mixed-up household of the dog lover. The other was married and had two children, a man with a nose like a plow iron. We would tease him and tell him that he would drown if he turned his nose upside down and walk in a rainstorm. He did not take kindly to that!

HANK OPDENDRIES

Anyway, my friend Dick and Albert were braiding straw on that faithful day that the Germans held a surprise raid. The underground must have been asleep on the job, and we were not forewarned. It came as a total surprise, and the Germans were up on us before we knew what hit us. Dick escaped out of the backdoor, and Albert left the front door to hide in a ditch in a field across the road. A hedge was overlapping this spot, and the place was almost impossible to detect. He might have been OK if he had made it that far, but he was arrested before he reached that place. He walked right into the arms of the soldiers and was transported to a concentration camp in the company of a dozen other unfortunate victims also caught in the oppressor's grasp.

No mercy was shown to any of them, and they were still lucky that they got out alive many months later. They ended in camp Amersfoort—a camp that was the worst in the country. Albert told us the following stories later . . .

Most of them were set to work braiding straw and making straw products. Others had to dig holes and fill them in repeatedly. Still, others had to carry rocks back and forth, back and forth. There was absolutely no meaning to any of these activities, only designed to degrade and subdue the strength and spirit of the unfortunates of that wretched camp.

A group of inmates was forced to lift a tree heavy enough for ten men, and they were forced to do this with six undernourished skeletons of human beings. Four men were kicked out from under that tree, and the two remaining were falling down with crushed arms and legs. Then the guards ordered them to stand up and go to work—something that was impossible for these wrecks. The larger of the two guards then charged them with disobedience and beat them to death. Changes for those men were next to nothing, and that's just what these guards had in mind. The treatment of the ordinary prisoner was inhuman; the treatment of the Jew was infinitely worse, if that was possible. The Jews were forced to exist in the middle of camp in a place with the colorful name of rose garden.

This garden was guarded by vicious dogs. These animals were trained to bite anything that moved, especially humans. And the Jews were forced to suffer among those animals. No Jew was allowed to defend himself if attacked by one of these dogs. One of those dogs might get hurt, you know! Thus the victims were forced to pass by those animals again and again in their daily routine. It happened that a prisoner would hold out his hands in fearful reflective action. And the dogs tore the victim to pieces as the guards stood by laughing.

The Jews were forced to haul water in baskets, getting nowhere, to the great delight of the sadistic onlooking guards. But the guards did not want to get too monotonous and had the Jews move sand in wheelbarrows with a square wheel.

The food for these creatures was next to nothing, and they were forced to crawl under the table of the SS on hands and knees, and they just might get a scrap of food if the Jew would bark like a dog, sitting up much the same as a dog. The SS found this greatly entertaining and never seemed to get bored with these kinds of games. The guard dogs were always around for the protection of the poor SS and ready to jump in action at the slightest command of the torturers with the silver death heads on their caps. That the guard dogs were fed more than enough stands for reason—the reason of the crazed German intellect.

Justice was far removed, and God seemed very far away to many in those dark days. Hope was gone, and no light shone for the hopeless and the lost.

Conditions were not quite as bad for Albert and his friends, but bad enough. The warped minds of the Nazis had strange twists and quirks. They would lash out to anything or anyone out of the ordinary, and it was this condition that made life for one of Albert's friends almost unbearable. The man was much taller than most, and that seemed very offensive for the mentally unbalanced overseers—capos were the name of these torturers, overseers for the German camp officers. They were prisoners themselves but would stoop to inhuman behavior just to please the SS guards.

This oversized man was on the receiving end of this inhuman combination of German SS and their slave drivers. He stuck out a head above the rest of the straw-braiding crowd. This was his undoing because the capos were always hitting him with their clubs just because he was different.

The man ended up braiding straw lying on his knees to escape the beatings that were measured out on a daily basis. The other prisoners thought this to be somewhat hilarious.

"Saying that this was hilarious is not a slip of the tongue but actual fact."

The lifesaving—or rather, the mind-saving—quality of those days was the humor and the hearty laugh that could be shared in the most unlikely situations. I have experienced that myself in more than one situation, and many others have told me the same thing. Albert could tell with a hearty laugh how they would lie behind the barracks on a nice sunny day enjoying the sun, and a capo would come flying around the corner with a big stick. The crowd would scatter like a bunch of chickens scared for some unknown reason or object. This would happen often on Sunday. The Germans kept Sunday as a day of rest even in those camps. This might be for the reason that the Great War lord Adolf had a religious background. He did advocate some unpredictable things, and some actions had a religious background.

Life has many mind-saving devices, and humor and laughter are some of the more important ones. But all this did not wipe out the fact that these camps were ruled by mentally defunct individuals, just to put it mildly. A fairly young boy of the hometown group was never to return, and Albert told me that he had seen how the German brutes had picked on him without letting up. The boy was not very strong and started lagging behind in more ways than was good for him. Anything unusual was punishable with death. The dictum of Hitler called for a strong and pure race. Anyone who was weak and had the wrong color of hair or the wrong nose or anything else was not desired and had to be finished off.

This is exactly what happened to this boy. The day came that they were to be transferred to Germany, and the group was lined up in a railroad station in Zwolle—a city in Holland. The camp commandant told this boy to stand with his legs apart and then kicked between the boy's legs with his soldier boots just as hard as he could manage. A last farewell of the Amersfoort camp commandant!

The boy never returned, and it is my hope that his family never found out what happened to him. Why did I tell these stories? So that the truth will be known! And that future generations are aware and watchful. Much more could be told, but that would fall outside the scope of this memoir.

We would like to look at the role of women in those days (a role that was extraordinary). Albert's wife was just a little person, yet she managed to visit her husband about once a week in near-impossible conditions. She and others like her spent days in front of that camp just trying to catch a glimpse of their husbands.

The camp was hours away from the place they lived, and the girls had to make the trip on bicycles with solid tires made out of strips of auto tires joined in the middle with a piece of wire. These tires would make a resounding thump every time this wire hit the surface of the road. Even a well-fed man would have a hard time under those conditions.

It would not be hard to understand the strain and wear and tear on these mostly underfed women. You have to take into consideration the effort it required to pedal the bicycles over roads deteriorated through war conditions. And then there was still something that I was to learn after the war.

Albert and his family had been harboring Jews regularly. Jews that had to be transported from one hiding place to the other. There were still Jews in this house on the day that Albert was captured, and there was one young Jew who has given Albert's wife a very bad time. But I will get into that later . . .

Albert and his friends were put to work on the trenches along the big rivers not all that long before the end of the war. This was a great improvement over the life in the Amersfoort camp. It might have had a lifesaving value for many of these men, not to mention the burden taken off the women's shoulders, for this was a lot closer to our hometown. This was the story of Albert and friends, but life went on for us in much the nerve-racking manner—only it got worse by the day.

A warning came through that another raid would be held. This time the Germans announced that several hostages would be shot if we did not report for work on the German defense system along the great rivers in the center of Holland.

Again, this was no idle threat. Some high-ranking Dutchmen were held as hostages. Men out of our district and the Germans were well inclined to do just what they said. This made our decision a lot harder. It is one thing to risk your own life! It's an altogether different story when someone else is involved.

We came together with a circle of friends who had stuck together throughout this war, for we were at a loss of what to do next. It was one thing to put our own life in jeopardy, but now the lives of others were at stake, and that was a way different ball game.

So we came together to discuss the situation, and it was on this meeting that we were informed that the underground advised us to stay put and not to report for labor at the defense works of the Germans. It might be quite possible that the Germans wanted to round up as many as possible to have their back covered if the English broke through!

Whatever the truth may be, we decided to stay right at home, or in hiding to be exact. We also decided to follow the advice of an underground member in the neighborhood. This man told us that he had a good hiding place, much better than ours. Now it happened that this was one of those men who are overenthusiastic, and he seemed to have more enthusiasm than insight. His hiding place was not satisfactory at all. We sure did not like the place all that much! Our own would have been better—but it was too late to turn back, and we ended up in a kind of double ceiling above his kitchen. Any policeman worth his salt would have dug us right out of there in no time flat. But there was something far worse! We had to share that ceiling with a couple of sacks of black market grain. There we were—the three of us and two Jews previously hidden in Albert's house . . . This was the same Albert who was caught that day.

One Jew was a girl and very knowledgeable in the Bible. She could quote almost every verse of the Old Testament by heart. I have never met anyone like that again. The other was a young boy, and he turned out to be one of the funniest people I have ever met, and here the same thing happened that I mentioned before.

The Jew was telling jokes that were so funny that we laughed beyond all reason, while at the same time we were eaten by nerves and anxiety simultaneously! We had to laugh so hard at times that anyone walking behind the houses would have had to hear the noise of it all. This was really stupid, and it could have been avoided.

The green police walked the street in front of the house but did not go near the back. God must have sent His angels to take care of us. Our end would have been certain if we had been caught in the company of two Jews! The fact that we were hiding in the company of these Jews did not upset us all that much. On the contrary, we would gladly have put our lives on the line for them, but we had some reservation about the young Jew and the way he was acting. I was even more concerned when I talked to the Jew, John, after it was all over.

We went outside afterward, and I said to John, "I laughed myself silly about the jokes and other stories you told us up on that ceiling, but it was not very smart of you to act like that. Your end would have been sure if the police had caught you!"

He looked at me and started laughing. "I am not worried," he said. "Nothing will happen to me if they catch me! I will tell them everything I know, and that will be enough to get me off the hook."

I stood there with a stunned expression on my face, while he laughed and walked away as if he had no worry in the world.

A member of the underground stopped by not all that much later and asked me how it had been. I told him like it was and warned him to watch this person, repeating the words that he said to me after the danger was past. Little did I realize the forces I had set in motion. This John had been to many transfer stations in the last four years already, and always with the same result. He got too careless and was too dangerous to have around. He must have been in many stations in those four years, with Albert as the last resort. The consequences of his capture would have been beyond the imagination, and many underground people would have lost their lives. They had John in the swimming pool, the headquarters of the local underground, that same night. He would have to be shot. Just like that! They were going to shoot him. It is beyond belief but absolutely true. It was too dangerous to let him live any longer!

A hole for his body had been dug already, and the underground members were all set to finish the matter once and for all. The mother of that underground group happened to come in at the last moment, and she begged the men to let him live. She would personally guarantee that he would not be any trouble from thereon, and this is what saved the boy's life. She kept him to the end of the war, and he was almost impossible to control because he became cell crazy, as we would call his condition. I talked to Albert—more than forty years later—and asked him about this boy, John the Jew. Albert told me that he had given his wife an awful time after he had been caught by the Germans.

This same boy came to Albert after the war and asked if he could have board and room with him and his family, and Albert told him,

"I looked after you when you needed it, and I would do it again. Nevertheless, the war is over, and I don't want you in my house after the manner in which you treated my wife when I was caught!"

Albert was one of the most sincere Christian men I have ever met, but there was a limit to his patience. I do not think that many Jews were like this, but there is always a bad apple in the barrel. War does strange things to the minds of people, judging by the way the underground was prepared to act.

John's life was saved, and he became a translator on one of the first Canadian troop carriers that entered our town and from thereon went on to an unknown destination. The little Jewish girl made it through the war and immigrated to Israel on a later date, fulfilling her wish that she mentioned to us on that dreary ceiling in that old Dutch town.

We lived through this episode, but the war was long from over. Antwerp was taken in the fall of 1944. France was liberated, and so were Belgium and the south of Holland—below the great rivers.

A desperation move of Montgomery to hasten the end of the war ended in failure after paratroopers had landed in great numbers around Arnhem and Nijmegen assisted by gliders and numerous bombers, all to no avail. Many died in the attempt, but Holland had to get through the worst winter of the war, and the underground was nearly wiped out by the efforts of the gestapo and secret police.

The Germans grew more ferocious than ever while huge armadas of bombers were flying over day and night on their way to pulverize the German homeland. The Nazis in Berlin were trying to buy a few more months, or even days, of freedom for the prize of thousands or even millions of human lives. The lives of friends and foes alike were thrown away in senseless slaughter of the innocent and helpless.

I remember one night that we sat together discussing the war. Hitler was a human wreck, according to one of the guys, crippled on one side with uncontrollable shaking and plagued with hardening of the arteries. The man was not able to function anymore and was giving in to fits of rage beyond any reason. How could we know this at that time while it has been denied by many later on? And how could an army keep fighting, slaughtering so many in the process?

We also talked about the secret weapons of Hitler, weapons to turn the fortunes of war in favor of the Germans. These were to be revealed in the near future. Most of us were very skeptical of the senseless boast blabbered around from the Berlin war command.

The Germans were supposed to have big cannons built on rails near the coast of Antwerp, cannons that could flatten London if they ever came into operation. They also had new submarine weapons with unsurpassed powers and abilities that had never been seen before—new delivery systems to deliver more and heavier bombs, bombs with no human pilots of any kind. All this was true. It is very strange that we should know these things right in the end of the war with no newspapers of any kind except the underground. It seems ironical that the majority of the German generals did not know what shape Hitler was in.

WE KNEW! We knew many more things through the grapevine with an accuracy that was absolutely uncanny as was proven later on. Many records say that the Allies did not know about the death camps with the crematories in Germany. We knew . . .

Books have been written that Eisenhower had to launch the Normandy invasion in bad weather because he feared the increased activities of the V-2 and the existence of the long-barreled cannons along the coast. We knew . . . The winter of 1944 was very cold, and there was ice on the pools and creeks. This was something that does not happen in a normal winter in Holland. It can be cold, but it seldom freezes to the point that there is ice on the water that is strong enough to go skating, but this was one of those winters.

Dick and I decided to go skating on a point not far from our home. It was cold, but we were in good company. A number of girls had shown some genuine interest in a little closer relationship. A combined warm-up session was just about to mature when we were shocked by the sound of some object that sounded like a dozen freight trains. A great high object rose very, very slowly from the ground not too far away from us. It was a beautiful sight. Great clouds blasted away from this machine, and it was enveloped in flames of all hues and textures, many times the colors of a rainbow. It rose ever so slowly, and it seemed at times that it was not going to go at all, but it rose and rose until it was a hundred feet from the ground. Then it accelerated at a tremendous rate far faster than anything we had ever seen before. The whole thing was out of sight in a matter of minutes, and only a vapor trail could be seen in the upper atmosphere.

We had witnessed the launching of the first missile, and many more would follow on short notice! It was one of the secret weapons of Hitler. The V-2 was the dreaded weapon of the later days of the war, and it was going up in the atmosphere almost daily and became the most dreaded weapon of the whole war.

I think that the war would have been lost if the atomic bomb had been ready a few months earlier. It is fortunate that the Allies managed to destroy the heavy water supply in Norway earlier. The atomic bomb would have ended in German hands months earlier, and the winner would have been Hitler and his cohorts. The world would have gone under in darkness and slavery. There would have been no escape for any of us who were fighting for freedom, each in his or her own way. Victory could have come to the Germans even when the Allies were preparing to invade the German homeland.

The Allies were fully aware of the danger as the attacks on the V-2 and V-1 launching areas increased manyfold. It was not all that much later when a one-engine airplane of unusual construction came buzzing over town. It seems to have been a lightning plane. We had never seen anything like it. A plane with two tails went straight for the railroad bridge to the east of town. It threw a bomb against one bridge pillar then turned around and shot a steam engine full of holes. Some bullets went straight through the railroad lines. This was the first of many visits by the Allied airpower, but I have never seen precision work like that of that first plane again. The guy threw a bomb and finished destroying a train full of German war material all in a day's work. The Hurricanes and other Allied aircraft came on an almost daily basis after that until the end of the war. A new phase in the hostilities had begun, and we were very encouraged.

The danger increased also to the point that many people had to move out of town around the target area and moved in with farmers in the most unlikely places. Townspeople of high standing moved with their expensive furniture in chicken coops and other locations like that all over the countryside. They adapted to the conditions in an amazingly good mood of cooperation and goodwill.

Danger and necessity brought out the best in many of us, and the mood became upbeat all over because the news was getting better by the day. One airplane was circling over our town night after night, shooting anything that moved on the road, and it was not only the enemy wagons that got shot up. Many milk wagons did not dare to go on the roads anymore, and all transport came to a standstill. This plane was nicknamed "the Jolly Frans." It was this plane that was feared and revered simultaneously.

I would lie in bed and be scared out of my mind every time that the machine guns would stutter and shoot at another item moving along the road. I had the conviction that the next strafing would end between my shoulder blades. I just had that conviction for no reason at all. This is not funny but very terrifying if you have to live with that night after night. I should know. I lived it! Several planes came out of the west on a day that I was at my friend's place.

There was also a man at my friend's place who was on the most-wanted list of the German secret police. He was in a very upbeat mood that day and was play fighting with the incoming planes.

He was standing there with his fist in the air and hollered at the planes, "Come and get me if you dare!"

He would run away as if he was scared when the plane took a dive at some unknown object.

"I won't say it again," he would yell with the hands over his head. "I won't say it again!"

This looked very funny at the time when the atmosphere crackled with danger and excitement. It was not very funny at all a few months later when another set of planes cut him in half with bomb fragments. My friend Dick tried to carry him away that day, and he fell apart in two halves. But that was later. We had a lot of enjoyment on this day with his playacting. But our joy was short-lived because the sky was filled with planes suddenly and for no reason at all. They came from every direction, and it was impossible to tell who was coming or going.

The planes had decided not to play anymore, and the bombs were raining out of the sky from every direction. I was lying in the porch flat on my stomach and made myself as small as possible. My friend was lying on top of his girlfriend, and his mother was trying to protect both with his own body. I could see big chunks of dirt sailing through the skies above me and bomb fragments hitting everywhere and everything. It was a very heavy winter, and the chunks of dirt flying around were of unbelievable proportions. This made me just as scared as the real bombs. But the screaming of the neighbor's wife was the worst of all. She was absolutely hysterical and had lost all sense of normality for the time that the ordeal lasted. She was not a Christian and had nothing to hold on to. This terror was the end of all things for her.

It is in times like these that the Savior's presence upholds us. We had something to hold on to when all else seems to crumble around us. We were just as fearful as the woman next door, but the outcome is so much different for a believer and an unbeliever. I walked outside after it was over and found the tail section of a bomb right in the front of the house. This section was still hot to the touch.

I left the house to see if anyone needed help and was met with an avalanche of people of every stripe and color. I have never seen so many underground people on the streets simultaneously since the war started. It was unbelievable.

They came from every crook and cranny and disappeared just as fast. Our friend John, the redhead, was there too. He had changed color of hair overnight, it seems like. All this gave some idea of the resistance that was growing by leaps and bounds.

The exodus lasted for a few moments, and then the streets were empty of men again; nobody was inclined to stay for a visit. It was too dangerous, and that stands for reason that some visitors could be Germans or German informers, whatever came first. It was not many days later that several German planes came roaring over, almost touching the rooftops. We were taken completely by surprise. There had not been a German plane in the sky for ages, and here they came flying at low altitude to escape radar detection. The Battle of the Bulge had begun, and the Allies were just as surprised as we were.

It might look funny at first glance but really was not funny at all. The Allies were taken completely off balance, and it could have ended very badly indeed. We could not know this then, but the Germans were trying to gain time to create more fearsome weaponry that would result in more horror and destruction. But worse was to come for us in our small little world. Many more were rounded up in a raid and put to work at the great rivers. They had to build fortifications for the enemy not all that much later.

Albert, the boy out of the family with the knitting needle in the meter, and his friends were warned one day that another raid was on the way. The guys were in a lighthearted mood discussing if they should hide in a hole that their kid brothers had dug in the side of the road.

Albert went inside to investigate and yelled, "Grab! A hare, grab him!"

His friend was right on the ball and grabbed it as a big cat was flying out of that hole. Albert was in the hole and his friend outside. And they laughed until they almost cried. Then the laughter froze on the face of Albert's friend. He got eyes as big as saucers and almost fainted on the spot. Albert who was in the darkness of this little tunnel was flabbergasted when his friend took a flying leap and took off like the whole German army was after him.

It was not quite that bad, but several Germans were standing in front of the hole to check out what was in there. Albert was lucky enough that he could hide behind some straw along the wall, and the soldiers did not see him in the darkness of the interior, and he was left where he was. As for his friend? He kept running like a man possessed, and others found one of his wooden shoes several hundred yards down the road. The owner of that shoe was found late that night way back in the country. He was too scared to come home.

This was George, the same guy that made me swallow the tobacco in days long ago. He escaped that time, but it did not help him much. He was caught anyway a little while later and ended up in the war area around Remagen. It was there that he witnessed the heaviest battles around the Rhine River.

Remagen was a place bombarded with two thousand cannons for several days. Albert told us the story as we were braiding straw in a different location. We had to work in shifts in that place, and my eyes felt as if there was sand in there during the nights that I had to work there. I could not handle the night work, and there were way too many people in one place, so one traitor could round up dozens of guys. The whole setup felt wrong from day one, and so I decided to quit. It is sad to say, but my premonitions were right. The place was raided not many days later. Most of the guys working there were caught and shipped to Germany, including a neighbor of ours. A friendly farmer's help and the fact that he managed to steal some tubers were the only reason that he made it through the war. He was skin over bones and covered with dirt and lice when he came back. He did not want to talk about his experiences over there until this very day!

Getty, the joker of the tobacco, came back in the same condition from the same area. We were lucky enough to escape the raids held almost every month after that.

Life became almost impossible, for the pressure on our nerves became almost unbearable and food was getting harder to come by all the time, compliments of Jolly Frans!—the plane that shot everything of the road, but I will say more about that later. It will always be a

HANK OPDENDRIES

mystery how our parents kept twelve people alive—Dad and Mom and ten children. However, the going was tough.

The man who was to become my father-in-law later knew of our need, and he brought us two loaves of rye bread, loaves about seven inches wide, three inches thick, and eight inch long. He would walk by our window very cautiously and bring us this bread from heaven. I'll never know why he did this! But he did it.

Then a strange and unforgettable thing happened. Our mother was very sharing and caring besides the fact that she was a good Christian (some people thought she was very uneconomical). But the Lord only knows what good she did over the years. Still, she might have carried charity too far that day.

She had received two of those wonder loaves from my father-in-law when a man out of Rotterdam came at the door, emaciated and skin over bones. He asked my mother for food because his family in the city was starving. Our mother did not hesitate but gave him one of the two loaves of bread, while we went hungry. Stupid and irresponsible you may think, but—you know something? We were a bit hungrier but made it anyway. It was like the oil in the jar of the woman of Zarephath. Mom gave, but we lived! Mom and Dad had a little business in knitting materials, wool, cottons, linen, and other material.

This business entitled them to a fair amount of rations. So she could have provided quite well for her household as far as clothing, etc. There was only one problem, and that was the fact that Mom kept giving away materials to people in need and without ration cards. And the well was more than dry by the end of the war. Sounds funny? It was not.

She had no business left by the end of the war! And I could not help but compare this to some folks—also from our church—who did nothing without gain and would not help if there was no profit margin. I will tell more about that later.

My parents never reached the stature of some above-mentioned people, but only heaven knows what the values of their works are. One thing is certain. There was nothing wrong with their love for their neighbors. It was around this time that we ran into the flare that night. I told you that story a while back. We also ran into Hermann Goring's troops around that time, also mentioned. The flares were a forerunner of a great flying fortress that came over the next day to take pictures of the town center. Only we did not know that at the time.

Many people might have been alive if only we had known! It was on that unforgettable day before March 22, 1945, the hardest day of the war and of the whole neighborhood!

The twenty-second was a beautiful day, a harbinger of spring that was about to rule all over this tortured and war-torn creation. I had been watching a fairly big-sized bug just moments ago—the May bug, as it was called. This creature had the habit of pumping its body in and out about forty or fifty times before it would fly away. We watched that many times when we were little, prodding them sometimes into a premature flight out of her lazy mood. These big bugs compared to the smaller ladybugs as a flying fortress to a small fighter plane. These little creatures proclaimed the beauty and peace that the Creator intended when this world came into being.

We would sing a song for the little bug when we were children: "Sweet, sweet ladybug; fly into heaven; father and mother are dead."

The meaning of this little song was that she would fly to heaven and bring the thoughts and prayers of a little orphan child to the parents. The little bug was regarded as something almost holy in our childhood imagination. It was a sign of good things to come. But no good was coming our way this time.

My brother and I were braiding straw at a leisure pace (there was no market for our product just then), when suddenly airplanes came droning in from the west. There was nothing unusual about that because airplanes were daily visitors then, and we welcomed them happily and selfishly if they would pound the German homeland into submission. We were a long cry from love to our enemies. We were also a long way from the peaceful world of the two little bugs and a host of other harmless creatures who were proclaiming the coming of spring all around us. But no peace would reign this day. Everything went wrong, and the most horrible day of the war had started for the little town between the mountains. We came on the receiving end of the Allied war machine. Machine gun fire erupted from the Mosquito airplanes overhead, and a series of bombs landed in the center of town almost at once, only five houses away from us. Many of these bombs were phosphorus bombs, and the whole neighboring street was on fire.

My brother and I did not lose a minute but ran over to the house across from us, and we said to our cousin Hans, "Let's go and help the people that are caught in there!"

Hans was a lot wiser than we were and saved our lives almost certainly with his sound advice.

He said, "There are specially trained people on the way to help out with the emergency. You guys are underwater, and the streets will be swarming with Germans in a matter of minutes. Stay where you are! We can do lots of other things later when this is all settled."

These words saved our lives. Marienus—Hans's brother—went over to the place where the fires were, for he had freedom of movement because he was classified as a food provider and free from labor. He landed right in the middle of the next series of bombs, and he was the only one that came back alive.

We were still speaking with Hans when a tempest of sound came thundering down like many freight trains. I have never heard a sound like that before or after that day! This was far worse than the time when the frozen dirt was flying over my head. It seemed to come from every direction, and there was no place to hide.

The tempest increased and swelled to a high keening sound, like steam escaping out of a thousand boilers. Nobody has to teach you how to take cover in moments like that. You do that naturally, without thinking. It is the instinct of self-preservation that blocks out all other emotions.

I dove into the neighbor's house just when bomb fragments and debris started raining all around us. A hundred-year doorpost in front of me was moving like a reed in the wind. It moved back and forth about three or four inches. Wooden carats were flying out of the hayloft, like leaves in a storm wind, while Hans's sister was standing in front of us, screaming at the top of her voice. She had lost all control over herself. Her screams were mingled with many other women's, and the world was drowned in a cacophony of thundering sounds like the end of days had come. I was lying there on my stomach, thinking, *This is the end.* It is strange, but I was completely calm and collected. Death was imminent for me, and I was not scared.

Judgment day might be a little like what we experienced in those moments. I would have crawled in a crack in the floor just to get away from that terrible torment. At that moment, I made up the balance of my life and found much that was wanting.

I will live every day in thankfulness if I walk out of here, I thought.

And I committed my soul to the Lord. This was too terrible! Nobody could live through this and live! But we did live through that moment! The bombing stopped, and everything became deadly quiet for a few moments. We were completely deafened by this awful turmoil. We walked out of that house dazed but in one piece and alive. And that is more than we could say for many others. There was not a tile left on our house. The explosions had ripped every tile and smashed it to pieces in the streets.

Still this was a small matter compared to the rest of the neighborhood. The town center was a complete inferno, and fires were howling through the streets, creating an inferno like I have never seen in all my life, then or later. Almost every house was in rubble in a half circle around us, and there was no hesitation this time. We ran out to the scene of disaster to help wherever we could.

I was hardly out of the yard when I ran into an old lady almost directly after that. She was cradling the head of her son in her lap, and the color of death was already spreading over the boy's face. This was a young man whom we knew very well. He was lying there against a big stone, the millstone, we called it. He was lying on top of it, and he was trying to hold his stomach with his two hands. Bomb fragments had torn his lower body in a bloody mess. The lady motioned us to go on, since I could not be of any help anymore anyway.

I found the oldest daughter of the same lady only a little further. She was recently engaged, and we found her and her lover pushed by the explosions in a fetal position in the corner of a hedge. The double tragedy was that this couple had found each other at an advanced age and had everything to live for. Someone told me almost forty years later that it was also this same lady who had saved the life of Red John the Jew. You wonder at these things, since these women were all believers.

The widow's faith must have been severely tested in those days. The Lord never makes mistakes, and we confess that with all our hearts, but we wonder at times why His children have to walk such a deep road. One day we will know and understand! We had neighbors who had two beautiful little girls of about ten or eleven years old. Both these girls had pitch-black hair with an almost blue sheen over it, and both were almost identical, although they were not twins.

I have watched them often go by our place and wondered over the beauty of it all—both happy and well-balanced children who had everything to live for. We found one of them without face. The other one was never seen again.

I could go on and on but would like to quit at this point. It is too hard even after fifty years!

We met my older brother only a little further on. He came out of that burning inferno of fire and smoke, and he half carried a well-known young man—a black market dealer. This fellow was hurt but not serious, and my brother turned him over to us. We carried the jabbering man to the outskirts of town. I felt like hitting the guy! He was hurt but only a little, and he jabbered as if the end of his life was at hand. He promised us all kinds of money if we would just get him out of there. I must say, in all fairness, that he might have been in shock. But it was a degrading sight at best! I met the guy a few weeks later, and he did not even say hello.

People who walk the low road in normal life will often become heroes in times of crisis. They are the quiet types whom you don't notice, and the so-called leaders will be in the back or missing altogether. This is remarkable but true, and I have seen this happen often.

Anyway! We trundled along with this guy and turned him over to a doctor outside town. This doctor, who was very young with little experience, was almost out of his mind too.

"This is no war anymore," he said in a high voice. "This is genocide!"

One thing is sure: he had a very important-sounding name for it all right, but it did not help the situation any at all. He was scared. It was as simple as that. He was scared out of his senses. I could not blame him completely but had some trouble understanding it. I must add that he did some excellent work later, and that made me respect him after all!

The air was full of gunpowder. This stuff seems to do different things to different people. It seemed to make me drunk and half crazy, and I would have attacked the airplanes if I had any weapons. I would have done just that, although they were supposed to be our friends. I would not have counted that in that moment. They were a danger to us and attacking us, and I would have fought back.

War does funny things to people! The planes used antipersonnel bombs, and that will always be a mystery for me. Why did they use those bombs against a harmless population with no protection at all and no military personnel around to speak of? The antipersonnel bomb has a rubber head on the nose so that it does not penetrate in the ground but exploded on contact. A very heavy shell produced untold many scraps with ragged sharp edges. These slivers will enter the body and work in further all the time, day after day, and there are people walking around with scraps like that in their bodies. These bombs mixed with a few air mines and many phosphorus bombs made a total devastation wherever they landed.

The mystery deepens if you take into consideration that there were almost no German troops in the whole town. In the middle of the street was a house with a little outbuilding. A little hallway between the houses about four feet wide gave access to the back of the property. My cousin was in the group of about nine people who had been trying to reach that little hallway. They all died under the deadly rain of fire and steel.

All of them were in the bloom of life and had a whole life ahead of them. They were lying in a heap as pieces of a discarded chess game carelessly thrown after the game was done. It was there that Dick found his friend who was daring the airplanes only weeks before. How is one going to describe the terror of these moments? No words can be found and no tears left to cry. The sadness and horror were just too great! But life does go on, and measures had to be taken to stop disease and sickness. Disaster would follow shortly if measures were not taken at the right moment.

The bureaucracy found back its stride, and savings operations became more organized. Ambulance crews were already carrying away the victims, and we were not allowed to help with this last little thing that we might have done for them.

The dead were brought to a school a little off the center of town since. All the steps were taken to stop an epidemic from breaking out because of careless handling of the bodies. I went over to the school to see if there was any of our family over there, and we found the departed in all kinds of positions, just in the form that death had arrested them.

It's just like a collection of Roman statues where somebody has spilled red paint in a careless way, I was thinking.

And then I felt ashamed of the thoughts that had entered my mind.

None of my family was there, and that was a little relief in all this sadness and depression. All might be well with them, as indeed it was. This is one of the miracles of the day. We had a family of twelve, and they were all over town that day, but none were hurt in any way. The house was heavily damaged, but none of us received a scratch.

Our task was still ahead of us! Some families had made a zigzag trench before this happened. We had looked it over and were a little skeptical of the construction at the time, but it turned out to be a wise move. The antipersonnel bombs fell on the edge of the trench in several places, but none of them was hurt—thanks to their foresight and the precautions they had taken. The laugh would have been on their side! But no one felt like laughing for a long, long time.

Hans and his brother carried my cousin to their house and put him to rest in the old farm for the time being. It was against orders, but our friends did not care much about orders then. My uncle Hank died of a broken heart only days later, and my aunt was left alone with her family to mourn the two who had died. This family was hit very hard also, and we do not know why. It was almost unbearable to see all the pain and sorrow all around us, but the sight of the animals that lost their lives in terror was also very tragic.

Two Belgian horses were lying in the mill yard in front of our house, also torn apart by the exploding bombs. These noble animals were lying there struck down and sharing in the violence of human kind, dying a violent and painful death just because the masters of creation had decided to make war. Men had sinned, and the animal suffered. Men made war, and the animals suffered! I looked at it and could not help but feel guilty in a strange kind of way!

Fear came to me personally a few days later. My brother and I were told by Dad that we should try and close the roof of the house with boards and tarps and whatever else might be handy. We were upstairs when several planes came over close over the roof of the house. The roof was covered fairly well then, and we could not see what the planes were up to. So we ran downstairs but could not get out because the doorknobs had been pulled out by the air pressure of the bombs, something I do not understand to this very day. We were locked in the house as the planes came over, and this put me in a complete panic. I just had to be outside to face whatever danger was coming our way, but there was no way out, and I kicked the door in just to be able to see those planes.

It must have been delayed shock or something like that! We went through something like that a few months earlier when a V-1 started circling over our town in the misty night. We had the same terror that time. To be in danger is one thing, but it seems easier if you can see it coming.

The same thing happened to Mom (my wife) in 1951 when a small air plane came over the place she worked and started buzzing the farmhouse. She dove right under the table and would not come out until the plane had left. This was six years after the war.

An unexpected explosion or anything in that nature can set off this reaction in many people for years after. And then of course the ever-recurring nightmares that never go away completely.

Our town was a very quiet place for days after. An unearthly stillness hung all over the place, and the next day was not much better—a factor that was awful hard on our already frayed nerves. All the hustle and bustle had come to a standstill, and the whole town was as silent as a tomb. Even the animals had departed, and not a bird was singing anymore. The slamming of a door could be heard from one end of town to the other.

Nothing moved and nothing stirred. There was just unnatural stillness—except the crackling of the smoking ruins and the falling of some debris or the falling of a burning log. It was with a sense of relief that we heard Father's decision that we should leave to another town about six miles away in the hope that all this would be over soon.

Dad and Mom went ahead with the little children and a horse-drawn wagon pulling the little household that we had left in a somber procession of despair and worry. I followed a few days later and ran smack right into a *veld-gendarme* control of the German army. The veld-gendarme had a kind of metal half-moon on a chain around their neck, and they were on the lookout for deserters of the German army. The war was ending, and they were well aware of that, but that would not stop them from shooting deserters on sight. They looked me over very closely but let me pass without any remarks. The story would have been different if these had been SS troops or if I had looked like a deserter.

And this is how I ended in Denham, in the house of a twice-removed cousin of Dad. These folks were friendly and helpful, and we had a place to stay, upstairs in a fairly new house in a quiet neighborhood that had never been touched by any violence or war actions. It must have been hard on them to have a big family intrude on their daily routine. But they never complained in the month that we had to stay around there.

The light-generating bicycle was set up again, and Mom's warm personality restored a semblance of normality to our war-torn existence. She was the kind of person that could make a conversation at any given moment in any situation to any given person. That's why she has been called "a mother in Israel."

I ended up on a farm not all that far in the country on the place of another of Dad's cousins. He was a short little man with a nose as a plough iron with a good sense of humor. And that came in very handily in those stressful times, although he was a bachelor and set in his own lifestyle and that he did not want to be interfered with. He had built up a cozy lifestyle living with his two sisters who were never married either. So we had to do some adjusting, but that was nothing new. Our whole life had been one adjustment after the other ever since the war began.

My uncle invited us to go to an open house where there was a feast along much the same lines as in Haarle with the same hand-slapping routine. I was not too interested, especially if you take into consideration that I might get my lights knocked out if I ended up with a girl of the wrong guy.

Our chances in town might have been much better, but we decided to lie low for a while. We had enough excitement in the last year or so. Even so, life went on pleasantly enough, except for my fear for the low-flying aircraft, and this was bad—mostly at night when you could not watch what they were doing. But we got more optimistic by the day outside these problems. The news was getting better always. The Allies had crossed the great rivers, and they were coming nearer all the time, until the day that a tremendous commotion broke out—still unexpected.

One neighbor boy came running in the yard, yelling, "The Tommies are here! They are coming from the east. We are free! We are free! The Tommies are here!"

CHAPTER 7

VICTORY

ONE OF THE best days of my life had started. We were free! The Canadian troops came in from the east. Several troop carriers loaded down with soldiers and even more civilians. Bedlam had broken loose. Many people were out of their minds with joy. Others were just standing there with tears rolling down their faces. They just could not believe this glorious day. Was it really true? Was the day of liberation finely come, and could we finally walk the streets any time of day or night without fear of capture and violence? Was it true after all the fear, sorrow, and death of the last five years? Were we free to walk and free to speak in every way we desired?

How does a person find words for the exhilarating feeling of freedom where he had to be in hiding and in fear of his life only hours ago? Were we allowed to fly the Dutch flag where and whenever we wanted? How can you describe the feeling of delirious happiness when you walked the edge of death less than a month ago?

I simply don't have words for this experience, and I can't explain what freedom really is—unless you have lost it and know what I am talking about. Dozens, maybe hundreds, of people crowded around the troop carriers to have a firsthand look at the liberators from close by, while the tank commanders watched the crowd with big smiles on their faces.

It must have been a very rewarding experience for them, although plenty tiresome at times. That's what I thought anyway.

The Tommies were throwing handfuls of cigarettes and chocolate bars all over the assembly like priests giving benedictions. We managed to make our way to the tanks, when suddenly both machine guns started firing with a deafening roar.

The crowd flew off the road, including me, and I was certainly not the last one to leave, since my nerves were plenty keyed up and not nearly recovered from the turmoil of former days. Some women were screaming in fear not knowing what was happening. The same people were beyond all caring a moment ago. However, the eyes of the tank commanders were ever watchful and had noticed enemy presence in the close surroundings, so they cleared the road in the fastest method.

They were shooting in the corner of a brick house, the best way to get the people off the road. And, sure enough, a German soldier came walking up the road, his hands in the air and white as a sheet. One Tommie motioned him to go in front of him to a gunner's nest at the side of the road. Cold shivers went down my spine as I watched the Canadian following the man with a revolver pointed at his back. I did not know what to expect, and the German was not all that comfortable either by the looks of him as he showed the Canadian around the stronghold.

There was no doubt at all that the man would be shot at the slightest sign of betrayal. Many people were cheering at the sight of it, but I just shivered at the show of naked force. We had seen that way too often already.

Much jeering and great pestering followed the next day as some girls were brought to have their hair shaved off in front of an overflowing crowd. These were the girls who had collaborated with the German in his heyday living off the good of the land as we had to go hungry. Many people enjoyed the spectacle, but I did not enjoy this at all. These were mostly low-class girls and not that good looking. The better-looking ones sought the protection of the Canadians and walked away shot-free more often than not.

It is very doubtful that the Germans would have put up with some of those unfortunate girls. None of them had anything that would have made desirable to any male in his right mind. But here they were on display for a crowd that was hungry for revenge, but the wrong people were suffering again. That's what I thought anyway.

The land stormers—turncoats—and other people who had collaborated with the enemy were also brought forward under much pestering, jeering, and ribald laughter. They were forced to roll eggs with their noses over the uneven ground, sweep the ground with a toothbrush, and more cruel activities that were on the order of the day.

It is true that they deserved just punishment for their behavior, but not like this. The whole action was more degrading for the perpetrators than for the victims no matter how deserving. This would have been way better served by the proper authorities.

All these things happened in later days, but the first days were pure and simple joy—irresponsible at times and not nice to look at, but joy even so. A strong reminder that the war was not over yet came only a little while later. Some soldiers ran to protective covering shortly after they had entered the town. An enemy force had been located not all that far away, and the Canadians set out to meet them without any hesitation. It was only a little group of weary German defenders trying to make it to the border in a horse-drawn wagon. One of the tank crew ordered them to throw away their weapons, and one shell was shot into the group when they did not obey fast enough. The rest were only too eager to oblige. These fellows were only farm boys and just as happy as we that the war was over.

They even waved at us as they went past. Those first days were days of celebration, and we went to a farmer that evening to have a good time with some close friends. This farmer was one of those blustery kinds of guys who are either in the tree or under it and never between. And this time he could hear nothing wrong about the Canadians. Something I agreed with completely. I felt the same way, until I remarked that the Canadians would be more harmful to our women then the Germans ever were. Boy oh boy was that a mistake! I thought the farmer was going to attack me and throw me right out of his house. Was he ever mad at me! My name was mud from that point on since I had dared to say something wrong about our liberators.

Later days proved that I was right in almost everything. One liberating soldier came later that day and wanted to buy some eggs, and the farmer sold him a whole helmet full—payment would come later, since the guy had forgotten his wallet. The farmer is still waiting for his money. There could be a good reason for that, of course. The man might have had to move along to a new battlefield or several other reasons. But it did prove the point of what I was saying.

There was hardly a girl in these days who did not date a Canadian soldier at one time or another. And the local boys had to stand in line for their turn to have a kick at the cat. The result showed up after nine months in an often unwelcome manner.

HANK OPDENDRIES

You might think that I say this with a chip on my shoulder, but nothing is further from the truth. Those boys laid their lives on the line for us, and we would have gone under without their help. I was just being sensible. Those boys were the liberators and were allowed to date our girls, while the Germans were totally ignored by all but a few of our womenfolk.

The regular German army acted in a civilized manner most of the time—in our part of the country anyway—and that's about all the good I can say about them. Mark well! I am not talking about the other units of the German forces like the SS, the green police, the gestapo, and a host of other Wehrmacht units.

Life became a little more organized, and my dad wanted to go back home the minute we were liberated, totally ignoring the request of the Allied high command to stay off the highways so that the movement of troops and materials would not be disrupted. None of that could stop my dad. He was absolutely determined that we should go home, and we hit the road again in a matter of days.

The same wagon was used again that was used before to bring us the other way, and the trip was a lot happier than the time before. All went well until we hit an emergency bridge installed by the Allied troops where a sturdy stream of army material was going in the direction of Germany. We had to stand there and watch until a control soldier took mercy on us and gave us a chance to cross over the bridge. But it was hardly a happy event. The soldier was cussing and swearing at us like you would not believe. I can't say that I blamed him, but we got across, and that was all that mattered to Dad. He was so reasonable most of the time, and this time was altogether different. He just had to go home!

We got home safe and sound after that with our miserly belongings and undaunted when we saw the shape that our house was in. All this could be rebuilt, and I remembered the words of a woman when we helped her to carry the furniture out of her house after the great bombardment.

"The furniture and the house are not the worst," she said. "That can all be replaced if we stay alive!"

The same people were fighting like cats and dogs for the last dollar only a short time later. Then you wonder! Are we ever going to learn? I will enjoy every day as it comes, I promised myself that day. And I never forgot.

Thankfulness and memories are short-lived among us *Homo sapiens* even so. Slices of uneaten bread were found again in the trash cans of the big cities only weeks after the liberation.

The amount of weapons pouring into Germany was absolutely unbelievable. Column after column went by our street. Heavy trucks loaded with cannons, tanks, and all kinds of weaponry went by in an unbroken stream and in absolutely breathtaking succession. Traffic was so heavy that the pavement was heaving and crumbling on the roads of Holland's countryside. There was absolutely no way that Germany could meet this onslaught. One major event after the other followed in quick succession as the Thousand-Year Reich disintegrated.

Hitler committed suicide, and so did many other leading figures in the Nazi hierarchy. The voice of the propaganda minister, Goebbels, fell quiet forever after he had his wife and children follow him in death.

The Russians entered Berlin amid total destruction of the Nazi war machine, and total surrender of the Germans followed in a matter of days. An end had come to the most terrible war that this Old World had seen in all recorded history. Hitler committed suicide with Eva Brown, his wife of one-half day. A war started by the half-crazed would-be painter of Austria was ended, started by a man who had the evil talent to organize and hypnotize an entire nation of misguided people, taking them in a war that destroyed a continent and ruined the German nation.

All this might never have happened if the Allied forces of the first war had made a just and merciful peace after the ending of the first war that was to end all wars. This might never have happened if the German nation had listened to some church leaders sounding a warning against the morality of the Nazi system. We could go on with many reasons and excuses and forget the real reason for this awful disaster. The real reason is in the Cain-and-Abel mentality of this sinful world around us and in us—a world that does not want to turn and repent, a world that does not want to seek the only way to salvation, the only way that would bring a just and peaceful world. If only they knew and understood! If only I knew and understood!

This world of today seems riper for judgment than it ever was then. Everything looks rosy, and many people think that a better way is just around the corner. The Communist countries are caving in one after the other as proof positive that the Communist idea is unworkable and degenerate. The Communist leaders are visiting with the leaders of the west, while a new cooperation with the west is including freedom of religion, open borders.

Even the pope and Billy Graham visited Russia with freedom of movement, and everything seems to fall in place! But have the nations changed? Are the nations repenting and giving God the honor? Or is this all the forerunner of much worse calamities that will come over this world in short order? What do I really see? Many disruptions in many places. Murder and violence are the order of the day, while the church of our Lord Jesus is discredited and abused from all sides. False prophets change the Bible message, and preachers are lovers of money. Breakdown of authority in a big way. Abortions and selfishness on a scale that has never been seen before. Homosexuals and lesbians claiming a center stage in many areas of life! The list goes on and on!

And many more churches are half full or empty. A small Gideon band of true Christians is still serving the Lord in a reverent way, but even they are torn apart by divisions on an ever-increasing number. The real peace is missing in many places. And the one thing that worries me most is the fact that the feminist movement has succeeded by and large to change the value system of family life.

A woman has only value if she lives like a man and thinks like a man and makes money like a man. A housewife is relegated to a secondary position and is portrayed as a baby machine and a slouch with no pride or self-value. Who is going to bring up our children if the home is without a mother? And who is going to rock the cradle of the leaders of tomorrow? The state? Is that not just what Hitler had in mind for the upcoming generation?

Only the reading and study of God's word can preserve us from sliding ever further into the abyss. Sorry, I forgot myself, and we will go back to the ending of the war.

The population of our hometown and Holland at large was caught up in a frenzy of joy making on a scale never seen before. Young men and women walked and danced in the streets till the middle of the night. Anything that could walk or stumble was out for days on end. They were drunk with the regained freedom and the restraint that had held us in check for those long and weary years. Community clubs came to the bright ideas of having dance clubs in the middle of the hard surface roads. Right in front of the houses, young and old were dancing in numerous places all over town accompanied by any instrument that would make an acceptable sound. Liquor was the only thing lacking in most places, and that was a blessing in disguise. May 10 was proclaimed as Liberation Day, and this turned out to be the most important day in my life.

The day started normally enough. A great meeting was called together on a sport field near the center of town "by order of the newly organized town council." There were flags all over the place, and many participants sported the orange color—the color of the House of Orange, that is, the Queen of Holland).

Some children came completely dressed in orange, and a mood of unblemished harmony prevailed. The brass bands were belting out a variety of marches and many folk songs, and there was an overall mood of goodwill. It was at that point that the mayor of the town came forward to deliver the liberation speech, and it was also the moment bedlam broke loose through the rank and file of the common man.

This man, the burgomaster, had been cooperating in an unworthy manner with the Germans according to the rumor mill. The man might have had no choice or maybe prevented much worse to happen during the occupation. Whatever the case: a tremendous jeering went up the moment he climbed on the platform to deliver his speech. The poor man was not able to get a decent sound across the sound system. He was jeered down any moment he made a beginning. He was lucky that the folks did not pelt him with rotten apples and eggs, but the food was of more value than the mayor just then. The angry crowd made up for the shortage of projectiles in boos and jeering—very undignified, and I could not help but feeling sorry for the man. It seemed all so degrading!

It was a relief for me when the whole farce ended, and the crowd started to disperse in a somewhat better mood. We started mingling with other young people, and I even had a conversation with the Johanna who had treated me so poorly some months earlier. She showed an unusual interest in my escape out of Germany. She and the other young girls around there would gladly have heard a little more about that episode, but this Johanna was a thing of the past for me. I politely, but positively, declined for the honor because my crush on this girl was all but over. I had no interest in any of the other fly-by-night creatures either. And I would have been much too shy if it had been another way.

It was then that I noticed two young girls dressed alike, and both had an orange scarf over their heads. The youngest one would laugh about the silliest things. She was a regular laugh on legs and much too young to merit any attention. The other one was a little older but not much and almost five years younger than I was, but she seemed like a nice enough girl.

They were the daughters of my father's friend, the one who brought us bread when we were hungry—and it was this more than anything that made me stop and talk to them. Only for a while, mind you! Because they were small stuff in the bloated world of us grown-up men, wise to the ways of the world. Our Lord must have a great sense of humor and might have snickered just then about the delightful foolishness of young men when they are in that overblown state of mind.

Anyway, I went home disillusioned with the world, and in myself in particular. I wanted to be left alone to settle down and gnaw on my bone of discontent. The feast would resume that night, and I was going to be there in spite of my disillusion.

Young men are quite resilient, and I came home that night for more punishment by the hands of the weaker sex. Now you got to laugh. This is a joke! Got it? My friend Dick had lost himself quite willingly with his sturdy girlfriend. And Dolf disappeared with some wild-eyed women over a fast-darkening horizon, and that left me to fend for myself.

And there she was!—the one and only!—the woman who would share the rest of my life! My mother told me once that you do not look for a woman! You just find her! This was so true and simple.

It was the same girl that I met in the afternoon, but now she had a blue leather jacket on—a nice wrapping around a nice package. She was just snuggling against me as if to say, "Here is where I belong!" She was there to stay. It was all as simple as that—no ifs, no buts.

She was five years younger than me! It was like robbing the cradle, and that is how I felt when I invited her for a walk. A strange feeling of pity overtook me almost as if I was going to rob her from a careless life and force her in a life complicated and full of difficulties!—that I was dragging her down to my level, as indeed I might have done through the years that followed! It might not have been as bad as my mind had pictured it, but another life had started for the both of us. She has raised me to a level that I might never have reached without her. She has slapped me around, verbally, sometimes when I needed it and often when I did not need it.

She was a beautiful mother for our children. She has helped us and guided us with infinite wisdom, endless patience, great endurance, and boundless love—that especially, boundless love—and a host of other excellent qualities too many to mention. But the one thing I thank the Lord for many times is this! That she has helped us to reach upward to heaven always!

I was longing for Johanna from the fast lanes. God said *no*. What he gave me was Johanna, heaven bound! She pushed me on often when I was slacking off. She encouraged me when I was downhearted, laughed with me when I was happy, and cried with me when I was sad. And we shared a million things—bad and good. I will never forget how she would come rolling down the mountains with her lightly bowed legs and shinbones flashing in the sun. Her head tilted slightly to the side—she still does that—and a big smile all over her face, like the full moon coming up in joy and glory. That is . . . *Johanna!*

The beginning was not all that good. We had a walk together through the quiet surroundings of our hometown, and we did some exploratory work of future possibilities. But the whole affair was lackluster in those beginning moments. The seven children of the future were not even a gleam in the eyes yet—but that was not all! Faith had in store that I ran right into her parents on the way down the hill.

They asked me where I came from, with a knowing smile, and I made some lame excuses, trying to get away as fast as politeness would allow me. There is little doubt that they knew what was going on, but they never said anything. Somehow this was very surprising. Johanna was only fifteen years and ten months old at the time, and that was not all—she belonged to another denomination, to make matters even worse.

I was twenty-one at the time and not yet ready for a sturdy relationship, so I struggled to get loose occasionally, but it was all to no avail. Jo held on for more than fifty years at the time of this writing, and she made me rich beyond measure.

Today is Thursday, March 1990. It is my wife's birthday, and we have many reasons to be thankful for. We have received seven children, and they are all good to us and besides that getting along really well with each other. Much of that is due to my wife, who always makes time to talk to the children as they tell their struggles and disappointments in a confident manner.

Yet I am very depressed. Last night was almost certainly the last time that I will sing in the church choir. I love singing, but it is harder to handle as time goes by. I am hard of hearing and have to follow directions by guess and thunder most of the time.

All the bass singers in the back row are hard of hearing, and directions were hard to follow. Up front were women with soft-spoken voices giving directions, and as a result, we have had to follow most of the directions by lipreading. It was at that point that we were ordered to the front, and one woman grabbed me by the arm and pushed me to the front as if I was a little schoolboy. It tore to scratch the little dignity left in me. Now I realize that there is not all that much time left for me and that I will walk a very lonesome road in the time that is left for me, the Lord willing. Yet it is only a minor detail in the long row of losses that I have sustained in the last few years.

One of my paintings that I donated was sold for peanuts in a silent auction for the organ fund, a good reminder of the opinion that people have of my work. No one has shown the slightest interest in reading my memoirs, and I carry on in spite of myself for some unknown reason. I might do some writing to release a little tension as the road gets a little more lonesome.

It is now December 2, 1995, and our CRC church is getting harder on the old people to the point that we have much difficulty to keep up! Our minister held a sermon last Sunday about the church of Laodicea and implied that many of us were much like that church. We do not want to follow through on his vision of a CRC church with a completely changed worship format. He implied that there was little hope for us unless we go the way he has advocated.

What that means, in fact, is a conditional salvation, and I will not be saved unless I fulfill the additional condition that I evangelize according to the blueprint laid out by our minister. There is not much left in life if they even make the saving grace of Jesus conditional in a one-sided way! We are living in a vastly changing world, and the changes in the former Soviet Union seem almost supernatural. Gorbachev has done in two or three years what seemed impossible only two years ago. Everyone is saying peace, and then sudden destruction will overcome them. The community of believers is under attack on a scale that I have never seen before. Hitler and Communism tried to get control over the masses by taking the children out of the families, making good progress, I may add.

The present form of democracy takes a way different approach—they take the mother out of the family . . . an approach that is much more effective with disastrous results in many cases. Everyone, including our churches, is taking this in, hook, line and sinker. Most women are after their rightful place in life.

The question is not so much "What is my calling in life?" The question has become "What are my rights?"

What is the result? Judge for yourself!

Society has not succeeded to bring happiness in a woman's life. On the contrary, a system has been created that has forced many women in the job market to help support their partner, just to make ends meet. And the former partners have become competitors. The empty space in the house and the children's hearts are filled with TV and junk food and, more often than not, with alcohol and drugs. The law departments are faced with an impossible task, and the day care centers have become money and time consuming beyond all reason.

Partner abuse is on the rise because the partners are not partners anymore but competitors. And the great masses are suffocating in a sea of lonesomeness and sorrow, unwilling to turn to the very source of life—"Jesus."

An overburdened Medicare and an unmanageable welfare system drive taxes through the roof. All this is followed by air and water pollution so that the world seems to scream for a centralized figure to bring things under control and put a stop to abuse and waste. I do not want to criticize either men or women in the first place but more so the system that we have created. This system will prove deadly to the freedom of all well-meaning people. Believe it or not!

The likes of Jimmy Swaggart and Baker have damaged the efforts of many evangelists like Billy Graham to a great extent, while one priest after the other is condemned for incest upon children. The latest efforts of the press and many so-called intellectual writers are working overtime to rewrite history. They are claiming that the mission schools of yesterday are to blame for alcoholism, incest on children, while the abuse of women is to be blamed on the mission efforts of the early nineties. Indians and third-world countries would have been better off in their natural state, is now the message. But enough of all that. We better return to the simpler times when I first met my wife.

We were told in the late part of the war that we could collect unemployment money from the employment offices. The manufacturers had seen the signs of the times, and the victory of the Allies was imminent. Steps were taken to secure a future supply of labor for the day when the war would be over.

I was told to go to work in the factory cleaning some underground tunnels from some water that had accumulated during the wartime. This would have been OK with me, but I had to cross the highway to get there, and that highway was heavily patrolled by the Germans, and for that reason the risk of capture was extremely great. I refused to go under those conditions and was cut off from all assistance, since I did not act according to the manufacturer's wishes—that did it for me! I decided that I would never work in that factory again.

Then Dad came home on a certain day and told me that he did not want me to go idle. He had hired me out as a bricklayer apprentice. I would have loved to be a machine bank worker. but nobody asked me what my wishes were. I was enslaved as a bricklayer only days after the war ended. My friend Dick had a very low opinion of my new vocation; a blacksmith would have been better than a lime-covered bricklayer, to his way of thinking.

And here I went from that day on, pushing a two-wheeled car from one place to the other, helping to repair what had been destroyed during the war activities. It was a strange turn of events indeed.

My teacher became the same. Albert had been put in a concentration camp only months before, but there was one consolation: he was a good bricklayer with a good sense of humor. More importantly, he was a good Christian. He had many good qualities and some interesting insights on our value systems.

He told me that we were entitled to the produce of some garden and fruit trees just when we moved into a house to do a major repair job. This was the unwritten law of the construction workers, according to the expert Albert. We were just out of reach of a beautiful apple that time on a tree nearby while we were working on the roof of a shed in the parsonage's garden. Right beside us there was a beautiful apple hanging on that tree, just out of our reach.

We had run the car into the tree several times already, to no avail. The apple stayed where it was supposed to be—on the tree. I wish that the apple of Eve had been as hard to get. We all might have been in Paradise if that had been the case!

The apple stayed where it was until one of us threw a trowel in desperation through the unbending tree. It was at that point of great jubilation that a window opened in the parsonage, and the pastor called in a very unloving voice, "Hey there, you sinners, cease and desist!"

That did it! There was not much left to do but go and return to more fruitful labors. We had more luck at another place with a very big prune tree. These prunes were a sight for sore eyes. Nice and ripe with a nice blue color covered by a golden sheen. Neither one of us could resist the temptation. We ran the car into that tree with great expertise (we had a lot of practice by then), and the end result was overwhelming. We got much more than we bargained for! The ground was covered with prunes, so much so that we could not get them out of the way in time and had to face the owners with the end result when she came with a pot of coffee.

Thus we ended up real shamefaced and with a bad case of the runs! There was some comfort in the fact that the homeowners took the affair good-naturedly with the message that we could have all we wanted if we had only asked.

Construction workers were highly regarded in those days. Our work was not always that pleasant. We found out on more than one occasion that the sewer never runs uphill, and we were called in fairly often to correct the wayward ways of an unruly sewer. We were richly blessed with the odors of a lively sewer as a result of that and passed the reward on to our families when the time came to return home.

Albert and I were told to repair a shed one day. Two old spinsters lived in the house nearby, and they told us that they had cleaned out the remains of a wooden wash machine out of that shed already. It had been lying in a fair-sized hole in the middle of the shed, while there was a hole in the roof of that little shed.

Albert told me to knock down the brick wall and dump it in that hole, and I followed the instructions to a tee as an obedient pupil of the great Albert. The wall came crashing in the hole with a very satisfying crunch. It was at that point that I had some second thoughts. Something did not add up!

The brick wall had a big hole in it, the wash machine was pulverized, and there were some branches missing from the tree nearby above the shed! Nothing should have been left standing if this had been a bomb and if it had exploded! Albert agreed with me right away, and the town officials were notified at once.

The Canadians came within days and dug a bomb right out of the hole where I had dropped that wall! The whole neighborhood had to be evacuated when these men dug out that big monster because of the danger of the situation. I had a near brush with death once again!

Bombs were found in later years on more than one occasion when people had failed to notice the implications of a hole in the ground and built right on top of them! A big one was found forty years later in a house not further than a half a kilometer from our home. Albert and I had to work at another bombed-out place not all that much later. That time we were accompanied by another young guy. He had become our laborer, and I became second man on the totem pole. It was at this place that I found a golden opportunity to get back at Albert for some practical jokes that he had pulled on me over the times that I had known him.

We had to repair a house in a bombed-out area. I should explain that there was always an element of danger in those places as you might have noticed in the foregone story. It was there that I found the end plate of a big bomb in a garden covered with holes where bombs had fallen not all that long ago. Antipersonnel bombs did not penetrate the ground much deeper than a foot at the most. Their design was to explode aboveground and bring damage to the bodies of anyone close by, and the ground was covered with holes of that type.

The end plate that I found was about two inches thick and about a foot in diameter. It must have been from an air mine, and a big one! So I took the piece that was quite harmless and hid it in one hole in the garden so that only the very edge was sticking aboveground.

Then I walked to Albert and Jake with a heavy hammer in my hand, yelling at the top of my voice, "I found a bomb! I found a bomb! Come and look! It's a big one!"

Albert and Jake came running along fast enough, and then I made sure that they were close to the hole and carefully scratched a little sand away from the surface.

When I thought they were close enough, I hauled out with the hammer and hit it with all my might, yelling, "That rotten thing!" while hitting it a few more times for good measure.

I have never seen a couple of guys run faster than Albert and Jake! They had turned white as a sheet and ran for their lives, while I laughed so hard that I rolled over the ground and could not control myself but giggled like a young girl on her first date. Albert and Jake did not think this was funny at all and were furious at me, not speaking to me for hours on end. Maybe it was not funny at all! But I am still laughing as I write this down. Albert and Jake never stopped running until they were half a block away. They thought I had flipped my lid.

Albert gave me a really good sermon after that while I listened with a sinner's face, duly impressed and promising not to do that again—a promise that was easily kept because I did not find any more end pieces of bombs.

The memory of Albert talking me into hauling two pigs in the middle of the war might have had something to do with my behavior. I had forgotten that episode, but it is worth repeating after all. Albert had bought two small pigs in the last year of the war, and they had to be picked up on a heavy transport bicycle. Albert asked me to pick up those pigs, while Dick and he followed in the distance. Albert claimed that he could not ride a bicycle with front transport. A big basket was in front of the steering wheel this time, about four feet wide. That is where we put the pigs. This had disastrous consequences because the two pigs had enough room to fly back and forth in that basket on the front of the bicycle.

It does not take much imagination to realize that the bicycle was swinging back and forth like a drunk sailor as the pigs were flying from one corner to the other. And here I had to ride that bicycle over some very narrow cycle paths, something that was next to impossible. Albert and Dick followed faithfully at a good distance behind me.

I don't have to tell you that they almost fainted laughing while I was wrestling with those pigs. But worse was to come! We entered our hometown at the time that the factories just had a break for lunch! And here I was riding with two unruly pigs in a basket, screaming at the top of their lungs, flying back and forth right through the afternoon traffic. I was lucky indeed that no police were around, or they would most certainly have arrested me for black marketeering, an occupation frowned on by friend and foe alike. But we would have to put this behind us now!

Live ammunition is nothing to fool around with. I remember the time when a group of boys found a supply of live grenades in the bush, and they had to experiment with that—true to the nature of teenagers. What were the results? One dead and two maimed for life! This was another sad experience that happened after the end of the war.

All this happened to others, but we carried on with the repair of one house after the other. In one house we found a whole supply of wine in a certain house and some hard liquor in a secret apartment. The story did the rounds that the son of the household had worked with the Germans, and we could well believe it, looking at that wine supply!

We had several carpenters working with us then, and one of them was the guy who ended in the TOD troops in Russia. This man was still plenty wild in his behavior, something that was not hard to understand. Not for me anyway.

The two carpenters took a hold of this unheard-of treasure, and it did not take long before they had drilled a neat little hole in the cork of one bottle. It didn't take all that long before they were very drunk, sucking this strong drink through a straw in little sips.

The Russian had to cut a board with a hand saw and started complaining loudly that the pencil line would not stand still so that he could cut a straight line. That is the way it looked to his alcohol-addled brains anyway.

Albert warned us to stay away from the stuff, but all to no avail. The natives had gone wild. The two men refilled the half-empty bottles with water, and everything came up roses, except one thing. The sticky stuff had left circles on the table surface—and this was discovered by the owner the same evening, and as a result, we all had to face judgment the next day.

Albert said with his woodpecker face, "I told you so."

He came out of that deal smelling like a rose, but he was no saint either! "Not by a long shot."

He used to tell me that the best people to work for were the really rich or the really poor. The people that wanted to pass themselves off rich—the tin rich, he called them—were not the best places to work for. Those folks wanted to act as rich people but had to scrape it together over the backs of the poor and the have-nots. He proved his point on the day that we left one of those tin rich. We never got a cup of coffee or anything else for that matter. These people had to squeeze every little bit of work out of us (laborers), and that did not leave room or time for coffee.

"They are going to pay for the coffee that we are going to get at the next job!" said Albert.

And so the coffee time of the next client was added on the bill of the people we just left. I found this a very reasonable settlement, since the next customer was a really old lady who was more friendly than clean, and the coffeepot went on within minutes after we entered the house. The surroundings in that house did not look all that appetizing, but the old lady had water on a coal oil heater even before we started working. The lady was old all right, but she moved way too fast for our taste.

The situation became critical, and I turned the heater down the minute the old lady left the room. She came back in and turned the heater on again. She went out, and the heat was turned down. She came in, and the heat went up . . . She came back and forth until a neighbor lady happened to come in when I was adjusting the flame again for a more pleasant lunchtime.

It did not take long for the neighbor lady to understand what the problem was, and she turned to the old lady and said, "Don't bother with making coffee for the men. I have some on already, and they can come over to my place next!"

She left us with a knowing smile in our direction and made coffee for us from that point on. We made sure that we did some extra work for the old lady without charge, for we really liked the old lady—dirt and all. This lady was a hundred times the host that the previous people had been. We appreciated her an awful lot more, no matter how she lived.

The women of the neighborhood decided to help the old lady to clean her house. Soap had been in short supply, but that was made up by the force of elbow grease, and the women were well on the way to win the battle by hard work and perseverance. The bunk beds were emptied of the straw underlayer that many folks used in the early days and new straw put in. The old straw was burned in a bonfire later that night, and the kids of the neighborhood had a whale of a time jumping through the straw and the fire until it was all gone.

A mighty roar went through the neighborhood later that night when the children brought the livestock home picked up out of the straw bundles of the old folks—fleas. These little critters had jumped from the fire unto the safer ground of the children's unprotected bodies. The children did not have that much fun anymore either when the newly immigrated guests started feeding in the new hunting ground.

And so we went from one house to the next until we ended in our church that was also damaged by the bombings not that long ago. My job was to carry the tiles up the ladder and onto the roof all day long—a load of about sixty or seventy pounds at a time. Up the ladder and up the roof, about fifty feet high, and all this work had to be done with an undernourished body. It's amazing that they did not design a more practical way to bring all that material over such a distance. One load at a time—it almost finished me off before it was all over. We went higher and higher until we reached the little steeple on top of the church, and we had to cover that with some kind of lead covering.

Another scaffold had to be built, even higher above the roof until we were about sixty or seventy feet above the ground. The scaffold had four upright posts on each corner with a tiny handrail on the side. The rails were more for moral support than help in time of trouble because they were only one-by-fours. I was standing there about seventy feet aboveground looking down on an ant-size community far down below.

Albert and I had some serious discussions way up there where nobody could hear us. I told him all about my love life and the problems encountered. It was a sad story, and I started singing.

A song that sounded something like this: "Oh! If only I was dead for the one I love I will not get."

Albert got really angry with me after that little tidbit. I had the wrong attitude and should have a more positive outlook, since I was a Christian. The sermon went on and on, and so I went down the ladder to a safer environment. This would give Albert time to get it out of his system, and I could go to the bathroom simultaneously. My good friend Albert was looking over the edge of the scaffold with his woodpecker face in wrinkles when I made my way back up the ladder. Things were returning to normal when I told Albert that I was just joking, and we finished the job on high in good harmony.

My wish was almost fulfilled a few days later when the boss ordered me to take that scaffold down all by myself without any help of any kind—an unreasonable demand "if ever I heard one." But I was the servant and had to do what I was told. I was lifting a two-by-ten board about sixteen feet long when a great gust of wind got under the board, and the board acted like an airplane wing. I was thrown over backward into the corner, hard enough that the whole structure was shivering, including me!

I was shivering a lot more than the scaffold and an awful lot longer. I would have gone down seventy feet if I had crashed against the one-by-fours in the middle. I tried to lift that board again after a lot of shivering with much the same result. Then I shoved the boards over the sides without any further ado. My life was more important than that one of anyone below—nobody as it turned out!

I can still wake up in a cold sweat, even now after all those years, when I relive those moments of absolute terror. It was very irresponsible of that contractor to send me on that mission all by myself, and that might be the understatement of the year.

Then again, Albert and I were not as clean as the driven snow either. We had done some crazy things in those days also. The church had suffered a lot from the bomb damage, but the structure had remained standing. The tremendous air pressure had thrown the Bibles and the songbooks all over the building, and many of those books were damaged beyond repair. These books would have to be thrown in the garbage. This was a pity, since some of those songbooks had very fine pages, just like first-class cigarette paper, and that is what we used it for. Not very high standing on our part but a little understandable if you know that cigarette paper was hard to come by in those days.

I asked Albert one day what he was smoking, and he answered, "Psalm 55."

It is very doubtful that those books have been used like that at any other time, and I still feel a little guilty when I write this after all those years, but life was like that, and you did things that you would not do in normal times.

Our morals had slipped somewhat in the last years, and this was also true for our upcoming generation as we would observe one day when the kids entered the emergency school next door. All children were on time with one exception! "An interesting specimen." This was a boy with the nickname of Tito. This boy was named "Tito" after the great Yugoslavian freedom fighter. His friends seemed to think that was a fitting name for the boy. The reason for that was never explained to me.

This most revered Tito came barreling around the corner on his father's big transport bicycle five minutes late every day.

"Shucks," he would say. "They have been too fast for me again!"

Marshall Tito used a golden opportunity when the architect and the contractor were standing next to a puddle of lavatory contents that Albert and I had dug out of the men's washroom. This really was an odorous mix, and Tito was not a man to pass up that opportunity. He threw a big rock in the puddle so that the architect was well concentrated in his work, carrying a nice aroma with him wherever he went.

Tito was a good-hearted person and believed in sharing the produce of many! The name of Tito might have been well deserved after all as a testimony to the strange and unpredictable forces that drive some people to strange and unpredictable actions. One story remains to be told before we say a sad and fond farewell to our beloved Tito.

This happened as follows. Albert and I were working away at the church when we were visited by Tito and his illustrious friends. Those boys were fooling around the baptism font in front of the church, and it so happened that the janitor kept his cleaning racks under the baptismal font. Albert hollered at them to stay away from that font and stay out of trouble.

"We are doing no harm," they told us with innocent faces—they were so right!

They only helped the deacons who found the racks back in the collection sacks when they had to pick up the collection on the next Sunday morning. The poor men were standing behind the Lord's supper table in front of the church, pulling racks out of the sacks with a very improved color on their otherwise pale and solemn countenance. How do you like that for apples? We had an attack of the cramps—Albert in his small corner, and I in mine.

The contractor had his share of headaches with his little flock—that was we fellows. This man was also involved with the making of coffins, and the carpenters were a little too familiar with the affairs of death when they worked on those objects on a daily basis.

One of them found it absolutely necessary that he should measure the size of it. It also happened that the contractor walked in there at much the same time. This guy looked at him over the edge of the coffin while the other guys were standing around with very solemn faces, faces that turned to consternation as the big boss progressed in a very unlovable manner.

The carpenter almost lost his job that time because the contractor was far from happy at these antics. The only redeeming factor was the fact that the perpetrator was the same guy who had been in Russia and was hardly back to normal. I am into the big words now and have to get that out of my system! My language will return to normal in a moment.

These antics were just another sign that our morals had slipped to a dangerous low, a fact that was especially true for the children of those days. They were taught to mislead and fool the enemy as much as possible, and now they had to switch around and become decent and trustworthy again all of a sudden. I honestly believe that these values have never been fully regained to the level of prewar years when everything was so much simpler. The authority of our parents was almost omnipotent before the war beside the fact that we never even had a radio until we landed in Canada. But let's get on with the story!

Life was not standing still as we did our daily rounds. Certain demands had to be met beside the fact that I was absolutely determined that I should be a good bricklayer if I had to lay bricks at all. And so I started to attend an evening class for bricklayers. It had a course on drawing of blueprints and reading of plans. The amazing thing was the fact that I was top of a class of about sixty students. Somewhat amusing if you recall that I was a (less than average) student in the lower grade school of my earlier days—a clear sign that my heart never was in it when I attended the elementary school. I could have done much better at that time of my life. It was around that time that my dad sprung another surprise on me.

He came home and told me that he had enrolled me in a volunteer recreation club, a club that was putting on plays of about three hours in front of a crowd of a thousand or more people from all walks of life. It was mostly in an effort to keep the young people off the streets at New Year's Eve. One of my former teachers had told me that I had very much talent and a definite calling in that kind of endeavor, and he was proven right in that it opened a whole new world for me.

It was at that time that I formed the opinion that many of our Christians have an unfounded fear of fun and laughter. For instance, the club that I belonged to had a policy that a dramatic play could be opened with prayer but that a comical play was not fitting to be opened with prayer. It was not quite right to put those two together. Spontaneous laughter and Christianity don't seem to be compatible. A person with a Christian lifestyle could not really have a good time when there is a lot of laughter involved. It was small wonder that the young folks sought for entertainment somewhere else, often in the company of booze. The training in acting that I received was quite intensive in those days, and my parts were getting bigger and bigger until I became one of the top players in that club. I have seen people with tears rolling down their cheeks, not only with sadness but also with uncontrollable laughter, then and over the next forty years, time and again.

Many people have told me that they had a tremendous lift after one of those episodes, and in those moments they had forgotten about all the downsides of life for just a little while. It was good to see the reaction of many otherwise somber people turn into hearty laughter. Although that is not always true. I have met people who absolutely refused to laugh no matter what we did. I will enlighten you about that later!

We were so nervous at times that we did not sleep for nights before the play until the time that I was on the stage in front of an overflow crowd, often more than a thousand! It was at New Year's Eve that I was on stage and my coplayer did not show. He had taken a drink before the play and became so sick that he could not perform. Another very talented player had to take his place, but it does not take much imagination to understand that I was in an impossible position. We had to ad-lib most of these parts in front of a critical audience, yet all went well. People enjoyed themselves, and nobody asked for his or her money back.

The performing group was a very closely knit bunch, but not free of common weaknesses. Jealousy was quite common among us. The older players were in control of the roll distribution and kept the better parts for themselves most of the time.

One older woman with a major role got sick just before we were all set to perform in another play, and so a younger woman was asked to study the role as a backup player, something that she was really good at, and she was playing this role every bit as good as the original player. She played that role instead of the other lady, and everyone was pleased with her performance that night. A repeat performance was requested, and the older lady had recovered somewhat, and she wanted to play instead of the younger. This did not sit well with most of the other players. They thought that the young one should play, since she had done all the work to start with.

This was the first of often that I have seen jealousy at work in a human being. The face of the old lady turned almost black with venomous hatred, and she quit right then and there, taking her husband, who was involved in backstage organization, with her, and all this happened right before showtime, putting us in a very precarious position; but the show must go on, and we still had a very good evening together.

Still this was not the end of the story. Our group had a secret criticizer who wrote a critical report after every performance, not something that was badly needed as a moral builder at times. Our local newspaper had launched a slashing attack at some older players, criticizing them a little bit unfair, and most certainly in a vicious manner, in another play earlier on. The group was really broken up about this journalistic piece of handiwork, and the spirits were at all-time low, mostly of the players affected. But our secret criticizer came to the rescue in the next meeting. He set everything straight, praising the acting of the players involved, and the people affected were restored to the former glory! This handiwork was also shot down as a parting shot of the husband/wife team who had been so grievously hurt when the younger actor had replaced the older one in one measly performance.

This husband/wife team had been the secret criticizers in company of another person. Thus our criticizer turned out to be someone who was less than knowledgeable about the whole acting business. Neat, eh? This was a real low blow to our self-esteem, but we carried on with tears in our eyes. But we carried on!

Then came the time that we were asked to team up with some other clubs to act in a play on the national holiday—Orange Day. We were to do in an open-air theater, and this young woman and I were appointed to represent our society (somewhat to our surprise!).

This might have been the best performance I ever did. There was a crowd of more than three thousand people on that football field. The night was warm, and thunder was growling in the distance, nature's sound effect that fit in very well with the seashore drama that we were acting out that evening.

Rescue boats had to go out on a dangerous rescue mission in that particular play. Many people were moved to tears, as they were caught up in the drama that enfolded as the play went on to its sad ending. The interacting of nature and the performance related to this, I think!

The highest praise that I received might have come from one of the older players, who said, "I could not have it done better myself!"

HANK OPDENDRIES

I hope that no one gets the impression that I was talking anyone down in the former stories. I look at it more in this way. The emotions I have described are more or less a portrayal of human nature at one time or another and that no one should ever have the feeling that he or she is irreplaceable. You are ready for a fall when you think that you are indispensable. I have seen this many times in my life. It has happened to me also!

I have seen the more negative side of life not all that much later when they asked me to become the director/promoter of a drama club started by our young people. They were to perform a play about the wartime years displaying the underground movement. The imprisonment and execution of some underground workers were displayed in graphic detail. It was especially the death of an underground worker that spoke to the heart of people.

The actor did a superb job, while the acting of the supporting cast was also very good. Some scenes affected the audience, so much so that a good review was written in the local newspaper. This sat not all that good with some older members of our drama club, and I was severely reprimanded. The rule was that no member was allowed to participate in another drama club, and I seemed to have broken that rule!

Something else hurt me very much more—a hurt that was to last to this very day—that happened not all that much later. I had written a short play for our young people and gave it to our minister to read. The man looked into it and started picking it all to pieces, making fun of it in a degrading manner. This took away all my self-confidence, and it was the end of my writing career or any effort in that direction. What was worse was it took away all my respect for the intellectuals and this man in particular.

This man objected to me and my future wife having a relationship. His reasoning was that two people of a different church should not associate together. My father approved of the relationship, lucky enough. He was very fond of my Johanna in fact. This minister never attended the farewell party for my parents when we left for Canada later. He did not approve of Dad working with people from another denomination trying to start a Christian day school in our town.

I look at many intellectuals as very limited in real wisdom; many of them are no better than a carpenter with a box full of tools without the knowledge of how to use them properly! It is too bad I feel that way because I have steered away from any close contact with any members of the learned profession. But my first impression of their limited abilities has been confirmed time and again.

Any skilled worker can tell you that they are hard to work for. They seem to think that all problems in life can be solved by adding one on one. If it can be done on paper, it can be done in life!—period! End of discussion! Real life is not at all like that.

I learned as a bricklayer that you can put sand cement and bricks together, but you are a long way from having a wall. Weather, sun and rain, and a thousand other conditions come into play. The human factor overshadows all calculations. That's what the intellectual cannot grasp. I learned the same thing as an auto bodyworker. You can mix thinners with paint, put it in a spray gun, and spray it at sixty pounds of pressure, and after all that, you are still a long way from having a paint job. Anybody can tell you that, but the intellectual cannot.

It is too bad that we can't find a better way of communicating. Wonders and miracles would happen if we could! I am sure that there is an awful lot of good in those professions, but many of them are so convinced of their ability to provide leadership that they look upon themselves as the saviors of the world, so much so that their minds are closed to everything else. You want proof? Look at the record of the Khmer Rouge in Cambodia. Look at the depravity at the campuses and the universities, at a man like Trudeau and a score of others like him. Sad to say, but nothing will shake them out of their ivory towers. Enough of that . . .

My good friend Albert had left me to go to a job that was paying more money laying bricks in the bombed-out areas of Holland. He thought that he owed it to his family, and you could not argue that point, although it hurt me very bad to see him go even more so for the fact that we could talk so well about the things that are not of this world. So I was promoted to the number-one bricklayer in the company. There was only one! Albert had told me often that I would have to go away from the small jobs and start laying bricks with the big boys if I ever wanted to amount to anything.

I talked it over with the boss, and he promised me that I would be laying bricks in a big way when he would line up a building project— but he told me to work as a laborer when he finally got some houses to build. The laborers that he hired had not shown up, and he told me to be patient and do a laborer's job—mixing cement and carrying bricks.

I should have been more patient, especially since he broke his arm and was hard put to get everything organized. But no! Hank had it in his stubborn head that he wanted to lay bricks and wanted to lay them—*now!* I was wrong in that. But being pigheaded, I walked off the job right then and there and left him out in the cold. He told me as a parting shot that I was not a bricklayer and would never be one either!

I often proved him wrong over in later days, but that did not help me then. I was out of work, and it turned out to be a lot harder to get a job than I had realized. Everyone was looking for experienced bricklayers, but nobody wanted to break in an apprentice. The construction work in the bombed-out areas was off to a slow start and bogged down in a lot of red tape. Even so, my friend Albert gave me some addresses, and I landed a job in a town about four kilometers south of my hometown. It was most interesting that the people in that town talked a way different dialect than we did. Those people had an awful lot of fun with my backward way of talking. Little did they know that their way of talking sounded just as funny to me.

"This was also a lesson for me, and I learned that our way is hardly the only way."

In other words, we should not degrade the other person if he speaks or acts a little differently from what we do. There are a lot of different ways of living, and everyone is entitled to his or her own way of doing things. I learned to look at the things that we have in common and not at what divides us. To laugh at someone who is different is always stupid and deplorable. It was a problem that the women of that town did not see or seem to care about the difference.

I was approached often by women who would have liked a little closer contact with a little adventure here or there, and that was all fine and dandy, but the risk was too great. My woman was just as big as any of them, and I doubt if she was very understanding in a matter of that nature.

But there was another risk that was even greater. The young men of that town were awful protective of their womenfolk. More than one reckless fool had ended in the canal or even a lot worse. I did not see much future in the prospect. Still, that did not mean that I was free to go and do what I liked. Age-old barriers were in place that could not be crossed without certain preliminaries. And on one particular day some unknown group of would-be lovers must have crossed into no man's land.

This set of a chain reaction involved me in an indirect way. The young guys from town got on the war path one day and knocked any stranger off the bicycle whether he was innocent or not. Caution was advised, and I considered it very prudent to take the back roads that day and try to get back home in one piece. Johanna would appreciate that much better too! I did not have an easy time of it at work either.

My wish was fulfilled, and I was among the real bricklayers now. For instance, there was one guy who was almost square. He was about five foot six high and almost as wide. This gave him the looks of a gorilla, and on top of that, he would start chewing his lip when he really got going. He would lay a thousand bricks a day, and even more when the lip chewing business started. It got so bad that I looked more at his lip than at my work. This slowed me quite a bit.

People like that were nicknamed "thousand planters," and he was one of them, if I have ever seen one. This was the kind of man I had to work with, and I was hardly ready for that kind of entertainment. He would throw bricks like twelve years old with marbles, and he would stucco with a board that was twice the size of anybody else. This made me feel like Lilliput in giant country. The days were cold on top of all other misery, and my underfed body had a tough time coping with that kind of onslaught. The only redeeming factor was the fact that we had to work at a factory, a place that had some very large boilers with fires that never went out. These boilers had a constant heat, and it would take days, or even weeks, to let those ovens cool to a temperature that some repair work could be attempted. There was a story doing the rounds that a couple of bricklayers had to do some repair work in an oven like that while they had been drinking a lot of beer to help them cope with the heat of the upcoming repair work.

One of those jokers was well filled out around the middle and had to squeeze to get in that oven through the narrow opening. The great quantity of beer that he had consumed started acting when he was at work in the heat of that oven, and he did not feel all that well, so he tried to get out, but the beer had expanded his body to the point that he could not get through the opening anymore. He was dead before they had broken the door to get him out. This happened in Belgium, according to the spokesman, and it is very well possible that it happened like I was told. I have worked on those ovens, and it is very hard on the body at the best of times. The story could be true or not!

The boilers were a blessing for me then. They gave me a chance to get really warm during lunchtime, and this might have pulled me through!—that and the fried eggs that Mom used to make for me. These eggs looked like wagon wheels but had a lot of kick in them, and that gave me the energy to stick it out. Even so! The going was very hard at the best of times.

Anyway, my training as a bricklayer progressed at a good pace. Not all that soft handed, mind you, but that is what I had asked for, and I only got what was coming to me! That's how the tough are made, and I was not complaining. Nobody would listen anyway! My stay with these people did not last all that long either. The biggest change of my life was just around the corner . . .

My father had wanted to go to the Americas as far back as 1920 when a score of families in the neighborhood had moved to Canada. Mom and Dad were just married then. Mom had always said that she would follow Dad wherever he would go, but Grandfather was still alive in those years, and Mom asked Dad if he would allow her to bring Grandfather to his end. This was the reason that the immigration of my parents was put off until the passing away of Grandpa. The crisis years were in full swing when that happened, and the immigration was put off until times would improve, but my father held on to his lifelong dream. It was fully revived in the closing years of the war.

We had all kinds of reading material then about prospective countries where we might go. Argentine and Brazil had popped up as places where we could probably go. Brazil, especially, had our interest for a little while. There was a great movement about a man who was planning a colony in Brazil, but that turned out to be a fraud, and the organizers turned out to be crooks. That was one down and more to go. Dad started to look into other possibilities much to the dismay of my brother Adolf and me. We each had a woman to think of. The rest of the family was in favor or lukewarm at the best of time.

My oldest brother was married and had a wife and an old mother-in-law to take care of. So he was completely out of the picture. Be that as it may, my brother Adolf and I had not much to say in the matter. Dad had decided. We were underage and would have to go along, like it or not. All this did not stop me from building some huge dream castles. I could see myself in the jungles of Brazil or Argentina and be involved in all kinds of adventures of course.

Then I was in Canada at other times and built a waterwheel in a fast-flowing river, generating my own electricity and making lots of money in the process. They were all daydreams with little sense of reality in it. Fact was that I was always trying to save money in my daydreams of course.

Making money did not seem to matter that much, a sign of things to come. I never was aggressive enough (the story of my life!). The truth of the matter was that we did not have the foggiest idea of what we would be facing in years to come. The planning started in the end of the war, but it still took till the spring of 1948 before we emigrated. It was quite an uproar when our plans became known to the public in general.

Most people called us crazy, but there was a handful who said that we were planning the right thing and that they would not mind coming along. Leaving your country to go that far away was a departure for life in those days. Jet travel was unheard of, and nobody had an idea of the great strides that air travel would make in the future. Still, a lot of water had to flow under the bridge before we were setting feet on board to sail into an unknown future.

I had broken up with my girlfriend in the meantime to go after another girl. She was interested. However, she hummed and hawed and could not decide whether she wanted to come along or not. I asked her twice and told her then that I never was going to come back a third time. It was at that point that she changed her mind, and she came after me a few days later, telling me that she was willing to come with me after all. But I was not interested anymore.

Then my future father-in-law came walking in the door one day, and who was behind him? My future wife, Johanna! That's who! I believe to this very day that he had arranged that on purpose. Quite amazing! I always thought that he was dead set against our relationship. Yet he had been fighting the same battle as Dad had. The school principal of their church was just as much opposed to our relationship as our minister was. My father-in-law resisted the pressure that was put on him just as stubbornly as my dad had done. So we were brought together again, Jo and me. This time for the duration!

I have always seen the hand of God in this, and I truly believe that our marriage was made in heaven. It was the best thing that happened in my life! This does not necessarily mean that it was clear sailing for the two of us from that point on. Nothing is further from the truth. I had to confront Jo with the question if she would go with me to Canada when the time came closer that we would be leaving.

She never hesitated but told me that she would go "where I would go."

She had picked her man and was ready to follow through no matter what the consequences might be. I went to her dad, who was sitting with the family in the cookhouse then, asking for his permission to let her go and follow me.

"Well," he said, "you go outside and talk to her again, and if she says yes, we will talk again!"

Of course she said that she was ready to follow me. I still don't know why, but that was her decision. That made the situation somewhat different for her dad. He had not expected that, and he started backtracking a little from that point on—quite understandable.

He then said that she could follow me after one year if she did not change her mind before then. I gave her another chance to back out in an honorable way only days before we were ready to leave for good. We were making one of our last walks through the bush, and I told her that we better break off the engagement, considering all things.

"I would give her the benefit of the doubt, and she had a chance to walk away with no commitment at all."

We parted ways at that point. She went one way, and I went another direction. I turned around when I had done a hundred yards or so, and she did the same thing right then at almost the same time. We both turned our footsteps, and that was that!

Neither one of us looked back from that moment on. She had chosen me for better or worse, and that commitment was just as solid as a marriage vow, although marriage was still four years away. The departure came only after a long and bothersome road. Canada was opening the borders for immigration, but the selection process was very severe. We had to go for a medical in a nearby city, and that was a very interesting experience.

The trip was made on bicycles, two beside each other, and about six rows long. Our brother Dick was closing the gate with a single bicycle at the end right in the middle. Some woman was walking on the bicycle path, and the row of bicycles parted neatly in the middle, and a bicycle passed on each side of her until brother Dick drove right between her legs. This was not nice of brother Dick, but I must say he acted like a gentleman, and he offered his excuse in a very dignified manner while she was sitting on top of the wheel, facing the world in a very unusual position, to say the least.

It was a hilarious sight, and we all broke up laughing, except Brother Dick and the woman, of course. This incident set the tone for the whole trip. Everyone was excited, and we rolled through the doctor's office like a bunch of young dogs in a kennel, much to the embarrassment of Dad and Mom. But it did not hinder the test, and we were cleared to go to The Hague to the Canadian ambassador to be interviewed. The impression must have been OK, for we had clearance there also to go to the promised land of Canada. After that came the task of finding a sponsor. Nobody was allowed in Canada unless they had a sponsor willing to guarantee their well-being for one full year.

Dad tried several people, with no result, until he tried his brother-in-law in Monarch, Alberta, and my dad was greatly amazed that his brother-in-law sponsored thirteen people in all for one full year. This was very unusual, for he was known as a very cautious man. Auntie Mientje must have had a great influence in that matter!

She was truly an op den Dries, small of stature and very persuasive if she wanted to be. You should have seen the tearful reunion when they finally met later, but that was a long way off yet. Father and Mother had ten children and more debts than assets only a few years before this date. They owned their own home but had a very heavy mortgage against it, and so the house had to be sold when the prices were still frozen by the government. We had some buyers but not all that serious, until I met the farmer from Haarle for the last time, and he was up to his old tricks, true to form. His son came over one day with a lawyer who was a member of our church. They offered a low price for the house and asked for a counterbid from my dad. I happened to walk in on the conversation and recognized the farmer's son.

So I called Dad in the kitchen and warned him not to state a price at any cost; he would be caught outside the law if he did. Dad went back in and canceled all conversation from that point on. The man's eyes spit fire, and he left the house in a terrible mood. Dad had been ready to state a price, since he trusted these men because a member of our church was in on the deal, and this had given him a false sense of security. What else is new? The old farmer came himself a day later with some tearful stories that he had to look after the welfare of his children. We should look at his problems.

He did not seem to realize that our dad was in much the same position—moral law comes seldom into play in matters like that—and that's too bad between children of one father. An engineer of the town came over not all that much later and did a bid for the town. This bid was well above the market value, and this was also a man from our church.

We heard later that he had run into some difficulty because he had bought at too high a price, but that's unlikely because this property served for many years as a maintenance yard for the town.

The sale did not bring much more than owed against the house, so we were a long way from having the money for tickets for twelve people. It was at this point that we got help from an unexpected source, as will be explained in the following.

No immigrant was allowed to take more than one hundred dollars in hand when they were leaving the country. And that was a real hindrance for farmers immigrating. Some of those farmers had a lot more money than that amount, and so they started looking for ways to get that money across. Some of those farmers contacted Dad with the proposition that they would lend the money to us and we had to pay this back in Canada.

The deal was that we would have a little time before the money had to be paid back. This was agreed on, and we held our part of the bargain later on, since we paid everything we owed. Nevertheless, the farmers got involved in money grabbing when they got in Canada, and some of them gave Dad and Mom a rough time once they were on this side of the ocean.

That is the story as it was told by my brother who had stayed behind in Holland. I really don't know if this is true, but Mom had written that to Holland. I have never been aware of this. Whatever is the truth, fact is that all things started falling together, and the way was cleared that we could leave for the new world—Canada.

Brother Adolf was in the army then, and he had a whale of a time ignoring the commands of the corporals and other low-ranking officers. He was either not listening or just acting stupid—this came quite easy for him because he has always been a little different, him being a stranger in paradise—in a manner of speaking—and it seems that he got away with it most of the time.

He was engaged, more or less, with a girl who was connected to the Salvation Army. She was baptized under the flag, and Dolf and his friends discussed the legal aspect of a baptism under the Salvation Army flag. "Many big words and no results!" Does that remind you of something?

Adolf was amorous one night, according to his stories, and he wanted to steal a few kisses from that girl while they were standing right under the light of a lamppost. The girl objected to the procedure if it had to be done under the light of this lamppost. She would rather have been under the light of the silvery moon without advertising Adolf's intentions in such a brazen manner.

So she said, "Let's go behind the hedge over there. We won't be seen so much in that place. I don't want to be seen like this by every Tom, Dick, and Jo."

(Jo was not even there at the time! She was with me!)

"Aha," said Adolf the wise. "You want to contact the forces of darkness," and he followed the girl as Adam followed Eve so long ago.

Dolf was left-handed. He was left-brained too! He was different all right and very unpredictable, but he was a lot of fun to have around, most of the time, but not always. I think that he must have had the hardest time to go along in this immigration bit, except my oldest brother. But my oldest brother was married, and the others went along because they had to, or were reluctant like me. And then you had others like brother Dick who was all for it. The bricklayers at work treated me like Noah must have been treated when he built the ark.

"We did not have the elevator going to the top floor, according to their folks' wisdom."

Canada was a world away, and they just could not visualize anyone wanting to go that far away to an unknown destination. The old man told me that I had been overpaid when I started working for them but had progressed quite well after their expert instruction. How is that for a parting shot? But they were generous about my limitations, and I could come back anytime if I changed my mind (something safe enough to say when I would be half a world away in a matter of weeks).

HANK OPDENDRIES

The narrow-mindedness of small-time Holland confronted me more than once. I was stopped by the police on my last trip to work. I was in grievous transgression. The bell was not working on my bicycle, and that was so dangerous that he had to write me out a ticket. He must have had many sleepless nights trying to figure out what happened to the man to whom the ticket belonged. I never said anything but let him write his ticket. That way he had something to do rather than going after other small-time folks with faulty bells or no bells. Many memories of my childhood came back in those last days, the times when we went fishing for salamanders, the many-colored lizard-type, four-legged animals that lived in shallow creeks and pools . . .

The times that I was almost worshipped as a hero when I had caught one of those much-coveted animals. Or the times that we were smoking dried chestnut leaves wrapped in a bit of newspaper—caught and reported by the neighbor's wife—and later the leaves of the real tobacco plant, also rolled in newspaper, during the war. One whiff of that before breakfast, and it hit you with the force of a sledgehammer, sending you in a spin with your breath wheezing like a worn-out bicycle pump.

Then there was the time that we went pole jumping, and one girl insisted that she should be treated just like the boys. She wanted to jump just like we did. This had the result that she was left hanging in the middle of a wide ditch. The pole was not going back or forth until she slowly sank in the water.

None of us could help her! We were laughing too much then.

I remembered the times of grasshoppers and earthworms. Of butterflies and dragon flies dancing in the sunlight. Of flowers with dewdrops sparkling in the morning sun. Thousands upon thousands of memories came crowding in quick succession, and I doubted often if it was wise to leave this versatile and beautiful country on the shores of the North Sea.

The engagement of Jo and me was one of the last things that happened before our departure. We promised to be faithful until the day that we might meet again—a promise that never was broken.

The engagement happened in a very unusual way . . . like almost everything else in our life. Jo got some really old gold from her grandmother, and we had that melted down into two golden rings. Jo had the gold, and I had to pay for the goldsmith's fee. I insisted that we should make our vows in the middle of a railroad track in the ravine behind Jo's house in a ceremony that is very likely unequaled in all of human history.

We were married more than three years later, thousands of miles away from that spot, and our vows of that moment were never broken. More than fifty years ago.

My father was uneducated but very wise in his own right, a member of the town council and president of the Christian Workers Union for many years, also numerous organizations beside these. Many high-ranking dignitaries came out to a big farewell party for Mom and Dad. Also many common folks were showing the affection that never came to the fore in normal days. Dad and Mom really had a great place in the hearts of many.

The minister who gave us so much trouble never showed his face. I can say that without bitterness. It was sad, if anything! The op den Dries family was remembered as much as forty years later for their very happy coziness and the hospitality that they extended to an unbelievable amount of people from all over. I can say that without exaggeration. Both Dutch and Canadian people will testify to this! Our mother was a very outreaching person who touched the lives of many with her unending cheerfulness.

Time went on, and the day came that our friends brought us to the train in the next township on that fateful day in the end of March 1948. The great journey had started.

My brother and my fiancée were among the people who brought us away. It is fair to say that my oldest brother never really recovered from the shock of losing his whole family in just one day and more so because he would have loved to come along.

I will never know what went through Jo's head either, but she was not laughing at those moments. My brother buried himself in his daily work and gave the cold shoulder to the little bit of family left in Holland. He made a success of his life in the years that followed, and it was a good thing that he had a good wife who stuck with him through thick and thin in years to come.

Jo was looking forward to a reunion in another year and had it a little easier because she had every intention of doing just that. She believed that this departure was only for one year and she would follow when that year was over.

HANK OPDENDRIES

She and my oldest brother grew very close over the next few years as opposed to Adolf's girlfriend. That girl promptly forgot Adolf after the train turned the corner, and she forgot him the minute she lost sight of him.

And so we traveled through the low country for the last time on our way to the boat in Rotterdam. Holland gave her departing sons and daughters a departing shot of unfriendliness when the customs stole a handbag full of the foodstuff given to us by friends and neighbors. Part of this was the famous farmer sausages of Holland that will keep almost indefinitely.

CHAPTER 8

CANADA

I DO NOT remember all that much of the voyage, strangely enough. We were pulled out of the new Holland waterway and reached open sea by the time the sun dipped below the horizon so that we did not see all that much. The yellow sand dunes were the last we saw of the receding shoreline, and Holland was a thing of the past.

I was not to see it again until twenty-eight years later when we returned for our first visit to the "Old Country," but that was a long way off, and all we could do was prepare ourselves for the long voyage ahead.

Some people were saying that the English coast could be seen in the distance, but that must have been because they had better eyes or a better imagination. I did not see anything except water and more water!

The name of our ship was *Kota-Inten*, and it was just an old troop ship used by the Dutch army to ship troops back and forth to the war in the former East Indies. It was a ship void of any comfort, just a bucket of bolts afloat in the great wide ocean. "Lost between the skies and the sea and very uncomfortable for us landlubbers . . ."

Almost everyone got sick after we hit the wide wavelength. I remember one family that was fairly well-to-do, measured by our standards. This family got so seasick that they turned yellow as cod liver oil, and the woman was mumbling that she would prefer to die rather than go on over this hostile ocean.

They used to more or less skate by on their wooden shoes on their way to the railing as they kept feeding the fish faithfully and without letup. One thing about it, they must have been well fed, for they kept at this for days on end, and this became even worse when the day came that we hit some really rough weather.

The waves came rolling over the side of the ship in ever-increasing voracity and greater volume until it looked to our inexperienced eyes that we would certainly drown. It took many people by surprise, and they were running for cover as if their lives depended on it. Especially one big burly person who threw aside anyone that was in his way, even women and children. I have never seen anything like it.

The man was in a complete panic and had lost all rhyme or reason. It was at that point that I got so angry that I grabbed him in the chest and told him to let women and children clear the deck first.

"I am no hero, but I fail to understand how he could lose himself in such a shameful way."

The sailors laughed and called it "a little breeze." Maybe it was. But who were we to know! It is an awesome sight when you see the rear end of the ship come clear out of the water with every heave of the big wavelength. The great propellers are threshing the air half the time. Then the rear end hits the water with a thunderous explosion, and the big propeller churns into the water again to drive the ship a little further to the endless horizon—nothing unusual, only we had never seen anything like that before.

The captain and his officers tried to bring a little life in the boring everyday life of the ten-day journey. A request came over the PA system for volunteers to do a little entertaining on one evening about the middle of the journey. Dad and Mom, simple folks that they were, talked me into volunteering to do a little acting in this event, and I was gullible enough to go for it. Little did I know what I was in for, since it was a critical audience that would be waiting for me after a nerve-racking time.

My name was called over the PA system on the day of the event, and I was put on the program. Several other numbers came first with a shady content. One of them was a Mokum guy (Amsterdammer). He was so bad that he even made the captain blush. And that's bad!

My turn came after that, and I did the best piece of acting and mimicking of my life, but I never heard if it was any good. Most people had a good laugh, but I never found out if they were polite or entertained. We could not count on my mother's judgment, for everything we did was great as far as she was concerned. I might have been set for ass by the good intentions of others again. Then again, it might not have been that bad after all. Who knows?

We had to sleep in hammocks throughout our stay on that ship. I wonder how hard that must have been on Mother, but she never complained. Brother John complained that much more. He fell out of his hammock and broke his arm when he landed on the steel floor. We were sleeping in three rows above each other, and it was a long way from the top one to the floor, too long for John's arm anyway. He entered the new country with a broken arm.

The odors of many people crowded in one room and the smell of cooking food mixed with the stench of oil hung as a blanket over the heaving ship. It made its way through the unending ocean from one wavelength to the next in unending boredom. A few Indonesian seamen were the exception to the rule. They sat in their cubbyholes involved in card games that never seemed to end.

We could go downstairs to the boiler room and watch the giant pistons laboring to push the ship ever onward to a faraway destination. Nevertheless, that was also monotonous and never ending. And so the journey went on from one boring day to the next.

Until someone started yelling, "Land in sight! That must be Canada!"

And indeed, a small shadow could be seen on the far horizon. This must be Canada! Too bad we lost it almost right away, for a snowstorm started blowing in, and Canada disappeared. We looked at each other in astonishment and dismay.

"Snowstorms in the middle of April? Who had ever seen such a thing?"

The flowers started to come out in Holland around that time of the year. What had we gone into? Well, we had not seen anything yet, as we were soon to find out. Canada was not only a wonderful but also a harsh land with many possibilities and many limitations.

We left Holland on April 8, 1948, and arrived in Halifax on April 18—ten days after we boarded the ship.

My mother was interviewed by Radio Holland when we arrived at customs, and that's the last contact we had with the Old Country in a long, long time.

The press wanted to talk to Mom because she had the largest family in that shipment of immigrants and considered quite a novelty. She was quite proud of that and claimed in later years that the neighbors in the Old Country had been standing around the radio with tears in their eyes. At least that's what they wrote to her in a letter in later days. Who knows?

There was a slight delay before we could board the train that was to take us to Alberta, and I went for a walk around the harbor in Halifax. It was there that I saw some peanuts in the store window, something I had not seen in six years since the early war years. Maybe some good would come our way after all, although it was mighty cold and windy along the seashore. But that is most likely common to most seaports.

The harbor was quiet and empty as far as I could see, except a few women who were sitting behind a store window. So I walked over to see if they needed help with something or another, but they needed help of the wrong kind as I realized when I came a little closer. This is not what Mother Geertje had taught us, even I could realize that, although I was naive and very innocent in many respects of life. The truth penetrated to my slow-moving brains after all, and I decided to go to safer territory heading back to the train that was almost ready to go anyway.

The train was just about ready to begin the five-day train trip, and I did not want to miss a thing. The "all aboard" sounded, and the illustrious company was on its way to faraway Alberta. None of us had the slightest idea what Alberta looked like, and right then nobody cared all that much as long as we would get there.

The countryside was fascinating with her wide-open spaces and the mighty mountain scenery alternating with sea and lake vistas of a beauty that we had never even dreamed of. We were used to the low flat countryside of Holland with the narrow horizon and the low skies where the clouds seemed to touch the church steeples more often than not. The sky was almost unending in this new country as we looked out of the train that was speeding through this land of rugged wonder.

The trains themselves were less than spectacular. The soot of the coal-fueled locomotives was penetrating everything, and we started to look like Negroes after a few days without bathing facilities and limited water supply.

Our family was allocated a section between two narrow wooden benches, and we had to sleep on the benches where we were sitting on during the daytime. It is no wonder that we became bone-tired of this menu of coal dust and sleepless nights.

I sometimes wonder what our parents must have been thinking at time; it was all so different from what we had been used to, but the way back was cut off. We carried on in faith and hope, enjoying the scenery. We even had a look at the Quebec Parliament buildings on a short stopover. This did not mean all that much to us then, since we had very little information about the new country that we entered.

The train had to go some ways through the USA, and a short stop was made in one station where we were treated like enemies. The detectives of the States were watching us like hawks. They must have been very scared that some undesirable person might jump off the train. One big fat guy even waved me off the platform when the train was gathering speed. It did not give a very friendly feeling, and it was a cold shoulder that we received from Uncle Sam as we went through his territory.

Health conditions on the train were not number one either, and the child of one young family on the train became sick as the journey went on. The inexperienced parents did not know what to make of it and asked my mother what she thought of it. It did not take my mother very long to recognize that the child was in serious trouble, and she advised that they see a doctor at the first opportunity. The boy had pneumonia, sure enough, and the little guy was put in the hospital at the next station. The rest of the family had to stay there for several days before they could continue their journey. This boy might never have made it if my mother had been less experienced. Who knows?

The rest of the trip was boring after the first excitement had worn off, and we continued, not much interested in anything. The whole company had only one girl worth looking at, and she was of loose morals, according to my mom. I remembered her from the ship and was inclined to agree with my mother's verdict. I could write something more about that but respectfully decline. Besides that, my own love would be less than understanding if I had thrown myself into another woman's arms.

And so we arrived in Lethbridge after a bone-jarring trip. The fieldman Nieboer and many other interested people were at the train station to give a warm welcome to the bedraggled group of would-be Canadians.

"Tired but not too tired to take in some first impressions of our new surroundings."

Our closest family came driving in an old Model T Ford, something we had not seen in a long time, and this was very interesting for us. The few autos in our old country were of a more recent make, but Canada had a war behind her, and all the materials had been directed to the war effort. Out of the Model T came a lady who was absolutely beautiful in our eyes, heavy on the lipstick and wearing some classy clothes. Only the high-class ladies in our country would get away with makeup like that, and then only barely!

It was strange, but those people talked a dialect every bit as flat as ours. They still do. And it never ceases to amaze me. They had been away from Holland since the First World War, and they still talked every bit like us. That made us feel at home a lot more right away.

We were loaded in a car and taken to one of the bigger houses where a really old patriarch welcomed us in the name of the whole Dutch community. The whole table was loaded down with sweets, cookies, and a great variety of cakes and other sweet stuff in all kinds of colors and shapes, more than I had seen in my whole life. It seemed as if we had entered paradise on earth.

One should remember that we had a very poor childhood. After that, our childhood was followed by the greatest war of all times. It's small wonder that we were so overwhelmed by this display of prosperity.

The farmer's sons welcomed us uproariously and had great pleasure in our reaction to all the new impressions that we had to cope with.

Many older folks had close family in the Old Country, and those old folks were interested in everything about life in Holland, especially during the war years. And we had many questions about life in Canada. The talk went back and forth without letup until it was time to go to bed. Dad asked us to close the evening with the singing of the Dutch national anthem, and the old-timers answered with the singing of the Canadian anthem.

Then the old-timers told us that we should not sing the Dutch anthem anymore. We were in a different country now, and it was wise to forget the Dutch customs. We should be falling in with the Canadian way of life.

One thing they told us repeatedly: "Never say to your future employer this is the way we did it in Holland!" or "The way we did it in Holland was much better!"

We had to adapt to the Canadian way of life no matter how strange it might look. There was nothing that would turn a Canadian off more than the words "this or that is the way we did it before!"

This was very good advice, and we made it a point to live up to it often in years to come.

The customs of our newly adopted country were strange and often hard to understand. For example, land was so expensive in Holland that every little corner had to be used, and a little corner was turned over with the spade if it could not be reached with plow and tractor. The Canadian farmer could not even begin to do this; he would lose way too much time while more important work would have to wait or not be done at all.

It has happened that an old Dutch farmer went to work with a spade in a field corner of a section of land. The Canadian would look at you with a benevolent smile and go his way. He was much too polite to say anything, but he thought that much more!

This all we had to learn and a thousand things more! Our new life in Canada had begun!

An unbelievable countryside unfolded before our wondering eyes in days to come. Our new family lived in dry country farming land. The rolling country undulated on in unending variety out to a horizon that was so far away that the Blue Mountains could be seen, and these mountains seemed only a walking distance away.

Reality was that a person would have to walk many days to reach those beautiful mountains. That was not all. After that, you were only in the foothills of an unending mountain chain going all the way to the Pacific Ocean, more than a thousand miles away.

Another amazing thing was the fact that all the farmhouses were built out of wood and were at least two stories high, and none of them had much paint on them. This country had also suffered from the war, as we were soon to find out. We were used to the tidy Dutch countryside with the quaint little brick houses with the nicely painted trim and the clean-scrubbed streets in front of the small but well-kept holdings. Everything had its own place in the order of things, secure and well ordered. Neat little Holland!

Everything in Holland was done by foot or bicycle, while now we had to travel by car. Traveling by car or truck might have been the greatest change in our lives. I had never even looked under the hood of a car when we left Holland, and here we entered a lifestyle where the distances were so large that a car was almost a must if you wanted to get anywhere.

This led to the thrill of my life the next Sunday when we went to church with a young family, and this young woman said to me suddenly, "You want to drive?" as she looked at me with those big, blue eyes.

I was absolutely stunned but gladly accepted the invitation, and so I drove a car for the first time in my life. The woman could have never known what an unbelievable pleasure she provided for me when she let me drive that car the little distance from church to her house. She was very good looking, and that made it extra special for me. I was terribly impressed with the panorama, the car, and the woman also, and I had therefore one of the heydays of my life.

The church service was another experience that was much different from the Old Country. The service was very tasteful, and the worshippers were very well behaved in the house of our Lord.

Another eye-opener was the women. They were very well dressed, while we compared almost drab in contrast to the clothing of most of the church members. This was small wonder, since we had just come through the war, and that made all the difference in our lifestyle, and besides that we were poor also!

Poor but honest, and our fortunes would change as time went on, but that was much later. I was young and engaged to a wonderful girl, but you are inclined to look at the opposite sex, like it or not! And I liked very much what I was seeing.

One thing that I could not help but notice was the very subdued manner in which the teenage girls were acting as they entered church. They were almost gliding to the front of the church with sedate downcast eyes, and they made an impression as if they were innocent as newborn babies.

Silent waters have great depths, I was thinking. And there was an element of truth in this as I got to know the people a little better.

I am fairly sure that they were a little disappointed with that scrubby lot from Holland who looked like they had been eating with the rabbits through the rails. I had never any proof of that, though, and it is a fact that we were not that bad looking as I look at the pictures of those days!

My brother Adolf had his first driving experience that day before a very appreciative public. There was a really old Chevy car on the yard, and the teenage member of the family helped Adolf to get that car going. Adolf went racing around the yard, taking the corners on two wheels with a big grin on his face—true to his nature.

The young farmer was laughing so hard that he rolled over the ground while he was holding his stomach with both hands. He just could not control himself as Adolf went through his antics with this prewar monster on wheels. This activity was not without danger for either one because the boy had a severe heart condition and could not stand too much excitement and Adolf was just himself. Faith had dictated that they would live through it—both Adolf and the boy. It's hard to say who was in more danger, Adolf or the boy!

Caution! I am going to recall the early Iron Spring years and later in the years in Rocky Mountain House exactly as I remember them. Let no one who might read this publish anything out of this document in the exact form as I write it down. People might get hurt if you do this, and even lawsuits could follow if you are careless in the way you handle these memoirs. I am writing down most of the facts as I remember them without any bitterness on my part. Some people have wronged us, maybe unknowingly, and others might have been hurt by us! And I ask for clemency if that is the case. We all need forgiveness for things we have done at one time or another!

Everything was new and everything was strange to us. It was as if we had landed on another planet and we had to adjust accordingly. We had to learn new customs and a new language, and I greatly admired the ease of my cousin as he spoke the English language without effort. We would never learn to speak the language that easily, was my opinion then. But one eye is king in the land of the blind, and I was chosen as the coordinator between my family and the farmer due to the fact that I had learned a little of the English language through the perseverance of my friend Dick in Holland.

And so it was that I happened to be one eye in this situation, since I was the only one that could speak a little bit of English in these beginning times. The rest of the family caught on fast, even so, and my services became obsolete in a relatively short time.

We entered Picture Butte only days after our arrival in Nobleford, and we had our first look at our future homes—two little beet houses the size of the kitchen in our former home. These beet houses were about twenty by twenty feet and had no electricity, no heat, or any luxury of any kind. We could not even sleep with the whole family in the same house together. Therefore, the grim company of pilgrims had to be split up in two groups: Dad and Mom with the smaller kids in one, and the others in the next house.

The houses had been cleaned thoroughly, although I think that the former Japanese occupants had left the house clean enough. Those Japanese must have been some very clean people, for they had left behind some kind of square tub that must have been used for daily bathing or something like that.

Let me explain that the Japanese were deported from the seaside in BC in the early war years. They were sent away from strategic places around the Pacific to the more inland locations around the prairies and elsewhere. There is a protest going on that they were not treated right. Neither were we, and I don't know what to think in that respect, so I reserve judgment! Fact is that we had to start at the bottom and take over from them as beet workers.

The Nobleford folks had told us that the little Japanese women only had to spread their legs and they were at the same level as the beets—a joke, of course. Fact is that these little people left some mighty big shoes to fill, for they were very good beet workers, and that kind of work is very hard on the back as we would soon find out. But that was later.

We installed Mom and Dad behind a curtain in the better beet house.

Dad was ruling the roost like "Mussolini in his war tank," as one brother liked to put it!

As for us? We had entered the world of the beet worker and had a lot of adapting ahead of us in days and years to come!

Our farmer was a nice enough person, and so was his wife. They were Mormons by faith, but there was never even the slightest form of discrimination in any shape or form either from them or anyone else as far as I can remember.

Charley was the handyman, a little fellow who was handy in every sense of the word. And the last in the row was a Polish guy. He was looking after the horses, and let me tell you, he was good at it. I have never seen a man who could handle horses better than this man.

He would come flying around the corner with his two-horse team as if there was a fire going under them. The horses were racing along with raised heads and stretched-out legs as if they were on show in a circus of some kind or another. It was amazing that these same horses seemed to lose all color and fire after we started working with them.

The Pole was a reluctant teacher. He had to show us how to handle these horses and other animals on the yard, since he was to leave not that much after the day we entered the picture. I could not blame him for that.

He tried to teach us the ways of a good horseman, but we were poor students and slow learners. Nevertheless, he persevered, and the day came that we had to fly solo with horse and wagon.

The whole farm family came outside to watch the show, and it was a show all right. Hitching the horses in front of a wagon is a little tricky. The outside bridles had to be a little longer than the inside ones, and we managed to do the exact opposite so that the horses were completely mixed up and impossible to handle.

Their heads were pulled together as if they were trying to kiss each other in a kissing spree. And this got worse the more we pulled on the reigns. I have seldom seen a man laugh so hard as that Pole did when he saw us coming. He called to the farmer and his family as we were thundering through the yard with a team of horses that was impossible to handle after we took control of them.

And so it went from one adventure to the next.

The farmer was shaking his head more than once with good reason, but we were willing workers and learning fast so that he started to like us well enough by the time we left that farm a year later.

Something happened one day that made a great impression on him and his helper Charley. They had many pipes lying around the shop that were useless because the thread was broken in the end of the pipes, and they did not know how to take them apart. So the farmer asked me, with a sly grin on his face, if I would take a few minutes and take those broken ends out of the pipes. I happened to hit on the solution just by coincidence. I asked for a steel saw and cut through the threads in about five minutes, and the two sections came apart without further problems. Even Charley was shook up about that—and he was no dummy!

They simply had overlooked this solution, but it sure improved my standing in the realm of things. But I am getting ahead of myself for all this happened later.

Our family came over from Nobleford just before the first weekend that we were at that place. I suppose Aunt Mientje was so happy to have a brother over with his family that she could not get enough of it. Anyway, they were at our place talking about this and that and everything else when it started to snow, and we had a foot of snow in no time flat. And so the little houses had another four people to handle. Quite a problem!

We did not know what hit us! Here it was almost May, and a family snowed in because it was too dangerous to drive over the road with a car. It all seemed like a bad dream. We had never seen anything like that in all our lives, and we sure had seen our share of things already. But everything moves fast in this large country, including the weather. The snow melted in a few days, and we were ready to go to work.

It was too early yet for the beet work, and so we were in for a mighty big surprise. The farmer brought us to a corral about an acre square with manure piled in there more than six feet in most places as we soon found out to our dismay.

The fortunes of the sons of Derk and Geertje had hit an all-time low when they were put in front of that mountain of manure. We would have the task of moving that mountain of cow manure by means of a pitchfork about five feet long with four teeth and a slippery handle. How low can you get?

There was no help for it and no way out, so we started to work with two manure spreaders, a little tractor, and the two horses. The horses started well fed and were very hard to handle at first, but they slowed considerably before the onslaught of Derk's sons to the point that they could hardly pull the empty wagon after four weeks of hard and sturdy work. The farmer should have fed them a little grain and we should have had more knowledge, and this would not have happened! We did feel sorry enough for the poor creatures, but it was all new to us, and we had to do as we were told. You guessed it—shovel manure!

We could take turns to drive the little tractor, and that made the whole operation almost a pleasure for us, and most of us were in a remarkable good mood, all except Adolf. He was severely homesick and not a little lovesick for his little "Hanyball," as he used to call his girlfriend of yore. Then came the fateful day that he got the "Dear John" letter, and Hanyball told him that the love affair had demised an untimely death.

Old Adolf fell in a pit of deep despair and was absolutely unbearable for many weeks until youthful optimism took over, and he returned to the land of the living, although we never really knew what Adolf's true level was. He is a real character and has proven that over and again.

Our working habits were very good in general, and I don't think there was a lazy one between us, and our work went on at a really good clip. We kept digging and digging until we dug a dead calf right out of that pile of manure, and we wondered again about this land of strange contradictions like we had done so often before. We would find out in later years and on other farms that this was not all that unusual in this land with its harsh climate on a farm with that many heads of cattle.

The beets were ready for thinning after about four weeks, and we had to start a new line of work, something that turned out to be a lot harder than meets the eye. The days were long and the sun was hot with no shadow of any kind in that whole forty acres of beets. The ever-present wind was blowing from one day to the next, blowing little dust devils over the moist beet fields. That and the fact that dried alkaline dust was also carried in by the blowing wind, which made conditions even worse.

No wonder the Japanese were good at this work—these little midgets were a whole lot shorter than we were, and beet thinning is the hardest job on the back I have ever known.

Our beet fields were covered with wild oats, and it got so hard on us that brother John was sitting between the rows and pulled himself forward on his backside. That and the large sombrero on his head made for a ridiculous combination. We would have laughed if we had been in a better mood.

"A large sombrero sliding through the rows of beets from one row to the next. It was a sight for sore eyes."

The farm was close to the lake, and the water had brought on the salt to such an amount that the soil had become quite alkaline. This is where the manure came in. Manure is about the only thing that will produce a good crop on alkaline soil like that. But manure has one bad side effect on the other hand. It brings out the weeds in great numbers so that we did not have an easy time doing those sixty acres of beets.

Even so, we hung in there in spite of everything. The farmer was well pleased, and that was important to us, for we all felt very insecure then and for many years after that.

The beet workers had to have food and drink in time that stands for reason, and brother John was the man to go and haul the vitals from our home, a distance of about a half a mile away because he was the youngest in the company of brave men.

Let me say that John was not all that happy with the assignment, since he could not get anyone to help him carry the stuff. But John is a resourceful person, and he found a way around the problem. He tied the wheelbarrow behind the tractor and arrived at the beet working company with a triumphant grin on his moon-shaped face.

Dad soon wiped the grin of his face with a mighty swipe of the flat of his hand. We all watched the proceedings in the meantime with the greatest astonishment on our faces. John-boy had to work a lot harder to keep the wheelbarrow behind the tractor than if he had just carried it nice and easy. John seldom did things the easy way, and that's a fact!

Then there was Adolf. He was the man that really could thin beets. He went through the rows like a storm wind passing by, and it would not take long before Adolf was sitting at the end of the row while we had a long way to go yet. Dad reprimanded him one day that he had left too many beets in the wrong places.

"The wind was blowing against my hoe, and I missed a few," he said.

A very interesting explanation if I ever heard one!

It was in that manner that our days were filled with work from morning until evening. Nobody went to town in that first half year, although we lived only about three miles away. We had too much to keep us busy.

Bert, as the youngest, had to do the chores in town. He had to travel on the bicycle all those three miles and back the same way. He hated this with a passion, but that could not be helped. Gerty and Bert were the only ones with time on their hands. They attended school in Picture Butte, and that went fairly good until Gerty came home one day and did not want to go back to school.

"They want to kiss me all the time," she said. "They say 'excuse me' every time someone goes past me."

("Excuse me" and "kiss me" in Dutch sound much the same way, and that's where the problem was!) She did not want to be kissed all the time.

The reality was that the other children treated them very nicely and nobody made fun of them. The Canadian people are very well behaved in that respect. I have never been made fun of by any Canadian ever because of my language or looks, to my knowledge anyway, and the Canadians should be commended for that.

Transportation was a great problem for the immigrants in that first year. Nobody had a car, and the distances were prohibitive.

The church of Nobleford, as mother church, with the help of the fieldman, arranged a school bus to take us to church on Sunday morning. The bus would pick us up in the morning and drop us off at the farm again in the evening, a solution that seemed to work nicely at first.

"Everyone was looking forward to the Sundays in those days."

You got to keep in mind that our lives were full of beets from morning to evening for seven days a week. We had no newspapers and no radio and nobody but the family to talk to. It was for that reason that we looked forward to the trip on the school bus to church Sunday morning. We all lived by faith and very much so in the first years, and we really felt comforted under the proclamation of the Word.

The church was also the place to meet people: the Friesian, the Groninger, and the Drent people, from North and from South Holland of Overysel, and mid-Holland. People from all over came together in one great melting pot. And in spite of all that, it was a very close community, and we learned to value different people from all kinds of backgrounds.

The ongoing gossip of the early years hurt us very much when we lived in that community. We had lived a very sheltered life in that respect and were not used to the farmer's ways of coping with the different impressions that came at them day after day. It is almost second nature to the farmers. Everything and everyone are taken under the loupe magnifying glass. And the story did the rounds for that reason that we were not much of beet workers.

Our day did not start much before eight in the morning, whereas most of the other farmers were out in the fields by six in the morning and even earlier. The whole family, young and old, was there. I am not sure if there was no child labor involved at first. But that's beside the point. The topic of discussion was usually how many acres of beets had been cleaned during the week, and it is true that most farmers were ahead of us initially. But, on the other hand, we were much fresher in the third and the fourth week and got so that we were way ahead of many others when it was all said and done, much to the amazement of the other farmers.

Brother Adolf brought that fact home to them when they were bragging about how much work they had done. Dolf remarked that we had done more than they had with all their bragging and hot air. Fact is we really did not care what others did if we could do the work to the satisfaction of our farmer.

Church was held in Picture Butte for a while, and then we moved to a church in Iron Springs—the United Church, I believe. This must have quite a sacrifice for the members of that church, but we did not realize the fact at that time that the Canadians have a deep respect for church buildings in general. They must have had more patience with us than we realized at the time. I am not sure that we always respected their sanctuary the way we should have. Our traditions are so much different from theirs.

I can clearly remember the initiation service where the emigrant church was ordained and the new church was begun. This was well before the Lethbridge and the Calgary churches came into being. The services were held in a hall in Picture Butte; I believe it was in a hall of the Knights of Columbus.

An emigrant farmer out of the town had built several benches out of two-by-ones. These benches could be folded up after the service and set aside so that they would not interfere with the normal business of the Knights Chapter, and those benches were used in the initiation services of the new church.

Many well-built people from the neighboring churches attended that ordination service, and there were some hefty dames in the crowd. They had not suffered much in the war years by the looks of things.

The congregation settled itself on the benches like a swarm of sparrows, and it became a very weighty matter indeed. One bench after the other caved in under the excessive weight, and the service ended with the whole congregation standing beside the wreckage.

The man who built the benches was the most interesting to watch in that whole drama. He stood in the back of the meeting with tears rolling down his cheeks—tears of utter enjoyment. He thought it all to be a great joke and could not get enough of it. He might have had the right attitude after all! I would have tried to crawl under the floor if this had happened to me. It takes all kinds to make a world, but this was strange material indeed.

He built several support latches under the benches after that fateful meeting, and the benches served us well until we moved to Iron Springs later.

My father had the privilege of holding a speech in that initiation service, and he said something like "It is a real blessing to see the start of this church. However, we should not stop with that but aim for the creation of a daytime Christian school."

I could not help but think that he was a little immature and overdramatic when he made these remarks. The fact is that he was well ahead of his time again once again. Schools were started all over the country within the next thirty or forty years, also colleges and high schools throughout this fair country.

I should explain that the desire for Christian schools lived already very strongly among the old-timers who came around the 1920 years. But it took the influx of the emigrant churches to make the desire a reality. Lethbridge has a fair-sized Christian high school, and that city did not even have a church yet when Dad spoke those faith-filled words in 1948.

Church life became stronger by the year, and I like to believe that in those beginning days, the foundations were laid not only for a sharing and caring but also for a giving church. We had transportation and we had a church. However, the young people had their demands also, and the school bus was pressed into service for the young people's meetings on Sunday nights. This made for some strange situations. The young people had been cooped up the whole week on their respective farms and were more than a little wild when they came together for these Sunday night bus rides. The driver had a rough time holding that bus on the road when about thirty or forty of those young folks set the bus rocking and swaying over the small country roads. It was the Christian rock movement of the late forties, and I liked it a lot better than today's kind of rock. It was not so loud either.

We might have been overreacting then, but it was the only recreation that we had. Fact is that we felt insecure most of the time in this country where we lived as strangers until we gained more possessions and got a better foothold later. Most people were insecure, and some became homesick, and this is a sickness that is very hard to fathom for people that live an easier lifestyle.

One woman was desperately ill with homesickness, but the way back was cut off. The family was too poor to go back even if they had wanted to, and this person had to work her way through that condition without much help from anyone. She had a strong prayer life and a living faith, and that helped her to get through in the long run.

We had many strong and faithful women all around us in those days, and that may have been a far greater blessing than any one of us ever realized at that time. My mother was one of these them, and she carried us through many a flat spot with her upbeat mood and optimistic outlook, something we needed very badly at times as we went from one extreme to the other.

The farmer sent us to another farm up north when the first stages of beet work had been done. A slow-talking individual ran this farm. He did not move all that fast either if I remember him in the right way.

The farm where we ended up was really Indian country. You could picture the Indians sitting around the campfires in this wild and rugged setting. Some stone circles remain in these places where the Indian had used the fieldstone to weigh down the edges of the tents in olden days. The country was untouched the way it was lying there when we had to work in those fields—dry and seemingly lifeless, but that was only a mirage.

The prairie was teeming with life in reality. The dry grass was rolling to a horizon ending in eternity as wave after wave rolled away in ever-changing patterns in a kaleidoscope of colors that contained every hue and color of the rainbow as sun and season shifted through the evolutions of time. Greenish-purple growth on moss-colored rocks dippled and dappled all along the background of the grayish yellow of the grassy plains.

Rocks are among the most beautiful creations on earth. Anyone who has never had a close look at the rocks of this world cannot appreciate the beauty of it all, and he or she has not really lived yet. I can say that now after so many years, but you would not have convinced us of this fact then, I don't think so.

Rock picking was our next assignment, another activity that had been left undone in the war years, and so we had to do it. All labor had been directed to the war effort, and there had been no time to develop new land. This is where we came in really handy. The farm help gave us a stone boat, a kind of sled pulled behind the tractor. We would not have to lift the rocks that far off the ground as long as we used this contraption. To lift them on a wagon would have been a lot harder. Not a bad idea really!

A relative of the farmer showed up when we were picking away at those rocks. This man was over six feet tall and a little high winded—if you know what that means—overbearing in his manners. He was going to show those Dutch men a thing or two!

So he walked to a really big rock and proceeded to wrestle the object onto the stone boat. He was shivering and shaking as if he were going to fall apart at the seams. Then he looked at us very triumphantly, like Napoleon before Waterloo. And he was at his waterloo indeed. Brother Adolf was not impressed at all.

He walked to a bigger rock lying a little further, lifted it without further ado, and put it on the sled without blinking an eye. The tall guy never said anything and left without saying a word. We never saw him again. It was in this way that we had the Canadians almost convinced that we were a little off the beam.

Adolf was a big help in establishing our place in the realm of things. He came to our rescue again not all that much later. We had to pick some smaller rocks in a manure spreader. The young sons of the farmer had to drive the tractor, and they turned out to be quite finicky and restless.

The tractor would go slow at times so that we could keep up at a reasonable pace. Then the boys would get bored and speeded up the tractor so that we had to run to keep up with the spreader. We could not blame the boys all that much; they were just kids. But it put us in an impossible position, and it did not seem to help if we asked them to slow down a little. They slowed down a while, and then it would be the same story—run or be left behind.

Adolf figured that some corrective measures should be taken, and he threw a few rocks so close to the tractor seat that the running boards were rattling on that tractor. The boys turned a little pale and slowed down somewhat, but the evil spirit got the better of them again, and we were running to keep up with the procession. Adolf landed a few rocks right behind the boys on the seat of the tractor. That settled the matter. The boys turned white as a sheet and left the premises without looking back. One of our boys took over the driver's seat, and things went in a more humane manner from then on. Those Dutch are crazy!

It was in this manner that we had to establish our rights time and again. Some work had to be done at the home place on another day, tidying up in the yard and doing some cleaning and things like that. The farmer's wife was always there, quite young and not bad looking. She was always watching every move we made, and it finally got on our nerves, and one boy suggested that we should wave at her every time she showed her face. That's what we did, and it worked like a charm! We were not bothered again from that point on.

It was a wonderful cure but gave us the reputation that the Dutch were a little crazy. Not that this mattered all that much, since we went to the hay fields from thereon anyway. This was also completely different from what we were used to in Holland.

The hay was pushed with a large sweep and then onto a giant forklift. A tractor could pull the load of hay by means of this fork and dump it on the haystack in one great heap. Some of us ran a tractor, and the others had to keep the haystack squared off on top until we reached a certain height where the stack would be capped off. The work was hard and demanding, but all of us were in a good mood, including the farmer.

He lifted us off the stack by means of the farmhand when it was time for dinner. Then the whole tractor tipped over because we were all sitting on one side of the farmhand singing at the top of our voices. Nobody was singing anymore after that episode. Still, no harm was done. The tractor snapped a radiator hose, and that was fixed soon enough. The main thing was that we were all in one piece, and so was the farmer. All were in good enough shape to go for dinner at the farm help's house anyway. That meal was also was interesting, as you will see in a minute.

Dinner was ready when we arrived, and this turned out to be a whole different food than we were used to at home. Mom always made a very solid meal with no frills or thrills of any kind. This meal had everything under the sun and then some. We looked at the corn served, and one boy said that this was chicken feed in our old country. This set off a gale of laughter by the farmer and the rest of the family. Fact is nobody in his right mind would eat this chicken feed in the Old Country. It was too bad that those people were so backward that they did not understand a little thing like that. But it tasted ever so good, and we soon became converts to this new kind of food.

Brother John was always the adventure type, and he wanted to experiment a little more than most of us, and he got hold of a celery stick. This looked very good to him, but he did not like it after all after tasting it. He tried to be smart and put it in his pocket. That was really good except for one thing, and that was the fact was that he had a hole in his pocket, and the celery came poking out of his pants like a newborn fruit.

The wife of the farmer happened to notice the outgrowth and had tears in her eyes from laughter. But she put us well at ease and told us that it really did not matter. They could understand our predicament and were not taking any issue.

It could have been different. But our education was gradually progressing, and we got more adapted to the Canadian way of life. This was a good thing because threshing the Canadian way was next on the list.

This was also very interesting and not without its hazards as we were about to learn not all that much later. The bundles had to be hauled from the field and pitched in the threshing machine. This was really hard on us, since we had never done this before.

Our younger brothers had a tough time, and the farmhand who ran the machine was not all that nice to us. He was really picking on the younger boys.

"Dolf had to come to the rescue again!"

The loading chute could take two bundles at a time, and we were warned never to throw two bundles crossways in the chute and never more than two at a time. We had a good understanding of that fact, but the pressure was on, and things came to a head when the farmhand started to push brother Gerrit just a little too hard. The good man had miscalculated on one fact, and that was our brother Adolf. He was not the man to stand back when someone picked on his little brother, and so he decided to rectify the situation. He threw three bundles crossways in the chute, with the result that the machine came to a crashing halt. It took the farmer and his help more than a half hour of hard work to get the machine going again.

The machine started again in due time, and the farm help came to reason for a little while until his bad nature took again. Adolf did not think that this was nice at all! Something had to be done, and he threw in four bundles crossways, including the fork. Wham! That was the end of threshing for the rest of the day. This was not nice of brother Adolf, but it was a good cure for the farm help, who never bothered us again!

We did overreact sometimes. There is little doubt about that, but we had good reason to do so at other times! One of those times came when we had to work about five miles away from home and it was late, but the farmer did not show up to take us home. It got later and later! No farmer! Until we got so mad that we hitched the tractor to the manure spreader, and the whole company crawled in the manure spreader, mad as hornets driving along the highway at top speed while the shit was flying sky high.

It was not pleasant for the sons of Derk and Geertje. The people we met on the road waved at us and thought that this was a hilarious sight—a manure spreader full of Dutchmen! Those crazy emigrants sure did not stop at anything.

It was not so nice for us though. We did not see anything funny in the whole situation. You can be sure of that!

Things had not even turned back to normal when the farmer ordered us to dig a septic tank with field. The whole operation had to be done by hand, and one can only understand the difficulty of that operation if you know that this soil was of the heaviest infernal clay. It was the so-called gumbo clay. That stuff was so sticky that more than half of the clay stuck to the shovel as we tried to empty the shovels full of clay on the wall. We could throw a shovelful out of that infernal pit, and more than half would come back down. It must have been the heaviest clay in all of Canada. It stuck like molasses, and we started worrying that we could end in China the way things were going.

We wrestled around with this for a while, and then I came up with the bright idea to use forks instead of shovels. That worked much better. The clay did not stick nearly as much to the tines of the forks, and we did more than twice as much as the days before. Adolf started thinking about Hanyball again and was throwing some awful big chunks on the wall. We were getting along better all the time.

There was only one problem! The fork handles bent like reeds, and one after the other snapped in half. It got so bad that we had used up all the three-tine hay forks. Only a couple of straw forks were left—forks with five teeth that were twice as long as the hay forks. None of us was really strong enough to handle that kind of equipment, except Adolf.

It was absolutely frightful to see him at work. He was not in a good mood in those days. He lifted those straw forks full of clay and slammed them on the wall so that the ground was shivering several meters away. Hanyball must have given him some extra incentive! Even the farmer started shaking his head, but he had seen nothing yet. It got even worse one day when we had to load a drum full of gasoline—about forty gallons.

Adolf called one of the boys. They grabbed that barrel one on each side, and with the slant of pot . . . pot . . . pot . . . pot, and another delayed pot . . . they lifted the whole barrel off the ground and set it on the wagon without further ado! This was too much for the farmer and his helper. They shook their heads and walked away from there. I do not think that they trusted us completely after that time. He even got a little more polite after that, come to think of it! I do not want to leave the impression that he was not good for us. He was polite enough most of the time. The fault was often on our side but not always. I remember one day that he asked me how he should reinforce the cover of a water pit. I suggested that the rebar should be put about one or two inches from the bottom. He listened very politely and did exactly the opposite, putting the steel rods about an inch from the top, and then he added insult to injury, for he told me to take the forms out about ten days later.

I had not been that scared in a long time. I fully expected that the whole shebang would come down on top of my head when I took the boards away without a way out in the middle of that water pit.

The water supply was something else that we had to get used to. The average household around there was getting water out of the irrigation ditches along the roadway at that point in time. The water out of the irrigation ditches was drained into cisterns or dugouts and stored for use in the wintertime. This never could be that healthy to our way of thinking, but it seemed to work OK, and I never noticed anyone sick because of that practice. The farmers were still using the same water dugouts when I was out there not all that long ago, so it must be OK.

The subsoil is very alkaline, and wells with good water are not to be found according to the farmers of that area. It is not that much different from the cities that take water out of the rivers that are much more polluted when you think about it!

Today is December 26, 1991.

I have become very discouraged about the writing of these memoirs. It is to the point that I might quit altogether. None of my children have taken time to read even one piece of my writing, and I doubt that they ever will. What is the use of it all? I am filling paper with words that no one will ever read. Maybe there is an outside chance that one of my great-great-grandchildren will, fifty years or so from now . . . thus, we carry on in desperation. Vain, it's all in vain! But that's what life is all about anyway. Or is it?

It is just before Christmas, and war is about to break out in Iraq. Little hope is left that it can be avoided. The Allies might be altogether too cocky about the outcome. It could well be a different world when this is all over. The countries have come to the point that it is almost impossible to govern them anymore. The selfishness of people and nations has grown in staggering proportions.

I fear most the developments in the former Soviet Union. Freedom seems to have come to the suffering eastern countries, and Russia seems to have been put on a democratic course—something I have never trusted completely. The dictatorial forces have been altogether too quiet, just biding their time. That's what the leader of that country needs the most—time. It is a foregone conclusion that people brainwashed in a dictatorial system cannot change course overnight. The dictatorship that looms on the horizon might be the forerunner of the Antichrist. Many books have pictured the coming Antichrist as a man who will be hailed as a savior at first but later will set himself up as a god. Will Gorbachev be that man? (This proved not to be the case!)

It is the fall of 1991 as I sit resuming this writing. The USA has all but eliminated the might and power of Saddam Hussein, and the world has returned to some form of normality. So we return to the events of 1948 as they unfolded in our lives . . .

Winter has arrived, and the weather is more than a little cold. Some of our number had to go and work somewhere else. A couple of the brothers were working on the railroad. They were spending the nights in a railroad car in some really rough company. The language that they had to listen to was hardly the kind taught in our sheltered family circle.

Two brothers went to work in Lethbridge, Adolf as electrician and Gerrit as carpenter. Both returned to that occupation in later years and made a good living doing this. The rest of us stayed on the farm to do the run-of-the-mill farmwork.

The farmer was feeding several hundred heads of cattle on his land to live off the beet tops and other produce left over from the summer farming operations. Beet pulp was picked up from the factory in town for an additional food supply, and the farmer hoped to make a good profit on this operation.

It was on one of those days that I found a cow stuck in the mud of the dugout, and I reported that to the farmer at once, but sad to say, these fellows were way too occupied with more important matters, and the cow was left where it was until it was late evening when she was pulled out of the water and left to the side of the lake, without food and without water for several days—a very inhumane way of dealing with an animal, and we went over there often to give it water and food.

The farmer in turn shrugged this off and said, "It's going to die anyway!"

He was right. She did not that many days later, but I thought that this was a poor way of treating one's livestock.

John was appointed to look after the pigs. Those animals were kept in a kind of rotunda operation: a round structure with the feeding station in the middle of a circle of pig pens. This was a setup that was quite modern for that time. Pigs would move from one stage to the other and were fed accordingly. A great mean old boar was doing the manly duties in that setup. He was a real freedom lover and was left to run loose most of the time. This beast was in an ugly mood quite often, and in the course of time, it would become so bad that a person was not safe in the yard anymore.

One farmhand told us to watch while he was going to straighten out the situation. He went for a pail of boiling hot water and threw that over the animal point-blank. This was effective for a long time until his mean nature got the overhand again, but the treatment was repeated—poor management, I figured, and cruel to the extreme.

We looked at these kinds of things and could hardly approve of that kind of behavior. I don't think that this kind of farming was standard procedure, but it was not pleasant to deal with.

The winter sky of the Canadian nights was almost scary for the boys of Derk and Geertje. We were used to the low-hanging skies of the Dutch countryside. Now we looked into a sky so bright and so wide that all eternity seemed to open up in front of our eyes. I have had evenings that I was so overwhelmed that everything else seemed to disappear and only the universe was present in my humbled being. One has to have lived on both continents to know what I mean.

Other nights were so cold that we had to walk backward when the wind was blowing. Our faces would freeze if we did not, and we were lucky that we never got frostbite. Old-timers have told us of blizzards so severe that they had to take hold of a clothesline to find their way back home in their own backyard going from the home to the barn and vice versa. I would not doubt for a minute that this was true, since I was close to situations like that more than once!

CHAPTER 9

PIONEERS

I HAVE SEEN snowdrifts blown against the buildings so high that a person could walk straight up to the top of the barn. This was in a year that the roads could not be plowed with a snowplow. A Caterpillar was brought in to free the road, but I am getting ahead of myself again; that was the following year when we had moved to another farm. That was the second year in Canada.

The first year was cold, but not much snow was falling, and we came through the winter reasonably well. The farmhand gave us hope for the future when he said that we could handle any winter if we had no trouble with this one. So we tackled the next shore in a better mood and with perseverance.

The old John Deere tractor had to be started daily; antifreeze was unknown or too expensive in those postwar years, and we had to fill the tractor with hot water. The outlets on the side of the motor block had to be primed next while turning the big flywheel simultaneously. This big flywheel kicked back more than half the time so that the instigator was nearly thrown over the front of the tractor, a fact that made us plump scared of that green-eyed monster, but there was no help to it. We had to start all over again, and the beast would come to life with thundering explosions after many false starts. The exhaust would fire back with the sound of a cannon every few minutes or so, and that might relate to my deafness in later years.

The John Deere was called "the workhorse of the prairies," a name that was well deserved. I can still remember how my brother Adolf was making a dugout for silage with the so-called tumble box. A tumble box is a steel drum scraping the dirt away out of the dugout in ever-greater loads. The grade of the dugout was getting steeper and steeper as the hole got deeper and deeper, and the front of the tractor would lift off the ground as much as three or four feet. It was an operation that was extremely dangerous, since the power of the tractor was so great that it could turn on its own axle.

It could flip over backward, especially on a steep incline like the one Adolf was working on. Adolf was blissfully unaware of this and let the front end lift so that the whole tractor was nearly standing straight on its rear wheels. He was singing so loud that we could hear him above the explosions of the tractor exhaust. Brother Adolf had a whale of a time, and he was enjoying himself immensely. We had not seen him so happy in months. He could have lost his life just as easily as many other farmers did before and after him, but that never seemed to enter his mind by the looks of things.

These machines were regulated by a hand clutch, and that made it so tempting to wait for the last possible moment before pulling the clutch. It is also the reason that one of Bert's friends lost his life behind the same kind of tractor. This boy's dad was in the process of hooking up the tractor to a one-way disk blade, and the boy wanted to put the pin into the hitch of the machine. All precautions were taken, but the clutch did not pull back the way it should have, with the result that the boy was crushed between the tractor and the machine.

It was the first of many boys in our circle of friends who have lost their lives by the combination of man and machine. The same thing could have happened easily enough to Adolf, but we were spared that tragedy, and all Mom and Dad's children are still alive at this date— nearly forty-seven years later. Ten children, eight boys and two girls! What a blessing!

No sign of that was noticeable at the time we were struggling through the winter of 1948, but we were in for a great change in short order. A change we did not really want. Also a change that we were not really prepared for.

One old-time farmer had bought another half section of land in partnership of his brother. This land had a contract for forty acres of beets, and the best way to pay for that farm was to let someone else pay for it. This is where we came in as gullible victims of some shrewd dealing of the two brothers.

I must explain that it had been our plan to work several years in the beets until we had a little more experience in the Canadian way of doing business. But this was not to be! We respected the man who came to see us one of these winter evenings. We also believed in the inherent goodness of men and of this person in particular. He was a member of our church and in high position in the emigration movement. It was the reason that we made the same mistake as our uncle, the carpenter in the Old Country, had done with disastrous results.

We liked it well enough on the farm where we worked at that time. There was only one fly in the ointment. We had some difficulty collecting the wages owing to us from the year just past. This was a difficulty we could not cope within our own right, but the prospective landlord could help in that respect. He straightened the matter out with the beet factory, and we received our wages in full. This was a great relief and put us morally in debt with this man.

We needed the money very badly to repay some money that was borrowed overseas from the farmers with money. The deal then was that we should pay the money back when it was convenient. The rich Samaritans started pushing for money shortly after they had settled in the new country, and they would not be denied. Some people get difficult when they have money on the brain.

One of them is a well-established businessman at the time of this writing, and this is strange because the same man was complaining then that he was so sick that he could not work. Miracles do happen especially when there is money involved.

It was small wonder that we did not want to get involved that early in farming! We had no money to start with and no machinery or anything else for that matter, but nothing seemed to matter—the anxious future landlord had an answer for all our problems . . . We could use his tractor to work the field, and he had all kinds of machinery that we could use to get a good start in the farmer's profession. To make a long story short, we accepted and were contracted for a good share of the profit to go to the landlord. Rumor has it that the farm was bought for roughly $25,000, and we were paying about $5,000 a year. Neat, eh?

Our family in the next town was very disappointed that they had not been approached before that deal was made. They would have known right away that this was not a good deal for us, but the farmer could only give us a day's notice, so he said, pushing for an immediate answer. We were hooked to make a long story short—hook, line and sinker. He even could arrange for a replacement family to take over when we left the farmer who had contracted us until that moment.

This new family fell in the trap that we had been warned to avoid. They had the attitude that everything in Holland was better than in Canada—that they were the farmers with better ideas and more experience, an attitude that did not go over all that well with the Canadian farmer, and the immigrant could not afford to be stuck up. Our replacements did not know the customs of the land and most certainly the weather changes that the Canadian farmer has to cope with. A hailstorm can come sweeping over his land without warning on a nice and sunny day. No amount of care and hard work can protect the farmer from heavy losses when that happened. That is not hard to understand.

The farmer and the all-knowing Dutchmen of later days just did not get along. Two of my brothers were hired back a couple of years later to do some work for this farmer. We might not have been farmers, but we were willing workers, and that was a fact that could not be denied by friend or foe.

Anyway, we became farmers and moved to the new location when spring was in the air. Let me say that the first year in Canada might have been the happiest in my dad's life. He had enjoyed the company of the neighbors across the road much more than we had realized.

The new life began, and so did our troubles. We had little or any money, but the fieldwork had to be done. We needed a tractor to do the work, but the generous landlord of yesterday had no tractor for us! He needed it to work his own field. It was up to us to find ways to plant our crops. The result was that we had to buy a tractor on credit, but that was no problem! Our landlord had friends willing enough to sell the tractor. Nice, eh!

The seed had to be planted not all that much later, and we could certainly get the machinery from our landlord to work the fields so that the crop could be planted! You guessed it! Our landlord needed the machinery himself, and we ended up going to a Polish neighbor. This man realized our difficulties and lent us a cultivator to do the necessary work so that the crop was put in the ground after all. His only condition was that we should grease the machinery so that the grease ran out of the joints. He had the best-greased machinery in that part of the country. This is the way it went time and again. The once-so-proud family op den Dries had to beg for help repeatedly.

The groceries had to be bought on credit! No problem! Our landlord had good relations with the shopkeeper, and our credit was good. What a laugh! I was deeply ashamed as I had a ride with neighboring emigrants who were paying for everything in cash money. We had to charge again . . . and again . . . and again . . . the cultivator, the seeds drill, the beet seed planter! Everything had to be borrowed, and we were living on the goodwill of the neighboring farmers from beginning to end.

And then there was the gossip! The ever-present gossips. Everyone had an opinion on the mistakes that we were bound to make, but the help had to come from the Canadians. But, oh happy day! Help was on the way! Was it ever!

Our landlord's brother talked Dad into buying a pair of horses that he did not need anyway! Was that not nice?

"Real mustangs?"

That's what we thought anyway.

We had good hopes that this would put us on top of things, but there was a tiny little snake in the grass—just a little one, mind you—but it was sneaky all right. The whole affair did not start all that well. We spent more than a day running after these animals, and they could not be caught no matter what we tried. They would make a run for it every time we had them close to the barn, and we would start all over. It took another day and several guys on horseback to catch the elusive and wayward animals. This was only the beginning of our troubles; more would follow.

We hitched them proudly to a wagon, and brother Adolf would break them in properly. Adolf had excellent intentions and asked Dad to come along for the ride. The old man needed a little diversion, and Adolf had the situation well under control, at first anyway. Horses and wagon left the yard in a nice and easy trot, and we followed the joyride as far as the eye could see. We were really impressed with Adolf's horsemanship when the trot turned into a gallop. The horses were a joy to behold; the front legs reached further and further to the faraway horizon as the team turned around in the far distance with the riders in full control.

A beautiful dust cloud was rising around the joyful crowd, but the cloud got heavier and heavier as it came closer to the front gate. Only the blinking of horse teeth in the dust of the road could be seen once in a while. We could see the situation a little better as the cloud came closer and watched with amazement as two horses and four wheels came thundering out of the clouds and into the driveway.

There was not a board left on the wagon. Dad was hanging on to the skeleton of the rear for dear life, while Adolf was hanging on to the front section with eyes as big as saucers. Adolf was sawing away at the reigns with all his might, but he would have had more luck with a speeding train at that point.

Adolf's smile was gone, and so were his cap and his self-assurance. The whole rigmarole came crashing in the front gate, and only the horses with the front wheels kept going. Dad was staying behind with the rear wheels—a spiritually broken man. The poor man was not ready for that much diversion. The rest was all right except some cuts and bruises. Adolf was allowed to take a rest when the horses reached the stable.

That's how Adolf trained our horses! Or the horses trained Adolf! Whatever came first. Nobody really ever figured that out!

The horses never were any good for anything. I worked with them later, but one of them would lie down in front of the wagon when it had to pull a load through the mud. He preferred the mud before the work.

The horses were just no good, or we were no good. There was no help for it. We had to do something. The boys slaughtered them later and made sausages out of them. Mom told us later that one of the folks who gossiped so much about us was first in line to share in the spoils.

He was even demanding a string for the sausage, as Mom used to imitate him, "*Een touwtje voor* the worst"—a string for the sausage.

The average Canadian did not have much of an opinion of folks that butchered horses, but we did not have much choice in the matter around that time. This is, by the way, the generous help we received from our landlords. It must have been partly our own fault, since we acted too fast and really did not understand the way of the world. The average farmer would have been more awake and better prepared. But that's all water under the bridge! This all had to be that way, and the landlord did something that was more or less to be expected among the farmers. Maybe? I have learned to understand that all these things had to come as they did, and I hold no grudges no matter how hard it was in those days. The rest of what happened in that community will be hearsay on my part, since I was not around to see the rest of the story.

The situation had deteriorated, and the shortage of money was so severe that someone had to go out and make some cash money. I ended up going. Some of my brothers could have gotten work better than I could because Gerrit had worked as a carpenter and Adolf as an electrician. Both were good in what they did and were well liked by their former bosses. George had also been working out already at other places, but all of them wanted to stay in the farm no matter how bad the situation was. I fully realized that this could not go on, since no money was expected to come in before the end of the beet season, and that was months away. I was getting plenty worried and decided to try my luck at a town nearby . . .

A school was being built, and they just might have an opening for a bricklayer. I had laid bricks for only two years in the Old Country and was still an apprentice by rights, but need breaks rules! And I walked about four or five miles to the next town in a very downhearted mood. I wanted to farm and instead was on my way to apply for a job. Life seemed very unfair just then, and I was far from happy. I was in this frame of mind when I walked up to the foreman of that job and asked for a job as bricklayer.

"Something happened there that I have never fully understood."

The foreman was a very intellectual-looking individual with a friendly smile that came out of a mouthful of gold teeth. He looked at me and seemed to have a good impression, since he told me that I could start laying bricks the same day he would give me a chance to show what I could do, with the words,

"I will let you try for three days, and you will have a job if you are good enough. You will be out on the street if you are not! I just fired two Polish guys yesterday who claimed that they could lay bricks, and all they did was plaster the wall with cement and lime! You will go the same way if you can't do any better."

It turned out that this man was very good to me. He told me what tools I would need and showed me the right way to lay bricks.

I had to get away from the grip-and-dip system practiced by the European bricklayers. This was much too cumbersome according to him. The Canadian way was better and easier on the back. The Canadian bricklayer spread the mud in a better way and would pick the bricks from the wall without bending any more than was absolutely necessary. That is how I became a Canadian bricklayer. I had to go to town and buy a four-foot level and a trowel, like a spearpoint. A hammer, like an ax, was also added to the collection, and old Henry was on his away to the hallowed halls of bricklayers.

It was my luck that the foreman spent a lot of time with me in the next few days and gave me a sturdy job after the three days of trial had passed. I believe that it was God's direct interference that leveled the road for me at that time.

The relationship with the other three bricklayers was not all that smooth with the exception of an English guy by the name of Tommy. He was the fastest bricklayer by far that I have ever seen—then or later. He showed me many tricks that helped me immensely in the work I was involved in on the jobs for many years to come.

The foreman showed me the proper use of the trowel: snap the trowel down with a fast wrist movement like this . . . snap . . . and butter the joint like this . . . swishhhhhh . . .

Tommy was teaching me the trick of building corners and laying bricks. Control of motion was a must, and I became fairly good at it, but never as good as Tommy; he could lay thirty bricks against anyone else's twenty, and he would have time to spare. He was also the best corner builder that I ever witnessed at work. He showed me how to put up a foot of brick and check it with the level and form that point onto sight down the wall the rest of the way so that the eye became almost as dependable as the level after the proper amount of training.

A good bricklayer would make every move count. Every unnecessary move was a loss of time and extra work. And finally, but not least, a good bricklayer had to roll the mud off the board instead of scooping it up. This would allow you to spread a nice even bead all along the top of the wall. This could cut back on the number of times that a bricklayer has to bend down during one day of work.

I never could understand why these two men, the foreman and Tommy, helped me out that much! But I trust that a Higher Hand was at work in all these matters.

A certain amount of friction developed between the other Englishmen and me, especially between a young Scot and me. This boy still had to put in several years as an apprentice, and this little Dutchman came walking from nowhere and was treated as a full-time bricklayer. He could not understand this, and neither could I. It was something that I could sympathize with deep down inside. It seemed to go against their pride as Englishmen. I was wise enough that I never told them the fact that I had been in the trade for only three years, and nobody ever asked me. My work was good, and that was that!

There was a certain amount of gossiping going on between the bricklayers, and it was at that stage that the other bricklayers started pulling dirty tricks. I remember that I had to leave the scaffold one day and came back when nobody was aware of it. Several bricklayers had made their own portion smaller and smaller, and I had to lay ever more bricks to keep up with them.

They did not see me when I came back from down the scaffold, but I heard them say, "This time he will get fired! He is way behind now, and the foreman is watching through a pair of binoculars way down the road! That Dutchman is finished for sure now!"

The foreman must have seen more than they had counted on because the whole crew was laid off a few months later. I was the only one to stay on the job from that point on.

Picture Butte was very hot that summer, and it became real torture to stand on the scaffold while the wind was blowing dried lime and cement from under the scaffolds along the wall right into the bricklayer's eyes. This and the wearing down of the skin on the fingertips must be the greatest trial for the average bricklayer. The wind in that part of the country is ever present without letup. It kept coming in over the flat prairie lands in great gusts, shaking everything in sight.

The pain in my eyes was almost unbearable at times. The sun would shine out of a cloudless sky for weeks on end, and the cement dust at the bottom of the scaffold grew by leaps and bounds.

The boarding house where I was staying at was one of those old-style three-story buildings right on the edge of the lake. It was also catching the full force of the wind when it came from a westerly direction, with the result that the top floor where I was sleeping was swaying back and forth like a ship in the ocean when the wind really started going. It set the superstructure creaking and groaning as if it had come alive under the pressures of wind and weather. It formed a combination of sounds and motions that were not all that unpleasant and would rock me to sleep after many days of hard work in the burning prairie sunshine.

The man who had built the benches for that eventful initiation of the Picture Butte Church was my landlord. He was a happy-go-lucky but very sharp little man—a farmer in the Old Country, and he was doing exactly what we should have done. He was putting in time and gaining experience before committing himself to a farming operation.

Dad's landlord had approached this man also according to this man's version of the story. But he had politely but definitely declined for the honor of becoming a farmer under the conditions that were set out by my family's landlord. His story may be true and maybe not! It really did not matter. Fact is that this man was sharp enough to see the limitations of the deal.

I heard some unbelievable rumors about that man and his family not all that long ago. His oldest son wrote a book about the history of this family. This was a story that stretches all imagination. It was about betrayal during the war years and several cases of murder by poisoning. His son wrote this, but it is very hard to believe, since they were very good to me then. His wife was the example of the clean Dutch housewife.

She was an excellent cook and set good food on the table. That's all I asked for, and I had no reason for complaints. His son and I would go walking through the coulee at night if we were not too tired, but the danger of rattlesnakes was always present. Nothing could be taken for granted in those sun-drenched coulees of Southern Alberta.

A completely new life had begun, and my days were filled with work under the direction of old Seven Up and his Marie Band. That's what he was called (Seven Up) because he never touched any liquor of any kind, and he never made a secret that he belonged to the Mormons— the Church of the Latter-Day Saints.

He did not drink, and neither did I. This fact sets you always apart from the crowd and makes you an outcast when it comes to the talk of the common folk among themselves. The ministers of the Word can talk easily enough from the pulpit that we are not supposed to be involved with that kind of lifestyle, and they might be right. But it is very hard to handle when you are living, working, and sleeping with a crew of workmen who have been brought up in a way different environment. I was to find that out not all that much later.

Most immigrants were only interested with saving money to buy a farm at one time or another. But the average tradesman has a way different lifestyle, and they are more pleasure oriented. I lived with people like that for the better part of my life, and it becomes a real challenge to walk the right way. I wish that all future preachers would have to spend two or three years under conditions like that.

"Enough of that!"

The brick wall became higher and higher as the days went by, until we were ordered to brace a high freestanding piece of wall. It seemed to me that this was an order that seemed somewhat ridiculous, but as it turned out, it was very sensible in fact. I was glad that I kept my mouth shut then. A brick wall or a block wall will blow over easy enough if the wind is right and if the wall is freestanding, and this wall was—just another lesson like so many others that I had to learn.

The events were strange at times but always exciting, and there was hardly a dull moment in the construction business. Even so, all good things must end, and so did this job. All the bricklayers were laid off.

Tommy and I stayed on to do another small job yet, and then Tommy was laid off too. The contractor had no more jobs lined up. I was the only one left to do the little cleanup jobs, something that amazed me to no end! I was the last one hired and the last one to let go. It just did not seem right.

I felt lonesome in those days and seemed to have some kind of inferiority complex going. This was not all that strange under the emigrants of the early days. We had been uprooted out of our old country way of life and had not incorporated into the Canadian fabric of life—not for years to come.

"Strangers in a strange land" is a fitting description for the average emigrant of the early days.

But there were exceptions!

One emigrant who had been here for a half year or less said to an old-time Canadian, "It's really funny, but I am having ever more trouble to speak the Dutch language! I can hardly understand the Dutch language anymore!"

The old-timer patted him on the shoulder and said with great compassion,

"That's all right! It will all come back by the time that you learn to speak English!"

It took a little while for the words to sink in. Some people never learn anyway, but I have often noticed the trend of many folks like that one—people who can't wait to get away from the Dutch background and seem ashamed of the fact that they are Dutch and different somehow.

This kind of inferiority complex was also something that made me overreact one day when I was ordered to build a block chimney in a new house. The chimney blocks were of a very uneven construction and about an inch wider on the bottom than on the top. It was impossible to make a straight chimney on all sides under those conditions, and I chose to make one side straight instead of all sides crooked. This was not to the liking of a young inspector, who walked in just about that time. He told me to divide the unequal sides so that the whole chimney would look lopsided—the same difference really!

I threw such a tantrum that I grabbed the whole chimney of about eight feet and sent the whole structure crashing down in front of his startled eyes. He did not know how to get out of that basement fast enough! The head carpenter came down a little later and helped me to repair the damage! You see what I mean. This was not normal! The whole episode was another example of the strain we were under to find our place in this new society.

My stay in this company would be ending also. One laborer told me that I should ask for higher wages. I was working under the wages, according to him anyway. He might have been another instigator who was making trouble wherever he saw an opening—whatever the case. There was no one to turn for advice, and I had to decide again. It might have been the wrong decision, but the overriding factor guiding me was the fact that I would not work under the wages and hurt someone else that way. And so I was on my way to the head office to ask the big boss for a raise, and that was promptly denied. I quit just as promptly.

Hank was out of work again and went to the only company in Lethbridge involved in brickwork then—and would you know it? I landed right back with the English guys that had been my partners before.

The contractors were two brothers, and one of them asked me if there was another really good bricklayer left working in the company that I had just left.

"Do you know the guy?" he asked me, and I could tell him truthfully that I had been the only bricklayer left in that company.

My English friend Tommy had told him about a bricklayer in that company who was supposed to be really good.

One problem cropped up almost immediately. This company would not hire a man who was not in the union, and they placed me between several other bricklayers to try me out. I would be hired as journeyman bricklayer—if I passed the test! That's how I became a union member and a journeyman bricklayer on full wages. My wages became real good, for the pay rate was really high for that time.

One of the most interesting periods of my life had started . . . The company was building a college in the north of the city, and my two fellow bricklayers were two Belgians with whom I had a very good relationship. We were involved with some precision brickwork that called for the brickwork to be exactly vertical over the whole length of the building. I happened to hit upon the perfect solution to keep the vertical joints nicely lined up above one another. This was of an immense value not only for the reputation of the company but also for us.

The Belgians told me that the name "op den Dries" was very common in their country, and it was very likely that our origin was in the Flemish part of Belgium. I am still inclined to believe that our roots are with the gypsies, but I can't prove that theory either. A person gets the impression that there might be an element of truth in the gypsy story if you look at our family members and the way they behave at times: the love for music and their impulsive behavior in the way they love to have a good time.

The older one of the two Belgians was an interesting fellow with his black fisherman cap and his set ways. He is the only one I know who managed to hang on to the Old Country–style trowel and the grip-and-dip system of laying bricks. He was good! There is no doubt about that, and he was allowed to build corners in the Old Country way of doing things, and that was really impressive regarding the overall moods.

And who else do you think showed up there not all that much later in time? The guy that built the church benches, that's who! He became our mud man, and he was a very willing worker—one who had his eyes wide open for any opportunity to better himself.

A new location asked for another boarding place, and that's how I met the two people who became the closest to me outside my own family. They were a childless couple from Brabant in Holland, the province with warmhearted people—and that's what they were: warmhearted. Strangers have asked me more than once if we were father and son. This was a mistake that could be made easy enough because we did look it.

HANK OPDENDRIES

He was not all that lucky in one respect, since he had a lot of difficulty in following the English language.

Therefore, I would act as the in-between person several times. He appreciated this and returned the favor in later years in times when I needed some help. His wife was like a second mother to me, although our relationship got off to a rocky start in the very beginning. It seems that she was not interested in having a boarder over the floor, and she allowed me to come and live with them after much persuasion of her husband. She told him that she was going to try this only once and would never do it again if this did not work out.

It worked out very well! Thank you! I was the first of many boarders to follow in years to come. This had an unexpected benefit for these two people, for it gave an entirely new perspective to the childless couple's life. I should mention that they were very devote Catholics, and the fact that most of the boys staying with them in later years were Protestants made it even more remarkable.

The evenings were cozy and companionable beyond belief. There was a really old country spirit prevailing. She had four boarders once who belonged to a different Protestant church.

Tonia—that was her name—called them on Sunday morning to get ready for church, but nothing much was happening, and she finally yelled in desperation, "I am going to call your ministers if you don't get out of bed right now!"

"You are going to be very busy this morning if you want to do that!" they said. "We all belong to a different church!"

This was the devotion of that woman, and she looked after everyone alike no matter what church they belonged to. I went with her to the Catholic Church more than once in later days, and that might have something to do with my attitude toward people of other faith. But let's get back to the story!

More than a half a dozen guys moved in within the next half year. The guy from the church benches whose name was Koos was one of them. He was a really practical joker, and hardly an evening would go by that he did not pull a stunt in one form or another. He had always a bottle of tea in front of him on the table, and it was this bottle that nearly cost me my head. It gave me the grand idea to put some salt in that bottle when he had left for a moment. The whole congregation was watching in great expectation as he was taking the first sip of tea after he came back.

The reaction surpassed all expectations, and he turned all the colors of the rainbow after he took a good swallow of the salt-treated medicine. He was after me in a flash and would have beaten me into the ground had he caught up with me. But I was flat-footed as the runners of David in the Bible. Fear gave me wings, and I needed those winged feet very much in that critical moment of my life.

A little cooling period outside the house seemed like the better part of valor. I waited for an hour or so and then went back into the house to test the spirits. All seemed well then, and I returned to the fold. Koos was cooled down a little but very grumpy for the rest of the evening. He was one of those guys who are always ready to pull a fast one on anyone handy but very unforgiving when they are on the receiving end of the joke.

The mood improved quite nicely when we stuffed a set of overalls, put some boots on the contraption, and set it on the toilet for the next beneficiary. This happened to be Tonia who had to answer the call of nature at a certain moment. What followed was very entertaining and educational. It scared the living daylights out of her when she sat down without turning the light on. She came screaming out of the bathroom to our great enjoyment. She did not get mad though. She got even later, and that made the fun even greater.

That many men in one house were sure to attract the attention of the womenfolk, and it did not take all that long before we had almost as many girls as men in the house during the evening. There were more than a few emigrant girls looking for a little action in those days. A little excitement in the life of those love-starved creatures was more than welcome. The girls were willing enough, but I was not, I am proud to say. I had my love in the Old Country and was not available in the playgrounds of that day.

Those were good days, both at work and at home. It is too bad that they did not last any longer. The college was almost finished but not before the time that I had another run-in with my friends of former days, the Englishmen. They were up to their old tricks. They could not lay bricks any faster than I could, and so the culprits did the next best thing. All of them were much taller than I was, and they delayed raising the scaffold. The result was that I had to work on my tiptoes most of the time. It would make me fall behind, and I became very tired from reaching above my head all the time. The Englishmen had great pleasure in this game and would repeat the situation as often as possible. The work itself was pleasant enough outside of the fun-loving Englishmen, and I came through this trial also without too much damage to my self-esteem.

My old friend Tommy, an Italian, and another Englishman were my next companions in the battle of the bricks. We had to build an extension to a school in Medicine Hat. This was to lead to one of the roughest periods of that time. The work was not too demanding, and we did the whole job in three weeks' time. This was a record for that kind of work. The reason was that Tommy was an excellent bricklayer, and I was getting better all the time, mostly through the advice of my friend and protector Tommy. The other two were no slouches either, and we had an excellent team among the four of us.

The carpenters were chasing us around at first, but that changed in a matter of days, and then we started pushing the carpenters around—a very satisfactory arrangement for us. We as bricklayers had a lot of fun, and the days were filled with good-natured teasing. It would have been perfect if it had not been so unbelievably hot.

Our mud maker was another drawback. This was a very cantankerous fellow who had fought in the Second World War, and he was a man who had little love for the Englishmen (Limeys—as he would call them). This man would make our mud so heavy that we almost broke our wrist getting it off the board, or he would make it thin as soup so that we could not pick it up. Besides that, he could always throw a shovel full of gravel in the mud as a last resort. Only a bricklayer knows how exasperating it is when you have to lift a brick two or three times because a piece of gravel won't let the brick fall in place. You have to lay the same bricks repeatedly. I should mention that this individual was going to give the English a beauty of a parting shot when the job was finished. I will show that later.

We had to stay in a company-paid room for those three weeks. The two Englishmen were sleeping in one bed together, and the Italian and I slept in the other bed. I got a feeling that the Italian might not have been all that happy with that arrangement because I had sweaty feet, and that must not have been very pleasant for this man. He never mentioned this in fact. The whole setup would not have been unacceptable in the present age. Things were different then and quite primitive by today's standards.

We would talk about all kinds of subjects including religion. I tried to tell them about the saving grace of our Lord Jesus, and the Italian, who was a Catholic, would agree with me. Tommy did not believe in anything, and Eddy, the other Englishman, was somewhat impressed, saying that he might see the light someday but was not ready for this step just yet. Tommy claimed that all of us had descended from the apes, so I told him that this was very well likely if you had a good look at the ape's and at his face. All this resulted in the spectacle that Tommy was hanging on the scaffold like an ape the next day. He was scratching his rear and acting the part of an ape in a very convincing way to the great delight of the other guys.

It was not too hard to understand that the Englishmen were that way. They had fought in the second war in the Libyan Desert with the desert rats. They told me a little about it.

Those English soldiers would warn their buddies as they were walking through the desert, "A Jerry ahead. Watch out!"

And the soldiers would be passing a half-buried German soldier with his boots uncovered by the ever-shifting sand of the desert surface. These kinds and more macabre stories they would share with us, and especially Tommy seemed to be a little unhinged at times.

Tommy had to go back to Lethbridge one weekend. He had trouble with his wife, and he was afraid that he would lose her. This is what he told me that day in a confidential moment. I went with him on that trip in his old Model A Ford because he wanted me along for moral support, I suppose.

This trip was a real adventure and very enlightening for an unlearned person like me since we broke down when the old Model Ford was halfway to where we were going. Tommy was very mixed up after that, and he ended in the middle of the railroad tracks—something that I don't understand to this very day! It turned out that Tommy was just as good in wrecking cars as in the brick business.

Then came the reckless day that might be hard to understand, but I will try to explain it anyway. The job was finished, and the head boss and his wife came over to pick us up in his brand-new '49 Chevy car. There was no way that I could get out of this trip, and I was caught up in the company of men who were very wise to the ways of the world, while I was just a babe in the woods.

The head boss was very pleased that we had done the job in record time and treated us all to the best dinner money could buy—steaks, two inches thick, with all the trimmings we could possibly eat. The whole dinner was started with a wagonload of beer or hard liquor, straight or mixed, in any quantity required.

The English kept pushing the beer in my direction, and I was in a very good mood. They treated me so good that I started feeling a little bit guilty, and something had to be done, since I wanted to return the favor. Therefore, I bought chocolate bars for the whole company. None of them wanted any of it; they all declined politely but very definitely.

We had to go right to the bar again after the meal was finished, and these guys kept on drinking up to closing time. This was not good enough yet, and they went to the Legion because that place stayed open a couple of more hours.

The company kept drinking until closing time in that place. I was ready to go home, but our cantankerous mud maker, who was also in the crowd, told us that he had a very interesting sight to show us. It was absolutely imperative that we went to see that before going home. He took us out on the prairie, six men in one car following his beat-up old truck. The ride seemed to go on forever until we ended in the middle of the prairie, close to Red Cliff. Our beloved mud maker gathered the whole crowd around a big rock in the middle of nowhere. He climbed on the rock with a lot of help from his willing friends—but he did not stay there for very long!

"Here," he said as he clung to his pedestal precariously. "Here the Indians killed four hundred Englishmen about one hundred years ago."

He sat there with an evil grin on his face and waited full of expectation for the English to come after him, but nothing happened. The others let him tell the story of that Indian feat of a hundred years ago! I thought that the English were going to kill him on the spot, and not just the English but all the rest of the company who were all very drunk then, including me!

Then a strange thing happened. They did a lot of hollering and then burst out laughing, and the whole crowd drove back to Medicine Hat to drink for a couple of hours more. It must have been six in the morning when we finally were ready to go home.

The contractor drove the car with the gas pedal on the floor at a speed of 120 miles an hour just as fast as the car would go. He did not even slow down when we went through the middle of a few small towns. It seems that I had been eating the chocolate bars with silver paper and everything according to the other guys who had to clean the car a day later.

I had to write this down, since it is part of the story, but I am still ashamed about the whole affair after all these years. Well, to make a long story short, I came stumbling home in the morning when the other men were leaving for work. My future father-in-law was the first person I met that morning, but he did not say a thing, not then or anytime after that. He must have been worried over his future son-in-law!

This was the last big job that I have been involved in working for that company. The construction business had hit a flat spot, and work was hard to come by. The head boss made use of that condition to force the wages down.

He came to me one day and told me that he could not pay me the full wages anymore; things were slow, he said, and he had to cut back.

I looked at him and said, "I have never worked under the wages, and I am not going to start now! I'll look somewhere else for work if you can't pay me."

"No," he said. "I need bricklayers, and I don't want to lose you, but you will have to work harder."

Everything went sour after that. I would be sitting on the sidewalk in the company of a few more unfortunates watching other bricklayers at work in front of us. We were told that we could work when more work became available. This just was not good enough. I hung on for a few more weeks. Then I looked at the other partner in that construction outfit—Marly was the man's name, and he could not believe that the other guy had said that I would have to work harder.

"You?" he said. "You of all people were told to work harder! I can't believe it!"

But he is like that, this man told me. He never gives me any money either, and it's as if he can smell it. He will show up with a little sum of money when I am ready to quit.

"You go and look for a job somewhere else," he said. "I will tell him that you are sick. You will find your place open if you don't find another job within a week."

This man kept his word. The main boss came inquiring about my health within a week, but I was gone.

My second father, Tye, had gone to Edmonton for work three or four months before that, and he lined up a job for me in the great city of Edmonton. It was in the fall of 1950.

Tonia gave me some of her best food and a lot of good advice, and I was on my way to the new location. I met one of our ministers on the train, but I found more sympathy from the Catholic priest at a later stage than I had help from this man. What else is new in the life of a lonesome boy on his way to an uncertain future? I was in the train and could not turn back even if I wanted to.

The train went past Nobleford, and it was with some nostalgia that I saw the prairie slide past my window. I left a lot of memories behind, but life must go on, and I entered my life in Edmonton on a cold and windy fall day.

The wind was blowing full force around the skyscrapers of the oil capital of later days. The oil boom had just started when I got there, and a lot of construction was on the way, but that was a few years away then. Too bad that I could not see in the future when the town really started booming, but I believe that was also predestined.

Tye was living the life of a hermit, without any warm meals at the best of time. He was a stingy little fellow then, and I was forced to fall in with his lifestyle. I had to agree reluctantly to this way of life; there was little choice, since he had the biggest shares in the company. Our main course was cinnamon buns, with cinnamon buns for dessert, and cinnamon buns for breakfast. This is what our life looked like for many months. Still, life had its rewards under his direction.

I got rescued at the least expected moment. Tye started complaining to a friend on another construction site. Many small bumps kept showing up all over his body, and my friend was getting worried that he had a sickness coming up. The man put on his glasses and moved to the other side of the room.

"That's no sickness," he said. "Those are bedbugs. You better check out the place where you live. It might be full of bugs."

The place was crawling with bedbugs, sure enough! The bugs would come for the light, according to Tye, and he turned out the light for five minutes, and then he would hit the ceiling with a brick hammer. The *toenten* (bedbugs) came hailing down according to Tye's version of the story. I had seen enough of them to turn me off, but it was no hailstorm. But you had to give Tye some leeway; everything came in a big way with my friend Tye!

It had a satisfactory result. We did move out in a big hurry after that episode.

The new place was an improvement, but not much, since we were still in the Ninety-Sixth Street, and that was a very bad section of the city. The front section close to Jasper Avenue was called the shit street, since it had so many beer parlors. While the street further east past Tenth Avenue was called the holy street, since that part was full with churches, including the first Christian Reformed Church. Be that as it may, it was a lot better than our first location. Our new landlady was a strange one, but she was clean, and that was important. She was also strange in other ways, as you will see later in this story.

Tye and I took a walk through Jasper Avenue on the first Saturday in Edmonton and had the surprise of the month when we met Tommy and the other Englishmen. This company of esteemed people had also moved to Edmonton, and they told us why we had to sit on the sidewalks watching the other guys at our former workplace during our stay at Lethbridge. All the other men were working below the wages, and that was the real reason why we had to sit this out. Tommy asked me to come with them.

Tommy and his friends did not like Edmonton, and they had a good prospect for a job at another place. But my commitment was with Tye at that point, and I did not accept the offer. I met Tommy again a year later in Lethbridge. He asked me again to come with them. He showed me the car that he had bought and assured me that he would look after me if I only would come back with him. I wish that I had known Tommy a little better in later years, since he did me a lot of good, and a mutual relationship might have been good for both of us. Alas, this was not to be!

We will have to backtrack a year or so, since many things happened meanwhile both on the farm and in the life of my future wife. Our family had a fairly good beet year that first year, but the debts were so high that the money disappeared just as fast as it came in.

Dad went to the landlord to ask for the beet loader that the land lord had promised when he had made the contract not all that long ago. The old, old story was repeated! The landlord could not help this time either. He and the neighbor had that loader together, and the neighbor needed it when he himself did not use it. This was disappointing but nothing new.

The family had not expected anything else by now. Need breaks rules. We had to go deeper into debt. The beets had to come out of the ground, and Dad decided to buy a beet loader and a two-ton truck to get the beets out and to the factory.

The native population understood our motives very well, but not the emigrants! The story was doing the rounds that our family felt so important that they wanted to be big farmers. So the big shots bought a beet loader, since the boys had to be too lazy to load the beets by hand. The busybodies might have liked it a little better if the beets had stayed in the ground. The story then had to be changed so that we were now poor farmers because we could not get the beets to the factory.

We were deeply hurt by this kind of gossip—maybe too much, since we were not familiar with the kind of gossip that is common in the farm communities. Among farmers everyone knows everyone, and judgment can be swift and harsh. Many a farm community is warmhearted and caring, but the flip side can be a lot more damaging. People can be destroyed by the destructive gossip that prevails in some of those coffee parties.

There is no defense against this kind of vicious criticism because the victim is not there to put up an honest defense. We have been on the receiving end of this malicious behavior more than once, and it can make a person very bitter!

Be that as it may, our family did what it thought was best to bring in the crop, while I was maintaining a small cash flow to keep the clan in food supplies. It was proven again that I was really a good guy, but nobody believed that no matter how often I have told this to the public over the years gone by. I will have to try to get that in the paper someday.

Bricklaying was for the summer only, and not much was going on in the wintertime. Not in those days anyway. I believe that the other boys picked up some work during the winter, but I am not sure of that. Like I said, money was in short supply. It is almost inconceivable that my parents managed to pay off that many debts with almost no money coming in. Our parents had to buy twelve tickets to Canada when they left the Old Country and made a lot of expense on the side of that. Now they had to pay for a lot of machinery, and that was an expense that they had not counted on. And then on top of that came the other living expenses. Last but not least, making payment on the church that was being built then also.

Payment for the building of the church was made financially, but much more in free labor. My share of work was also included in our commitment to this great work. I had to build a long, tall chimney. The chimney was the only thing left standing when the church burned down a few years later. It was the only thing that would not burn in fact. A spontaneous combustion in the furnace room was the cause of that fire. Don't blame it on the brickwork please.

Local politics had decided that the church was to be built in Iron Springs. Picture Butte would have been the much better place of the two. Iron Springs is an almost-dead town by now, a town of a few grocery stores, a gas station, an elevator, and one church. It is even less of a town the last time that I saw it!

This church was very important to Jo and me after all is said and done. It is the church where we got married, but we will tell that sad occasion at a later date.

My father-in-law had promised Jo and me that she could follow me after one year if she had not changed her mind by then. He was hoping, most likely, that Jo would forget me in that space of time. In that he was very mistaken. This commitment was made for life in the spring of 1948. Jo held to her conviction without wavering through all those years, for better and for a lot worse at times. Conditions had changed during that time because Jo's mother was expecting a child, and Jo's grandmother started ailing so that Jo could not come after one year—a real disappointment for me—but I was also a good guy and lived up to my end of the bargain!

My father-in-law decided to follow Jo along to Canada after Jo's grandma passed away, and he asked us to sponsor his family. This was something that left us deeply worried. It was the most unlikely family for demanding work in the beet fields. Jo's mother had a little baby to look after, and Jan, my father-in-law, was six feet tall and had a very poor back. That left Jo, of nineteen years, and this laugh on legs that went by the name of Henny! The boys were not even ten years old at that time.

My dad sponsored them anyway but with a very heavy heart. Not only did we sponsor them but we sponsored the family Ekkel also, another unlikely family of beet workers. I still don't understand to this very day why those families wanted to leave good old Holland for the uncertain future in Canada. All this was very risky for us, but this was not all of it. We also ended up sponsoring the boyfriend of this laugh on legs, Henny—another unlikely customer if I have ever seen one!

Miracles do happen. They all made out very well, and all became successful citizens after the customary grievances and setbacks. It was in this condition that we started looking forward to the arrival of my girlfriend, Jo, and her following.

Tonia and Tye and all the boarders came along to the railroad station to watch the arrival of the family Kranenborg. Everybody was there, except one! The most important person in that little drama. That was old Hank himself. He had no intention of putting on a show in front of everybody. This lover boy was in a theater in town watching *Tarzan of the Apes.*

And so it came to pass that the train arrived, and everyone was lined up for the welcome but no Hank! I did go and got a hold of my girl when no one was around, taking off with her before anyone noticed what was going on.

It stands to reason that we were very happy to be back together again, yet it did not feel the same as when we parted in Holland only two years ago. We had grown apart in some way or another, and it would take a time of adjustment to get back on the old footing of former relations. The problem was mostly on my side. We had been thrown into a very different world, very insecure and struggling to find a place to stand.

Then here came my little girl, not much more than a teenager. She was to claim her rightful place in my life, and I am really blessed that she is a woman of great wisdom, and she guided me back with love and patience until she had me back on the right track. Everything fell back in place again after a short time.

Nothing happens by chance. The beets of the Kranenborg's farm developed a disease, and father Kranenborg ended up working as an electrician somewhere else in Lethbridge, and I should mention that he did very well indeed. The boys were that much older a year later and were a lot of help in the beet fields already. I believe that my family helped sometimes. This was before our marriage and lasted only a short time. This was in 1951, a year later.

Disaster stuck our family in the summer of 1950. The boys had done well enough under the circumstances, although the relations with the landlord had gone from bad to worse. It had been a cold spring, but the beets recovered and looked really good after the first setback. It was always a great pleasure for me to walk through the growing crop over the weekends when I was home from the city. The boys held me up to date fairly well, but it was not the same as being there where the things were happening.

They told me that the neighbors upstream of the irrigation ditch would partly close the gates that were regulating the water flow on days when the weather was hot. That way they would get more water when a lot of water was needed to keep the beets growing. Our boys did not get nearly enough water when they needed it, but the blessings overflowed on Sundays when the neighbors had to go to church. They were very religious and could not miss a church service.

The gates were thrown wide open on Sunday, and the boys got all the water—thanks to the pious nature of our religious neighbors. Our boys had to work like slaves to handle all the water on those days. It was not much of a Sunday for my brothers.

There are many ways to celebrate the Sunday, but this hardly can be the right way in my humble opinion. The whole action was against the irrigation laws. Nobody was allowed to touch the sluice gates on Sundays or on any other day. But that's beside the point. Or is it?

These same guys could pay cash for the groceries when I had to stand there and charge with a red face! It is not so much a question of what we have but what we do with it, for that is what matters in the long run. That's what I think anyway.

One reason that I never became rich is the fact that I could never bring myself to manipulate the other guy for my benefit. Life is just too short for that. I believe that the Lord calls us for another purpose here below!

I came home one weekend from my work in Lethbridge and marveled at the beauty of the crops on our two quarters. The beets looked good, and the wheat came clear up to my chest as I walked through the ripening fields. The ears were filling nicely, and the wheat should be ready to be harvested in a matter of weeks. A bright future seemed ahead of us! Everything promised a rich and golden harvest. The wheat field was undulating in the golden sunlight when heavy dark clouds came rolling in over the horizon, and I was still a half mile from home. Swirling gray clouds mingled with an ugly black overtone accompanied by a grumbling faraway sound. It sounded like a heavy-loaded freight train coming closer and closer. A great gray blanket rolled in over the neighbor's field while I was still a little ways from home. Things did not look good, and I started running to get to the house, and just in time too. I had no time to spare when I reached the front door of the house. Hailstones as big as golf balls and many more like chicken eggs started pounding our beautiful crop right into the mud. All was gone in a matter of minutes. Even the windows on the west side of the house came crashing into the living room at the feet of our unbelieving family.

Mother started crying, and all of us felt like doing the same. None of us was in a laughing mood. So much for our high hopes for the future! Even so, Dad and Mom never complained, not even in the middle of total disaster. They started putting the pieces back together again in the knowledge that our Lord is the ruler yet! He must have a meaning for this if He wanted this to come over us. This is the faith that strengthened them also in those dark moments.

It was very remarkable that the hail started exactly on the west side of our quarter just at the border of an irrigation ditch. It also ended at an irrigation ditch just at the edge of our eastern quarter. Our entire field was destroyed, and the neighbors on both sides had hardly any hail to speak of. It is a known fact that hailstorms act like that, playing hopscotch over the fields and hearts of the terrified farmer below—over the farmer who has no defense against the awesome forces of nature as it causes havoc to man and beast.

All this was of little comfort to us. The landlords were hard as rocks and wanted their share of the remaining beets just the same as if nothing had happened. The leaves of the beets were destroyed, but some beet part below ground could be salvaged!

The grain crop set off another argument between Dad and the landlord. The landlord wanted us to plow the remnant of the grain crop under to control the weeds that might come in a year down the road. Dad wanted to follow the advice of our cousin from Nobleford in the hope that some grain might come back out of the remaining grain root system. And so it's not hard to believe that the relations between the two parties became even worse.

My family felt very isolated, since it seemed that hardly anyone cared. The Ekkel family (whom we had sponsored earlier) was not much comfort either. They became the best of friends with our landlords for the time being anyway! Some jealousy might have been the underlying cause by some, if not most, of the immigrants around us.

I left the farm not long after that hailstorm, never to set feet on that place again! I can only reconstruct the continuing drama on the farm from hearsay! The fact that I left for Edmonton was another burden for me but might have been fortunate also in another respect—the situation had reached the boiling point.

Several factors came together to force a conclusion to the whole miserable affair. The big tractor for the heavy work was the straw that broke the camel's back. The quotation is a little lopsided, but the results were the same, since this tractor was always overheating. So the boys had that repaired in the garage in Iron Springs. This tractor created the spark that made the explosion.

It seems that my father tried to cash in on another promise made by our beloved landlord. This man had promised us several thousand feet of lumber if we ever needed it. Dad asked for some of that lumber so that he could build a little barn to hold some milk cows to carry us through the coming winter. The answer was as expected. The landlord needed the lumber himself.

It was at that point that one of the boys—his name is Johan—got the bright idea to try out that tractor on an old building on the west quarter. This was a cement building—a landmark, since it was the only one in the country—never used for anything. This barn had nice wood in the roof section, so Johan suggested that they should try the strength of that tractor on that old building. Adolf was all for it, and Dad did not object all that much either. The pull was on, and the tractor was at full strength again. The garage had done a good repair job. The barn came down like a breeze. So did the landlord!

He was boiling mad and told Dad that he was going to take away the better west quarter—the only one that was not poisoned by alkali due to over irrigation by the former owners of that land.

"That's OK!" said Dad. "You can have the other quarter also! We are leaving! You have fooled us for the last time. We rented both quarters when we made the deal. You go and ask your brother."

HANK OPDENDRIES

This is what the man did, since he was quite taken back by the stand that Father had taken. Sure enough! He came back a little later to say that Dad was right—we had a right to both quarters, and they would like to leave things as they were. But this made little difference at that point. These men had pushed Dad around just once too often. There was no power on earth that would stop Dad anymore at this point. The die was cast. We would be leaving in short order.

This brought the question to the problem: Where do we go from here? There was little work around the prairies in those days. There was no alternative. Our future was elsewhere, and so their eyes fell on Rocky Mountain House—the most likely place to find work in those days.

The lumber camps could place people quite often, and we had a contact point in Rocky—the Konynenbelt brothers. Our beloved friend Hans, remember him? And Prince Marinus the Great!

The op den Dries clan settled their affairs in Iron Springs, and the move was onto the promised land of Rocky Mountain House. Our destiny would have been way different if we had stayed around Lethbridge a few more years. There would have been work in abundance only two or three years later.

I believe that this hailstorm was sent on our path to break us loose from the prairies so that we would go where we never would have gone if we had brought in that beautiful crop that looked so nice in our eyes, and that was a balm for our pride. The Lord works in ways that are not easy at times. But in retrospect, our future was in the West Country!

It is beyond any doubt that our family has been a very strong driving force in the church of Rocky—be it bad or good. I have no bitterness left in me about those days. The reader must see this document as a memoir of facts about days long gone. I am writing the facts as I remember them and might be out on some small points, but the overall picture is as I have been showing in this writing.

We will have to return to Edmonton to the existence of cinnamon bunch and bedbugs. Tye was desperately trying to make enough money to bring Tonia back with him to Edmonton. We hardly had a warm meal in those months, but Tye gained the objective—Tonia—in this case. She settled her affairs in Lethbridge, and she asked my family to move her to her beloved one by the name of Tye.

The boys moved her over in the old Fargo truck, and that was not a pleasure trip, since it was thirty below at that time, and antifreeze was almost unknown in these days. The truck had no thermostat either, thus no heat of any kind. The two boys and Tonia sat in that truck wiping the inside of the windshield with a salt bag. This was the only thing to keep the freezing breath from sticking to the inside windshield. They looked at the shifting scenery through a little peephole that was left open by the salt bags. It is fair to say that they did not miss much, since it was winter and the ground was covered with snow.

The journey continued, and they almost missed a very important thing. That was the railroad.

It was in Granum that one of the boys was saying, "There must be a railroad not far away from here!"

He was still speaking when a train thundered past them. Right in front of the truck! They had been just seconds away from eternity at that moment.

"A person would be with our dear Lord before he knew it!" said Tonia.

She was not making fun. She was very serious and quite near to the truth of the situation. They had a very cold trip the rest of the way. But Tonia never complained.

"Everything is OK," she would say, "as long as I go to my Tye!"

I was wandering with Tye through Jasper Avenue at about that time, and it was then that I got the crazy notion to ask Tye if he was still praying for the sinners who had gone astray from the mother church—who were us!

"No," he said. "We only pray for the foolish ones now. And you are standing in the front row of that crowd!"

So much for that! I had that coming, don't you think? It shows how close we had grown together in the time that we had been together. People have carried a lifelong grudge for remarks a lot milder than what I was making. Tye took it in strides.

Tonia landed in this kind of atmosphere and took up the slack without pause. The food improved a hundredfold, and life was more pleasant to live all the way around. Our beloved Tonia settled in that front room of the Ninety-Sixth Street house as if she had always been there. We lived in a boarding house run by a middle-aged widow.

This woman was something else. I remarked once in a crazy mood that it would be nice to have a date with her teenage daughter. This woman said that I should look for someone a little older—she would be able and very willing to fill the void that existed in my bachelor's life of that time. She claimed that she was a Jehovah Witness, and she would come to our room to sit on my bed, trying to convert me to a different mind-set. She wanted the wrong kind of fellowship, according to the wisdom of my friend and companion Tye.

This same woman asked me to visit her after she had sold her house to a pair of Ukrainian bachelors. I can tell you the joyful tiding that I never did such a thing. I needed all my strength for the bricklaying in the very cold winter weather.

We have laid bricks when it was more than twenty below with only a firepot to warm us, or the mud to be correct. You could not knock those bricks off the wall less than five minutes after they had been laid. They would be frozen solid in that time. My feet would be cold only minutes after starting in the morning, and my feet would not warm up again until I came home at six in the evening.

A bladder infection was the result of that abuse to my weary body. I honestly thought that I had Vanerial Disease. The water that I passed in the toilet was as heavy as syrup and as brown as coffee. No wonder that I grew desperate, and so I asked the Jehovah Witness woman about the symptoms of venereal disease. She enlightened me about the fact that these bacteria would never survive outside the body, not on a toilet seat or anywhere else outside a person's body. She was quite willing to take a peek, but I denied and was only too happy when Tonia was entering the room at that same moment.

My bladder infection did not improve any at all. I was still worried that I might have the dreaded disease, although I never was close enough to touch a woman, let alone have any close relations with any of them. Tonia advised me to go and see a doctor, and they gave me the address of a former army doctor.

A very humble person set his footsteps to the offices of the famed army doctor. I came in the office, and the secretary asked me to explain the nature of my problem. It was at that point that my problem had taken on proportions of its own. How do you tell a good-looking young woman about a problem of that nature?

But there was no help for it. I had to confess that I had severe troubles with my waterworks. Some corrective measure might be required, I told the woman. I thought that she would burst out laughing, but she managed to get out of the office with a very cramped look on her face.

I did not make out all that much better with the doctor, who was a really tough hombre who must have seen a lot of action in his army career. He was trying to keep from laughing before I even had said anything. I had to show my unmentionables, and he assured me that I had nothing to worry about. I would be a man free of worries again. Nothing was done, and nothing was settled—just the bill for services rendered. My conscience was clean, but my bladder was still in trouble. The doctor had done nothing about the infection.

I did the next best thing and went to a Chinese herb doctor on Jasper Avenue. This guy charged me twenty-five dollars and gave me four different kinds of pills: one for lunch, one for bedtime, one for noon, and one for the morning. But I was very optimistic and wanted to speed things up just a little bit. I took two pills in the evening. This had the result that I got the runs so bad that I could have split a one-inch board without effort. The second pill dried me up later in the evening. The morning pill took the stomachache pain away, and the afternoon pill made me feel good!

The evening pill started the cycle all again—I wonder what would have happened if I had mixed up those pills? I might have killed myself if Tonia had not taken the pills away from me. Nature took care of itself for the time being. It would have been much better if I had used those twenty-five dollars and bought a pair of good winter boots. But no! Hank wanted to save money to bring home. I think that suffering like that was a very stupid thing to do, and I had to pay for it in my health at later days.

My situation got so bad in time that I could not even step on the sidewalk anymore. The little step from the street up to the sidewalk was less than six inches, but I could not do this one evening, and Tye had to get a taxicab to bring me home.

Home was Ninety-Sixth Street and 102nd Avenue, one of the roughest sections in town. Our first Christian church was in that east part, and I went to church there twice every Sunday. It is sad to say this, but nobody ever invited me for coffee in the one and a half years that I spent in Edmonton.

I was made welcome in the Catholic Church. I would go with Tonia to a Catholic church sometimes, and we felt completely at ease in each other's company. I even went to the monastery on one occasion and found that very interesting. I did not think that those monks lived that badly after all. They even had a pool table and other recreation in that place—a lot different from I expected it to be. I never would become a Catholic but always had a deep respect for the Catholic believer that never diminished as time went by.

One of Tonia's friends was a Catholic priest, a man who had to finance himself and his ministry for a reason that I never could grasp. He had to be some kind of home missionary, but the church did not support him in any shape or form. It was up to the common people to raise the money for his livelihood. Tonia and Tye and the rest of the Catholic immigrants would help him with money and special attention. I even put in a few dollars off and on and never felt regret about this action, especially so when I heard later on that the man died of cancer not that many years later.

This priest was a farm boy and a little coarse in his manners at times but a very good Christian by the looks of his actions, although you would not think that on the day we stopped for a beer in a beer parlor. He tagged right along and had a beer with us in the best of harmony. One thing he did—he took off his priestly collar to hide the fact that he was connected to the priesthood of the Catholic Church.

It is a good thing that our clergy was not aware of my lifestyle of that time. I might have been in trouble if they had seen me in that kind of company. Not that I had much to worry about. The city church of our denomination did not pay any attention to me anyway.

Our church hierarchy of that day was really worried that the Catholic Church immigration movement might overtake our CRC church! This never happened and would not have been that bad anyway. Many Catholics were excellent citizens and had very high standards. This was a well-known fact, also by the priesthood of the Catholic Church.

CHAPTER 10

MIDDAY

I T WAS GOING toward the end of my stay in Edmonton. Many more Catholic immigrants were looking for a place to stay in or around Edmonton, and Tye acted as some kind of contact man. He was looking for work and housing for many young families that entered Edmonton around that time. The result was that Tye and I walked great distances from one neighborhood to the next to find housing for the incoming families.

This was not always as easy as you may think. We would be asking for rooms to rent in some place or another.

Rooms would be available, sure enough, but then came the inevitable question: "Do these young folks have children?"

The rooms would not be rented if the family had children. It was as simple and as cruel as that.

It was then that I decided that I would not want to rent a house under circumstances like that! This had the result that I ended up building four houses over the coming years. I did not want to be caught in the renter's trap where every little thing the children do might set of a conflict that's embarrassing for a landlord and the person renting the house. It may also have made a difference in my stand on the location of the church in Rocky not all that much later. I was concerned that our young people might be a nuisance to the people that were living around there. And the young people of that day have been a nuisance on several occasions, but that's another story. I also decided at that time that I would never try to raise a family in the city!

Bricklayer wages were good in those days to the point that one bank teller remarked to me that she was jealous of the kind of money printed out on my paycheck, but Tye still was not satisfied with the money that we were taking in, and he was looking for still more income. He lined up some houses in snob hills where the very rich live. We would go cutting grass and do the landscaping for a supplementary income. It seemed that Tye never would be satisfied no matter how much we brought home in cash money. This was not the best side of him, but he has shown a way different side in later days when I lived on my own farm in Rocky.

Edmonton was a cold and windy city with wind blowing in icy blasts around the skyscrapers, and I never felt really warm in this cold climate of the gate to the north. I should have bought more warm clothing to make me more comfortable in these situations. Instead I walked around with plenty of money in my pocket without spending a nickel—I wanted to bring it all home because the family might need it!

I traveled from building to building in the cold heart of Edmonton with money in my pocket and feeling cold most of the time. The brickwork itself was interesting and varied. We worked on a fire hall one week and on a church or beer parlor the next. It was also an insecure existence, since we were going from one boss to the other, never long in one place.

Some considered me to be an excellent tradesman, while I was just one of the crowd in other places. The saving work mode that Tommy had taught me made an impression on many tradesmen I worked with using Tommy's little tricks and innovations. It was this fact that set me apart from many other bricklayers, but bricklaying was an insecure existence and only good in the summer months. Most bricklayers would be sent home in the winter with no income at all.

A young guy was a foreman on the last job just before Christmas. He was very insecure but had the privileged position that he was the son of one of the bosses. This is what got him the position of foreman when he was not ready for that at his age.

He kept worrying about getting a "pig in the wall," an expression for a condition where the brickwork of an old and that of a new building don't match up.

He was plenty worried, and none of the other guys knew what to do either. Finally, they asked the Dutchman as a last resort! I explained the situation to them and showed them that it was really quite simple if they followed certain procedures. That did it! They were on easy streets again and did not need the stupid Dutchman anymore! I was like the poor old man who saved the city by sound advice promptly forgotten when the enemy was gone . . . The boy himself was grateful, but that did not mean that he would look after my interest any more than before. I was to find that out in short order.

The job was half finished, and we were all laid off. All work would cease until further notice. We walked home with the young fellow and his young friends in the company of some other older workmen. We even had a very animated conversation for a block or so. Then the boy said that he had to turn off in a side street. He went right back to work! I found that out not all that much later. Not that it mattered that much to me then. It was getting close to Christmas, and I longed to go home.

My girlfriend would be waiting for me in the grand district of Rocky Mountain House. I would also see the farm that the family had bought after leaving the fertile and inhospitable plains of Iron Springs.

A Greyhound bus made its way to the upcoming city of Red Deer. Another bus with the final destination of Rocky was waiting to trundle me over one of the roughest gravel roads that I had traveled up to that very day. The country appeared more desolate by the mile as we traveled along in some thirty-below weather into a winter wonderland of snow and more snow.

"This wonderland was some long ways from the winter wonderland of Bing Crosby!" You can take my word for that!

The trees seemed to come at us, mile after mile, with no letup in sight. Neither was there any traffic in the whole fifty miles from Red Deer to Rocky. A light of a remote farmhouse could be seen very dimly here and there with great gaps of trees and more snow-covered trees. No fences could be seen—"nothing." We might drop off the end of the world any moment by the looks of things.

This is the way that I was mangled to the grand country of Rocky.

Several young teenagers sat in the back of the bus and a few older women with their children. Beside them sat a number of fierce-looking Indians in the front of the bus. Those people were the only participants in this fearsome adventure for a long way, and the end was not in sight.

"Not by a long shot." I feared for my life more than once in the next hour or so, since the bus went through impossible antics to overcome the different obstacles on the road between Rocky and Red Deer. It was a really mangled company that finally ended in Rocky.

The town itself was not all that mind-boggling either. It appeared like a one-horse town with some ramshackle buildings thrown together on the hillside not far from the foothills leading into the mighty Rocky Mountains. The town itself had almost no appeal for this little boy when he stepped off the bus and headed for the main store where a cousin of ours was working.

It was "Red Marinus," our old neighbor from Holland. It was almost closing time when I got there, and Marinus was anxious to go home.

I had walked along to the rough wooden counter over the creaky hardboard floor and made my way around all kinds of boxes and crates standing in great diversity all over the store, all but hiding the familiar face of good old Marinus. I would have liked to make a little conversation about old times and about the new country that I was about to enter, but Marinus was not at liberty to do much talking of any kind. Jobs were hard to get and even harder to keep, so he gave me some hasty instructions about the whereabouts of my family.

This was my first time in Rocky, and I did not know where I was or where I was going. His directions were to go up the hill and straight ahead, just follow Main Street up the hill. As simple as that! Very simple indeed. I followed the directions to a tee. Right up the hill and down Frisco Road I went. Further and further away from home.

Trouble was, I did not know this and kept going and going for hours on end, but nothing looked even close to the kind of scenery explained to me by the family and friend Marinus. There was supposed to be a graveyard somewhere, but all that I could see were trees and more trees all along that lonesome road. Nothing came even close to the descriptions of dear old Marinus. It was hopeless, and I finally decided to turn back.

There was not a car in sight, not even a farmhouse or little shed. No light could be seen anywhere, and it was getting colder and colder. The town of Rocky was pitch-dark when I got back there, and not a soul was in sight. Everyone had gone home. It was close to Christmas, and the folks had been anxious to get to the warm surroundings of family and friends.

Another road was angling off a little to the right of Main Street, and I started following that one. This might just be the one that Marinus had been talking about. It was getting colder and colder all the time, close to thirty below.

My bag of bricklayer tools was starting to weigh like a ton, and I was in great danger of getting frostbitten, but I decided to carry on. There did not seem to be anything else I could do. I had been reading a book once with the title *The Eternal Forest*. I was reminded of that in that cold but glorious night of 1950.

The forest was crowding into the road on all sides, but the sky above seemed to reach in all eternity. I could see for miles ahead over a moon-shaped road that seemed to have no horizon and no end. It was so bright that the trees were casting shadows of giant proportions, and the sky itself seemed to take on a pathway to eternity.

It was in this eerie landscape that I approached the landmark pointed out by my elusive friend Marinus—a graveyard just to the east of Rocky! That's the place I was supposed to pass. It was so cold by then that the trees cracked open with the sound of gunshots due to the frost that forced the moisture in the tree s to expand beyond the breaking point. The moonlight cast weird shadows around the graveyard, and a light mist could be seen swirling around the distant gravestones.

The coyotes were howling and coming closer and closer. The lonesome traveler felt very ill at ease. Fact is I was plumb scared in that bright but lonesome night. It seemed as if I was a lost soul all by himself with no place to go.

Never a car in sight in all the hours I spent on the road. I was getting so very tired and started looking for a place to lie down for just a little while. Just a little while! It was around that time that I decided that I would try one more farm. After that I would return to a haystack not far from the road. Just to lie down and rest! It would have my last resting place if I had followed through on that decision—but the Lord was good to me, and the next farm was the right one. I had made it home close to midnight!

It was not a happy camper that entered the door of that one-story farm building two miles out of Rocky. More than a dozen smiling faces were beaming in my direction when I entered that room. None of them seemed to have the slightest idea of the ordeal that I just went through. It seemed that they did not care even if they had known! It is slightly amazing that a caring family could be so callous about the whole episode. It was thirty below after all!

There was always a big crowd at our home, and this evening was no exception. Adolf's girlfriend had come in on the same bus as Jo, and the whole clan was gathered around the airtight stove, while the women were busy in the kitchen. Everyone was counting on a great Christmas, and they had a great time among themselves to the point that they must have forgotten me! It would not have been so nice if they had found me later, stiff as a doornail in the haystack of the neighbors. You can take my word for that!

I am not kidding! It was as serious as that, but nobody seemed to realize the danger of the situation. How callous can you get?

We lived in a wood-framed house in those days, and the inside was also covered with wood paneling. A really old-fashioned round table with matching chairs added to the charm of the place, and only the old pump organ in the corner could make it complete. This instrument was put to good use often in the following years.

The coffeepot was always on, and some cooking was going on most of the time, while the room was filled with smoke, a little from the fire but mostly from the boys. Fact is we were smoking a can of tobacco a day, which is seven cans a week. That made thirty a month. We had a great pile of empty cans behind the house by the time the winter ended. We smoked like chimneys. Everyone had mastered the art of hand rolling the cigarettes while stories with unbelievable content were handwoven, or rather mouth-woven, through the fabric of smoke and confusion most of the evenings.

This evening was no exception. A blast of hot air hit me in the face when I opened the door of my future home. No one had the slightest idea how close I had come to the haystack at the neighbor's place, and I never told them either. Our family was a little careless often and plain ignorant at other times. They could have descended from the gypsies. I think that even the gypsies would have shown a little more care.

It happened often that I had to walk home from work, first in Iron Springs and later in Rocky. I had to walk long distances without assistance. Time to get groceries or as little as a tin of tobacco could always be found, and the old truck would be wheeling to town.

Nobody ever seemed to know the time that I would be arriving. Curious, is it not? Henry would be hoofing the way home again, often in the company of brother Bert in later days. My parents simply did not seem to understand that it would have helped us a great deal if they had taken a little extra care for us in that respect. Life was hard enough as it was.

It was altogether different from life in the city. No electricity or any warm or cold water, and, worst of all, no inside toilet. A coal oil lamp was giving us light in the evening, and that lamp was an institution in itself. It was quite a ritual to get that light going. The lamp was filled with high-test gasoline, and then the little hand pump was used to fill the little tank with air. The heated gasoline mix was blown into a mantle connected to the top of the lantern, and extra care had to be taken that the brittle mantle material did not get damaged. A match was lit to the mantle, and, plop, we would have light on the subject matter of the evening.

It was not simple and could be dangerous. Most folks had a healthy respect for those lanterns, since they could explode if not handled properly.

So far so good! Light was half the battle, but then followed the problem of heat! We heated the house with a wood-burning airtight stove in those days. This was very messy but extremely cozy when the sun went down and all life turned inside both human and animal life! I like to say that airtight stoves are an invention of a person with an evil mind, if you ask me, but nobody asked me. These stoves cook the front, while the back is slowly freezing before you know what is happening. There was an alternative. A person could turn around and warm his back, but you would miss out on all the fun that way!

A very unhealthy situation at best. We as early settlers would be freezing at night unless you kept the stove going of course. None of the family was brave enough to put fire in the stove after you are just warming up under the warm blankets after a hard day at work. We would wake up with frost on the blankets on many winter mornings.

A layer of frost had accumulated from the outgoing breath of the unwary sleeper. Even the greatest coward is forced out of bed by the necessities of nature, be it a large or a small errand forced in your way. You had to go to the outhouse for that, and that was real torture when there was a cold wind blowing.

This useful little building was located over a hole in the ground, about four or five feet deep. It all depended on the guy who had to dig that hole. It was a workable solution, but there was one problem. The produce of about twelve people, give or take a few, was piling up in a hurry to such an extent that it started to look like the Tower of Babel.

HANK OPDENDRIES

It came clear out of the hole. The stuff froze just as fast as it was put down. It was at that point that Dad would come to the rescue with a bag full of lye. This usually worked like a charm, but then came the day that he spilled some on the toilet seat. One woman became the beneficiary of that free gift. Her husband had to look at the blisters the same evening.

The facilities for a little get-together with the girlfriend were virtually nonexisting. Jo and I had to go outside in the cold if we wanted to talk under four eyes, standing in the cold around the corner or sitting in the cold on a haystack. The choice was limited. I tried to bring the warming element into the situation by stealing my mother's overcoat, an overcoat made out of very coarse material. The necking went as planned, but my mother was in for an unpleasant surprise the next morning when she made ready to go to church. Almost half the haystack was hanging around in her overcoat. Such were the times we lived in!

Nowadays the young people have cars to complement the romancing, but it might seem a little strange. There were not many cars in those beginning days, and hardly any of them had antifreeze. The job of filling the radiator with hot water was enough to cool down any desire for a little adventure. Another factor that slowed me was the fact that none of our units had a thermostat so that it was colder inside the truck than outside. Cold air would blow along over the inside of the windshield, and our exercise was never fierce enough to defrost the window. We were coldhearted lovers by the looks of it!

Heat was a problem in those days—heat, or rather the lack of it. We would go to the bush with our horses and cut some firewood and pull that home. You should know that we had progressed into a two-horse farm in that beginning year.

We had one horse by the name of Champion. This little horse had been relieved of his manhood by someone incompetent. The job had not been done properly so that we could not build a fence high enough to keep the dear animal inside when there was a woman in the neighborhood. He would clear the fence with inches to spare and go on a mission impossible. We had to keep him locked up in the barn always. This was really too bad for the horse and for us.

Brother Bert took him along to the planer mill often, and it was a sight to behold when he came barreling around the corner, he and the horse going full tilt. The horse and Bert had somewhat the same nature. They were both a little stuck-up and made a perfect set on the mantelpiece.

It looked as if Dad loved that horse more than any one of us. They practically lived together. Dad would have him in front of the wagon to haul hay in the summer and put him in front of the sled in the winter to haul wood. Dad was where the horse went and vice versa!

Our father had the best time of his life in those later years. He had things he never could have dreamed of his own farm with his own horse and some livestock to take care of. He even had his own car in the last years of his life. The matter of money was not all that pressing either in those days so that he could live fairly well and carefree.

We had our troubles to be sure, but some troubles were of our own making. Other difficulties came over us to keep us on our toes. Some of these things can be told, and others are better kept out of the limelight of public scrutiny.

Strange things could, and often would, happen in those pioneer days. The boys told me that they caught one of Dad's heifers. The poor animal was in bad shape. A piece of wood, almost a fence post, was sticking out its abdomen just as if she had been running with great speed to get away from some animal, a wolf or a cougar or some other wild beast. The poor thing had to be destroyed because gangrene had already set in. There was no hope for the animal anymore, and it was a reminder that we had a lot to learn about animals, tame and wild.

We were told to be careful when walking in the bush. Many bears were roaming in the district, and bears can be very dangerous when provoked. A grizzly bear can outrun a full-grown horse. Their speed is incredible, although they look clumsy at the best of times. The cougar was another dangerous animal. They could lie on the limb of a tree so that this animal could not be distinguished from the surroundings at the best of times.

The animal could pounce on the unwary traveler and hurt or even kill a person before the guy knew what hit him. This is what we were told in those days. I have never met any cougars or any person who had been attacked, but there is little doubt that they are some very dangerous animals indeed. Wolves have the name of being dangerous, but I have never heard of anyone who was hurt by a wolf. This is in contrast to the bear. They have attacked and even eaten human beings. Coyotes are still very common when I am writing this. They are not that dangerous, unless they can separate a weak animal from a herd of cows. These coyotes will gang up and kill the outside calf or sheep, giving it half a chance.

Horses are the farmer's best friends, but even they can be very dangerous if they are approached unaware. We were told to talk to the horses always as a warning that people were in the neighborhood. A horse will never hurt anyone if it's treated respectfully and if it's behaving normally.

Machinery is the number-one enemy of the farmer, with the bull a close second. There is a saying among the farmers that a tame bull usually hurts people. This is true enough! A young bull may get pampered and cuddled when it is young and never act bad for years on end. Then he will attack for no reason at all. Many farmers have found that out and been left crippled for life—after they woke up in the hospital—never to be the same again.

The cows will be just as dangerous when it is calving time. Several farmers end in the hospital almost every year. They did only one thing wrong! The farmer came too close to the cow after calving, and the protective animal would attack just in case something or someone might hurt her newborn calf. I ought to know! It happened to me!

One of our cows had calved, and I bent over to check the calf. This was an absolute no-no. The mother attacked me without warning, throwing me to the ground while it was butting me with the head until the air was driven out of my lungs. My heart was going like a trip hammer, and I ended with bruised ribs and a few other injuries.

It happened that I was one of the lucky ones. It could have been much worse. Most cows will eat their own afterbirth as a remainder of the wild state. All traces of birth had to disappear so that no wild animal would come visiting. Strange but true that this has to be so in most of our domestic animal world.

It was in this environment that I spent the winter of 1950 in Rocky. Most of my brothers had found work in the little town of Alexo and in the mines of Nordegg later. The wages were not all that bad, and they might have had a good enough income all around if the work had been a little more secure. The brothers were knocked from pillar to post in fact—work on one day and at home the next. This would not have been so bad if they had been a little closer to home, but the brothers had to live in a bunkhouse when they worked the mines of Alexo. We heard a lot of hair-raising stories about the miners—mostly Italians—who worked in the mines in those days.

Those men had their own way of doing things, and the boys did not always fall in with the unwritten status quo of the mining population. The brothers did not see eye to eye with the foreman in charge of the trip—a place where the coal is loaded. The dignity of the brothers was offended to the point that they just sat down on the job. The whole loading platform came to a standstill and everything else further down the line.

The union job steward came down in a flash to calm the troubled waters, explaining to the boys that disagreements had to be settled in the union way! The job steward should be notified whenever problems arose. The poor man left shaking his head after he had a little run-in with our brother Adolf. He did not know what to make of the crazy Dutchman! He was in good company. The foreman did not, and neither did anyone else. Alexo was a most interesting place, and I had the opportunity to visit that place when a friend of Dad wanted to buy a load of coal. He asked me along for company. It was most interesting, and we were even invited in the washroom of the miners, since no one was in the least bit inhibited about the nakedness of the mining population.

Everyone was wandering around, naked as a jaybird, and nobody seemed to care! There were men in that place in all shapes and forms. Some were almost as wide as they were tall in contrast to men as skinny as beanpoles. Others had king-size beer bellies. They looked like little teakettles come to life in an unseemly manner.

Everyone was as black as the coal that they had worked in. The white men returned slowly to the present world as the water rinsed the black coal dust off the many variations of human bodies. Most people were honest, but there is always a bad apple in the crowd. It was for that reason that everyone had his own lock and key to a chain reaching to the ceiling of the washhouse. Each miner would tie his clothes and other belongings in a bundle and pull it to the ceiling. The chain could be locked with a padlock, and the belongings would be secure until the miner lowered the chain and retrieved his own belongings at quitting time. I had seen the very same setup in the mines in Holland before the war.

A very sensible way of storing the miners' belongings in all the dirt and coal dust that were always present in and around the mine.

My memories of the Alexo mine are not all that clear, since I did not have to work there, but I do remember a car in that town. This car had an engine like a locomotive, since this engine had eight cylinders in a row, and it must have been six or seven feet long. Some important person of the mine was the sole owner of that contraption.

He was welcome to it, I may add. Parts must have been hard to come by because this is the only straight eight I have ever seen. Even so, this was not the only antique in that town—not by a long shot—not counting in the people of that town.

One Dutch boy was the proud owner of a car with a straight six. Beautiful to look at, but one problem marred the perfection of that jalopy—it lost the backup gears! The owner of that car had to always stay on the straight and narrow. He was absolutely stuck when he ran into a road with no exit!

This is fairly well what happened when he ran into trouble halfway to Rocky. He could not go back or forward when his friends found him the next morning in the company of a woman of uncertain virtues. He had driven in a narrow road with no exit, making it a one-way trip with no way to turn around. It was no wonder that this boy became the talk of the small Dutch community. Not many believed his excuses that he had ended in that location by accident!

It turned out that the work in the Alexo mine did not last, and the brothers went for work to the little mining town of Nordegg. This is a little town resting against the foothills of the Rocky Mountains.

The mighty mountains are embracing this town with possessiveness, unearthly and assuring simultaneously. Summer and winter exchange the same sense of belonging to the weary person that has to seek refuge in the close embrace of that little mining town. Little romantic company houses in colorful setting follow the road in helter-skelter fashion, dictated by the crusty cinder road winding up the hill to the hospital.

A recreation building with a dance hall, and behind that the weathered outbuildings of the mine site completed the picturesque sight of that little town. One of the most inviting churches of the west was resting against the bottom of the hill. The surrounding countryside is undulating in harmonious fashion up to the towering mountain range—the gateway to one of the most beautiful scenarios of Western Canada.

The overpowering mountains make everything look small and insignificant. How great must the Creator be! All this glorious might and power rest in the hollow of His hand, and He can shape it and reshape it according to His slightest wish!

This reminds us of the story of an unbelieving person who asked once, "How long is eternity?"

And a wise old farmer told the following story, "There was a little bird that came every year to the same mountain. It would sharpen its little beak on the top of that mountain. The mountain will wear down over the length of time if bird after bird keeps up this ritual!"

"Will that be the end of eternity?" the blasphemer asked.

"No," the farmer replied, "less than one second of eternity!"

Your heart can only respond with adoration and say, "My God! How great You are! You made all this."

How mighty is He who makes the clear mountain stream to tumble over the rocky bottom, while it is shimmering in unnumbered variations through vales and streambed, over falls and through gullies, shaping and reshaping much of the creation in ever-changing adoration of the Mighty One.

It was in this little town of Nordegg that a few Dutch immigrants tried to hang on to their old country values: "A job and a half in the middle of the rough-and-tumble population of this rough mining town."

The work was very demanding, but the pay was fairly good. This made the difference between going or staying. Members of my family had to work with horses that had not seen daylight in many years. Total blindness was the result for those poor animals. The boys were feeling lost at times, much the same as these abused creatures, ghosts of the underground shafts of the Nordegg mines.

Some horses had a mean disposition, since they had not always been treated with kindness and consideration. Care had to be exercised always when working with these horses. Some would kick back at the least provocation, and others would bite in the direction of the person who had to work with these bitter-disposed animals. It is a known fact that the bite of a horse is very slow healing and very painful. More than one miner has found that out over the years. Added to that was the danger of runaway cars. This was always a possibility, and this increased the danger that the brothers had to work under.

They did not have an easy life, but there was one great consolation in this kind of life. The evenings were always cozy and filled with lots of fun and good food. I can well imagine that they must have had many a tall story when they were on visits in one house or another. I should know! I heard some over the years, not always suitable for repeating though!

The powers that be had decided that I did not have to go to the mine. I had spent enough time away from home already and deserved a place in the house, for the winter months anyway. I went to work in a planer mill on the other side of Rocky. My share of trouble was waiting for me over in that place, and those troubles would keep me more than occupied during the winter. I ended up working under the direction of my younger brother Bert. Life sure is strange at times! He was running the mill, and I had to pick up the rough boards in the yard. A very backbreaking job! It was all very unorganized at that mill, since the lumber trucks were allowed to dump the rough lumber in one great pile, boards from every size and description. Several feet of snow would mix in with the lumber piles, and others loads were dumped on top before the first ones were cleared away. It turned into a mess beyond description. Even the lengths of the lumber were never alike.

An order would come in for two-by-fours. We had to pick over the whole pile to fish out the proper size. Another order would come in for two-by-sixes, and the whole process was repeated. We often had to turn over a dozen truckloads to fill one order. This is how we wrestled through the days in clothes altogether insufficient for this kind of cold weather.

In ordinary leather shoes soaked with cold snow water before the day was half done, no amount of heat can cancel the chilling effect of cold feet. It works through the whole body, and a person will still be cold right in front of a red-hot stove.

The day would start at eight in the morning, and my feet would be cold at half past eight, never to get warm again until quitting time at six in the evening, and all this suffering had to be endured for minimum wages. Insult was added to injury, since we still would have to wait several hours for our paycheck on Saturday.

Twelve o'clock was quitting time, but we would not get our pay until one or even later if we were lucky. But that was only the beginning. The greatest embarrassment was to come yet. We had to cash the check in a grocery store, but most of the clerks would take off when they saw us coming with our checks. They were not worth the paper they had been written on, and we had quite a hassle getting the checks validated.

There was not a clerk in the store who wanted to take the chance of cashing a rubber check, and I can't say that I could blame them. Life has strange twists and turns . . . I had gone from riches to rags again, from top wages as a bricklayer to the bottom of the ladder!

Our employer was one of the brightest men in the machine-building business. He was reckoned as the best in town. You could be assured that anything he fixed would be running just as he had planned it without any readjustment to speak of. This does not mean that everything was in the best of shape! It just means that he could repair anything running on wheels or bearings, and the risk he would be willing to take were out of this world. The resaw motor was a big old Massy-Harris tractor motor that he had rebuilt so that it could drive the band saw, while antifreeze was obsolete in his book.

He had ordinary diesel fuel in the radiator of that motor, and it worked like a charm, if the engine did not catch fire. Nobody knows what would have happened if this had happened! The motor had to be started with a swing handle, and that was always adventurous, for the machine would kick back like a horse when the spark backfired. The handle would throw a person back like a rag doll when that happened. There were a lot of dangers in that infernal place, but we were more scared of that motor than anything else in the whole yard. This machine was so bad that it got the employer himself caught in an almost deadly embrace. The boss was trying to fix the rollers that feed the lumber into the circular saw, and his foot got caught in those rollers while he was working on this.

The rollers grabbed his feet, and he was inexorably drawn into the hungry teeth of the roaring circular saw. It seemed like a certain deal that his foot would be cut in two halves before anyone could do anything.

Brother Bert was fast acting enough to pull the stop switch on the motor, and this would stop the motor just at the last moment. One of the older workers tried to be smarter yet and pulled the clutch. This set the machine freewheeling along so that it still would take too long to stop the rollers. The boss saw the danger and screamed in great desperation to push the clutch back in so that the motor that had come to a standstill would stop the saw blade. Bert did as requested, and the saw came to a standstill with the foot less than an inch away from the saw. The boss was almost green in his face when he noticed his foot approaching the saw without letup. Small wonder! Bert could not do much wrong with his employer after that episode, and that is not hard to understand either.

I had my moments too as a forklift driver. The front of the forklift would get top heavy when I had too big a load on the front teeth. The driver's end would rise higher until I was almost vertical to the ground, about fifteen feet in the air. Part of the load would slide off, and the pull of gravity would restore lift and driver to a more normal way of operating.

This was the normal way of things until the day that I had an interlocking load of boards on the front teeth. The load did not slide off like it was supposed to. I went straight into the air to the highest position, and it was at that point that the whole load slid off at once. The poor driver came down with a crash that could be heard in the next county!

The generator broke off the motor, and I had a few bruised ribs. The boss inspected the damage, and he was real put out over the generator! My condition did not seem to matter that much. The motor was important. I was dispensable in his opinion.

But that was not all that was wrong in that place! The people working there were just as lopsided as the machinery. We had a man who was always picking on religion. He seemed to have a thing about that! He was not bad in himself, but he might have had a secret longing to have someone convince him of the truth in religion and of the real meaning of the Bible. We never found that out.

Bert and I would say our prayer before eating our food in the afternoon in spite of his sarcasm, and that could be very annoying and biting at times! Until the day that we sat in his shed on a nice winter day when the whole story started all again. I should explain that the airtight stove was going, and we had to open a window to get a little cool air in the room.

We had just said our prayers, and this man started again, true to form. The subject was an article that he had brought along with a photo of some unknown tribe of little people. They had little tails on their backside—proof positive that they had descended from the apes, according to Clark, the man in question. Man was created out of species in the sea and other matter, and we were a bunch of fools that we could believe in the stories of man being created, etc. He went on and on until I had enough for that day. I was in a goofy mood and a little reckless.

So I said, "Clark, what are you eating there?"

"An orange," he said promptly.

"Are you sure that it is an orange?" I asked him. "It might be a banana or maybe an ostrich egg, a melon, or a potato. Your mother must have told you that it was an orange, but that does not prove a thing. You don't want to believe everything that somebody tells you. You believe that you have a nose in front of your head, but it could be an eye or an ear. You believe all those things because somebody told you so."

Old man Clark turned red in the face and became more upset with every word I said. I should have known the danger signs but went on like that just a little too long. Clark jumped to his feet and came after me with murder in his eyes. There was no time to lose, and I had to jump out of the window to save my frail little being from the wrathful hands of Clark the avenger. The other guys were all a little white around the nose.

We had never seen him so mad in all the time that we worked there. He turned out to be just another person who liked to poke fun at everyone else but was unable to handle a little fun at his expense.

Clark was not a mean person, just a little unreasonable.

Some other guys in that outfit were indecent and cruel in the way that they treated another man who had left the Old Country and his wife had stayed behind. This man had been away from the Old Country for more than three years when he got the news that his wife had a baby. A feat somewhat unlikely after a separation of at least three years' time! He was so unwise as to tell his problem at the mill, and this sent off a wave of pestering and jeering by his fellow coworkers. Questions were asked if he had sent it by mail and got his wife in child by that process and many more lewd suggestions. One suggestion was even more degrading than the other in an endless succession of abuse.

I really felt sorry for that man, since nothing could be said or done to stop these other fellows from abusing the man's feelings for many days until the novelty finally wore off. A person is almost ashamed to belong to the human race in situations like that.

The onslaught of the devil in swear words and filthy language is hard to imagine for people who have never had to work in places like the one I was just describing. This was mild by some other places where I had to work. I have known many people who could not say even one sentence without a swear word.

We were fortunate in a way that we had to keep working most of the day. We had to listen to this kind of abuse in the breaks when there was no other place to go. One of those breaks came very unexpectedly.

A heavy fan with blades of a half inch thick and about a foot square was moving the shavings and sawdust off the planer in a sturdy stream of air and shavings—that is to say, until that particular day. One blade broke off in that fan and got caught in the rotating rest of the broken contraption.

It was like World War II all over again! This fan was turning at a thousand or more revolutions a minute, and the broken blade was thrown into the heavy casing with such force that the whole mill was shivering from beginning to end. The little fellow with the unfaithful wife who was feeding boards was running so fast that we thought he was never going to stop. To be truthful, we were not very far behind him. We were all saved from serious injury because the casing of that fan was at least a half inch thick.

You will understand from these stories that we never had a dull moment. Bert and I have never understood why our family could not find a way to pick us up when we came home tired after a day of very heavy work. Almost never!

Bert and I would be hoofing it home too tired to walk straight, and it happened more than once that our little sister was passing us on her way to town just to get a pound of butter or some other little errand—things that could easily have been worked out in a way we would have had a ride home.

The family never seemed to remember that we were on the way in. It was up to Bert and me to find a solution to this problem, and the two desperados started to look in the most unlikely places for help in their desperate situation. And sure enough, a neighbor of ours was willing to give us a ride home, and that seemed the ideal solution, except one minor detail! The man was in the habit of picking up a beer in the lower bar. Bert and I would be sitting in the truck box in front of the bar for hours on end every evening. It became debatable as to which was the worst of the two evils—to walk all the way or to wait all the way! The fact that the man was sitting in the bar poking fun at us, in all likelihood, was even more discouraging.

We came home in this truck one evening, and the low-lying road before the graveyard was one lake of water. We will never know if the man did it as a challenge or out of necessity, but he went through that body of water at top speed, and Bert and I got a free but an unwanted bath of ice-cold snow water.

But there was light at the end of the tunnel even so. Bert and I were allowed to take the half-ton to work. We were on easy streets now! Our happiness was so great that we just had to share it with other people less fortunate than we were. That is how we caught up to three of those unfortunates on our way home from work. This was a situation that could not be ignored, since it was common courtesy in those days to pick up any hitchhiker forced to walk for one reason or another.

Those three fellows were walking on the road and trying to thumb their way to an unknown destination, a place that my brother and I would bring a lot closer in our well-meaning efforts. We decided to give them a ride, with disastrous results! I had to step out of the cab to let the three guys in, and they turned out to be drunk out of their collective skulls. These jokers piled in that cab, and I was standing outside with no room left to sit inside. We squeezed them together like sardines in a can, and I managed to crawl inside.

It was too bad that I had to sit right on top of one of those inhibited beer-loving boys. The result was that the guy under me relieved himself in an unexpected way—he dirtied his pants. There must have been too much pressure when I sat on top of him so that I literally squeezed the stuff out of him. The smell was unbearable and our choice limited. We had to bring them the distance until we could unload them in town. I must have squeezed him dry by the time we got them into town. I know that this sounds like a strong story, but it is true nevertheless! It was also a strong-smelling story, I may add!

I picked up an old Indian hitchhiker in later years, also with the best of intentions, and this joker refused to leave my car once he was inside it. He made me drive all over town two or three times. It was so bad that I finally stopped in front of the police barracks in desperation. It was there that I persuaded him that he either get out or be hauled out by the police! One will learn by doing!

We were catching on fast to the dos and don'ts of life in the truck driver's world, and we progressed to the point that we could take our two-ton Fargo truck to work. This truck was next to impossible to start in the hard winter weather. This called for strong medicine, and we had to use strong measures.

The ritual went something like follows every morning!

First, we had to fill the truck and a little McCormick tractor with hot water. We had to steel the hot washing water from the women to fill the radiator. Then we would turn the swing handle on the little tractor till it started coughing and running with a lot of sputtering and backfiring. The big truck was jacked off the ground next with one rear wheel. A drive belt had to be laid over the rear wheel and the tractor pulley in the next sequence of operation. The clutch of the truck was pushed in. The tractor pulley turned the rear wheel of the truck. The clutch of the truck was slowly released, and the truck motor would slowly start to turn over. The truck might sputter and backfire and then thunder to life—if we were lucky! The whole procedure would take close to an hour. It is quite understandable that Bert and I were tired out before we even started working in the mill!

We were pioneers in every sense of the word! We had to rumble to town over roads with rock-filled gravel of unbelievable proportions. Many pieces of rock were as big as a good-sized football and very unforgiving, to put it mildly. This was the undoing of a little Austin car that came from the direction of town one evening. The guy was driving much too fast and rolled over twice in a row after he had hit one of those boulders on the road. The car was facing back to town where it came from after that adventure, and the guy kept on driving right back to where he came from! This is absolutely a true story. I have seen this with my own two little beady eyes! And life rolled on with no warning of what would happen in the next turn of the wheel.

Threshing was an activity shared by the whole neighborhood. The neighbor from across the road had a threshing machine, and according to tradition, all close neighbors were expected to participate in the threshing crew. Anyone shirking his duty was banned from the neighborhood. Something that never happened to my knowledge! It was along those lines that I was volunteered to do my duty in the neighborhood community. The little tractor was started, and we went to the folks living to the east of us. There was a lot of good-natured bantering going on over a cup of coffee (or something stronger, if you asked for it). After that we were off to the grain fields.

Old uncle George was in front of me with his two-horse team—a team that was very freaky and hard to handle because it was pampered and fed grain by the old man without doing any work!

I noticed that the old man was a little overexcited and had a tough time of the whole threshing operation. I wanted to do a good deed seeing this and decided to help him unload his wagon with oat bundles. I had to wait anyway!

I jumped behind him on the wagon and started pitching bundles in the loading chute of the threshing machine. The old man coughed a few times when the load was half finished and then sat down in front of me. I never realized what was going on and kept pitching bundles. It was at that point that the machine operator started to wave with his arms to catch my attention and threw the machine to a standstill.

By then it was too late already. The old man had passed away of a stroke. The woman of the house came running along with the whiskey bottle with the words "Maybe a shot of whiskey will bring him around!" But a shot of whiskey did not help anymore in this situation. Uncle had passed away for good!

Events like that make a deep impression on a person, and I was no exception. A passing away like this is a shaking event and a sure reminder that we are not here to stay.

The winters in Canada are also a reminder of the infinite depth of space and of the entire universe. People who have never seen the winter night in Canada and of the Canadian Rockies can't begin to understand Canada and its people. The stillness of the Canadian night is beyond description. I have seen those nights that the pure blanket of the winter snow seemed to blot out anything but the majesty of nature supreme. Pine and spruce trees next to the poplar tree seemed to reach out vainly to the impossible dream of human wishes to a mastery of power invested in the Creator of all! There is nothing in this world that He cannot say, "It is mine!"

He will always be in full control no matter what the little creature here on earth may say or think—those little ones who are trying in vain to reach into the powers and resources that the Creator has laid in this creation from the foundation of the world. The human being who is boasting power and might trying to build another tower of Babylon, they will only reach that pinnacle until the Ruler of all will say, "It is enough!" And time will be no more!

The northern lights will send its beams of light over the winter nights, frozen in a stillness that no human can disperse—the light that still proclaims the mighty power of God the Creator! The main driving force in our lives, and my own personally, has always been the unshakable faith that God is ever present—has been and always will be!

I have believed from my very early childhood that not one hair from my head will fall without the will of my heavenly Father. I know that my Redeemer liveth, and although my body be eaten by the worms, yet in my flesh I shall see God. I shall behold Him and no other! I shall see Him and no other.

God is equally present on the wedding as in the funeral home. He has proven that at the wedding of Kana! How could it be any other way? If God has made the tear ducts and the muscles for laughter, should they not be used if they were created in the first place for just that purpose?

I am not exaggerating when I say that I have used my talent to make people laugh much in the same way as Red Skeleton has done. Some people laughed so hard at times that they could not control themselves. They came later to shake hands with me and told me that a great load was lifted off their shoulders for just a little while. They had received new strength to go on to the days ahead with new courage and a renewed optimism.

It is strange, but some members of the drama clubs that I belonged to had the opinion that only an evening of drama could be opened with prayer—a comical play was not fitting to be opened with prayer. Nothing is further from the truth! A comical play should not be acted out if a person can't say a prayer beforehand. A person should never be found in a place where he couldn't face the Lord if He decides to come and visit that place.

There is another evil that I have seen under the sun! I have seen very dedicated people involved in the building of the church pushing their point at the expense of others who were not as fluent in the powerhouse of windy debates. The Lord said that "the meek shall inherit the earth!" I believe that this also applies in these situations! I have seen more sinning in these places than in many a wedding party where the proceedings were not always within the bounds of good taste. I had to go a little in detail about these viewpoints of absolute commitment because I believe that this life is but the Christian's journey to a life in eternity. Jesus paid for that journey and thus committed me to a life of service to my fellow man, empowered by His Spirit—a presence for which I pray every day of my life.

We would like to elaborate a little about the role that the Christian has to play in the life of clean and sound entertainment. It seems that the youth understood better than most how we were approaching the role of entertainment in our life. I have the feeling that many of those young folks were feeling instinctively that we were for real! The young people did not always feel too comfortable with the attitude of well-meaning people who always seemed to have the right words. But, alas, their actions did not always cover their words. Mark well the words seen in the above example because I know only too well that we all have the same shortfall when it comes to living holy! I will give an example without malice intended!

I was one of several boys' club leaders in later years. We realized that simple Bible instruction would not be enough to appeal to our young people. Another way had to be found if we wanted to get the point across that all our lives are dictated to the service of our Lord—not only in Bible class but also at work and very much so at play.

Our lives are an example for anyone around us who might be watching our way of serving Jesus—that is, be responsible in serving Jesus! This is what we tried to teach in those days, and to get the message across, we started making short weekend campouts to build a lasting relationship between counselors and boys. Much of our own time would be given in spite of the fact that times were very valuable to us as beginning farmers.

We also had to drive our own cars and supply our own gas and oil, a fact that was well noticed by most of the boys. They realized what we were trying to do. These boys realized full well the efforts we put into the commitment that we had taken upon us. They responded very well indeed when we instructed them in the way of life that calls for caring for the person next to them. They in turn were inclined to care for the person next to them even if they did not always understand or appreciate his attitude or motives.

This compares to the fact that I have known many ministers and teachers who will do nothing unless they are reimbursed for their efforts. It is small wonder that teens and older people listen politely then turn around, thinking, *Do after my words but not after my works!* There are many very dedicated professionals, but they seem to have missed out on this reality altogether—words are empty unless accompanied by works.

We better get back to our story!

There were several immigrant families already in the Rocky district when my family arrived in their new dwelling place during October 1950.

It is not my intent to mention any names. Contact First CRC in Rocky if you want further information on that!—some hardy families had settled in the district before we did. A large new family was more than welcome in this beginning group of people. Our welcome was friendly enough, but we ran headlong into the church politics of that day. Plans were in progress to build a new church, and that is where the trouble started. One group wanted to build in town and another group in the country. It seems that the fieldman of the district had expected to see a farm community developing in the direction of Eckville. This last sentence is hearsay—someone told me that later.

Our family landed into this dispute without any prior knowledge of the problem, and we really did not care either way. But it seemed that a vote was taken at that time regarding a church in town. The vote was a little unusual, to say the least. My father suggested another vote should be taken, and that vote fell in favor of a country church.

I doubt if anyone ever knew if this was the right move or not. But an argument has been brought forward—for many years after—that the church should have been in town for evangelism purposes. I do not know if that argument holds water. I know many churches that were built often in the middle of other cities that have no more and often much less influence on their surroundings! Evangelism calls for a different approach as far as I can judge.

Our young people were also a factor. To have them in the middle of town might have proven a little embarrassing. Those kids used to do some strange things and not always in line with the Canadian code of ethics. This could prove to be a problem to my way of thinking, since I lived and worked among the average Canadian, and I could form a reasonable good opinion about what the citizens in town were saying and thinking. We had our troubles as you can see, but it is amazing that all those people from so many different backgrounds and opinions still could find ways to work together for a common goal. We were inspired by a home missionary—Van Laar was his name.

"We are called to start a church here," he said.

That was easier said than done, since none of us had any money. Nevertheless, a church building should be our first priority.

"I came to tell you that if you seek first the things of the Kingdom, the rest shall be added unto you!" were the immortal words of Van Laar the minister.

One person responded that he was first responsible to his family. The farm had to come first. The rest of the meeting was most of one mind. They were called to build and would fulfill this commitment to the best of their ability. All those people had emigrated from Holland and were not allowed to take any money with them, a fact that should be well remembered! All of them were acting out of an empty wallet! This is even more remarkable, since they were divided about almost everything.

There were people from most provinces of Holland, and everyone wanted to do things as they were used to in the Old Country. There were too many chiefs and not enough Indians! And yet we built a church because we were walking by the power of the Spirit in spite of the divided opinions—which were not directed by God. The grace of God is indeed above all imagination! It was a close-knit group in spite of everything. No one had money to spare, and all had to work for a living.

One family came to church with horse and wagon, while others had to have a car or truck because they lived too far from town. One man came to church in an old Model T car. It had still a two-inch belt replacing a fan belt. That jalopy was a real antique even in those early days.

Our own family had to go to church in three shifts. The first group was way too early, and the second group a little bit early, while the last group came in around the middle of the sermon. This continued until we bought a 1928 Chevy car. Then we made it in two shifts.

Brother Adolf was the man who could play a little organ then. He was the guy who supplied the music for that reason only. Adolf was a good friend of the minister, and this man would overlook the shortfalls of Adolf's playing until the Sunday that he announced a song in the middle of the sermon.

The minister's intentions were good, but no music was forthcoming from behind the curtain that shielded organ and organist from the eyes of the faithful congregation. Van Laar repeated the demand for music and ripped the curtain aside to see what the holdup was. And here was brother Adolf fast asleep with both feet high up on the table, out to the realities of this cruel world. The whole congregations had great pleasure out of this unusual break in the service, and even the minister was making excuses for the unfaithful organ grinder by the name of Adolf the Great.

This was somewhat unusual but nothing compared to the time that Dolf joined forces with a policeman when both were making music in like manner—but that was later!

Several young couples joined the little community of "would-be" saints. This made the little get-together between the services even more joyful and a lot noisier because the young families were working vigorously on the future Jerusalem—there were many mothers with babies, and that set the stage for some interesting meetings mixed with pabulum and milk bottles. The children of that time were truly brought up in the church.

Those days might have been the best years of Rocky CRC, since nobody had any reason to be jealous because none of us had any possessions. It looked like the first Christian church with saints and sinners all in one batch!

Brother Bert was a farsighted person and was in touch with other religious people in the community because of that. One of these saints in blue jeans was an interesting man. He was supposed to be a minister of one of the spin-off churches—that made him trustworthy right from the start. This man did Bert a great favor! He sold Bert a beautiful panel truck.

The man told Bert in a great demonstration of trust, "This was one of the best cars that ever rolled off the assembly lines."

He really had an interest in Bert's well-being, and that's why he was willing to let that truck go at a sacrificial price! The deal was made, and brother Bert brought home this wonder on wheels with great pride of possession.

Nobody was allowed to touch that favored machine. He cleaned and polished it and then painted the proud slogan "Op den Dries and Sons" on the side of that panel truck. A trip to town was next on the list, and our brother drove that wonderwork to town, proud as a peacock.

It breaks my heart to tell you the rest of the story, but it is my painful duty to do so. The truck never got past the graveyard, and that's where "Op den Dries and Sons" was parked in the ditch, never to go on its own power again!

The pride of "Op den Dries and Sons" was no more! It was standing for many years in the weeds and the long grass behind the barn, a reminder of past glory and of things that might have been but did not come about. Another impossible dream has gone down in history!—but we never gave up! No, sir.

We persevered in spite of all setbacks. Fact is that we tried to fix everything so that many things ended in the trash heap long before its usefulness had ended.

"My boys fix everything!" said my dad one day. "Then it costs more!"

It was one of those occasions that his quiet wisdom came to the surface in a most colorful way of expression. We did wreck some machinery over the years—that is true. But we gained a lot of knowledge in the process, and that paid off handsomely in later years. We lived in the do-it-yourself days. We tried our hand at everything. A testimonial of this was that we were able to construct our own church building with the help of much free labor—an understanding banker—and some crafty dealings by the church leadership of those early days. Above all, it was the providence of God that provided us with the money and the means to start building.

Everyone was working with all hands to build up their farms in different places, but time for free labor at the church could always be found by hook or by crook. A local gravel pit supplied the sand and gravel for the building. We did not know then that this sand had a high content of clay, something that would prove costly in later years. We had to gain experience also in this matter. The clay has a tendency to eat the cement as years go by, and that makes much of the cement work brittle. But even so, the church is still standing after more than forty years!

We had article 31 folks and synodic people along with Reformed and Christian Reformed people laboring beside each other in touching unity. It looked like the reversal of the tower of Babel. Stubborn Friesians and the staid Groninger, the self-assured Hollander next to the sober Drent . . . The folks of Gelderland and the people from over Ysel all managed to work together and somehow build a church in Rocky.

You could tell none of them much of anything! They all had an answer all by their own. They were a smart bunch of people all right, but build a church they did. The old boys were pumping water in unison, and the younger generation called them "the hewers and water haulers," in reference to the tribes who made a covenant with Israel—Old Testament!

The women were holding the fort meanwhile at home! They were the ones who milked the cows and slopped the pigs and a thousand and one other chores on a growing family and farm holding. They also supplied us with a variety of foods that surpassed all imagination.

We all lived strongly in those days. Strong in almost everything! Strong at work and strong at play, and this gave us a deep satisfaction that was never surpassed in later days. It is my conviction that there is more love for a project if one is involved directly on the building of it! This is maybe the reason that Rocky church is still the deeply caring community that it was until recently.

I have seen this process at work time and again, and it was a bad day indeed when the church authorities started to organize one society after the other so that all but a few lose interest, and hardly anyone feels like participating anymore.

I am almost inclined to say, "Let my people go!" Please!

Enough of that for the time being. We will go back to the story and also to back to Edmonton. I had a phone call in the spring of 1951 that construction was opening up again after the winter break, so I returned to the loving arms of my second mother, Tonia. Tye was also very content with the return of their number-one boarder. Nevertheless, there was a little fly in the ointment, just a little one, but it turned into a big one before the fall of that year.

Work was slow, and I went from one employer to the next to find work, but it was piecemeal at the best of time until I could go to work in the building of the Macdonald Hotel. This was in the late fall, and things started looking up until the moment that I would start working. Then I was notified that the ironworkers were going on strike, and all work came to a standstill, and that was the final straw for me. I figured that this kind of work was not for me if they were sending me home even in the summer.

To be without work in the winter was something that I could handle, but I had enough when work came to a standstill in late fall. I said a tearful farewell to Tonia and Tye and headed back to Picture Butte.

It was there that I was in for the biggest change of my life, since I headed into voluntary boundaries. We were to be married in the near future. Jo and I had decided earlier when Jo was over for a visit in Edmonton that we should marry and build on the future Jerusalem.

We had decided that but had forgotten to tell our parents about that great vision of ours. Jo's dad had some strong objection but was persuaded by Jo and me in an unethical way. I told them if we could not marry with their permission, we would have to do it another way. I pointed out to them that we had been engaged for more than six years, and that is a long time for two healthy, young people. We lived in an honorable way up to that point, but it became more difficult as time went by. We were near the breaking point. It was Jo's mom who intervened at that point, and that settled it.

Jo and I would be married in the near future, but I promised to help with the beet work first. Frost had come early that year, while most of the beets were still in the ground. The ground was frozen for at least six inches deep, and the beet plows lifted more mud than beets out of the ground. There was more mud than beet in every clump. It was like playing hide-and-seek—peekaboo—where is the beet?

This is a joke, of course. It was much worse in reality. My father-in-law was more than six feet tall and had a poor back, and the task of lifting those monstrosities of the ground was almost too much for him. Digging a beet out of all that mud was more than he could handle. The rest was up to Jo and Henny. These girls were little more than teenagers, but they had a lot of spunk. Spunk was little comfort against that mountain of mud that had to be faced from morning till evening. Then there were the brothers of Jo and Henny thrown in as an afterthought into the realm of things. They were some help sometimes but fought with each other most of the time.

It was my luck that I wandered into the midst of all that misery, and I was obliged to pitch in to do my bit. Added to all this was the problem that my old enemy from a former story acted up again. I had pain in my stomach. The cold had affected my performance, and I would have to go back to the Chinaman or find some other solution—Jo would not marry much of a man if this kept going.

Mustard liniment seemed to be the answer to my drastic situation. I went to the outhouse and applied a liberal amount of the stuff all over my lower body. A warm comforting feeling set in just below the midriff, but not for long. The comfortable feeling turned into a burning inferno that seemed to burn me alive. The fact that I had put some of that witch's brew on my unmentionables made it much worse. A burning fire was eating away my whole lower body in unbearable heat, all this in thirty-below weather.

I sat there and sat there some more for the longest time until my "bride-to-be" came over to see what was going on, since I should have been back inside a long time ago. She could not do much either. She could not even hold my hand, since both of my hands were holding on to my stomach. The thing had to work itself out, and Jo was standing outside in thirty-below weather, while I was suffering inside of that little building with the heart-shaped opening in the door.

I learned another lesson once again in that cold November evening. I was not good in medicine. I should leave it to the experts. Jo had to be in care of the medicine from that time on, and I am still alive after forty-eight years of marriage. How is that for a testimonial to the expertise of my little woman?

All things pass, and so did that period in the beets. We made it through the war about five years ago, and we also made it through the muddy beets. Many beets stayed in the ground that year all over that district. The beet plows could not even get in the ground anymore a little later on, and the farmers had to give up a part of that year's harvest.

It was after that fearsome period that we arrived at our marriage day. It was about one o'clock on November 30, and everyone was ready to go to church. The bride was there, and her family was there, but not the bridegroom.

He was lying under the family car to do a last-minute job on the brakes of the father-in-law's car. This genius fixed the car so good and eloquently that the brakes did not get fixed in time. We had to borrow the neighbor's car. I have never seen a person who was so afraid of his employer. He was almost crying before he could bring up the courage to ask his farmer for his car.

By the way, his crawling must have been successful! I heard that he bought the farm from his former employer in later years. Whatever the case, we should be thankful, since he helped us out at that time anyway.

The bridegroom appeared on the scene with dirt under his fingernails and a crumpled suit, but everything was in place on this very promising young man. Don't laugh! This is serious business!

Johanna and I went to church for the wedding ceremony on one of the windiest days of the year. We were greeted by a mighty and joyous crowd of about a dozen people, give or take a few. That number included the old minister, a very sympathetic man, and we liked him very much. But he was as dry as a crackerjack. His voice used to sound like the crackling of a bushfire. I mean no disrespect when I say that! On the contrary, we respected that man more than most people we have known over forty-four years of marriage. I just want to describe the true picture of our wedding day.

This minister performed the ceremony with the text, *"Go to the ant, o sluggard! Consider her ways and become wise,"* Proverbs 6:6.

It was with great consternation and utter amazement that Johanna and I were listening to his words. We always thought that he had a high opinion of Johanna, and then he comes and hits us with that text! The sermon was good enough, but the meaning cut us to the quick. It scared the living daylights out of us, and we started working like people possessed after that day and hardly ever took time to rest.

None of my family was there on that great joyous occasion, but it was in the middle of the sermon that my mother came stumbling into the church. She was one of the lucky ones. She missed the worst of it all.

Mom had come from Nobleford with another member of the Nobleford family, and they were the only representatives on my side of the family. Not only that, but they also had to leave almost right after the service, and that was that. Another boy gone into the wild blue yonder!

Our wedding picture outside the church shows Johanna and me in the company of the old minister. We were almost blown off by Mother Earth—so bad was the wind. That was fairly well the story of the day.

The important part was over, and the feast was about to start. But we were in for another surprise once again when we went from the church to the festive hall. We found the janitor and his wife sweeping the floor in a complete dust storm. It was just as cold in the building as it was outside and twice as unfriendly, since the janitor had completely forgotten our wedding party.

It was at that point that I showed my mighty intellect. I made my first manly decision as man of the house.

"Forget about your clumsy old building," I told the janitor. "You have done us very much harm. We are going someplace else!"

That someplace else turned out to be the dwelling place of my brand-new in-laws! How is that for apples? Was I a man of the moment or not? You don't fool around with guys like me and get away with it.

I am as hard as a rock, and my decisions irrevocable . . . as long as the wife is not around . . . !

There must have been about twenty-five or thirty people at the party that night, both male and female! We had a very good time in spite of the poor beginning. No one had money for liquor, and we all got high on tea and coffee.

Even so! The spirit was excellent and has stayed that way throughout our married life. Still, it was not the end of that troublesome day. The house had many guests that night, and it was decided that the folks from outside had to go in the spare bedroom—and would you believe it! Johanna and I ended on the couch. We had too much roof on the house to do much of anything.

"Roof on the house" is an expression used to explain that there are too many watching eyes in the vicinity to do much of anything—or to say it in brief terms, nothing happened. The two of us were sweating out the night, but it was hands off! Let alone anything else! How is that for a wedding night?

We had no honeymoon to speak of since beside that. Our honeymoon was in the beet field like an afterthought. Very unromantic!

We helped Dad and Mom Kranenborg for a few more days until the end of the week. The whole affair had left us so short of cash that father Kranenborg and I had to scrape the lining out of our coat pockets on Sunday morning to find money for the collection.

That, my good friend, was the beginning of a beautiful marriage that has lasted for forty-four years at the time of this writing. We have been very blessed! We always had enough but never were rich in worldly possessions but unimaginably rich in everything else!

It is as the saying goes: "I asked for money that I might enjoy life! I received life that I might enjoy everything!"

Fact is I did not even desire to be rich in money. Yet I have more than enough of everything.

And so the saga continued. An old friend of the family picked us up on Monday morning. He and his wife would take us along to our future home in Rocky Mountain House. You have heard of the yellow submarine? We went along in the yellow Studebaker, the pride and joy of our good friend John.

He was very proud of that machine, and he was very upset when I put the whole kit and caboodle on fire when we were halfway to

Rocky. I should explain that the floorboard of that truck was a little lower than the place where Jo and I were sitting. Some straw and paper had accumulated in that lower part of the floor. This had to be a very dangerous combination, since I was smoking like a chimney in those days. To make a long story short, I put some fireworks in our honeymoon and dropped some burning ashes in the tinder dry material on the floorboards. Presto! We had a nice fire going!

It was put out quickly enough, but the near disaster was not very conducive for a good relationship between me and our good friend John and his lovely wife. I must add that we became the best of friends in later years. It was in this kingly fashion that we arrived in Rocky in the Studebaker truck of John and his wife.

John bought a farm in the Rocky district not all that much later. Their house was an old railroad car with a built-on addition. The whole dwelling would tilt and shift with the frost and the changing seasons, like a ship on dry land. The floor had a slope of at least four inches, and it took a little engineering and nifty footwork to balance your way through that little building while visiting the friendly folks. But that was not the end of his riches. He was also the proud owner of an artesian well, a possession that he could never get enough of—this really was his pride and joy, and he could talk about his well as if it was one of the Seven Wonders of the World.

You might think that people in surroundings like that would be very dissatisfied and unhappy, but nothing was further from the truth! They were two of the happiest people I have ever met. He moved to BC later to live in much improved conditions, but he told me once that his best years had been in Rocky.

This brings to mind another story. This same man was at our place just before he bought the farm. And it was on one morning during that stay with us that I have seen him laugh so hard that we thought he was not going to pull through. My mother was in the habit of buying real bargains in the army surplus store. This started already in the first year in Canada. She would buy prisoners of war uniforms, and we would be wandering in the beet fields with great red circles on the back of our coats. But it was a bargain, and we had to put up or shut up.

Mom was still in the coverall-buying business in the first years of Rocky, with the exception that there was a slight variation in the pattern of things! She bought coveralls that would fit men of six feet or larger. This might have been a problem for other people, but not for Mother. She just cut the bottom off our pant legs, and we went to work in coveralls with the crotch hanging below knee level.

Friend John was at our place when brother Bert started complaining about those oversized wonderworks of our mother.

"Mom, I have had enough!" Bert was saying.

He had tears in his eyes, and his skinny little frame was shivering with agitation.

"I go to work in the morning with these oversized army tents of yours around my body. I feel like a snowplow. The snow starts to pile in front of me when I walk through the yard, and I have more snow than a snow plow that is piled up in that low-hanging crotch between my legs. Two-by-fours and two-by-sixes and bundles of shiplap mixed with snow have to be dragged along, and it has happened that I had complete trees in front of those infernal machinations of yours. I have had enough. I am going striking if I don't get decent clothes when I go to work!"

This was a complete exaggeration, of course, but it sounded so funny that the tears were just streaming down the face of our friend John. I have seldom seen a man laugh like John on that morning. It was really nothing to laugh about! The source of the trouble was the fact that we did not understand our mother. She was just forty years ahead of her time, that's all. You can see schoolkids dressed like that all over the place in this day and age.

Mom had mercy on us, and she did not force us to wear earrings at that time. We would have fit into perfection with the young people of today if Mom would have had the foresight to make us wear earrings. Too bad! She was good though.

Jo and I lived in the front of our parents' home in the first years of our marriage. The men would sleep with the men, and the girls with the girls in times of stress or if we had guests over during the weekends that the boys were home from the mine.

This had some queer consequences at times. I remember one of those evenings that the boys were in a really crazy mood. Swanney was born already, and she must have been about two years old at that time. The evening was filled with music and singing and a lot of laughter.

All the boys had underwear made of long johns. Not that evening, mind you—Adolf was the only one dressed like that on that particular evening. The long-john underwear was a one-piece undergarment with a flap on the back, and this contraption could be lowered when someone had to make a trip to the bathroom. This piece of underwear could be buttoned up in front and had a wide slit on the side.

It was on this evening that Adolf got caught up in the spirit of the moment and shoved Swanney in the back of his long johns. The little girl was sticking her head out of the side through that slit like a little kangaroo, while Adolf was prancing through the room like another version of Santa Claus caught in a time warp.

It might sound a little unfresh, but it was funny beyond belief at the time when this happened. Although, I must say, Johanna did not appreciate this kind of fun!

It was around that time that the young people of Red Deer decided to come to the West Country, to the end of civilization—Rocky Mountain House. They were looking for a little adventure, and that is just what they got—adventure, more than they had bargained for. Something went wrong with their car in subzero weather, and the fun came to a complete standstill when they were stranded with two cars full of young people and nowhere to go.

Good advice was hard to come by until someone suggested they go to the op den Dries family. They always had an open house, a fact that was well known through most of the province.

I should explain that many people recall a stay at our house at one time or another in the early years when many found work in the bush camps! The young people arrived at our place and were bedded down all over the kitchen floor. They were to try and sleep through the night. A very liberal mix of Christian Reformed future Jerusalem was spread all over the floor of our humble abode. There was even a future minister in that crowd of adventurers.

Dad was in bed when this all was arranged, and he slept through the whole thing. Nobody can describe his amazement when he stumbled into a room full of boys and girls right in the middle of the night. He had to go to the outhouse and did not get dressed for company as you may well imagine. This was the pioneering spirit of the first order!

CHAPTER 11

THE EARLY YEARS

MY FATHER HAD a dream, and that was an absolute belief that a great future would be ahead of our family if we only worked together and pooled our resources. All our efforts were directed to that ultimate goal in the beginning years. All the money coming in was put in one communal pot with our mother holding the strings of the purse. Several things were wrong with this setup. Not one of us had the killer instinct needed to be successful in business in the first place, and that might have been the greatest shortfall of my father's dream. But that was only part of the problem.

Our banker—that was our mother—was not very economical at the best of times and much too good-hearted. This had the result that the money was not accumulating as it should have been. The money was shifting like water through our fingers, and we did not gain much of anything during the time that our cooperated efforts lasted.

Many parents have found out in later days that bringing up teenagers is very costly at the best of time, but we were among the first to find that out in this great country of Canada. Jo and I were caught up in this dream so that most of my efforts were put into the farm in the beginning years. We lived in the front room of the old farmhouse, and the first three of our children were born while we were living there. Jo was very hard up for money at times, and I am ashamed to say that I never noticed how difficult life had been for her in those first years of our marriage.

The winters were not all that bad. I went to the planer mill for a supplemental income, and that was a little bit of help. It was the summers that were so hard on her. I would be helping Dad on the farm, and the income was next to nothing. It seems that my parents were just as naive as I was because they never seemed to notice anything either. I have only one excuse for my absolute ignorance in that respect—Jo never complained. Not that I can remember.

It was not until the first cracks in our common dream appeared that the situation improved for Jo and me. Adolf got married and pulled out of the company. He had another boss to look after him. This combined with the closing of the mine and the departure of another person. This was one who had been working together in the great dream of the op den Dries clan. He is also the only person who had brains enough and was hard enough to leave with money in his pocket. This man was very seldom mentioned after that in our circles. He did nothing wrong, and yet something did not click!

Dad and I would work together on the farm in the summertime. This must have been the best years of my father's life. We did not have all that much money, but we had not many worries either. He was involved in work at the church in a big way. To that I must add that our contributions to the building of the church were very impressive—both in money and in labor.

I had a dream also, a tremendous drive to clear the brush of that quarter section of land. My greatest dream was to get a Caterpillar and clean our land and many other farms. The result might have been the fulfillment of my father's dream, if only I could have obtained the money. That's where the problem was in those days.

It was almost impossible to get a loan from the bank in the beginning years. Most of the other farmers had money coming in from the Old Country during the early fifties. That allowed them to buy good farmland and pay for it in cash. This had the added benefit that they had enough collateral to receive loans from the bank.

We had to do it the hard way—work for it!

It is not hard to understand that this had to be very slow work. And it was for that reason that I would go into the bush with an ax to cut as many trees as possible. It was like mission impossible. But I did clear a fair amount of land that way on the old home quarter. Our neighbor across the road did a little bit of breaking land for us with his Caterpillar tractor. It stands for reason that he did not do that for nothing. Dad and I had to go and work on his land to help with the haying and later with the stooking of the wheat crop; this was also very heavy work.

The neighbor, who was a Norwegian, must have been more than disappointed with my skill as a stack builder during the haying time. I just did not have the knack of that work. The stack would start well enough, but I did not know how to finish the thing properly. I started pulling in much too early, and the poor guy had a bunch of stacks in the field that looked like the pyramids from Egypt. This fact must have been well advertised, since I know one farmer who could not look at me without a smirk on his face for many years after that.

Our efforts in the stooking of the wheat bundles were a little better—but not much. It seems that the farmer was on the losing end of that deal—but we were trying!

I remember that this farmer had his tractor so stuck in the heavy gumbo soil that only the exhaust was sticking out of the ground. I did a lot of work to help him out on that day and made up for the poor efforts earlier.

I designed and built a sawmill in those days, and we did saw enough lumber to build a barn with a round roof. It might have been cheaper and easier to buy the lumber and build the barn that way. Whatever the case, the barn became a very comfortable dwelling for the livestock of Dad, and he had a nice and warm place to putter around during the winter months. This was because we built the barn according to the plans of the district agriculturist. This man gave me some up-to-date plans for that barn. He gave me much other advice about the whole farming operation of that day.

Again, our life might have gone much different if I had the money and the resources in those days. This was not to be, and I realized that we were not going anywhere. I understood well enough that I would be working out for a long time before I would have a farm of my own. It was with that in mind that I applied for a job as a mechanic at a garage in Rocky. I might just as well learn a trade if I had to work out for many years by the looks of things, and because of that decision, my path was directed in another direction, again!

I was to start as an apprentice mechanic to replace a good but moody character who had walked out only days earlier. I was to start as an apprentice mechanic, but the man changed his mind and came back at the last moment. That's how I was sent to the body shop instead.

The foreman of that place turned out to be one of the hardest people to work with that I have been associated with in all my years. He had served in the navy in the last war, and his language was so bad that it surpassed anything that I ever heard before. I won't go into details about that, but it was bad!

The fact that I was too scared to move when he was in one of those moods might have worked on him like the red scarf on a steer. The only difference was that the steer had more influence to back him up than I had.

Another man with the name Rick worked also in that place, and he had a very comforting influence on my dreadful existence of those beginning years. He must have been the nicest person that I have met in all my life!—I have never heard him say one bad word about anyone in the years that I worked with him. The nice part was that he did not care that much about the tantrums of the foreman of the joint. The fact that he was a born Canadian might have had something to with this, and the saddest thing was the fact that both of them had one thing in common.

They were both alcoholics in the worst sense of the word. Carl, the foreman, was in a divorce proceeding, and that might have related to his bad mood. His wife had left him, and he was living with Rick.

Nobody will ever know how hard that must have been on Rick's wife, since she was a very nice person, and she must have loved Rick very dearly because she stayed with him as long as she did Even so, everything has its breaking point, and I was to witness this on a day that I was involved in a drinking spiel myself. I am by no means proud of the episode, but it went as follows . . .

We had a reason to celebrate something or another. I have forgotten what. It is one of the few times that I participated in one of those celebrations. Fact is I drank too much. All three of us ended up at Rick's house. I was not in good shape, and the other two were well over the limit, to put this mildly. It was small wonder that Rick's wife was not happy to see anyone of us. Little Rick did not know enough to keep his mouth shut and gave her some smart remark. This was the last straw, and the little woman hit him a good one under his chin so that Rick fell over backward on the couch. He was to stay there the rest of the day!

I remember Rick as one of the saddest and most forlorn men in my life. Brother Bert and I helped him at a later date when he was doing a job for some outfit. He could not finish that job because he had pneumonia from all his drinking, and the job had to be done in time.

We did the job for him, but only a little time was gained! He died not all that much later after his wife had left him, and he went from bad to worse.

How I wish that I could have done more for this little man! You have heard the expression "Ships passing in the night!"

I believe that the interlocking of relationships is a lot more than ships in the night! It is more like the interlocking of links in a net or chinks in chain armor. Good relations make a strong armor to protect each other from the hardships of life.

The Dutch have a saying, "Burdens shared together are cut in half."

There is a lot of truth in that statement. To find ways that allow your fellow man to let down his or her guard and allow you to help to carry that burden—that's the crux of the matter.

We might have failed not only Rick but also many more people crossing our path. It is this that can bother me in the closing years of my life. Matters and events that happened in those years cannot be recalled, but we can try to pass on our experiences so that others may be able to learn from our mistakes.

My relationship with Carl took a strange twist in later days. Neither one of the two other guys could paint very well, so Carl asked me to do a paint job, more in jest than that he was expecting anything good to come of this experiment. It turned out that I was an excellent painter, and they could not even match the kind of work that I was doing with the paint gun. This changed the whole relationship almost overnight in a manner of speaking! I went from low man to nearly the top of the totem pole.

It got so bad in later years that Carl became more and more dependent on me. He was almost unable to do any work on account of his alcoholism. More and more of the workload started coming my way, and I made full use of the situation. It came to the point that I had Carl running in circles, and he was doing what I wanted him to do most of the time.

I had become the crutch that he had to depend on more and more as the months slipped by. This came to a head one day. I told him that I was through working at that place. It took the intervention of the main office to get me back on the job, and that made the situation even more lopsided. I became more and more overbearing to the point where I was almost as hard to live with as Carl was in the beginning. Rick had left a long time before this happened.

I became the number-two man on paper but the number-one man in reality becoming better in bodywork than in Christianity! I was not really aware of this at the time, but I can see this in hindsight. The trouble is that matters in the past cannot be undone. I am not proud of that episode in my life. And more situations arrived in my life's pathway later that were just as deplorable.

Enough of that for now! I will have to backtrack a little to get back to the story line.

It was in the early fifties that I bought a raw quarter section of land. No land was broken at the time that I bought that place. This turned out to be one of my most serious mistakes . . . if you can call it a mistake! I was to spend the best years of my life to bring that land to cultivation. That's the best way I can describe the following years. I would have been much better off if I had bought a quarter with some ready-made pasture and some cultivated land. This was not the case, and I wasted the following years in hard work and little profit. And still, these years might have been excellent if I look at what my children are doing right now on the same land, but that is up to the next generation to judge!

Fact is that I had to start from the bottom, building a house first—a project without any help from anyone. Not only that! Everything had to be done by hand.

Electricity was an unknown thing on the countryside in those days, and a telephone was even further away. I built a house with a handsaw, a hammer, and a bag full of nails. The wood on the house was made of so-called lumber, or buttermilk wood, since the wood had the appearance of buttermilk, and the stuff was just as red as a hotheaded Irish woman. It is remarkable that this house is still standing in the town of Rocky now, forty years later.

The walls were filled with shavings, and the ceiling was covered with the same material—very primitive by today's standards but good enough for a starter, since all this work was done in my spare time. It was a very rewarding day when Jo and I finally moved into this house. Only the shell of the house was standing then, since the inside of the house had to be finished later as the money came available. Jo was with me in all these endeavors through thick and thin. I doubt if there is a woman around in these days of luxury who would do the same thing without a word of complaint, but that's exactly what Jo did.

We had three children when we moved in that house, and Jo had to do all the housework without electricity or any other convenience of any kind. Our well was a dugout—dug by hand, and the water was really nothing else but groundwater. Cooking and heating of the house had to be done on an old furnace.

One of the ironic happenings that I can clearly remember was the occasion that I was supposed to get home visitation from the minister and an elder, a visit that did not fit in well with my feelings at the time. It was at that point that the shady side of my character had the overhand, and I put a few mighty big lumps of coal in the stove just before the two arrived. It got so hot in there that the visit did not last any longer than was politely possible. You could say that I heaped burning coals on that visit. Not very nice, is it? I do believe that my manners were less than acceptable many times!

The building of the house was only the beginning of the great task ahead. The land was to be reclaimed in spite of the neighbors who said that I should have my head examined. I was trying to bring land in production that was so low that nobody could probably grow anything on it in a hundred years, according to their infinite wisdom, but we carried on—undaunted by the criticism of the folks around us.

We were wrestling a farm out of surroundings that were a complete wilderness at first. More people were moving in all the time, and we felt less lonesome as the years went by. That was in later years, but the road conditions were so bad in the first few years that some Dutch immigrants, who lived south of us, had to leave their cars at the railroad and would walk home. The roads were one great mud puddle when the rains fell down or in the spring when the snow was melting.

It was small wonder that the neighbors were laughing at our efforts to reclaim these sloughs if even the roads were unfit to travel on for the better part of the year. It was scary at first when the eternal stillness surrounded us like a blanket. No sound could be heard, but the whistling of the wind and moaning or baying of some undefined animal somewhere in the virgin woodlands.

We started with the lowland covered by willows. I had bought an old John Deere tractor and started working the willows down with a disk that I had borrowed from another beginner in the neighborhood. The old tractor was huffing and puffing through the sloughs interrupted with some mighty thundering explosions when the old machine was backfiring. But some land was cleared, and I could go through the process of breaking the first acres of land. It was like dragging a plow through a waterlogged bird sanctuary.

The water was filling the tracks wherever I went so that I became stuck in this wallowing mud hole every other round. I was stuck so bad in one of those holes that I could not even see the top of the axles anymore . . . a situation that called for desperate measures.

I put logs in front of the wheels and tried to make the tractor climb out of the hole. No go! Jacking up the wheels up so that I could fill the tracks with dry sod was another desperate measure. This helped sometime but not this time. I tried every trick in the book. No results! The tractor was there to stay—in the mud hole.

Only one thing remained to be done! This was to be a cure of last resort. I lugged a tree over to that mud hole and wormed that under the body of the tractor, just in front of the rear wheels. This was an immense amount of hard work, but everything else had failed. Even prayer does not seem to help in times like that!—I mean no disrespect when I say that. Most farmers can testify that the lifeline seems to be closed in some situations, almost as if heaven is telling us that we have the wrong approach.

I tied that log with heavy chains to the front of the steel wheels and pulled the throttle wide open. I realized full well that I was putting my life on the line in the next few minutes or more. This tractor is well known for its tendencies to tip over backward, crushing the driver in the process. But I was desperate at that point and pushed the clutch as far ahead as it would go. The tractor jumped three feet in the air and then fell back where it was before. I had pulled the clutch back just a fraction too fast. I had to try again. It was now or never!

I pushed the clutch in again and held it a little longer so that the machine was jumping at least three or four feet in the air in a vertical position. It stayed that way for the longest time and then fell forward into a new position. I had gained a foot or two and went through the same procedure again until I finally came on more solid ground.

Haying was done with just as much difficulty. Mom and I had the dump rake tied behind the old blue car, and Jo was handling the controls of the rake, while I was driving around the puddles to rake as much hay as possible. Much of it had to come right out of the water as I was driving as close to the edges of the sloughs as I possibly dared—but that was only part of the procedure!

Jo and I carried the rest of the hay out of the puddles by hand and piled them in little haystacks so that the hay would have a chance to get dry enough to bring it home. The whole operation must have looked like a couple of adults going back to childhood days. It looked silly! No person in his right mind would do a thing like that. And yet Jo and I did it, and we built a farm over the years while bringing up seven children as a byproduct of our whole lifestyle!

We were strictly following the value system that dictated our style of life. God in the first place, and, second, the family! Last but not least, the church! It has always been our belief that if we put Jesus in the center of our personal and family life, the church would be built because of this action, and God would be glorified through our love and sacrifice in support of the coming kingdom.

The coming of the kingdom seemed a long way off in church at that point in time. Troubles abounded in almost every sector of church life in those days. Part of the newly built church had burned down. It seemed strange that both churches where I had built a chimney burned down, one in Iron Springs and one in Rocky. It was true, nevertheless. But it had nothing to do with my brickwork, since the chimney in Rocky was used for many years after that.

I would get involved usually in spite of my good works of building a chimney that would stand the test of time and fire. The wise men in the consistory had made me a member of the stewardship committee in the company of a Friesian and some others. I have forgotten who they were. We had expected that we would be sharing in management affairs besides managing the finances, but this was not so! (We had been turned into tax collectors.) Our job was defined as a committee to encourage people into giving faithfully to the church and the building program. It was through the fire and the rebuilding of the church that our position took on a whole new dimension of priorities.

I would suggest that you read this story with the understanding that this will be a strictly personal record of the history of that time. It is completely without malice of any kind. Two views of commitment were involved, and it is by no means a sure thing that our view of the situation was the right one.

The church was partly burned down but saved from total destruction by the heroic efforts of the Rocky volunteer fire brigade and many volunteers. They have been struggling in subzero weather to contain the fire to its smallest dimension. Quite successfully! The church was insured, and that was good up to a point, but it also set off a struggle of mighty proportions. The committee of stewardship believed the church should be rebuilt in free labor just as had been done when the church was built.

The consistory thought a contractor should do the work, and little or no free labor should be involved. A lot of personal pride got mixed up in the whole argument, and it went so far that one of our committee was threatened with censure. A lot of emotion was displayed at both sides of the table, and it looked like the young church would fall apart in two halves—even before it got off the ground, in a manner of speaking. The issue was resolved at the last possible moment, and our little group made the resolution that none of us would bring the matter up again! This is the first time that this fact is recorded, and I hope that nobody will take conclusions out of this matter. It was just written down because it is part of history, that's all.

I dare say that I was not too well liked in some circles of the church community after that episode. One thing is for sure: they were awful careful in later years before I was put into any other leading position in any shape or form.

This issue was hardly settled when matters with the garage came to a head again. I quit again, and this time for keeps, but not before I had put in my first term in the technical school in Calgary. Carl did a very nice thing for me in those days. He talked the apprentice inspector into giving me two years' credit in a four-year term as an auto body apprentice. I don't know how he did this. They were wartime buddies, and that might have made the difference.

The students in the technical school were mighty upset when I attended tech school at a later date. It seems that nobody else got a credit like that in the whole history of SAIT—as the school is called. There were some mighty big shots in that school, and they gave me a plenty rough time when I attended school there. Even so, this cloud had also a silver lining, and that was my faithful Fargo truck. I was the proud owner of a very good-looking three-quarter-ton truck. The head office had talked me into buying that truck, and luck dictated that the instructor at the school had much use for that truck, and that equalized the situation in my favor. He asked me to move him over into another apartment, and that raised my standings to an acceptable level.

The school itself did not amount to all that much. I was well ahead in the three Rs but behind a little in language. The training was more practical than it was technical, and we learned most from looking at the techniques in other shops of that day, a fact freely advocated by the head instructor of our class.

It was a happy-go-lucky bunch of people gathered to gain a little experience. This was the overall picture of the class of 1956. The fact that I had just quit smoking made the situation for me almost unbearable. There were intermissions every hour, and the smoke that was twirling around the future body men was so thick that you could cut it with a knife, a situation that is hard to handle for a brand-new abstainer of the delicate art of smoking. It was so bad in that school that several body men masked a car with paper in preparation for a paint job. This was a laudable procedure in itself! What followed was a little more on the shady side . . .

Six of the guys went missing, and the instructor was looking all over for the missing people. No results! It was after a half hour of frantic searching that one guy noticed an awful lot of smoke coming out of the cracks of the car that had just been masked in. It looked as if the car was on fire and the instructor yanked the door of the car open and six guys came rolling out of there in a real cloud of smoke.

It looked like the war all over again, judging by the amount of smoke coming out of that car. The guy looked really sheepish and made excuses galore to the overwrought instructor who was really angry after that episode. It took them jokers the better part of the term to get back on good terms with the very frustrated man. He went out of his way for his students in other situations, but they had trespassed the level of tolerance of the good man. Remarkable enough!

Everything else went on a fairly even keel in all the other aspects of that year in school, if you don't mention the food and lodging—this left much to be desired. Food and lodging were another problem for the students and fellow sufferers. The good folks of Calgary tried to make an extra dime by taking in the students of SAIT for a more or less reasonable fee. Food was to be included in this progress. Some people tried to squeeze even more money out of the students by the food that they gave along to school and afterward.

We were not lucky in the family where we had our lodging, except one thing, and that's the fact that we never had to guess what would be on the menu! Baloney and more baloney! This was on the menu for four weeks in a row, except the last day. Then we got meat that was so rangy that I could not eat it so that I slipped the substance in my pocket in an unguarded moment. I simply could not eat that stuff. Let me tell you that I have never been choosy in my food, but this was well past the acceptable limit as far as little Hank was concerned.

It was a brokenhearted man who stepped in the truck and headed back to the loving arms and the good food of mother Johanna. Way back in the sticks! Life was a little better there. Johanna was the essence of life for the little crowd of helpless beings in her care, including me.

I finished my schooling as an apprentice the year after that. It was also the first time that I heard a record of Elvis Presley. This happened when we were on our way to the coffee shop, down the hill from SAIT in Calgary. It was an altogether different kind of music, and it shook me up quite severely, but I learned to like his spirituals a great deal in later years. It is too bad that a great talent like that ended in the wrong hands, a lifestyle that was to destroy him completely in years to come.

The music of that man has still got a great hold over the masses even now, almost forty years later. It must be for reason that he was deep down a very decent man who was very loyal to his friends and kind to people in lower positions. A combination that one does not see all that often after a person reaches success and rises from the lowest to the higher rungs of the ladder in society. I feel a strange kinship to this very talented man!

This was also the year of the great uprising of the Hungarian people against the Communist regime of that day—an uprising smothered in the blood of many innocent people but reminded us so much of our own struggle not all that many years before that. It also marked the year of my own uprising . . .

I quit the employ in the body shop of Rocky. I don't think that the head boss in the main office was all that happy of my resigning, but the facts were there, and little could be done about the whole situation. I was out of work and mulling around in my mind what to do next. The house was only half finished, and the farm was a long way from supporting a growing family with three children. My hand was forced again, and my father-in-law lined up a job for me in the city of Red Deer in one of the main body shops right in the center of town.

Our newly built house was left standing empty in Rocky Mountain House, and we hired a great and wide older house in Red Deer close to the house of my wife's parents. It was a house as square as a cubicle and just as unappealing, two stories high and with rooms downstairs as big as play fields in the neighborhood. The lower room was heated with gas, and the upper rooms were heated by a great roster in the ceiling of the front room of the house. We bedded the children in a safe place, and it was in the upstairs rooms that Jo and I had our own play garden. But I was not supposed to tell that to anyone.

Then came the night that we heard a great racket downstairs in the middle of the night not long after we had moved in that house. Jo forced me to go downstairs by making an appeal to my macho image, an image that had shrunk to almost nothing by the time I reached the lower room. And what did I find? Our friend from Alexo, the one with the car with no reverse gear!

He was driving in circles around the bottom room on the three-wheeled bicycle of my oldest son. It was absolutely ridiculous and awe inspiring. The guy was sitting on that bicycle with his knees touching his forehead, making circles like a man possessed. And you know what Jo did? She put the coffeepot on. That was my wife Jo in all her goodness and glory. She was also in her underwear—we forgot to get angry and had a great time drinking coffee and talking about the days in the Alexo mine. This guy was a queer but very likeable person, and we regret to have lost touch with him in the years that followed.

My acceptance in the new workplace was somehow strange and unpredictable. I have clearly seen the hand of God at work when times were difficult. Also in this place! That I was used, there is no doubt about that, not in my mind anyway.

A great black hearse from the funeral home was rolled into the shop only months after I had started working in that place. About six men had been working in the shop, and it was as busy as a beehive. Then all of a sudden the place was empty the minute that the black Moria was rolled inside the door. Only the foreman and I were left in that place.

The foreman said to me, "It looks that you will have to take care of that job! Everyone else has left!"

It was as simple and as neat as that.

It seems that the other men had been working on another black car only months before I had arrived on the scene. Let me explain that black is the most demanding color in the whole automotive industry. It will show every scratch and nick, and it is almost impossible to do a satisfying job on a black car. The other body men had to do the same repair and a paint job three times over, and even then the result was anything but beautiful after all that effort. This was the reason why everyone dropped out of sight the minute this car came in the door. The other guys were playing it safe and let me do the job with all the risks involved.

My work turned out very well! Not because I am so good, but my work was blessed, and I prospered in the handling of that more-than-difficult assignment—something like Joseph in the house of Pharaoh.

Another episode came along not all that much later. The son of a Chevy dealer in town came to our shop one day. He said quite bluntly that he did not want his black car painted in his dad's body shop. That was the reason that we had the privilege of sharpening our teeth on that job. I say we, but it really was me!

The situation was much the same as with the hearse earlier. Everyone was scared to tackle the job, and I ended up doing that paint job, with the same result. The owner of the car was more than pleased with my work, and the rest of the men were more than impressed. I believe that my work was blessed in an unnatural manner just like the time before. The foreman got a free case of beer out of that deal, and I got some credit, but not all that much. I might as well finish with the story of the same kind of special blessing on a later date not all that much later.

Times had toughened a lot, and work was getting slower and slower so that the foreman took in jobs that he would not have looked at in normal times. This included the stranger in town among cars—the lowly Beetle Volkswagen. The Beetle Volkswagen was an almost unknown commodity at the time. They brought one of these little beasts into the body shop. The other men had worked on a Volkswagen van before with the same poor results as with the black cars. They had to repair the side of that panel truck, and it kept buckling repeatedly. The result was so poor that they had lost a lot of money on that deal also. This was also the reason that nobody wanted to work on this little machine. They were just scared. The insurance adjuster did not even have a flat rate book on this car, and the foreman pushed the job off on me, again!

"You are half a German anyway," he said to me. "You know the German mind and how it works. You take that job and write your own price. Take your time!"

The job turned out to be a breeze, and I had a lot of time leftover . . . much to my advantage. This settled my reputation as a body man, but I never really did belong in that place in spite of my success.

This was mainly for the fact that I was not a drinking person even though the pressure was tremendous at times. Almost half the men working there would go straight from work to the beer parlor and spend most of the evening drinking in that place, a preoccupation that was totally unacceptable to me. The fact that I was praying before meals did not go unnoticed, and that did not make me any friends either!—this and the fact that I was not always handling in a very Christian way. Most of the guys respected me as a body man but could not understand me as a human being, I am sad to say. Christians can be very narrow-minded in their ways, and I was no exception!

These men had the strangest notions about recreation on Sundays and weekends. They had a spell that it was an absolute must that each person build a boat out of plywood. They spent endless hours building these flat-bottom crafts. Then the whole assembly would float down the Red Deer River on the long weekends. The boats were loaded with beer in such a way that neither craft nor men would dry out on these adventures. They had also weekend fishing trips of unbelievable proportions.

Cars and trucks were loaded to the hilt with provisions for those daring expositions to the wilds of Slave Lake. Twice the amount of money was spent on liquor over the money spent on food, but this was only heightening the adventurous aspect of those trips, and no one was complaining all that much. I wonder how the wives felt about it.

It happened that some guys got really angry with other members of the group. They set to work in dead earnest to chop down some trees to drop them on the tents of the intended victims. It was fortunate that all of them were so drunk that nobody could saw down a tree anymore. So they had another drink to settle their differences. The whole bunch would come back as the best of friends only days later.

The mood was even so good that plans would be made to have another campout in short order. I believe that many of those excursions were set up as an excuse to have a drinking party! But some of them sure sounded funny at times.

It was during the last summer of my stay in Red Deer that the lover boys in the shop had the absolute conviction that their presence was absolutely necessary on a lake in Central Alberta. This operation was set up along the same lines as the previous campouts with a lot of liquor and little food. The day was beautiful, and the spirits were high, boosted by the abundance of all kinds of liquor products.

Three of the guys were fishing in the middle of the lake in a leaky old rowboat. They had been toasting the fish frequently, and the festival mood went from good to excellent. And so it was around noon that they had a great desire to go back to the shore, but none of them were in shape to row the boat at such a long distance.

The help of one of the better-to-do boys was requested, and he hooked the harmless little rowboat to his really big speedboat. This speedboat had one of the biggest motors of that day. He started pulling the rowboat with a wide-open throttle at such a speed that the boat was sloshed full of water. It was only the speed that held that rowboat above water. The proud speedboat owner cut the throttle back close to shore, and the rowboat sank out of sight when the speed was cut to nothing. The ardent fishermen sank along with the rest of the equipment; only their heads were sticking out of the water by the time the boat had settled to the sandy bottom. You would think that this would be enough to shake them out of their drunken stupor. Not so! They fished out another bottle of beer out of the sunken vessel and went back to what they were doing before the power trip, and that was—you guessed it—drinking more beer.

You will understand that my communication was not all that smooth if I did not want to participate in these kinds of joyrides. I had a wife and three children waiting for me at home and had neither the money nor the desire to go along on those trips. My place was still at home with Johanna and the kids. Johanna! Heaven bound! That was really the overriding factor in our day-to-day lives—to seek the things that are above.

I joined the choir only weeks after I had moved to Red Deer. Our director was a person who had a great love for the Old Country style of folk songs. He could dwell on that in a very emotional way to the point that it started bothering some more—liberal-minded people and the same division developed that I had seen so often before.

They started yipping at the man's heels like a bunch of hyenas with the ultimate aim to bring the man to the ground and finish him off. Have we not all participated in the kind of exercise at one time or another? Well!

The strategy succeeded not all that long before I left the bright city of Red Deer. The situation came to a head when some members called a special meeting to vote on the capabilities of the unfortunate director. The opposition was so well organized that they had the man almost railroaded out of his position.

I had a feeling that a lot of animosities between some women were the underlying cause of the disagreement. I did not like the way that some folks were ganging up on the man and his supporters. The chairman of that day was a weak personality, and this was also adding to the confusion.

I could not help but speak my conviction, and the whole meeting voted with a majority to support the director. The whole board resigned, and someone nominated me for the job of new chairman of the board— an honor that I politely declined. You know why? I felt like a hypocrite, since I was not a stitch better than anyone else in the whole room. I just had used my peacemaking speech to come out the shining hero of the night! That's how I felt at least!

The decisions made at that meeting only postponed the inevitable ending. The man was ousted later and ended up in another church altogether. I do remember with much pleasure how we used to sing under his direction the old songs that I loved so well. The result was that we became involved in church matters in a very short order. We felt right at home in the church community.

A recreation society was started, and someone suggested that I should be the director of that society. The play director had to do his work under the supervision of a board with a chairman. This turned out to be an excellent working relationship, and we put up some very entertaining programs in the next year and a half. This had also the result that Jo and I were fully accepted in the church community of Red Deer.

The pinnacle of success was reached when the minister of that day wrote a three-hour review of the immigration movement of the early fifties. A drama club in Calgary had volunteered to study the play and put on a performance on the "Calvinists' *toogdag*"—a big word in Dutch. The meaning is "young people rally." The purpose was to bring together all the young people of South and Central Alberta.

The drama group from Calgary canceled out of their commitment six weeks before the rally was to be held. All the speakers had been contacted, and the Jubilee Auditorium of Calgary had been hired for this special day. The whole big day was threatened to turn in a disaster. Good counsel was hard to come by! It was at that point that the Red Deer minister remembered our little recreation club and approached me. You got to keep in mind that disaster creates its own laws. We were the last line of defense, and a very feeble defense it was! To say that I was overconfident would be an overstatement, but I could have been a little more cautious. I accepted under the condition that we would have all possible support from the congregation and the board had to give its consent. Both conditions were agreed on, and we started the most ambitious program of that kind at that time.

I have never worked with the kind of resources made available through the influence of the minister. We had to work with a cast of sixty-some people and then the supporting cast. The demand for organization was unbelievable in spite of the tremendous task of studying the parts and directing the different actors to the point that they would be enjoyable and believable. The Jubilee Auditorium where we would have to play was the most prestigious building of all Southern Alberta, and the stage was as big as a good-size barn.

The Calgary Club had said that the play was poorly written and was impossible to act out with believable results. We proved them wrong on all counts. The Calgary people did agree to make the backstage props and charged an unreasonable amount for their services. And not only that, but they were also strutting around as proudly as peacocks in their much-acclaimed Jubilee Auditorium. This did not wipe out the fact that the little city of Red Deer had to do the work that they thought was impossible.

And a success it was! If you take into consideration the type of material we had to work with and the very short time span to organize the whole production of that play. The Red Deer minister enjoyed the play so much that he arranged to have the play performed in Edmonton also. We acted on the most perfect stage that I have performed on in all my life. This was in the Ukrainian Hall on Ninety-Seventh Street—a beautiful building with all the comforts that an actor can ask for. It was an actor's dream. The back rooms had the most colorful costumes you could think of. It had hats and sabers and all the finery of an eastern play included. We had nothing to do with those costumes as you can well imagine, but it was a showcase of stage material, the likes I have never seen before or after. I think I would have liked to be a Ukrainian at that particular moment.

All good things must end! Also the story of that adventure . . . We will take a step back in time to cover another aspect of our life in that city. We had been renting this big old house in the first year of our residence in that city. It was then that I remembered the time in Edmonton that I vowed not to live my life in a rental home. We decided to build a house in the north of the city. Finances were a problem, since I could get no money without collateral. Father Kranenborg went out of his way to help us out in that respect. He went to his own bank and asked for a loan so that I could build a house.

His bank would not help him out, and Jo's dad canceled all his connections with that bank without any hesitation. He went to another bank where he could get me a loan, and that was something that I have never forgotten—this generous gesture on our behalf. It was mighty big of him! He also helped me out in another respect. The building inspector was making a little fun of the blueprint that I had submitted for approval of the building side.

My father-in-law went promptly to a higher official, and this old man said, "Give the man his permit! We don't care what the inside looks like. He can chop it up to matchsticks if he so desires! We are interested in the outside. He can have his permit if he sticks with the outside plan."

Now came the busy time of building the new house in that particular part of town. I contacted contractors to dig the hole for the basement and men to bring me blocks for the same purpose. I had the advantage that I could do my own block work, and this made a lot of difference in the cost of the project. This had to be done in my holidays, as you can imagine. The father of my brother-in-law was over for a trip from Holland, and he did not know what to do with his free time, and so he came over to do a little work for me in the basement right in the beginning of that project.

We had neighbors at that place who could have been sun worshippers. They believed that a lot of sunshine was the best thing for their half-year-old baby. The result was that the baby was lying in the boiling hot sunshine for the better part of the day. This was supposed to be healthy? The old man was so upset about that behavior that he was shivering in his workbooks, and he most definitely would have ended it if he only would have had the authority to do anything about it. This was not to be! The little ones had to suffer in the sunshine for better or worse. It is a funny thing because these mothers were very conscientious and really thought that they were doing the right thing, while the old man suffered right along with the children. He must have had a very low opinion about the young mothers in Canada.

My brothers, the carpenters, came out from Rocky and helped me to put on the roof in one day. It was the talk of that part of town, and the neighbors were watching the herculean task finished in record time. Brother Adolf did the electric work, and he was just as fast, but this did not show all that much, since this was inside the building. We got a furnace installed just before the cold set in and moved into the new house, in the basement for the time being!

All things were falling in place except my income. That was sliding to a lower level, since all businesses were dead around that time. No one was spending any money, and we were lucky if we could put in two days of work in one week's time. All the body men were suffering to the point that most of them became quite desperate.

I picked up a little rockwork in that time, but that was more grief than profit, since it was at Sylvan Lake, and I had to travel a long distance to do the job. I can't say that they treated me unfairly at my place of work in spite of all our troubles. On the contrary, it was just so that there was no business going on anywhere.

It was at that particular time that my old employer came from Rocky to ask if I would accept the position as foreman in my former place of employment. Another body shop had opened in Rocky, and the former foreman Carl could not compete, since he lost a lot of business to the other body shop. Carl had quit.

The decision was not easy, but the fact that we had to share so little work with so many body men in my present place of work had the effect that I was not free to deny the opportunity placed before me. I accepted out of the motive that I should make room for others. The Lord directed our future back to Rocky Mountain House. The bookkeeper of the shop said that I had been the highest-paid tradesman in that position. I don't know if this is true, but it is possible.

Now came the job of selling the house that we just built. I received a reasonable bid to be paid in cash money from one fellow at work, but I declined. I felt that I should help a young couple from our church instead. They were just married and needed all the help they could get. That's what I thought anyway. Our feelings of goodwill betrayed again the better part of judgment. I fought to get my money in later days and lost half the money to a collecting agency.

It reminded me of the advice that I received from the foreman when I left for the last time. He told me, "Never do a favor to anyone when you are in business"—advice that I have been reminded of time and again. It just seems to work that way. A favor done with the best of intentions seems to backfire usually. I am not cynical when I say that! It is just a fact of life. And yet I kept trying! And sometimes it did work out.

Nobody was crying when I left with the truck full of household stuff. I think that the men were glad that there was one person less to share the work. Our future seemed to be in Rocky. The trouble was I had just sold my house in Rocky to brother Bert, and it had been moved only a month before we returned to Rocky.

This did not leave many options, and I was forced into another rental house! This house was a very romantic one. It had all kinds of nooks and crannies, and it was a pleasure to roam through the different sections of the house. But looks can be deceiving even so. This house was not very comfortable, and we found to our sorrow that the house was colder than Toby. A person could stick his hand outside the kitchen without opening the door. There was a crack in the door of at least four inches or more.

The landlord seemed to think that a little crack like that was a small matter in a country as big as Canada. He refused to fix it. Not only that! I even had to pay for the repair of the plumbing when it busted because of the frost. It is easy to understand that we were not all that comfortable in that place of many tribulations. Yet we did have a lot of fun in that house after all, since the weather was fairly mild, and life was quite bearable for the time being.

Mom (Jo) and I wanted to go to the folks in Red Deer to celebrate New Year's Eve over at her parents' house after we had settled in and things were more or less organized. We left the house when the sun was shining, and the temperature was well above freezing. Things were looking up, but, first, I had to stop at the highway to change a sealed beam in the car, and the sun was still shining. We started driving when the sealed beam was installed, and the snow started flying before we had gone one mile. We were in for one of those quick weather changes that can happen in the unpredictable Canadian climate.

The temperature dropped at least twenty degrees in a matter of minutes, and we were in the middle of a snow blizzard before we had gone two miles. Sight became so bad that we ended in a ditch after a few more minutes. Trouble was upon us, and we were stalled for the duration. The trip was off; there was no other way. We had to return home after someone had pulled us out of the ditch.

This was the fastest weather change I have ever witnessed in this fair country of Canada. I have never seen anything like it.

We went to Jo's folks the next day and ran into trouble again when we came back home the next day. The oil stove had the nasty habit of quitting when it was most needed. She had figured to go on strike when we were in Red Deer. She did not quit only! She decided to enliven the situation and started spewing soot throughout the house. It was soot here and soot there—soot, soot everywhere. Even the children were under the soot after a little stay in the house. The place was not fit to live in when we got back home, and Jo had to bring the kids to Bert's house. Soot like that is the most impossible stuff to clean, and it was only after a lot of hard work that the place became livable again. It sounds so very easy when I write this, but it was so very hard to handle at the time when we had to live in there.

One sister-in-law became sick around that time, and Jo and the other in-laws started sharing the workload and the children. After that, we had three more kids to take care of; this added to the four of our own. It was a lot of extra work but also a lot of extra fun. This old house had a lean-to against the main building, and a person could walk up the side of that lean-to as easy as pie. This is just what I did on one nice and sunny day.

The children were in no hurry to come out of bed in spite of our repeated warnings of very dire consequences. This called for the ultimate weapon, and I crawled on the roof with the garden hose. It was with a great sense of accomplishment and a lot of enjoyment that I sprayed the kids soaking wet before they could get out of their precarious position escaping behind the skirts of my lovely Johanna.

It might sound a little rude, but it was great fun for all of us, including the victims of this rude awakening! They still talk about that at times. Come to think of it, we had an awful lot of fun in those days when the going was tough, but when the tough got going, I would not want one to do it again! But I would not have wanted to miss any of it either. We lived very strong in those days!

The sharing of the problems among the women was one of the nicest things that a person can think of. Nobody had any reason to be proud or stuck up because no one had anything to be proud of in the first place. One woman would take over for the other if there was any kind of problem in anyone's household. There was hardly a year that one or the other of the women was not expecting a child. It is for that reason that we often had the double amount of kids in those years. There was always room for one more! It also was one reason that I started to think about another house. The rented house was romantic, but romance does not keep you warm. Not very long anyway! Although it can be a lot of fun!

We started looking for another lot to build on in the spring of 1959. There was a building lot in the lower end of town that looked fairly good, and I had a notion to put a bid on that place. It was on a sloping hill overlooking the brush land to the south of Rocky, and the mountains could be clearly seen on a clear day. I was almost persuaded when a fire broke out in the nearby lumberyard. That did it!

Jo did not dare to live that close to the mill. Another place had to be found! I would have liked to build on the farm again, but Jo did not want any of that either. There was no electricity on the farm and no phone, and she absolutely refused to go there again under those conditions. I could see her point and accepted her reasoning against a house on the farm. She had to work too hard as it was. But it did double my workload!

I wanted to develop the farm, and I had to build a house simultaneously. And last but not least, I had to build up the business in the body shop, since there was almost no business left when I arrived in the former thriving body shop in the old location. I will go into that later!

It was back to square one after the fire. We started to look somewhere else and ended in Tin Pan Alley. I bought a lot in the north side of town and built a house there. An old man across the road was my supervisor. He watched every move I made, since he had nothing else to do. Well, we gave him something to watch all right!

I still was a good cement worker and a very good block layer. We went to work while many eyes were following our every move in those days. I was a good tradesman, and Jo had a very winning personality. This made us many friends in a short period, and I got, as an extra bonus, lots of free advice from the old guy across the road. The right display of appreciation, at the right time, can do wonders for future relations.

Another Dutch family was living down the road. This lady was one of the kindest and winning personalities in the neighborhood. Jo could not go outside, or this lady would call over and tell her that the coffee was on. Mom has many good memories of her, especially since the children were always welcome. Nothing was ever too much for this kind woman if she could help Jo in any way at all. We should have more people like her, kind and good.

I had built a three-wheeler bicycle for my oldest son beside all my other commitments—a wonder of engineering if I have to say so myself. The boy was even smarter than I was. He broke one pedal off that bicycle in no time flat. You might think that this would slow him. Not a chance! He went faster with one pedal than the other kids with two! That self-made bike has seen a lot of use in the years that we lived in that part of town, much to the frustration of the old man across the road. The nicest stretch of sidewalk was in front of his house, and the children had regular races in front of his property.

The old man was forever on the road to squeeze some oil in the pedals and wheels of the bicycles as they went squealing over the racetrack in front of his house. There was a good side to all this. It kept the old man busy, and this might have done him a lot of good.

This man was very precise but not without kindness, as he would prove to his own desperate wife on one nice summer day. He went to work in the old lady's garden. It was her pride and joy. The old man had a mission to improve on the old lady's gardening skills. He set to work when she was in town. Cleaning the garden but good!

He chopped down everything that he could see, and a lot that he could not see. I should mention that he was almost blind! He went into battle without fear or favor and cleaned the garden from everything that was green, including the beans and most of the other plants. It was a proud warrior who was facing the old lady who was crying when she came across the road and told Jo about the powerful works that her husband had wrought. I wonder why she did that.

We had good neighbors, but not everything was moonshine and roses in that part of town. I found a neighborhood girl in front of our cupboard when I came into the house unexpected. She was rifling through our cupboard drawers to try and find some money—mission impossible! We very seldom had any money, but it did not make me happy to see this fairly young girl in front of our cupboard.

It was even worse at the time that we had about forty dollars missing out of the money bin where Jo kept the household money. It turned out that this neighbor girl had talked one of our children into taking some money out of Jo's wallet. The poor child did not even know that she had stolen such a great amount of money, a great amount in those days anyway! We retrieved the money that time but did some worrying about the situation. The problem became even worse when we were told that some ten-year-old girls in the neighborhood would go in the bushes with some older boys. There they would strip naked for the price of a chocolate bar. All this gave us pause to think about the future of our children, and this would lead to another move—this time to a place where we would stay for the duration.

I am running ahead of myself again. Many other things happened before we made this last move. I should not forget that my brothers helped to put the roof on this house also. I was amazed at the fact that they could figure out the pitch of the whole roof on the carpenter's square. The brothers figured out the whole roof without crawling up the ladder. Something that I do not understand but respect till this very day!

We moved into the new house just before the winter. The shell of the house was ready, and some paneling was ready on the inside, but a lot of work would have to be done before we would be really living in comfort. Heating was the main problem when we moved into the house. We had a new gas furnace, but it had to be checked by a qualified plumber before the gas company would turn on the gas.

Our number-three son had to go to the hospital for an appendix operation around that time. This made matters even worse. The surgery went over without problems. Nevertheless, we were told that we would have to pick up the boy because he kept crying and whining all day long.

Some other guy in his room was ready to kill the little fellow. We did not have much choice in the matter and brought the little boy home. The child was so sore on the stomach area that he could have no blankets over that part of his body, and this created a big problem.

Our plumber had promised time and again that he would come out to check the furnace, but he never showed up. We needed heat very badly, and we had to go to another plumber to ask one of those men to check the furnace so that we would have heat in the house. The new plumber was at our place within the hour and hooked up the furnace so that we had the heat that we so badly needed. He might have headed off far more serious problems by his humanitarian action, and I am thankful for that to this very day. Naturally he did all his business with us from that point on!

It looks all so simple when you read this, but the problem was very serious when we had to struggle with it.

I had been heating the house with an old coal furnace up to that point, and the unloading of coal in the basement gave me the injury that has maimed me for the rest of my life. There was a broken window in the basement, and I was grabbing for it as that window as it was sliding into the basement. A piece of glass cut into the center of my hand and cut my hand wide open. The doctor had a very hard time cutting through the calluses in the inside my hand, and he broke more than one needle trying to stitch the wound edges in that place. The pain was almost unbearable, since he could not freeze the wound enough to take away all the pain. It was bad as it was, but that was not all. The worst was yet to come!

I found out that I could not move one of my fingers when I got home, so I went right back to the butcher, for that was the only solution. The doctor made his excuses that he had not checked my finger movements before doing anything and spent the better part of one hour pulling the two ends of the tendons back together. This operation was even more painful than the first time that he worked on my hand. Nevertheless, he came too late with all his efforts, since the tendons had shrunk so much that he could not hold on to the slippery ends. They slipped back into the wound repeatedly. My finger was standing straight ahead and bothered me in every small operation from then on especially when I was working inside a closed area. It was by the doctor's incompetence that I lost the use of that finger. I never made an issue out of this at the time, but it is his failure as a doctor beyond any doubt!

He sent me a reminder when I was a little slow in paying. That's the part that galled me the most. He bungled the job to start with, and then he sent me the bill for it plus a reminder! How stupid can you get!

I spent close to a thousand dollars a few years later for corrective surgery and ended with a crooked finger instead of a straight one. I remember that episode only too well. My insurance would not cover the whole bill, and that doctor treated me as his worst enemy until he had my promise that I would pay the amount that was not covered by the insurance. The whole affair left a very poor impression of the dedication of that particular doctor. His dedication did not seem to reach beyond the thickness of the patient's wallet, and that was not all that much in my situation. The doctors did not know how lucky they were, and neither did I.

We have a condition called malignant hypothermia, a condition that can react to the anesthesia of an operation. It can send a patient into a high fever, and death is almost certain if the reaction can't be arrested. This reaction could have happened then, and they surely would have lost me. It seems to indicate that I had some work to do yet! The result was the fact that I went through life with a crooked finger, and I got along quite well, thank you!

It is about time that we record the adventures in the body shop as they unfolded in horrid detail over the next few years. Carl had left because the opposing body man in town had moved in with the agencies of the chief Pontiac dealer in the town of Rocky. These guys belonged to the Kinsmen organization and to the Legion, both very influential organizations. It was a clever move of the opposition. He came in full control over the Chevrolet and the Ford dealership and all the business connected to these agencies.

My brother Bert told me that the old foreman had started looking for another job almost immediately after the rumor that this deal was in the making. Our main garage had only a subdealership under the Chrysler dealer in Red Deer, and this amounted to almost nothing. The headman in the main office did not want to do any dealings in used cars to speak of, and the result was that the shop did not get any used units to repair either.

I was not a drinking man, and all the business of the legion went to the opposition. My only hope was the people from the church, and their support was next to nothing for two reasons. First, those people did not drink much, and more than half the accidents in those days were caused by liquor. Second, most of the church people took their business somewhere else! Hard to believe? But it is a fact that any Christian businessman will confirm.

I am not bitter! Just stating a fact! Most Christians are very narrow-minded, a fact that I have seen confirmed repeatedly time and again. The worldly people are much more open-minded due to the nature of their dealings with each other. I have known many worldly dealers who were defrauded by certain people. They were very upset, of course, but started dealing again with the same persons only weeks later. They knew only too well that it is a long road that does not take a turn, as the expression goes. Tomorrow might be different, and the shoe might be on the other foot. This is the code of the world.

It is an easier code of conduct than the command, "Love God above all and your neighbor as yourself."

This I do know: the later code will prevail and have value for eternity. Our downfall is that we are so incompetent of living in harmony with it. Still, is this not what it is all about?

Oops! I got carried away again.

One of the biggest battles for me as manager of the shop came about almost immediately. A wrecked car was sitting behind the shop, and the insurance adjuster from Red Deer phoned me to make an estimate of repair on that job. I went to work full of optimism and phoned for prices and figured out the hours it would take to do the job. I was still working on this when a tow truck from Red Deer came to the shop and hooked onto the wrecked car and pulled it away to a shop in Red Deer.

I was absolutely livid with rage and went right to the main office to phone the head office of this young adjuster. I would not settle for anything less than the head guy himself. The boss of the main garage was standing with me in the office when I told the guy that he would have to repair the small jobs in Red Deer also if this was the way they would deal with us. My own boss was standing behind me and told me to back off. But old Henry was on the warhorse, and I told him that they would have nothing to lose, since we would not have a shop in the first place if we allowed them to pull away the better jobs.

The fellows in Red Deer understood very well what was at stake and assured me that we would get a fair bid on all jobs from that point on. I advised them that they better because I was in touch with the insurance agencies in town, and they would know where to go the next time that they needed an adjuster. This young adjuster who had pulled that one on me came in the shop not that many weeks later, and he was so angry that he was shivering on his feet.

"If you have something with me," he said, "be a man and tell it to me face-to-face!"

I replied, "I won't even talk to you if I have something with you after a stunt like that! I am going to hit you where it hurts. I will go right to the top, and don't you forget it!"

He never pulled another job out of there. All jobs were equally divided over the businesses in town from that time on.

A woman who was also the mayor of the town sold most of the insurance. She agreed fully that our shops should have first chance on estimating, and the work should stay in town if our prices were reasonable. This was the first and perhaps the heaviest battle that I fought with the adjusters, and I won that one hands down. We had a fairly good relationship with most of these men, and that came easy enough at first. Fact is we did not see much of them in those first few years.

Business was absolutely flat. There was nothing going on. We had at least two months that we had not one job in the place. Work could not be bought because there was not any. There is absolutely no punishment that can compare with an existence without any work. The days become unbearably long, and a person grows tired beyond compare after a day of doing absolutely nothing. Sounds strange? It's true nevertheless. All your bones start aging after a day of no activity. Yet we had to be there in case some work might come in at an unexpected time.

That's how we spent our days—just hanging around.

I am still grateful for the patience and the forbearance of the head boss. Our paycheck would be waiting without fail at the end of the week, and we never heard a single complaint from the old man in those lean and hungry beginning months.

There is a saying like this: "Ask a busy person if you want something done!"

I can vouch for a fact that this is absolutely true. We got so lethargic in the end that we did not feel like doing anything. Even a little job was too much for us, and we would try to get out of it, if possible. Strange but true, such is human nature. We used to be behind for an average of six weeks in later years, but then we would always find time to do a little more. As a matter of fact, my workload became unbelievably heavy in the last years in that place, but I always learned to cope with it at the expense of my health. People are that way. That's why I can understand and sympathize with the generations of people who are caught in the welfare trap. It takes a lot of understanding and patience to turn people around who have been brought up in a system like that.

We better explain at this point that I am referring to my brother Bert and me when I talk about more than one person. Bert had started working in the body shop just before I left two years earlier; he had spent those years with the other guy, Carl. This made him a second-year apprentice by the time that I took charge of that shop, and we went through some hectic years together.

I don't think that I was the most ideal boss most of the time. He was not the ideal employee. But we were brothers, and that seemed to level out all the rough spots—most of the time!

We used to pull together when the going was rough, although we might not agree on all matters. It was in those years that we had a very active civic choir, with Bert playing the organ at first and he became our director later. The choir had started as early as the winter of 1950 when we would sing under the direction of our old neighbor Marinus. He made up with enthusiasm what he was lacking in musical knowledge.

Marinus would give us a ride to the place of suffering, the house of one church member where we would practice under the heavy hand of our director.

"I got to give some disciplinarian action to night!" he would tell us on the way down there. "Don't be surprised when I start screaming at you guys tonight. You are family, and it won't hurt you if I scare the dickens out of you fellows. I can't do that to the other people! I might hurt their feelings. Be prepared. Somebody is going to get it tonight. There has to be some order in the place."

That is how my brothers and I would be sitting there with meek and sorrowful faces when Marinus was pouring the vials of wrath over us in generous measure. It was all for the good of the choir . . . I hope that you understand that! We tried to!

This happened in the early, early days of the church in Rocky. Some people out of the Rocky community joined our choir a few years later when we had a church building and a good choir director, but we must never forget that Marinus laid the basics in the first place, and it was on this basis that the choir of later years was built.

It was in those years that brother Bert sat behind the organ playing line by line the cantatas that we tackled with very inferior talents. Bert played this repeatedly until we finally would get the time and the tone in the right order. It sounded almost like singing after the right amount of time.

The general repetition was the most nerve-racking of all the practice evenings. We were totally unprepared most of the time and scared stiff. This might have made it so interesting. I have been on general repetitions in those early years with a feeling that we never would see the end of it. The sopranos would go in one direction, and the altos would make a composition of their own, while the tenors were wandering in another dimension altogether. The basses would be all right always, since I was singing bass! That made the difference in this stentorian and herculean task.

The opinion of the suffering public was very important to us, and we never could get enough of even the little crumbs of praise falling in our direction from the weary public in general. The reaction varied a lot and was almost predictable from the different sectors of the public. My parents found always some good that could be dug out of the ashes of our dream concert. They would praise even our clothing if they could not find any good anywhere else. They would always be positive.

It was only after a long time had elapsed that they would say, "Could you do this a little differently?" or "Would something like *that* not work a little better?"

Never in the middle of our triumph but always before a new wrestling match with a new musical piece! Such were the times of our earliest steps in the world of well-renowned musicians. Then there was the other group of people who seem to have made it a lifelong task to criticize and cut down any creative effort, no matter how great or how small. This group was a natural balance for our overbearing optimism—A group that could cut us down to size without any effort restoring the balance and setting us on the path of "We'll show you that we can do better!"

We have to say farewell to our friend Marinus for the time being, but not before sharing an anecdote that happened in later years when he was directing us in a little male choir. He was just as powerful in his directing then as what he was in the early days. It seems that we had not sung according to his vision of the composer's debut.

It was at that illustrious moment that Marinus uttered the following immortal phrase: "Hey, you guys. Look at me! I am standing here in the front of this outfit to help you men, and not as an ornament, if that is what you think. I might be right and you might be wrong! That's when we are all wrong together!"

His bald head would be dancing in front of our eyes like a crystal ball in front of the hypnotist.

He would point a finger at some unwary person in the front row and continue. "You might be right and I might be wrong! Then we are still wrong! But . . ." (we would be laughing our heads off at that point) ". . . But! If you are wrong and I am wrong, then we will still be right as long as you watch me and do as I tell you to!"

Most of us would be lying on the floor by then and double our efforts in his behalf after we had recovered to a semblance of normality.

Marinus was also the guy who gave us new courage in the churchyard on Sundays. He would tell us that he would go back to Holland and marry one of the princesses. He planned to return with a lot of money, and then he would set us all up in business, and all of us would get a nice farm. Beautiful words out of a beautiful person. I believe that Marinus could have charmed the birds out of the trees if he had wanted to—in those days anyway.

But we will have to do some more singing in the early day's choir. We kept learning by trial and error under a succession of directors and ended up with Bert directing as a last resort. Not many of us had great expectations of his talents, but he set us all up for a surprise. The choir kept getting better and better, and more members out of the community joined in our singing efforts until the day that we decided to tackle *Messiah* of Handel.

We had people join from all churches and backgrounds with an abundance of talent also in the solo sections, but one of the most valuable men was our pianist, a man with an English background—we did not hold that against him!

Bert kept pushing and pushing with our ardent help, and the pianist kept playing and playing line by line and note by note until we had the right timing, and after much practice, a good rendition of this immortal piece was rendered for many years in front of a fair-size crowd. I will never forget how the audience would rise to its feet again and again at the first notes of the incomparable hallelujah chorus. Not in respect to

HANK OPDENDRIES

the choir efforts but in adoration for the Lord of Lords and the King of Kings! I will carry with me till the day of my death the haunting and immeasurable comforting words of the composer.

I know that my Redeemer liveth, and although my body be eaten by the worms yet in my flesh, I shall see God! I shall see Him and no other as He will stand on the latter days up on the earth! There is no other message that's more penetrating and more meaningful in the entire world if it is seen in connection with the all-important message of the saving grace of our Lord Jesus. No message is closer to my heart!

Our outreach and presence in the musical world of Rocky and the district have never been more powerful and penetrating than in those days of the late fifties and the early sixties. We would sing *Messiah* in the Presbyterian Church for two evenings in a row and have a well-filled church both times. Not only that! We reached a lot of people in the joint efforts of people from different denominations.

The strange thing is that the average person in our church never caught on to the importance of the work we were doing in spite of the fact that this was evangelism and outreach of the first order.

All efforts are combined in the worship services at the time of this writing. Everything has to be crowded in the one-hour or one-and-a-half-hour service—Sunday school, Cadet and Calvinettes—and a host of other activities at the expense of the proclamation of the Word. It is all done in the name of outreach, and our worship gets muddled ever more as time goes by.

We might not have brought many people in the so-called Dutch Church, as it has been called scornfully and even shamefacedly. But we did proclaim the message in song and music in a very effective way in those days. It is too bad that we did not realize then how effective it really was until we lost it all in later years. It is too late to turn back the clock now. We will not get a second chance. Not like that anyway.

The trips that we made together to the choir festivals around Christmas are remembered by many as time goes on. We hired a bus and went to Red Deer to sing Christmas carols together with many choirs out of the Central Alberta area. It was an unforgettable sight to see that many choirs in their colorful robes one after the other in joyful succession proclaiming the birth of our Savior. Each in his or her own way!

This was the stuff that Christianity made a living experience for many of us. Even more so for the fact of the deeper meaning of all these things created for all of us. We will leave the music scene for a little while and follow a different area of activities that had almost as much, or even more, influence on our future generations . . . youth work!

CHAPTER 12

THE HISTORY OF
THE CADET AND
CALVINETTE CAMP

I WAS ASKED by some consistory members to write a little piece of history and of the background and the vision that led to the creation of this camp, so here is what I remember.

The minister of that day approached me on behalf of the consistory to become discussion leaders for the young people of that day, something I was quite willing to do, and so I spent my Sunday evenings with the young people! It did not take me long to realize that those young people had an abundance of energy and free time. The sad thing was that they were not enthusiastic about bible study—not in the way we used to be in the Old Country, before the war. So I started looking for a way to get them constructively involved.

It has always been my feeling and belief that every moment of our life is lived by the grace of our Lord. By that I mean all our time—times at work, time in church, time in recreation! It was with that in mind that I went to John Brouwer and asked him if he would be willing to sell a piece of land along the creek beside the Crimson Lake Road.

A movement was afoot in Lacombe at that time to obtain land from somebody along the lakeshore. This project had the backing of the classis and consequently of our minister! My aim was to get the young people involved on a volunteer basis on a project of their own. You will have to keep in mind that this land had practically no value then! All this changed, of course, in due time, but we are dealing with the times of April 1963—about two years before the time that Reverend Binnema left Rocky to go to Ontario!

John Brouwer was right away in favor. He had been thinking along the same lines! I will quote his exact words of that time, and this is what he said:

"I will do better than that. I will donate a parcel of land, but I have to talk it over with my dad—he is still part owner."

John was good for his word! The deal was on, and I had the go ahead to try and get the young people involved, but this turned into a disappointment. I could not get any help from the young folks— nothing, no matter what I said or did!

This was a real disappointment for me, but something else happened in the meantime . . . The consistory was approached by several parents about the Boys' and Girls' Club (boys and girls were meeting together simultaneously at that time—a combined club). Details of that problem are unimportant in this review!

Klaas Kikstra, Albert Jacht, Ben Simmelink, and Hank Op den Dries were asked to become leaders of the Boys' and Girls' Club! The problem area in this club showed up almost right away in the first meeting! It seemed that the former leaders gave only importance to the before-recess program. After recess did not seem to be of any concern to them! The leaders talked it over, and steps were taken by the new appointed leaders to become involved just as much in the after- as the before-recess programs!

It was also the feeling that the approach of girls and boys mentally and physically is way different especially at that age. It would be better if the boys and girls met in separate meetings. The boys and girls were very much opposed with this arrangement at first, but one girl admitted to me—after only two or three meetings—that they got a lot more out of the meetings! The Girls' Club leaders at that time were Stien Tensen, Mrs. Binnema, and Gerty Pool, as far as I remember (see Stien Tensen!).

The Boys' Club had a few very successful campouts after that— camps that are remembered to this very day. We also had some combined meetings during Christmas, and that went over very well.

We remember one meeting when it was *forty below!* The leaders went to church just in case some kids would show up and to their amazement found the place full of kids. A wind started blowing late in the evening, but nobody wanted to break up the meeting, none of the kids anyway. They had too good a time so that the respective leaders, feeling responsible, had to go with their cars along with the children to make sure everybody got home safe and sound. Just think of it! *Forty below and a wind blowing!* There is no exaggeration in this statement, but the honest truth as I remember it!

Things were happening fast in those days. We were approached by the Cadet and Calvinette Clubs of Central Alberta with a request to start a Cadet and Calvinette Club in Rocky. Four clubs were needed to make a club core, and Central Alberta was one club short. It was important to get that other club, and that was why we were contacted.

A core could form a depot to store badges and study materials at a lot cheaper price than when each club had to order it individually (the taxes were so high at the border). Everything had to be brought in from the States at that time. Let me point out that Cadets and Calvinettes were not a CRC organization as such at that time but were warmly supported by our CRC! We were requested to ask the consistory for permission to form these clubs and ask for their help and guidance!

John Brouwer approached me about a year after the first time when we had the first prospective agreement of camp donation to the young people!

The discussion went as follows:

JOHN BROUWER: Did you make any progress with the young people about the land?

HANK: No, I could not get the young people involved, but will you donate this land to the Boys' and Girls' Clubs?

JOHN BROUWER: That's perfectly all right with me, if it goes to the youth of the church!

But we still could not find the insight to the possibilities of this project until we mentioned it at a ring meeting of Central Alberta Cadet and Calvinette core later.

Those people were completely jealous and said, "We would give anything if we had a farmer in our neighborhood that would do the same for us!"

Things started shaping in a hurry after that! John Brouwer donated the camp on the following conditions: that within the following five years, a road should be put in and some buildings should be started.

"I do not want to donate that land and have it lying idle with no improvement!" he said.

To that we agreed. We owe a lot to the insight and support of John Belder, who helped us right from the beginning. His kids had joined the clubs after the separation of boys and girls into individual clubs. John Belder cut several pine trees and donated them to the camp. We had to cut the branches off and do the necessary work to make them ready for the mill! The idea was to cut the logs on three sides and make cabins out of the logs, just like it was done later with four of the cabins!

It was at that stage that Mr. Conie of Conie's Store told Klaas Kikstra that Crimson Lake wanted to increase the beach area at Crimson Lake. Several cabins were to be moved out of the beach area. One of them was the L-shaped cabin owned by the Curby family, if my memory serves me right. The government would sell this to us at a reasonable price.

We had received a lot more support from the parents at that stage. Too many to mention without missing a few, but with the buying of the cabins, we were still on our own. There was not a dime in the kitty just then, but we decided to go ahead and bid on the L-shaped cabin anyway, getting that one at a reasonable price! I have forgotten how we financed it, but we were prepared to raise the money out of our own pocket if necessary! This led to an episode that is still one of my fondest memories . . .

Several parents joined in the effort of cutting the L-shaped cabin in sections, since it could not be moved in one piece. The floor was cut up, the roof was cut in sections, and the walls were cut up so that it all could be transported!

It was during dinnertime of a certain day that I left my work in town to have a look at the proceedings. John Brouwer was working around the cabin with a front-end loader on his tractor and a wagon to move the different sections. Mr. Altwater came walking up to us. He was the park warden and overseer of the Crimson Lake area. This man told us that we could have the little cabin, the one next to the kitchen, for nothing, if we could get it out without cutting any trees—something that was next to impossible. I will tell just what happened without claiming any credit!

I suggested to John that we could lift the roof section and take the logs from underneath to put them back together again at a later date. John, resourceful as ever, borrowed a little Cat with a front-end loader from the work crews who were having a break for dinner. Then John forgot to ask for permission, but that seemed like a small matter then!

In that way the whole roof was hanging on the two loaders not long after that. We could lift the logs from underneath one by one. The whole operation took less than one hour. It was one of the slickest operations I have ever been involved in! The other leaders and I, with the help of some boys, rebuilt that cabin in the evenings.

Some boys involved were Bas Belder, Albert and Bill Tensen, John Feddes, the Smid boys, George Kraal, and a few more! We had that roof section hanging on a couple of Jackals, and underneath those raised logs, we replaced the following logs one by one. The boys had a whale of a time, but I was scared stiff most of the time. It looked like the whole kit and caboodle would come crashing down on our heads at any given moment, but it was all great fun and a great morale builder.

Something else happened around that time that was very important to the Cadet Camp. Reverend Binnema came to see me one day and told me that a couple of families had some objection to the fact that we were trying to start a camp. He told me that our efforts would be better spent if we traveled with our children to Gull Lake Camp; that camp was supported by classes! I replied that I had neither the will nor the authority to cancel the operation then. We agreed after a fairly heated discussion that we should bring it up at the next congregational meeting. That meeting was to be held not long after that day.

On that congregational meeting, it was agreed that the Boys' and Girls' Club leaders could go ahead if they thought it would benefit the children. There was almost no opposition to the project at that meeting or any time afterward! This must have been late 1964 or early 1965.

The founders of camp had the following vision: primarily, that this camp should be and remain a low-cost camp served by volunteer efforts; second, that this camp should promote and encourage the creative efforts of children of any color and background, not in a teacher-people relationship (there is enough of that in our schools and elsewhere) but in a counselor/Cadet-Calvinette relationship—just as the Cadet program advocates; third, a point strongly visualized by the late Klaas Kikstra, that not one tree should be cut unnecessarily. If any improvements should be made, that improvement should blend in with the character of a nature camp!

The one point that struck me when we entered the Cadet program was the following quote:

"Beware that you do not turn your Cadet program into a glorified Sunday school!"

Cadetting means that counselor and Cadet walk together, talk together, and experience together! Counseling is sharing and caring of the highest order!

Our following minister was Reverend Sluys, and he got involved enthusiastically almost from the beginning. Other paths had to be explored!

Our youth's movement was growing by leaps and bounds, and new resources had to be created! I have to mention something important before going any further. Permission had to be obtained to put a road in the camp. Mr. Hardolt, the Municipality District Manager of that time, insisted that the access road to the camp should come in on the bottom of the hill. An entrance at the top of the camp would be way too close to the crown of the hill.

Accidents would surely follow with cars coming over the hill at great speed. There would be no warning of traffic coming out of the campground. I should mention that this road was the main road to Crimson Lake at that time!

I could pick up a culvert after that and asked Art Herman, who was a cat skinner at that time, to plow in a road at the place where it is now. We had no money but enough faith that money would come in time. We could always pay it out of our own pocket at the last resort. This was in the first year that Reverend Sluys was with us. It was suggested that a camp out should be held for all Cadets and Calvinettes.

This was a spur of the moment decision at a time that we were not quite ready yet for such an undertaking. The small cabin was standing in fairly good shape, and the shell of the L-shape was standing, that was about all. This camp was not ready yet to receive some fifty or sixty children!

Bas Belder and I went to the campground on Saturday morning before the camp week. Nothing was ready and nobody else showed up, so Bas and I started pouring some much-needed foundation blocks under the L-shape cabin and lined the walls with plastic and plywood. Things did not look very promising, for it was pouring rain that morning, but we carried on and got more helpers coming in later in the day. Some tables were built, and, lo and behold, the sun came out on Monday morning. We had a good but somewhat hectic campout together in the week after that. A little premature and a little primitive! But it was the start of about thirty years of campouts.

This was the end of my involvement with Cadet Camp, and someone else will have to carry on the story! It has been a great privilege for me that I was asked to serve as camp director for four years of the beginning years. Most were very good. The cooperation between counselors was very good.

We held a name-giving contest in those first years, and the name chosen by general consent turned out as follows: Sonrise Cadet and Calvinette Camp!

Now a few personal remarks that you can read or ignore as you please: There is one cabin in this camp dedicated to the memory of my grandson who was called to be with his Lord at an early age. He was eleven years old when he passed away. Sometimes I wondered why? The answer is *Jesus!*

I was asked to write the early history of camp as good as I could remember, and I tried to do this faithfully to the best of my knowledge. I have grown old enough that it does not matter if I get any credit in my involvement, but I am very thankful that our early efforts were blessed far beyond our expectation.

Every moment of our life we live by the grace of God, and every moment should be dedicated to Him! Our Creator made muscles for crying but also for laughter, for work, and for pleasure. There is a time to cry and there is a time to laugh. It is all in His hand. This is the message we tried to pass on to the Cadets and Calvinettes. We have seen all those things in Sonrise Camp and more.

Things are bound to clash at times when some sixty odd people live out their feelings for a week in camp. But feelings can be directed and attitudes can be changed. People on the fringes can be drawn in. Loners can be reached—but only IF YOU LET PEOPLE BE THEMSELVES AND BE CREATIVE.

We can bring our kids up in a protected environment, something like a modern monastery! Protect them and shield them, but someday, somewhere, they have to enter the real world! We can also bring up our kids with a feeling of compassion and feeling for that what *seems to be inferior!* I have found time and again that even the roughest boy will come through if you make him responsible for someone else. After all, is that not what love is all about? To give yourself totally! And on the end of the road, there is only one being left—*Jesus.*

November 12, 1995, Hendrik op den Dries
PO Box 242
Rocky Mountain House, Alberta

I would like to add some additional information—some things that I wanted to keep out of the official report on the camp history as recorded in former pages.

We realized full well that we would be wise to act and have everything in place before the rest of the congregation woke up to the importance of these campgrounds. Opposition was sure to follow when some segment of the congregation would get a feeling of being left out. This is exactly what happened when the minister of that day tried to block the development of that camp. It was not official, don't you see?

The second blocking operation was more successful. This happened when the second minister got involved. He acted real fast when he realized that he could not take complete control as long as I was around. He called a meeting of all the counselors after the first campout in the new campground.

I was fifteen minutes late for that meeting, so they started without me. The minister informed me that they had voted in another head counselor the moment I walked in the door—they had delegated me to the sidelines.

Really neat and really effective, since I was unofficially the head counselor up to that point. This operation hurt my feelings in a very deep manner, but I have learned to understand that the Lord will delegate a person to the sideline when that is better for his own well-being, especially at those moments that he gets too big for his britches. It is all for the better in the long run!

The fact that the church got title to this camp at a later day is also for the better. We knew well enough at the time that we were in an untenable position. Two or three youth counselor should not be in possession of property of that kind. The most important thing is the fact that we were well guided by the Spirit in spite of our stubborn self-service!

CHAPTER 13

THE PRODUCTIVE YEARS

I WILL MAKE a remark that is way out of line, but it is a good illustration of what I mean! It was a little bit like Elijah after his battle with the Baal priest. He thought that he had done so well, and then the good man was put on a sideline. It had come to the point that I was standing in the way of the real progress of this camp and I was retired, so to speak! Do not get me wrong. I did not think that I was fighting against the Baal priest, but there is little doubt in my mind that the devil will fight against anything constructive.

Enough of the camp! We will go on to other important things.

It was during those years that my brother Bert asked me to become a member of a brass band, a band started by members from our church and some others from outside our denomination. Bert did not have much confidence in my abilities but must have figured, if it does not help, it won't hurt! History has recorded that I did rather well as a baritone player. I remember studying on that instrument until the walls of Tin Pan Alley were shaking on its foundation. Mom hung on for dear life, and so did the rest of the neighborhood. Our neighbors deserve real credit for the fact that they left me unharmed and the windows of the house in one piece. I got to be so good that I could play the valves of the instrument with the right or the left hand. A real accomplishment, I would say!

My right hand was in a cast after I cut my hand in the accident with the window that I have mentioned before. I was fingering the baritone valves with my right hand and getting fairly good at it. The injury put a stop to that, and I learned to do the same thing with the left hand instead. My commitment to the band was irrevocable. I kept practicing in spite of all obstructions. Even Johanna could not stop me. My opinion has always been that no activity is attractive at first stages and few people have the insight to join a beginning movement. It was that way with the choir and with the band and a host of other activities that we were involved in.

It takes a visionary person to get things done. Very few people will jump on the bandwagon until it starts rolling. Only a few people will start the rolling process. It is my conviction that the Spirit used the talents of a few individuals to start the different movements that have been a blessing for so many. I am thinking about the creation of churches and schools in the past fifty years and not so much about the other activities, although these activities also had a place in the development of Christian outreach in all areas of life.

We reached people also through the lowly efforts of the Rocky community band. I remember a woman who was beating the big drum with vigor and precision while the joy would be shining off her face as she walked with us in the parade. She was beating the skins of that drum as if her life depended on it. One of the most successful businessmen in town would be sitting along the lowly Dutchmen blowing the saxophone in the company of another businessman out of town, also a saxophone player.

This man was so fat that we had to sew two uniforms together to make room for his ample torso—to put it nicely. I must add that this happened at a later date.

I would not say that they members were top musicians, but they most certainly were the most faithful members you could think about and most certainly a lot of fun always. Even my oldest brother has played in that band when he was over here from Holland. He is a top musician but was not too proud to sit with our underdeveloped little group.

This was in sharp contrast to one member who had excellent talent as a musician, but he considered himself as a class in himself. The result was that he came irregularly, and we had to be very thankful when he came down to our level and played with ordinary folks like us. Members like the saxophone players might have had less talent but were a lot more useful. They would not miss a practice, and that's the kind of stuff that builds organizations and keeps them strong. I should mention that the lady of the lowly drum was an excellent piano player also. She did not think that it was below her dignity to beat the old drum. On the contrary!

The band was getting bigger and bigger, and the time came that we had to look for uniforms to satisfy the local population. A colorful character with the name Charley Bruce—a respected person in the community—went for a drive among the population to line up enough money to buy uniforms for the band of about forty-some members.

It was at that occasion that we had to sew two uniforms together for one person. Our new uniform turned to be plenty loud for the taste of some members but was gladly accepted out of respect for the goodwill that was backing up this generous gift.

Old Charley was walking in front of the yearly parade with a chamber pot on his eighty-year-old skull, a fact that might have looked ridiculous on anyone else but Charley. He had a standing ovation all along the parade route. This was not that remarkable, since everyone was standing anyway! But you get the picture, I hope.

It was the heart that counted. This gesture was bighearted and well appreciated, but we had almost empty halls when we gave a concert. It was so bad that we had a practice march through the center of town on a Friday night just before the parade. Down the hill we went right through the main street all the way to the bottom of the hill with not a soul in sight. The street was as empty as if someone had shot a cannon through the middle of town. The reason for that is not clear, but I have the feeling that we did not get accepted as Dutchmen who were replacing a band directed by a man named Platten. This man was remembered with a certain amount of nostalgia, and we could never live up to that image. This and the fact that we did not want to play for dances! We would have been an instant success if we had combined our efforts with a dance band.

The band went in a slow decline when brother Bert left and when the minister's wife and her daughter resigned because the music was too banal and ordinary for their refined tastes. It is fair to say that at least two dozen people picked up the first elementary knowledge of music in those days. We had some very accomplished instrumentalists then, enough to start another band even now, more than thirty years later.

But I said it before, the clock can't be turned back.

Our civic band often supported Remembrance Day and the parades in those days, but it did not seem to leave much of an impression! Not by the looks of it.

One thing was curious even so. One of the most influential businessmen in town was a band member. He was also a veteran of the First World War, a man who had fought in the trenches around Verdun—a fact he rarely mentioned except occasionally when he sang the tune of "Mademoiselle from Armentieres," a song depicting the fast women behind the front lines of the first war.

This man was of very high standing and did not want to go to the Remembrance Day parties unless absolutely necessary. I believe that he was worth a million or more, but you would never have known it. He was playing his instrument the same as all others. No fuss. No bother!

The battle over the Dutch and English services was heating up in the church around that time. One section wanted only English, and the other half wanted half-and-half. The feelings ran very high to the point that some members of the church refused to go to church unless their demands were met. Everything had to be English. Their argument was that everything had to go aside for the welfare of their children.

The attitude of my parents was in great contrast to these folks. Dad and Mom went to church as faithful as anything. They never skipped a single proclamation of the Word, no matter what the language was, as long as I have known them.

The issue was not that clear cut for me! I had a terrible time accepting the fact that my parents who had helped to build this church should be relegated to the basement if they wanted to hear a sermon in their mother tongue. I thought that this was disgraceful! And I still think that way, but no amount of persuasion could change the mind of some English language supporters. It was for the best interest of their children!

That was that! No ifs, ands, or buts . . .

The interest of the older generation was subservient to the interest of the children. I was of the opinion that all things would fall into place if due respect was given to the older people first. The behavior of the children would fall in place because of that. I do not have the impression that their children turned out any better than any of ours, in spite of their attitude. On the contrary!

We go through a period like that again presently. The old ways are obsolete and have to be changed—no matter what the cost. All

HANK OPDENDRIES

methods are sacred if it leads to the ultimate goal of watering down the worship services. My parents have taught me that it is a serious thing when a person goes through the congregation and starts building up pressure groups to overthrow the order of things. Total chaos and a total breakdown would be the result if we all did that.

The Bible calls that "creating divisions."

Yet it is exactly this that is propagated and encouraged by the ruling bodies in Calvin College. This and nothing else!

All this reminds me of Jesus's days on earth. He must have been convinced of the total depravity of the church system in His days. Yet He went to the church repeatedly to show another and a better way. He never discouraged or advised His followers to stay out of church. On the contrary! He called this house "the House of His Father" even though the destroyers were not far off in the future when all that earthly power would be eliminated.

I receive new courage when I think about this example, new courage to go on and do my duty in the hope that His judgment over me may be covered by the sacrifice of Jesus of Nazareth!—Nazareth, one of the most insignificant towns of Israel.

Is it not significant that the most exalted woman on earth, the mother of Jesus, had to travel through the cold and weary night while carrying the most exalted being that ever was born? Would we deserve any better if even His own mother was not spared the hardship of life? Would I deserve any better when they gave the example and had to walk through life in the most humble manner? It is with this in view that we go on and enjoy life because of their sacrifices. It is also along those lines that we carried on in the early days of church and our marriage.

We have covered the choir, the band, and our involvement with youth work in those hectic but very satisfying days. Recreation was another area that was quite central in our life. I was asked to become director of the recreation society in Rocky not long after our return to the area. There was no other activity that gave us more enjoyment than the study evenings in the different members' houses. We had some members who were very enthusiastic but not all that talented. They could not be bypassed when it came to the dividing of the different parts in the individual plays.

This was to lead to some difficult situations, like the time that we had an evening organized for the acting out of a dramatic play. The play was written in the setting of a dramatic rescue at sea and the emergency efforts of the different lifeboats and their crew. One player was a key figure in the club but had the bad habit of losing his nerves when he came on stage so that he could not remember his part. This is what happened in front of a hall full of people. The results were disastrous. We had to send a stretcher—*brancard*—on stage, time and again, to break the deadlock and give him a chance to be prompted on his parts. The play could drag on for a little while after that, with the cast suffering and the public suffering even more.

This does not mean that we were unsuccessful in general! We had some very good performances with a great audience and a lot of laughter and enjoyment by all. We also directed a review with a sailboat and singing involved against a beautiful background and a fair-sized children's choir. This performance was very appealing to the eyes and very pleasing for the ear. It was also acting and organizing of high quality and very well received by most of the attendance in the room.

We even went for a repeat performance in Red Deer with another comical play. This was also a success excepting one part in the comical play where one female player froze and could not be persuaded to go on stage to do her part. "She was completely freaked out." We had to throw her on stage where she recovered immediately and did an excellent job of acting from that point on. The most fun might have been the evenings when all these disasters and near disasters were rehashed with a little different viewpoint from every conceivable angle until the subject was exhausted and we started looking for another play and more punishment.

We had a practice that was called potverteren. It would sound something like this in translation: "spending the kitty" or spending the money left over after expenses. Food would be plentiful on those occasions—even though no liquor was involved but everything else. A good humor was a must! No one with a sour disposition was allowed on evenings like that. I remember one party at Crimson Lake especially. We had eaten all we could handle and decided to play a game of soccer, a very noble game! One woman decided that she wanted to be in the goal, and that would have been OK at any other time but this.

One player kicked the ball so hard that she was thrown back—ball and all—for five feet or more in a very cramped position. The results were so devastating that the game came to an unexpected standstill.

The sinner came forward to make sure that the lady was not hurt all that much. She took it good-naturedly and helped us to build a bonfire with flames higher than the treetops. Even the park warden came out to join in the fun.

One of us told a spook story at that occasion that was so spooky and scary that this park warden turned white around the nose. He was somewhat reluctant to leave the scene to go through the dark forest after these enlightening moments.

One farewell party for a certain female member was even more revealing and sidesplitting funny, although it will be next to impossible to tell the story in a way that will demonstrate the spirit of the evening with no dirty intent or thoughts of any kind. Our relationship was void of any smutty thoughts or actions! It was just straight clean fun. Here goes!

A member had got the crazy notion to buy the lady in question a panty—just an ordinary panty, but every member of that august society put his or her signature on it. Several faces had been drawn on the object, and on the back was a great black circle with the word "exhaust" written under it. This might not sound all that funny for the reader, but for us it was. The faces and the expressions of the different members were priceless.

I can remember only one evening that I laughed more than that particular night. I will envisage once again!

It was an evening without one dirty expression! The fact was the lady in question had so much fun that she framed in the object behind glass and had it hanging on the wall in her room for a long time after that. Let me add that she was single at the time!

Another thing occurred around that time that I like to mention before going on to something else. It is one of my actions with a somewhat dubious intent, and I really don't know if I should be sorry about it or not. It did teach brother Bert a lesson that he remembered and put into practice often when he had a business of his own in later days. He had moved to BC then! His wife's family had moved there, and she wanted to be closer to her folks.

This particular anecdote is about a female member of the recreation society. She was a likeable enough woman but a little bossy at times. This did not sit all that well with me. I am afraid that I was a little domineering in my role as recreation director. This led to a head-on collision between this lady and me so that I made some remarks that were not all that complimentary at the address of the poor girl. The fact is that I was really sorry on the way home and regretted my behavior with real sorrow and repentance. I am not kidding! This was one of the few times that I have gone too far. It seems that my leadership was acceptable most of the time. I never heard any complaints—not to my face anyway, and most people remember those days as some of the best in memory.

It was no surprise for me that her husband came first thing next morning and told me that my behavior was unacceptable. I agreed with him immediately and said that I was sorry about my handling of the situation.

"No!" he said. "That is not good enough. You have to ask for forgiveness!"

I agreed with him and asked for forgiveness right then and there.

"No!" he said. "That is not good enough! You have to ask for forgiveness and be sorry!"

I agreed with him again and told him that I was sorry and that I regretted my behavior very much. He must have been looking for an argument, since he started all again on the theme that I had to ask for forgiveness. I was very patient about the whole affair and told him that I really regretted the incident and asked to be forgiven. This must have gone on for several minutes, and it got to the point that it became somewhat ridiculous, and I set him outside the door with the assurance that I was truly sorry.

My brother Bert had watched the whole incident and was lying flat on his stomach on the paint room floor, laughing until he almost threw up. It must have looked very funny, and he told me in later years that he had followed the same method often when customers came in his shop looking for an argument. He would agree with them wholeheartedly, in most cases with much the same result. The procedure seems to take away the fuel from the fire or the sting out of the argument—not all that unbiblical.

It seems to refer to the words of proverbs: "A soft answer turns away wrath!"

There is a lot of truth in that, but I am afraid that my behavior might not have been as acceptable as that. I was still feeling guilty, even more so after this incident with her husband. I should have gone and talked to the lady herself as that would have been the better way of handling this affair. There was also the fact that this man seemed under great stress that morning, and he might have been close to a breakdown.

So much for that! It is time to go on with the rest of the story.

It was time to build a house, again! This would be the last one! I have mentioned already that we were having trouble with the children in our neighborhood, and it came to a head when the older boys started messing around with the little girls. We realized full well that our children were more than just a little gullible, and the results could be disastrous if we stayed in town much longer with our children.

My wife—Mom, as I will call her from now on—told me that we would have to take steps to get out of that neighborhood. A thing that was easier said than done. I was flat broke! We still had the farm, but there was still no electricity and no phone and no natural gas either. All the modern conveniences would have to be left behind, and we had to make a new beginning. Too bad in a way, since I was practically debt-free at that moment—debt-free and the owner of a house!

We chose for the benefit of the family again. Mom made the greatest sacrifice this time, but I was getting the bulk of the extra work on my already overloaded and bent shoulders. I had to build a house again. Everything had to be done by hand this time! No power tools of any kind could be used, since there was no electricity, and the little power generators were still locked in the brains of some ignorant Japanese pot licker.

I had to level the floor of the basement by hand and pour the cement for the footings and the laying of the cement blocks. The two-by-fours and all the other lumber in the walls? All cut by hand, my friend. Insulating and shingling of the roof! Painting and landscaping? Even the clearing of the brush for a prospective house side! All done by hand, my friend! I even had to water witch—or douse—the well by myself, although brother Bert and my own father were good at dousing also. We found excellent water vein among the three of us.

I really don't know about this dousing business, but it seems to work. I have doused for many people over the years and never missed once. It is either one of the two. There is water all over the country or it really works! I really don't know.

Many people have asked me about it, and I always say the same thing: "It won't hurt and it might help!"

A multimillion dollar resort in the heart of the mountains has even called for my services. No drilling has been done at this point, and so I don't know the results of that one.

Oops! I got carried away again! We better get back to the house building or we will never get finished.

Electricity was already in the country then, and it was just a matter of applying and waiting for the installation of the power poles. It would take the better part of a year, but it was in the works. I still had to do everything by hand! You can't build a house out of promises. Right? The house almost did not get built. Not by me anyway. It happened when I was working on the south side of the house on the eaves of the roof, about twelve feet from the ground. I was trying to bend a stubborn two-by-six in place so that I could nail it to the roof, an action that forced me in a position that put me sideways beside the top of the ladder. I should have known better but forced the issue.

The ladder slipped away sideways with the ineffable result that I fell straight down in a sideways position—just as if I was lying in a floating bed! It is hard to believe, but I was adding up my life insurance on the way down in the hope that there was enough to keep Jo and the children. I realize that this seems a little far-fetched. It is true nevertheless. A person can do a lot of thinking in a split second!

I might have sailed to the ground in a bedlike position, but the landing on the ground was anything but that. I landed in the mud with a resounding smash and stayed there for an indefinite period while the misty rain was seeping down on my half-unconscious form. The pain was unbelievable, and it took a long time before I could drag myself to the little Volkswagen. I'll never know how I made it to the doctor. However, I ended there somehow, and it was there that my old acquaintance—the doctor of the lost tendons—prepared himself for another blunder. He told me that I had bruised ribs, in seven different spots. I would not need to be bandaged, however, because he had a new drug that could be injected that would replace the more cumbersome bandages. He pulled out a needle of at least two inches or more and started injecting me all over the back of my bruised and painful body. The pain was excruciating, and I almost fainted right on the spot.

He must have seen something was not the way it should be, and he asked me if I was OK—a silly question if I ever heard one! I was not OK! Of course not!

I dragged myself to the faithful old Volkswagen and made it to our home place in Tin Pan Alley. That's as far as I got! Mom got me to the couch in some way or other, and that's where I passed into oblivion.

It was a funny sensation, and I could feel the air leave my lungs until there was only a very narrow passage left to breathe through, less than one inch on the right side of my lungs. I am absolutely certain that my life would have ended in a matter of minutes if Jo had not been so decisive and fast acting. She phoned the doctor immediately, and this worthy person came flying in the ambulance to our house in Tin Pan Alley. He did not have his own car and came with the town police in the ambulance without delay. This is what saved my life—and, above all, the fast-acting policeman.

I still had some work to do! The Lord did not call me home yet! I was close! Oh, so very close. Dying will not be bad if it comes like that. I would have slipped into oblivion in a fairly peaceful way the way it felt at that moment in time.

I should tell you a little about the ever-faithful Volkswagen! We were the proud owners of a little Volkswagen, a most endearing little machine that almost came to life in a very realistic way. I had seen the nostalgic movie *The Love Bug*, where a pint-size auto seemed to have a life of its own. There is more to this than just a little make-believe.

My darling seemed to have the same qualities. It might be the only thing connected to the Germans that I really appreciated. This little love boat would take me back and forth to the farm or to my work, and it hardly ever let me down.

It was on a trip to Edmonton that the little powerhouse reached the very pinnacle of success. We had taken the backseat out of that machine and had about six or seven children romping around in that small but surprisingly sufficient area. Mom and I were in the front with the baby, ten or eleven people in all. Great and small. I have heard of students trying to set a record by piling into a Volkswagen! We did surpass all records and had a great time doing it while going back and forth to the amusement park in Edmonton.

These simple pleasures really put the sun in our lives. We were young and we were strong. All this happened when we had three or four more kids of one sister in-law; I forget whose children, and it really did not matter. We mixed the whole bunch together and had a great time. I would not trade these memories for all the tea in China!

It was the same machine that almost put me in the hospital in the following winter. There was more than a foot of snow in the fields, and the road had not been graded in a long time. Ruts of more than half a foot divided the road in two sections. This made the whole shebang a complete skating area. The trouble was the fact that the little car had a smaller wheelbase than the average car of that day. This might be the only drawback in the whole makeup of this wonder on wheels. It was either the left or the right wheel that was in a rut, and the other side was trailing on the high side of the other ice-covered rut. I was going at a fairly good clip and made reasonable progress until I hit a spot where another spoor crossed the two that I was trailing. It was as if the hand of a giant lifted the little car and me and threw me right into a telephone pole—Hank was in the same boat again, bruised ribs! I played it smart this time and stayed away from the doctor and did the lifesaving bit all by myself with the help of my personal doctor, Johanna. She put me in bandage and kept me warm at night. Smart, hey?

I could write a book about my experiences in the body shop but would dabble in a few spots of my memory. This book is boring enough as it is. Don't you think so?

We did most of our work in the days of the so-called power cars. The average car had eight cylinders in those days, and most cars were a lot bigger than the later-day cars. Fuel was not that expensive in those days, and pollution was a nonissue then. That's the reason that little cars were frowned upon and considered dangerous. The little car had no protection in the front, and that was a scary thought for most auto buyers. This was one reason that many people would buy the heavier automobile of that day.

Big cars were in vogue for the average car owner, and then there was the ultimate power car with some heavier engines like the Super Bee and more cars of that make.

We had to repair one of those power cars and do some framework on it. I should explain that framework was a scary thought for most people. It would put a mental block on almost anybody. I met many customers who would see defects in a car after it had been in an accident—defects built in at the factory but were not noticed until the car came out of the body shop. A great discovery would be made then! The flaw would be pointed out as a result from the accident and the following repair work—flaws and defects that had been there all along but never been noticed.

We had finished this great big monster of a car at that particular day, and the customer came to try it out. He brought two of the mechanics along, and then there was my humble person. I was forced to sit in the passenger seat with the owner in the driver's seat and the two others in the back. It was in this fashion that we started at the edge of town. Then things really started moving, and this man brought the car to full speed in less than one half mile, from zero to 120 miles an hour or more. Hard to believe but true!

We had to go over an overpass with a fair-sized hump in the very center of it. It was at that point that this car left the road for at least eight feet. We were completely airborne for the space of a second or two. It was one of those moments that the third son of my mother, Geertje, would have liked to be anywhere else but in that car. I huddled close to the dashboard in the hope that I might have just a little chance in case something went wrong. Everything was all right, and our work got a passing mark, but I was almost sweating blood when the machine was put to the test. I swear that many of those young guys would rather be without their wives for three weeks than one week without the car! It was a sign of the status quo. A person was judged by the size of his car in those heady days of the mighty power units.

I had a friend with a self-made car. It had a fiberglass body and a high-powered motor with frame. He came to me with a problem. His rear wheels would start squealing when he went through the five-mile corner. This was a corner five miles out of town, and it was at least one mile long with a nice sloping curve. I told him that the best approach would be to go with me for a drive.

A person had to stretch down lengthways in that car, less than a foot from the ground with his feet forward. The whole structure was no more than two and a half or three feet from the ground—just like a professional race car.

My friend and I were lying beside each other like a just-married couple on a honeymoon. But the trouble was that it was anything but a honeymoon. It felt more like a ready-made coffin. The driver of the would-be honeymoon car pushed the pedal to the floor, and we went into that corner at a speed of better than 140 miles an hour.

The trees on the side of the road looked like a solid wall at that speed, and it felt more like an airplane than a car. Then it happened sure enough! A penetrating squealing noise started when we were well into the five-mile corner. It went on and on until we reached the end of the corner when everything turned back to normal.

"If you can call a speed of over 140 normal."

Little Henry was lying in the honeymoon couch with the sweat of fear all over his body. I asked Andy to stop the car for a moment so that we could have a look. And, sure enough, just as I thought, the air pressure against the side of the fiberglass rear fender was so tremendous that it had pushed the flexible material against the side of the very wide tires. This is what made the squealing sound!

"Shoot!" Andy said. "I wish I had known that before! I replaced the bearings in the rear wheels once already. I was ready to do it again!"

He told me that he drove once from Red Deer to Rocky in the middle of the night. It took twenty-five minutes to make the trip of about eighty miles. You take out the calculator and figure the speed. It is mind-boggling! He was not a man who would exaggerate or brag. I have known him too well for that.

A close friendship had developed between Andy and me after he came knocking at my door with the request to help him build a cement block coffee shop. He was at the end of his tether when it came to laying blocks. This had the result that we were laying blocks in an April snowstorm that was almost a blizzard. I was laying the blocks, and he was the laborer. The snow was so heavy at one point that I could not see him anymore at the end of the wall, a distance of about thirty or forty feet. The weather was soggy but not that cold in temperature so that we could carry on with the job without the problem of frozen cement. He enjoyed that so much that he mentioned it every time when we met in later years at irregular intervals. The fact that this business turned into a real moneymaker later might have had something to do with our friendship. He had to prove a point, you see!

This coffee shop had belonged to a joint enterprise of the family on his mother's side. It was a losing proposition when he took over, and the rest of the folks had given up on it. Andy was a man after my heart. I visited him one day after the block laying was finished, and he had two ten-yard cement trucks coming in to pour a cement floor. This is so much cement that it would normally take at least four men to work it down before it was setting, a process that does not give you more time than two hours at the most. He did it all by himself. I don't know how! I could not even begin to do that herculean task!

Andy would help me in turn to build some mighty heavy and up-to-date sound systems—amplifiers—an art in itself! Those systems became so cheap and well built in later years that it does not pay any more to spend your time to build one. This was not so in those days. I became almost addicted to this kind of work but never was much good at it. It was a counterbalance for the tremendous pressure that I was under, and Jo understood enough to give me the leeway that I needed to keep my sanity . . . up to a point at least. It was this and the old John Deere that kept me from a breakdown. Things could get very hectic at times.

I could go on and on about our work with cars of all makes and all shapes over a span of nearly twenty-five years, but this would fall out of the scope of these memoirs. I will have to quit after a few more stories.

Our company had an old car in the parade for many years. It was not just any old car but some old clunker that we would paint in all kinds of colors in all forms and description. It had many more colors and hues than a rainbow, and that's a lot of color. That was not all! We would weld the rear wheels in an offset position so that the car would make a jump with every turn of the wheel. This was a ridiculous sight but got even worse in later years when we welded the wheels in an offset position, also in an unbalanced position so that the old colored dinosaur would waddle through the parade route like an oversize duck.

Half the town would be looking forward to the contraption that our company would enter the float when year after year slipped off the calendar. A long twelve-foot-two-by-ten with a saddle tied to the end of that two-by-ten was added as an additional sensation. On top of that sat a saddle with a rider, all to the great enjoyment of the onlooking public and the great discomfort of the make-believe cowboy. He would have been better off if they had run him out of town on a rail like they did in the old days.

I believe that it is better that I don't mention that I got quite drunk once. That was one time that Mom was ready to belt me a couple of good-intended haymakers. I was not acting like a father of five children who was a deacon in church beside. I have an excuse though!

I was volunteered into the job at the last moment and was so scared that I tried to drown my fear with the help of Johnny Walker rum. All the boys on that float were sauced up pretty good, and it was nip and tuck, or the Mounties would have hauled us off that float before the parade started. I think that the mayor of the town did a good word for us, and we were allowed to go our way. I do remember that I was chasing balloons right in the center of Main Street in front of hundreds of onlookers. That would not have been so bad, but I was naked from the waist up and from the knees down. I thought that the minister of the Presbyterian Church was going to have a fit because he laughed so hard.

It was on the bottom of the hill that I tried to get a laugh out of a woman with a very disapproving face. Everyone was laughing themselves silly, except—you guessed it—the woman! She never cracked a smile! Not even a twitch . . . Yuck!

It was not a happy homecoming for me that evening. It was one time that Mom was really angry with me. She wanted to go to her parents that same afternoon, and this seemed quite unlikely under the circumstances. I was not in a good condition, certainly not for a trip to Red Deer. The skies of our married life cleared considerably in the late afternoon of that day. We went to her parents after all but not until I had a few hours of sleep to get over my reckless behavior.

I have hardly worked with anyone that I did not talk about my faith in Jesus and of my hope for the life in the hereafter. This was not always as effective as it should have been, and I often felt guilty that I did not make a better witness in matters that are so important for the well-being of every creature that ever walked this earth.

Andy had a friend who was a so-called blue baby. He had some kind of heart problem, and he was trying to escape the limitations that he was living under because of his sickness that would lead to an early death. I talked to him also about the eternal hope that should be in all of us. This man needed support!—more than anyone in those days, yet he could not be reached. He believed he lived a good enough life and that he did not need any help from any source—natural or supernatural. It is my hope that he found a better way in later days!

Andy himself was much like this unfortunate man. He was close to the truth also, but he did not want to make the last step that is so important. I hope for him also that he might be touched someday in the future.

"You can lead a horse to water, but you can't make him drink" is a saying that has a lot of truth in it.

I still believe that our prayers have more persuasion power if witness accompanies them. I am fairly sure that our attitude is not always conducive for a powerful witness, but I don't think that you have to go to church to find the good people. All sinners need redemption! And that becomes possible only when we realize that we need help.

My brother Bert was also a very committed Christian, and he was not afraid to stand up when it was necessary. He put me to shame more than once, especially in later years when he was in business for himself. His calendars had always a background with a powerful message—much the same as when we would sing in the choir or when we would play in the band and all the other activities that we were involved in. It was a real shock when he told me that he was leaving for another life close to the parents of his wife—in BC. The overall burden of running a business because of that came crashing on my shoulders without his moral support, and that turned out to be a lot harder than you would imagine. We had been very close indeed, but matters of the past can't be brought back.

I got me a new sidekick in the form of Garth the Cutting Torch! He was a great man with a cutting torch. This was the result of his work in an auto wrecking outfit in his former place of work. Garth turned out to be a terrible man. He was a lot of fun to have around and a willing worker, but he was not a precision man who was cut out for the more demanding work of bodywork and painting. The precision work involved for a good paint job is much more demanding than even the most broad-minded person can imagine. It is also the reason that I did not want to work for the average intellectual! People like that have been trained in a mode that seems to indicate anything possible on paper should be possible in the workplace. Nothing is further from the truth! Any working man can recall experiences where the logical thinker on paper is awfully hard to get along with. I have heard bricklayers who were ready to throw away their tools when they had to build projects that some smart-thinking architect had figured out on paper. The same holds true in the body shop.

My boys will laugh their collective heads off when or if they read this. I do not want to work for schoolteachers or church ministers or professional fire man or, last but not least, women! Not in the body shop anyway. Neither one in this category has even the remotest idea of the amount of problems connected to a good piece of work.

I will give an example of this in the following story. The church counsel of one local church approached me. One of their pastors had rolled over his car. This particular parson had not even been installed in his church yet when he rolled his car somewhere in Montana. He was on the way to his new parsonage in the town of Rocky. One counselor of his church came to our shop and asked me if I would be willing to help in this particular kind of emergency. The man was very short of cash, and the church counsel had lined up a few members of the church who were willing to put together an amount of money to get the man back on wheels. They asked me if we could do a fairly good roughening-out job so that the pastor would be able to drive again.

The fact that he was a man of the cloth made a big impression on us. We were only too willing to do our share in the reconstruction job of the man's car and his career. We really went out of our way to do a more-than-adequate job and put many more hours in than was billed out in the final repair bill.

The result was astonishingly good, considering the fact that it was supposed to be a roughening-out job in the first place. It's hard to describe our astonishment when he came to pick up the car and started complaining about the space between the two side doors. These were about one-eighth of an inch wider than before the accident. We had worked our butts off! The job was almost perfect for the condition as was agreed upon, and here is a man who is complaining about an item of no consequence. Can you beat that?

There was another side to this man that left a great impression on us. This was the fact that he brought many to a commitment with our Lord Jesus. He would tell us that this was the greatest experience that a person can go through. He must have been sincere because his church was growing with leaps and bounds in the following four or five years. And yet he ran into trouble with his counsel in later days and had to leave Rocky in a troublesome way. This is hearsay and recorded as an example of the contradictions seen so often in the life of God's children.

Enough of that. We will return to . . . Garth ʼhe Cutting Torch . . .

Garth was a happy-go-lucky sort of a guy, always in good humor, and a man with many talents—none of them connected to the trade of auto body repair. He had a father who had been a professional wrestler and boxer so that Garth had a calling to make me familiar with the art of boxing.

He would stand in front of me, locking eyeballs with me, just like the snake and the little birdie. We would stand there locking eyeballs, and he would tell me to hit him. I did not want to do that, of course! Then he would tell me to hit him or he would beat the tar out of me. It became a matter of self-defense after these threats, and I would strike out at him in great desperation. The sad fact is that I would not even be able to lay a finger on him. He had been watching my eye movements and shifted out of the way as easy as anything. There was nothing I could do to even touch him. He was always a fraction ahead of me. All movements could be avoided by watching your opponent's eyes.

This is how his dad had taught him.

Garth would teach me in turn! He would hit me so that my teeth rattled in my head with the only result that I was even slower than before. This happened before I had my teeth pulled. Garth just kind of loosened them up a little to make it easier for the dentist! He used to slap me around to the point that I figured that he was the boss in the outfit.

Knife throwing was also on the prescribed list of instructions by my various teachers. We used to throw knives in the walls and in the doors and in anything made out of wood. It was so bad that we did not have a knife left in the place. But this was no problem!

A little thing like that could not stop progress. A heavy punch would work just as well, and the building was shaking with the sound of chisels and punches flying all over the place. Our friend Andy had the misfortune that he came to the shop on an afternoon that I was having lunch. This was a time that was set aside to have a rest in my often-hectic life, and I could not by bothered by anyone during that time of relaxation. The door was locked, so he gave his famous cowboy yell—a sound that I would have known out of a thousand others, but I could not be bothered. I wanted to be left alone, and I took a knife of about eight or ten inches and threw that in the door that the wood chips were flying all over the place. It was at that point that I heard a mighty big "yowwww"—a sound like a cat with the tail caught in the doorjamb. My beloved friend had been standing with his back against the door when the knifepoint came peeking through the door. He claimed later that he was swinging along with the door when the door was opened to let him in. This was not altogether true, but it was close!

Knife throwing . . . boxing . . . wrestling, and shooting with bow and arrow! We have done it all. I just don't know how we found time to work with all those diversions. But we did! But all was not fun and games, I can tell you that.

It was a very brokenhearted Garth who came to see me on a Saturday morning. His wife had left him. The fool came home the night before, all dirty with grease and grime of a motor job, more than half drunk, and so he did not know what he was doing.

He slipped in bed with his wife without taking his clothes off and settled down for a good night's sleep. It is not hard to understand that his wife of less than half a year of marriage was more than just a little upset. Garth was an undivorced widower when he returned to the land of reality the next day. His wife and most of his household goods had disappeared before the morning sun.

This called for desperate measures, and Garth knocked on my door for help and condolences, and it was a very contrite Garth knocking at my door that morning. He begged me to come along and help him to get back at the good side of his estranged wife. It took a fair amount of persuasion and humble pie on the part of our friend Garth before the tide was turned, and the lady was persuaded to help load the household stuff and return back to the humble abode of Garth the Torch.

We were doing our work in a ramshackle building only two buildings away from the mounty barracks. This was very convenient at times, since the Indians had made it a habit to sit in the old wrecked cars behind our shop. This was a sad and degrading sight. The white man has addicted the Indian to alcohol to the point that there is not much pride left in many of those once-so-proud people. They would sit in those old cars and drink anything that had alcohol content. We have found bottles of rubbing alcohol that they used as a replacement when the money was short and they could not afford liquor. I am afraid that I never was able to do anything for those poor people. We have found many of those cars with the seats ripped into pieces smaller than a one-inch die. They had destroyed everything in the car, and nothing could be done about it.

I met a trio of Indians in the back alley one day when I came back from the main garage. They told me that I would not have long to wait and they would take care of the white man. This was in the high day of Communism, and there seems to be little doubt that some agitators were working among the Indian tribes—not with the best intentions, I may add.

We had an Indian woman coming in our shop one night, and she begged us to put her car inside for the night. She told us that the other members of the tribe were angry with her and that they would destroy her car if she left it outside.

Things came to a head on a nice sunny summer day when my helper and I came down the alley from the main garage after a little interview with the office people. We were in a good mood and heard some Indians having a party in the wooden shed behind the main building. It was then that I got an impulse to throw a fist-size rock against the wall of that building. It was on our own property, and we would pull little pranks like that all the time as a token of good relationship, and no one would get mad—just even.

The Indians did not share in this kind of good-natured kidding at all! They were really drunk at that point. One fellow flew out of that building and down the alley as if all the evil spirits were after him. He looked really funny. The other guy was not funny at all. He was in a much different frame of mind. He was in a fighting mood and started throwing rocks after us even when we had entered the rear door of our shop already. He had gone absolutely berserk and kept throwing rocks through the shop. It would only be a matter of time, and the cars in the shop would be pelted with rocks so that there would not be a window left in the place. It was at that moment in time that the mounted police came to the rescue.

One policeman had heard the racket and came over to investigate. He calmed the Indian down and locked him up for the night. It was touching to see the kindness of that officer as he worked with that person and showed full respect to the rights and dignity of that particular person.

I could tell many more stories about the Indian and his decline but will let that rest for the time being. One thing should be mentioned. The Indians themselves are in the process of rebuilding their dignity, and that is a hopeful sign. We will let the Indians do their thing, and we will go farming for a little while.

I had been working the farm a little when I lived in town, but that did not amount to much of anything. The real farming started after we moved back to the country. Cutting the brush with an ax would have been an impossible task, and so I hired a Caterpillar to start the clearing of the land. All these operations had to be done piecemeal in small operations when money came available. The banks would not give any big loans in those days, and we had to work with a few hundred dollars at a time.

It is here where the more prosperous immigrants had the greater advantage. They had money coming in and could do big stretches at a time without worrying about paying off a loan. This and the fact that we had a growing family made all the difference in the world.

I still remember the thrill of the moment when the Caterpillar operator invited me to come and sit with him on that monstrous machine, and we headed for the high timber, trees of eight to ten inches thick or more. I had to close my eyes for the first few minutes when we walked right into those big trees. It was the scariest feeling when that machine walked through that timber as if it was on a leisurely field trip. The engine did not even slow down as tree after tree folded to the ground, and the brush was shoved aside like grain before the sickle. It was majestic! And yet a feeling of sorrow was filling my soul when I saw the destruction of so much that was pure natural.

"Chips will fly when you chop wood!" It's an old saying.

I wish that wood could be produced without the flying of chips. This does not seem possible, and that's too bad.

The brush and trees were pushed together in great long brush piles over the length of the field to be burned after a period of drying when the wood would catch fire and snow would cover the ground. I had such a big fire going at once that I was getting plenty scared myself. This was later . . .

I had a dozen brush piles stretched out over the full length of the quarter section that time, from one end to the other. The piles were as high as a house in most of the places and no snow on the ground. It must have been Thanksgiving Day or someday around that time. There were haystacks in the neighbor's field but a long way from where I was going to start an operation firework. The day was without any wind when I started, and I put fire at almost every two hundred yards or so. My intentions were sound enough if it had worked out as planned. I was under the impression that most of the piles would be burned out before nighttime if I lit a starter fire in enough individual sections of brush piles. It worked wonderfully. For a while!

Then the wind started blowing, harder and harder, until it was almost a storm wind. The fire swept through all those brush piles at an incredible speed to such an extent that I have never seen a fire like that! Not even during the war.

It was majestic and incredible, beautiful, grotesque, and fearsome to the extreme. It is hard to understand that no one came to the rescue, but the whole neighborhood stayed out of sight. The piles burned down to a manageable size in the space of about two or three hours, and that was to my advantage. Guardian angels must have been working overtime on that special day of the great fires. The haystacks did not get on fire either, and that was my greatest fear at the height of that inferno. The fact that the piles burned so fiercely helped to reduce the amount of cleanup work later, and that was the big advantage of that mighty tempest of fire and wind.

There was a silver lining on the clouds of that fire also! My little boys were a big help in the days of the brush fires. I would have a five-gallon pail half full of diesel fuel and mix a little gasoline to get a better start on the fires. All the little boys carried a dry stick also and would dip these sticks into the diesel mixture until the stick was wet enough to catch fire. With these sticks they would light another fire a little further down the pile, just the way it should be done, but there was a fly on the ointment or a snake in the grass or even closer to the truth.

"My boys in the brush piles!"

Children don't have the right understanding and respect for their parents as they grow up. The parents have to do a lot of growing up before they can appreciate the wisdom of their children. I did not know that yet! I would learn! Would I ever learn!

Educated by our children! It is a great privilege when parents are allowed to participate in the journey of discovery from childhood to adolescence. I was just starting to participate in this privilege when we were burning the brush piles on that fateful day in the fall of the early sixties. The boys were dipping their little sticks in the five-gallon pail of diesel and gasoline mix and lighting fires all over the place. They were having fun, and that made me happy also . . . I was having fun because they had fun for the time being! Until . . .—that is always the spoiling factor in this life of ours; there is always a but, an until, or an or!—until the boys were dipping burning firebrands in the fuel pail behind my back!

The lover boys set the old man on fire as well as the brush piles. I felt an extra warm feeling on the back of my coat. Something did not feel right about this. I was supposed to be warm on the front and not on the back. The boys were halfway home by the time that I had my coat off and inspected the damage. A great shuddering sigh went through my weary body. My education had begun!

It was not all that much later that I got the second segment of my educational process. I had a beautiful 1957 Dodge Royal car with push button automatic. This is the car with the long wide fins on the back and the extraordinary eye-catching front and side moldings. This is maybe the most beautiful car that has ever been built.

I had painted this unit in a three-tone color, bright red against pitch-black with a white roofline. It was an advertisement on wheels for the shop I worked in. This car was sitting in front of the main door of the house; the keys had been left in it, and the great tempter persuaded my boys to crawl in the car and try all the button and knobs. They found the key also on their journey of discovery. The car started without any difficulty!—that was the miracle of it all. I never had that kind of luck myself, but that is how it was. Our oldest daughter had to take matters in hand before any more would happen with all the wrong results. The cure was even worse than the ailment!

She stepped on the gas pedal, filled with the best intentions. This did not do any good. After that she started pushing buttons and pushed the drive button! My showcase car came wandering through the front door of the house, moving the freshly built chimney in the process. It was a blessing that it came to a standstill after that. This and the fact that none of the kids was in front of the car. It must have been a direct intervention from their guardian angels.

Our Father in heaven kept us from an unbelievable sorrow and gave us time to live with our loved ones for many more years after that. It could have been so much different and sorrowful. Life would never have been the same, especially for the fact that I had left the keys in the car to start with. No one will ever know from how many dangers our children have been delivered before they are old enough to look after themselves. I believe that this time never comes!—not really. We all need the protecting hand of our Lord every moment of our life.

One of the children got in the habit of sniffing on the gas barrel. Neither Mom nor I realized the danger of the situation. We would not have understood the implications even if we had known what the child was doing.

A yellow jacket wasp was directed to that barrel at a time that the child was in the sniffing process. The wasp stung the child on the upper lip so that he was walking around with an upper lip like a monkey. It was ridiculously funny to look at and a blessing in disguise, since the child was cured of that addiction for the rest of its natural life. This story is absolutely true!

Another one of the boys got caught in a hole when they were playing hide-and-go-seek. I wanted to put a clothesline post in the ground and had dug a hole of about one foot square. One boy thought that this was an ideal hiding place and lowered himself in that hole with his knees touching his chin. The result is not hard to understand. He could not go up or down, or any other direction. He was stuck for the duration, and he was lucky that the other kids found him in due time. We will let the kids play and better go back to the farming. You do not get anywhere running after those kids anyway.

We started with two heifers. I had fenced a great deal of bush and chased the animals in that wide and woolly surrounding bush land. They had enough feed to last them for the rest of the year. After that I forgot them—but not for long. They went missing the very first day. The wanderers could not be found, although I searched high and low, over hill and dale. It was only thanks to the honesty of the neighbors that I found them after days of searching. This man was honest enough that he sent a message that my wayward cattle were on his land. He even helped me to round them up with his saddle horse. Good manners dictate that you always have to be thankful in a situation like that, although the service is rendered with a superior and knowing smile. We had a long learning process ahead of us and would never catch up to the settled farmers with years of experience.

The head boss of the garage gave me my first milk cow, a high and chunky animal with an udder that was utterly ridiculous . . . I mean, *udderly!* Its udder was so big that it was dragging through the mud when the rainy season was in the land. It was a producer! I must admit that. For the first half year, that is! Then it dropped off to next to nothing in milk production. There was absolutely no reason for this but a fact nevertheless no matter how you looked at it. It was almost as if the animal was pregnant—an absolute impossibility! I never had a bull on the place, and the neighbor's bull was so far away that he never came near the place. There was no help for it.

We had to wait and see what happened, and sure enough! A little calf was born in due time—a little hairy monster that was all hair and no flesh. It was the strangest little calf I have ever seen. I believe to this very day that it was the product of a male moose, something that was next to impossible. I have never heard of such a thing. Not then! And not later. The thing was dead when it was born, and that put an end to that story. We were back in the milk business again.

The name of that cow was Jessy—the forerunner of many cows with women's names. We had named this one after the wife of my employer, for it was just as gentle in disposition as the owner of the name. It was also the reason that we let her stay until she died from old age. This was an action just as illogical as many others that kept me from becoming too materialistic.

We had a Johanna . . . a Clooky . . . a Klooster . . . a Terpy . . . a Terpsma . . . a Micheleen, named after my granddaughter . . . a Nicky . . . and a Lady. We had a Rosie, named after my brother's daughter. There were Abby and Mugsy, names of Irene's friends. Misty and Peppy. A 3/T because it was a three-titter. Gryhech and Nancy, named after the wife of the former owner. We had a Stolty and a Tinker, named after Tinker Bell! We had a Sylfia, my brother's daughter, an Annebell and a Wooly. Then there was a Rosebud and a Swanney, named after my oldest daughter. A Georgy, a Pookey, and a Crook. We had a Sqeecky and a Pia—my boys did not like that cow and named it after the minister's wife. They did not like her either! A 363 and a Valentine, that one speaks for itself . . . and a Judy, who was the girlfriend of one of the boys.

We even had a The Devil. This cow received that name because she could kick like a horse.

It would sound awful funny when someone asked, "Have you put the kick chains on The Devil?"

The Devil was one of six cows that I had bought on an auction sale south of town. I bought four and was talked into buying two more on reasonable conditions. We brought those cows home and put them in the pasture, and I went back to work in the body shop. It was somewhere during the afternoon that my wife looked out of the window and saw several strange creatures running over the public road somewhere in the distance about a mile away. She never thought anything of it, and it was only when I wanted to milk the new cows that we realized that the happy wanderers in the far distance had been the cows that I had bought in the morning. So we had to round them up, and I put them in the milking parlor. It was there that The Devil went into her antics.

She kicked me with milk bucket and all in the corner of the milking parlor! She kept on doing that no matter what I did or tried. It was in final desperation that I asked one of my boys to help me, and he tied a rope to the cow's legs and let it kick until it was too tired to stand. Then we put the milk machine on and got a little milk out of that cow.

It needs no imagination to understand that actions like that were not very conducive for the milk production. In other words, I had been cheated. A second cow was even worse and could not be milked at all. She almost broke my wrist, and I ended under the cow instead of beside it!

I don't understand that people will stoop so low that they will sell cows that are absolutely useless. It goes against all decency and all codes of ethics. This was proof once again that we have always been too easy of believing in the good of men in general and had to pay the price accordingly. What else is new?

It was at a later date that I was really going in the milking business. That's what I thought anyway! I bought some high-quality cows from an up-to-date farmer close to the town of Didsbury. This was supposed to be the pick of the crop! The best of the best! I have to say one thing. They were big all right!

The boys and I put the cows in stanchions in the barn, and I left for a meeting in town to return a couple of hours later to witness the most remarkable scene of the day—maybe of the year. The new cows were wandering in the pasture with the wooden stanchions around their ruddy necks. The suckers had gone away with a whole section of the barn around their collective necks.

There is another evil under the sun as I was to find out in short order. One cow had the habit of milking herself. This was contrary to all the unwritten rules of agreement between the milk cow and the farmer. A cow is supposed to give the milk to the farmer, and the farmer will give feed to the cow! It is as simple as that! This is an agreement that is beneficial to both parties, but this cow was writing her own rules and ended up with a steel collar—studded with four-inch nails—around her *snosola* (nose). It helped for a little while, and then this cow started milking other cows. She was in the milking business for the duration. I had to sell her not long after that, since it is awful hard to break a cow out of these bad habits.

It is not hard to understand that I was overworked most of the time, and this got worse as the farming operation grew. But we carried on in faith and hope. In spite of all my tribulations, we started looking around for support and comfort, and it was not a long time later that my wife had an experience that proves how strong the power of prayer really is.

We had about thirty milk cows on one quarter, and the pasture was very skimpy. In other words, the cows were going hungry and still had to produce milk simultaneously. That is a very bad combination.

The pasture was next to a field of alfalfa that was more than two feet high. I have to explain that alfalfa is a kind of legume, grass that is extremely potent for a milk cow if it is eaten in great quantities and in green condition. A cow will bloat in a matter of minutes and swell up until it dies within a very short time. You can always put a knife in her belly and relieve the gas. However, that works less than half the time and has to be done almost right away after the cow has eaten the explosive mixture.

It was in this kind of situation that the hungry cows broke through the fence and headed straight for the rich alfalfa. No power on earth could have stopped them then, least of all my Johanna, since she was all by herself. She told me how she started praying, and the cows turned around as if an invisible hand was driving them back from the rich green fields into the skimpy and worn-down pasture. You don't have to be a farmer to realize that this was a miracle that was surpassing all human understanding. This story is absolutely true! Just as I have told it.

I got a little careless after that and found out that the angels do not always seem to act in that special way as you will discover in the following story. I have always believed that one has to build his fences as well as possible and live in a trusting relationship for the rest of the time.

It was with this in mind that I went to church on a beautiful hot summer day. The cows were grazing in the pasture across the road and were well cared for. There was an abundance of feed at that time.

The neighbor to the west of us was the owner of a herd of sheep. It is a well-known fact that the coyotes will go after an unprotected herd of sheep and drive it in a corner somewhere where the poor animals will crowd together to the point of suffocating. After that they fall easy prey to the hungry coyotes. There is a cure for that, which will help most of the time. A sheep herd owner can put a donkey or a billy goat with a herd like that. That animal will protect the herd and keep the coyotes at a safe distance. This neighbor had a billy goat with his sheep. But once again there was a snake in the grass—a snake in the form of a billy goat.

Cows can be spooked by a billy goat and do great damage in the process. This is what happened on that Sunday. The billy goat must have been lonesome and started looking for company—quite understandable, and it would have been OK up to a point, but that crazy goat looked in the wrong place, which was the fly in the ointment! Or the billy goat in the cow pasture! Or the snake in the grass!

More than three-quarters of my herd of cows were spooked out of their collective wits. They started running, and the billy goat started hopping along, love sick and with the best of intentions. The crazy goat was just looking for company, and the cows did not want anything to do with that. My prized milk cows kept running and running, while the friendly goat kept hopping along.

The end result? The cows broke through six fences before they came to rest in the neighbor's field to the east of our farm. That's where I found them when I came out of church. They were sweating as if somebody had thrown pails full of water over each cow, and that is a very unusual condition. You never see a cow that is putting up a sweat under any condition. That was not all. It was only the beginning of my sorrows.

The blood was pouring out of their udders, and even worse out of their teats! They had cuts in those nipples that a person could lay a pencil in the wound. That wide! It was nearly impossible to milk some of the worst cases. They kicked like horses and were scared and jumpy beyond imagination.

It was such a disaster that I lost my cool and went outside with the .22 shotgun, walked up to the goat as close as I could get, and shot a bullet in his head or just against it. I could see the hair flying in all directions! But the goat kept going! I shot him in the head again, and the goat kept going, although he had slowed down a lot! I handed the gun over to the boys and asked them to finish the job. It did take several bullets more to bring the animal down. We left that animal in the pasture, and then I phoned the neighbor.

I asked him, "Do you have a billy goat?"

"Yes, I do" was his answer. "What about it?"

"You have that goat no more," I told him. "I just shot it!"

This man really was mad. He was going to sue me, and I told him to go right ahead.

"You do that and you will have a bill for damages in the following mail!" I told him. "My damage exceeds thousands of dollars. You go right ahead and sue! We will see who has the most rights in this particular case!"

Well! To make a long story short, I have never seen hide or hair of the man. He must have known that Henry O. was on the warpath.

It looked as if the angels had a day off on that Sunday. I say that in all reverence! The Lord leads us along difficult trails at times. I hope to see the reason for that someday, hereafter. He did not promise us an easy journey! But He did promise us a safe homecoming! This is my comfort.

We had to build a milk house somewhere around that time! My two oldest boys were helping me to lay the cement floor (we were cementing our relationship, so to speak). The number-three son had to put the cows in the stanchions.

Stanchions are a headgate to hold the cows when they are in the stable. These stanchions could be opened and closed in a kind of a V-shaped form. We also had a cow with the illustrious name of Horny.

My number-three son, the stanchions, and the cow named Horny turned out to be a bad combination. The cow had horns in the shape of a half-moon, and that is where the name "Horny" came in! The cow hooked his half-moon-shaped horns around number-three son's arm and pulled back through the stanchions. The arm was caught between the stanchion sides and the cow's horns. Something had to give, and that was the boy's arm in this case. It is small wonder that the boy was upset and came running out of the barn right through the freshly poured cement. His arm was dangling at a funny angle somewhere in front of him.

"Look at what the cow did!"

He was crying! The boys who were helping me had hardly the time to be bothered with a little thing like that.

"Jah," they said. "You broke your arm, you nitwit, and now get out of the cement!"

You can draw your own conclusions of that episode. I had my own! Still! It does not mean that they were indifferent. They were just busy. These things happened and were taken in strides unless it was really serious, but what happened here was small stuff in the world of my lover boys.

Something happened on another farm that was a lot worse, by far! The farmer and his boys were pounding posts with a post pounder. These machines are very tricky and very touchy. And so it could happen that this man tripped the handle of the pounder at the wrong moment. The pounder came down and hit him on the head in a kind of scuffing motion. Luck was with him up to a point.

He would have been dead if it had been a direct hit, but he was knocked out cold, even so! Let me explain that this man was a funny character and could not be trusted in all situations, and so the boys figured it the better part of wisdom to vacate the premises. They went home to drink coffee with their mother. The man came back by his own locomotion. That's how the story was told anyway. I find it a little far-fetched to tell you my opinion. Still, funny things did happen, and you have not even heard half of it.

We have covered a lot of farm stories, and I wish that I could read your mind whether you are getting bored or not at this moment. I think that I will take a rest and then come back to insult your intelligence again in an accelerating manner.

Nice, hey! Are we happy yet? It is with great reluctance and a certain amount of diffidence that we will cover some stories of the sons and daughters of my parents.

My brother Jan had stayed behind in the Old Country when we immigrated to Canada with the rest of the family. It looked like a separation for life at that time, but times changed, and also the traveling possibilities. The near impossible became in reach of the ordinary people. Air travel became a big thing.

It was with this in mind that one brother here in Canada called us together and suggested that we give Jan the opportunity to make a trip to Canada. Most of us put in a few dollars to make this possible. This was done, and brother Jan made his way to the wild blue yonder of Canada.

No words can describe the tearful reunion when Jan met Dad and Mom for the first time after so many years. So I will skip that part and go to the meat of the matter. We had the oldest brother recruited into the band in no time at all, and he was blowing hot air in great volumes along with the rest of us—with one difference! He was much better than any one of us, and that stands for reason. He had been in the band as one of the youngest members in the local band in our birthplace in Holland, but that was not all. He was also an accomplished organist who will have his fifty-year anniversary this month at the time that I am writing this memoir. He could make circles around us in the music world but never did. He sat there quietly taking directions from his younger brother who knew far less of music than he did.

This might give you the impression that he was the kind of man who would not speak his mind or voice his opinion. Nothing is further from the truth. He had one big problem, for he had stopped his mental perception of his family at the time that we left Holland. This had often-hilarious results, since the younger brothers had grown up and had families of their own. They were not going to take lip from a brother who was coming over for a blue Monday to straighten our affairs here in Canada. The other boys would laugh him out of the house when he started his correcting lectures. And the joy of it all reached a high point when we gave him a .22 bore gun to play with!

He shot everything in sight, including the chamber pot of Mom and Dad. It had a neat little hole in it when Dad was going to put it to use in a desperate moment. Dad was not all that happy with that crazy Dutchman when he started blocking the natural functions of his well-being in such a drastic manner.

But sad to say, Jan had been hunting small game up to that point. He was ready for the big stuff now! My youngest sister had her bra hanging on the clothesline. He shot that full of holes also. He was going to add an amount of fresh air on these subjects.

It was with fear and trembling that I watched the arrival of the nineteenth-century nimrod at my farm. We had brought the cows and calves to the back of the quarter, and I had told the wife that she would have to go without bra for the day . . . you could never be sure. He might shoot at the bra and forget the part that was in it. The wild man of Borneo went through the whole neighborhood, but nothing happened. Everything stayed remarkably quiet around our place. The wife stayed in one piece, and the cows lived to fight another day.

It was not until the evening when I started milking that I noticed what he had been up to. I had a bucket full of paint standing on the roof of the milk house, and a sturdy little trickle of paint was leaking on my neck when I had to do some work under the edge of the roof.

Lover boy had shot a hole in the bucket that was full of paint and put a little twig of wood in the hole to cover his evil deed. I did not know what to do—laugh or cry! It would not help any if I would get mad. He and my other brothers were in such an uproarious mood at that point in time that I could not get through to them anyway. Grin and bear, it was the logical course to follow, and that's what I did.

My patience and forgiveness were so great that I went with him and his wife for a trip to BC—a trip that was a revelation in more ways than one. We were driving an old car of my employer. He lent me that car free of charge, a gesture of goodwill that I would not soon forget. The roads to the lower coast of British Columbia were narrow and dangerous in those days. But the mountains were beautiful beyond imagination. It was the first trip through the mountains for all of us. The majesty and grandeur of the mighty Rocky Mountains was an inspiration and a revelation.

I could not help but think, *How great must be our God and Creator. He made all this and sustained it from the moment that time began until the end of all being.*

We went over and past mountain ranges with a never-ending variety, and our eyes wandered from wonder to wonder in awesome adoration. We went past valleys and canyons of such depth that the women had to close their eyes and started praying for the better part of the way. The depth was threatening to swallow us. The overhanging rock formations seemed to be destined to fall on us and crush us, while mighty mountain streams and thundering waterfalls proclaimed the glory and might of the mighty Creator in a kaleidoscope of colors and light variations. The mountains were changing from moment to moment with the changing of the light reflections and the ever-increasing contradictions of conditions.

"This was . . . harmony in diversity . . . to perfection!"

Most of the first day was experienced in stillness and wonder by all of us. I must admit that I was very afraid as we traveled along the bottomless ravines. One little slip of the steering wheel or a minor defect in any of the four wheels could have sent us over the edge in those bottomless pits. You must keep in mind that the mountain roads are at least twice as wide in this present day and age. The outlooks on the ravines are much less to fear because the road construction of later years has improved the overall picture beyond recognition. A traveler can drive those roads in a much more relaxing mood in the present time.

It was a very welcome sight as we had our first look at the city of Vernon. This place is nestled in the Okanagan Valley in a landscape that seems a lot less threatening than the stretch between Rocky and Vernon. The mountains have receded to a respectable distance, and the habitation seems a lot friendlier for man and beast. There is even some green grass!—I was just kidding! There is a lot of grass in that valley—not only grass but also field fruits of every form and description.

Crops can be harvested as much as three times a year, and the dairies and livestock production are among the best of Western Canada. Fruit orchards are all over the valley, and these provide a fairly good living to many inhabitants, although the district does not have much industry outside the lumber industry. This is the reason that the economy is a little stagnant. It is hard to find work in that corner of the world.

We were not aware of all this, and we did not care much even if we had known. We had outlived the first part of the trip and were very thankful that we had reached the house of Jo's younger brother. I remember that we had a good time, and that's about all! Except the episode where brother Jan was ordered by the women to take a bath. This was something that did not appeal all that much to him at that particular moment.

Even so, he was fairly nice about it and went into the bathroom like the renowned fearless Fosdick with the difference that he made a lot more noise than Fosdick ever did. It was so bad that his wife went after him and found him on his knees, splashing with his hand through the water of the bathtub. You would have believed that Goliath was in that bathroom by the sound of it all. You can take my word for it that his wife took some corrective measures, but good! Peace reigned in the valley for a moment, until he reappeared and had the brasserie of my wife over his ample breast. This looked so outrageous that the women sent him to bed, all by himself.

You might get the impression that my oldest brother was a bit of a dolt. Nothing is further from the truth. He was the brightest of us all and maybe the most successful. He was acting like that because he was relaxing completely, and he might have been one of the happiest men in the whole district. He was with his family again!

We said a fond farewell to Jo's family the next day to start the last half of our journey. This was even more beautiful, if that is possible. We drove by the lakes of the Okanagan in the direction of Princeton through a landscape of rocks and dazzling heights looking down on lakes that had most colors of the rainbow. No one who has not seen this can fathom the beauty of the lakes—blue and green, red and purple, and all colors between. It was gorgeous and awesome to behold but even more alarming as we went past the deep gorges along the lakefronts moving further and further into the heart of the mountains.

We went higher and higher until we ended at the Hope Slide. It is at this place that years ago the whole mountainside came tumbling down in a sea of mud and covered a car full of people and several others in a grave that never could be reclaimed. A wet mist was hanging over this place of destruction. It gave us an eerie feeling of unease, and none of us felt all that comfortable in the stillness of that *Wet Moon*-like landscape. Just two more young couples were in that place, and everybody was talking in whispers. It was too depressing. We would not like to miss it but were glad to get out of that place where the ghost of past disaster might be wandering around in the swirling midst of the evening sun.

We carried on from there and had our first look ever of the coastal area of BC. This has been called the most beautiful region of Canada. Our first visit gave credit to that statement. The mountains fall away when you leave the area of Hope and you enter the fertile valley along the Fraser River. That's about all I remember of that first visit in that district.

Bert had found work in the Surrey District but was too busy to go anywhere with us. It is for that reason that we left the coast after only a few days.

Our return journey went past the Hells Gate area to follow the Fraser River in all its glory and wild attraction. It was around there that Jan and his wife had a dilly of an argument. Dina, Jan's wife, became an expert on exploration at the turn of the moment. She claimed by high and low that these mountains would have marble content. This was hotly denied by the other expert by the name of Jan! Mom and I were caught in the middle and did not have to say much of anything; the argument went way over our heads.

The war cries went all over the mountain area of BC, and the noise was deafening when Dina found a pebble that looked like marble. Everything fell back in place in the universe. Dina had her marble and had the proof that brother Jan had lost his marbles.

A grim silence fell over the interior of our four-wheeled troop carrier after that. It was so bad that it came to the point that somebody had to break the deadlock.

Jan discovered a butcher shop with some outlandish-looking sausages. This was our salvation. The stuff looked so appetizing that we bought an immense quantity of the stuff. The day was very hot, and I started to wonder where Jan was going to stuff all these sausages, but this problem was solved without any effort!

We were going to sample the remainder of the sausage treasure at the next stop. All other food had been rejected in the joyful anticipation of the upcoming treat, but we were disappointed again. The women were proven right, again. The sausage stank to the high heavens and proved to be another complete disaster for my already suffering brother Jan. We had to throw the whole kit and caboodle out of the window and go hungry to the next town, and even that went all wrong. We hit the town all right, but at the wrong side of the lake. It became a complete mystery trip.

It was at that point that I told Jan in dead earnest that we were right but the map was all wrong. We would have to turn the map upside down and everything would fall in place. He thought that this was so hilarious that he told that story repeatedly for as much as forty years later. It's sad to say, but I did not see the humor in the situation, and that's understandable. I had to do the driving.

His jocularity came to a high point when I recalled the story of one of our former prime ministers. His Excellency had a friend who was not high on the scale of appreciation, not in his opinion. He told the man that if he had the horns of a moose and if his brains were gunpowder, he would not have enough to shoot his horns off! I made that remark after we had come past one of the largest moose heads that we had ever seen. It was a lame joke but had the effect that brother Jan laughed his head off and was in a good mood the rest of the way.

The rest of my brothers did not want to be left behind when it came to the activity of entertaining Jan and Dina. A fishing trip was organized of immense proportion. We went to a lake to the east of Red Deer. This is a lake where we had to row our butts off to get to the fishing grounds, but that was part of the fun. The flotilla of two rowboats was anchored in the middle of the lake, and the fishing could begin. A great battle developed when one boat denied the other one to fish in the water of a brother who was an elder in church. This was pronounced to be a form of character assassination, and the rest was absolutely forbidden to fish even near that particular spot.

The remarks that went back and forth were out of this world, and the argument became so noisy that even the fish did not want to stay in the neighborhood. This had the result that we began the homeward trip in high state of excitement.

All eight brothers had a ride in the station wagon of brother John. He was laughing so hard that he began to swerve all over the road, from right to left and vice versa. We never noticed the fact that a black car had been following us for quite a distance, and none of us took notice. We had way too much fun. The fun came to an abrupt end when the red cherry on the following car started flashing, and we were ordered to the side of the road. Two members of the mounted police ordered the whole joyful crowd in the ditch, while they started taking the car apart. It was then that Bert tried to talk the mounties into buying some of our fish—we had about half a dozen small samples.

Bert and the other boys started to haggle in earnest with the mounties. They wanted to sell them fish in the worst manner. It was so ridiculous that even the police left the scene with shaking heads. They had been under the impression that we were stone drunk and that's the reason that we were pulled over. Nothing could be further from the truth! We have never used liquor in all the times that we as brothers had been together. And I hope we never will. This is in memory of our parents.

Brother Adolf was in the habit of telling stories about flying saucers and heavenly bodies. We had stopped for an ice cream cone in one little town, and the serving lady was giving a display of the abundance on the parts of her upper body.

This left little to the imagination, and it was in the middle of one of Adolf's stories about heavenly bodies that Dick remarked, "We had a good look at heavenly bodies this afternoon when we bought the ice cream."

The whole assembly sat stunned for a few seconds, until the remark sank in, and the scene that followed was priceless. We laughed ourselves silly, but the women did not know what to do—laugh or cry. There were some raised eyebrows in the crowd, and the rest started crying. It was so sad to hear a grown man talk like that!

The education of brother Jan came to a standstill, and we managed to send our oldest brother back to Holland to continue his good works, while we went back to our everyday lives with all its ups and downs.

I had another helper in the body shop again, a very easygoing sort of guy. He was so easygoing that he forgot to work most of the time. This was a little bit of a problem. It was not all that conducive to the spirit of goodwill that is supposed to be an interchange of pleasantries and goodwill.

His home life might have related to this. He had a wife who was even more easygoing than he was. She visited us once in the shop, and she had two or three little children lying in the back of the station wagon. None of them were any too clean. The little toddlers looked like a litter of little piggies as they were crawling around in that rear section of the station wagon. It was with an uneasy feeling that I looked at that little tableau of human misery. I feel even worse at the time of this writing. We seemed to have failed somewhere along the line that we did not have more compassion in one form or another.

The frustration of this young man came to a flash point one evening, and he was so upset that he shot a hole through the ceiling of the house where he lived. It went from bad to worse, and the whole marriage came to a breaking point when he came home one evening and found his wife in bed with a half-breed Indian. This time he handled it differently. He did not get angry that time. He was past that point!

He just walked up to the half-breed and shook hands with him with the words, "You want her? You can have her!"

This was his farewell to the unfaithful wife. The tragedy of this story does not need any more explanation.

This ending came several years after he quit working for us in the body shop business. I held on to him for quite a while, but the going was tough. I could sand a car down and prepare it for painting in two days. It would take him all week, and it came to the point that I walked to the head office and told them that I could not carry him much longer under the circumstances. Who will understand my amazement when he came that weekend real happy and content?

He said, "They must be satisfied with my work. I received a raise in pay!"

I was absolutely flabbergasted and asked the guys up there what the meaning of this kind of disciplinary action was. They told me that they had given him a raise so that he might have a little more incentive and ambition. I can't understand the logic of that statement to this very day. Fact is that I had to do the work for three and did not get an incentive as a pay raise.

The fellow who followed this man was even harder to handle. He had been laid off in another shop under the pretense that he was lazy. I could not believe that and had never any reason to complain about his work habits. He had other habits that were much harder to control. He was a three-year apprentice when he started working with me, but he had the allures of an accomplished tradesman with years of experience.

It was only a matter of time, and he took control of the buying of paint and materials—not only that! He believed that I was not a good manager and a poor estimator, and it became so bad that he would be at the front door to meet the customers to be taking over the estimating. I was degraded from manager to ordinary working status. As simple as that! What to do? I went to the head office again with much the same results—no action of any kind.

There is a statement in Proverbs that goes something like this: *"He who digs a pit for another will fall in it himself!"*

This is just about what happened not all that much later. I will call him Jo. Well, it went like this: Jo had a very demanding wife. She was so bad and stuck up that his life became next to impossible. This woman wanted to be in the upper class of society. She was just an ordinary but a good-looking woman with an impossible high opinion of herself. Her problem was that she could not see this, and that made life very hard for my partner.

"This might have had something to do with his attitude!"

Anyway, she was so insistent on a higher status that she started an affair with the employer where she was working. This went along for a little while, and she must have had good hopes that she could replace the employer's regular wife. Those actions and interactions started demanding a heavy toll on our relations all around.

Jo was demanding more money and started talking about a job in the city of Red Deer. The pay would be much better in the city. No amount of persuasion on my part could change his mind. He was obsessed with the idea of a better life in the city. I tried to explain to him that the pay would be better but that the cost of living would be much higher. All to no avail, and it was only his wife who kept him from moving.

She had high hopes that her project of wife replacement would be successful and should not be interfered with in the inconvenient manner of a move to Red Deer where her employer's wife was living. This all came to a drastic end when this employer's wife came to Rocky and put in her ten-cent worth, and then some. She chased Jo's wife out of the office and out of the life of this unfaithful man.

To make a long story short, the move to Red Deer was on within a week. The woman had seen the light and started another approach. It is sad to say, but this was not the end of the story. She forced Jo to build a house within a year of their arrival in the big city. That was the beginning of the end. She promptly left Jo after the house was built. She had her house and hooked Jo on an alimony payment to insure her lifestyle.

This is one affair that I don't feel guilty about. I tried to help Jo in spite of the despicable way he had been treating me. It is sad to say, but Jo did get his wish in another aspect of his desires. He became manager in another shop on the other side of Red Deer. It was there that he could put his ideas into practice, with the results that he had many comebacks on his paintwork, and the shop went broke. Sad but true!

This is the story of the man who had lost everything—his wife and his three children, his house, and, last of all, his illusions. I have seen him again in later years when he had married another good woman and lived quite prosperously.

I would like to correct the impression that I had nothing but bad luck with my helpers. You have to keep in mind that I was far from perfect myself! I just want to point out the human factor in those stories and others who have been told before and the stories that might be told yet. Let me envisage that we live in a world crippled by sin. Our reactions to our fellow man are far from perfect most of the time. We just wish that we had done better when I look at my life in retrospect.

I will tell the experiences with another man who worked with me—a story of misery and human weakness. The main office hired that man when I was so loaded down with work that I did not know where to turn anymore. Bill came wandering in the door on a day that I could not look over my workload anymore. This was a far cry from the conditions in the beginning days in that shop. I have had Monday mornings that I unlocked the door and was looking against a wall of auto repair jobs. I could not even imagine the end of all that work stacked up in front of me. It was like the proverbial cake that this person had to eat through to get to the promised land. It was in those days that I got in the habit of tackling a job one by one. Everything else had to wait till the moment that the first job was done. Then and only then did I begin on the next one . . . and so on. This was not half as easy as it might look.

Customer after customer came in the door asking for an estimate on repair of a damaged vehicle or a paint job. I would have no choice but to tell them that they would have to wait their turn or go somewhere else. I refused in a polite manner to work for some people like teachers and doctors or ministers and other intellectuals. They were too hard of understanding, and I could not be bothered with that. There are exceptions to the rule of course. But I was dealing out of the corner of a desperate man.

Bill came wandering into this kind of environment. I asked him if he had any experience. Oh yes! He was a very accomplished man by the sounds of it. I asked if he could paint. Oh yes! He was one of the best and had many jobs finished in his days as a tradesman. This clinched the matter, and I told him to go ahead and paint a car that was all prepared for painting. It was one of the great mistakes of that time! He went to work with an abundance of enthusiasm and a minimum of experience. The result was a paint job that looked like a rainstorm. It had runs all over the surface in all kinds of patterns and formations.

I think that he was a little ahead of his time. It would have made a perfect modern painting. He would shine in abstract paintings in the style of Picasso. I could say that I had teardrops all over my face in all patterns and formations, but that would be stretching the truth. I fell in a pit of despair and told him to clean up the mess, and I had to finish the job by myself after all that hassle. We ended with more work than I had to start with.

It was in a mood of resignation that I looked into the future with Bill as my new sidekick. Things were going from bad to worse as time went on. I found myself in the impossible position that I would take on work for two men, and Bill would not show up for work half the time. This combined with my growing farm operation put an impossible strain on me, and I was ready to break under the workload, until the day that Bill did not show up on Wednesday, and I had to work harder and harder to keep ahead of it all.

It was on the following Monday that his mother phoned if I had seen Bill in the last few days. I could not help her—I could not even help myself under the circumstances. The only advice that I could give her was to phone the police for information.

This is what she did, with the result that I was told not all that much later that Bill was in jail on a charge of possession of marijuana. He had been picked up in his apartment, and the police found a regular greenhouse. He was growing his own marijuana. This explained why his work habits were so irregular most of the time. He applied for a job again less than a month later. I refused to hire him that time.

This did not go over too well with the correction authorities. I had a phone call with the message that I was not a good citizen if I did not hire old Bill again. I sought the advice of the head office, and we decided to hire the boy again. Then came the straw that broke the camel's back. We had a job in the shop with a verbal OK from the RCMP but no repair sticker. Bill kept begging me to let him start on that job, something that I refused at first, but he was so eager to please that I told him to go ahead with that machine.

It was then of all times that a young RCMP officer walked in the door and started charging me with a criminal offence. Bill was working on a unit without a repair sticker. I had the responsibility, and I would have to answer to the charges. This was more than I could handle. I told the man that I was going to fight this charge—toe and nail! The main office was not that much help in this little affair either. It looked as if would have to fight the battle all by my lonesome self, again.

The young mounty came back in the shop not all that much later with the message that the corporal had told him to drop the charges. It must have been a disappointment for the young officer. He had gone out of his way to prepare his case. Bill was told to stand in front of the vehicle in question and had his picture taken and everything. The rookie had been overreacting in his zeal to serve the law. But I had enough. I told the guy that I had worked my butt off for this kid with no credits whatsoever. I was getting out of the body shop business at the first opportunity.

We are getting ahead of ourselves a little bit! But I would like to end the body shop affair. We had a customer who was the friendliness of people. He would come in the shop and talk with us about everything under the sun. It made no difference whether I was busy or not. This was very bothersome, since we had fallen very far behind in our work, with the result that I rushed a repair job that this same man had brought in for repair. The job was not done properly—it was as simple as that! What did the man do?

He displayed it on Main Street in front of a number of spectators and said, "This is the kind of work that Hank does!"

Just imagine this! He was supposed to be a friend! He came to the shop after that, and I told him that I would do the work over. This would be the last job that I would do for him. Not only that! I would give the main office notice that I would be quitting at the end of the next month.

He was related to my employer, and he went away with that message for the main office. With an unexpected result! They promptly put a "for sale" sign on the building with the excuse that they could not run that place after I was gone. It was unlikely that another trustworthy person could be found to take my place. This was the end of my career in that body shop. I had served that place for more than twenty years, and that was more than enough!

It turned out that this unreliable friend had done me a great favor. My weekly paycheck fell away, and I never noticed the difference. It was that simple. My farm operation was more than adequate to support my family, which included a wife and seven children.

My own life improved immeasurably, and I had some very good years in the coming years. Not only that, but our children also gave us the present of a trip to Holland in the spring of 1976. We had to pay for the trip, but the children would take care of the farm when we were gone. It is with great respect and thankfulness that I remember the way they handled the farm affairs in the time that we were in Holland. We could not have done better, Mom and I!

What shall I say about that trip to Holland? It was an experience like none other—the thrilling moment when we set feet on the soil of our country of birth. Thousands of memories came crowding our memory, one after the other . . . We recognized many friends of former years, and the relationship with my friend Dick continued as if I had never been away. Our houses where we were born were still standing there then, the road where we used to walk to the church of our childhood. It was all there—untouched by the sands of time. I could even find back the bomb marks that my friend Albert and I had repaired on the church and several places all over town. The home folks were very friendly and gave us a great welcome, although brother Jan did not have all that much time for us. He had a business to look after, and he invited me to go along on his trips as a driving instructor. It was along this way that I recognized many old places and many more new ones.

You have to keep in mind that we never had traveled further than a bicycle could carry us in the days of our youth. Everything traveled by car or bus in this modern Holland, and the trip by car was a real eye-opener. The country of our birth seemed to have shrunk in size. We went past the sloughs where we had dug the so-called turf for burning in the stove. The nesting place of the dragonfly and the bumblebee, the butterfly and the grasshopper; also a myriad of insects and birds of every description were still residing in the peat moss-covered grasslands.

This land had become a protected area a long time ago, and the habitat of that slue land was secured for future generations. The mountain slopes—"hill sides" would be a better word—covered with heather were also off limits to the wandering public. Nobody was allowed on the areas outside the wandering path. All the areas of our youth were forbidden territory. We were not allowed to visit the places where Mom and I had been walking, huddled close together, in the height of our courtship and young love.

Many of our old friends and acquaintances were still alive, and it was a great pleasure to visit my old friend Albert—the man who had taught me the elementariness of the bricklayer trade. It was still the same old Albert with the same sense of humor. He reminded me of many little facts and events that I had lost in the midst of time. He also confirmed the story of John, the Jew, who had come so close to dying that time when the Germans arrested Albert.

The stichen darkness of the midwar years had disappeared from the more-civilized areas, but we found the same darkness one night at the lakes of Friesland—the highlight of our visit since my friend Dick and his wife, Tiny, had taken us for a week to their camper at a lake in the heart of Friesland; Waterland of no compare. It was early in the season, and most of the campers were still empty. No light was shining for miles around. It was during the evening when I made a little trip outside the trailer that I discovered that nothing had changed in respect to darkness and light. It was so dark that I could not see a hand a front of my eyes, and it was a good thing that the trailer was nearby where a glimmering of light could be seen through the shades in front of the windows. This was my guiding light that brought me back home.

We were camping in some kind of harbor with many camping units all around us. Some sailboats would be passing by, but the bulk of the tourists were still locked in their winter sleep. This made it very peaceful, and we could enjoy the sight of the occasional boat drifting by, cutting a furrow of phosphorus light in the deep black waters of the Friesian water world. Several ducks made their own trail through the waveless water world, and everything was a picture of peace and harmony.

The architecture in this country was somewhat disappointing, but the rest of the trip more than made up for this. We went over the Afsluit Dike to the west of Holland. This dike is the barrier between the North and the South Seas—a marvel of engineering that only the Dutch can put together. You will have to forgive me if this sounds a little like bragging. The Dutch do have a reason to be proud of this titanic wonderwork—work that could be accomplished by the grace of God and by the knowledge of the Dutch engineers.

It was a scary sight to drive in the middle of two mighty waters divided by a fewer than two hundred yards wide barrier. All kinds of fowls like ducks and quails, kingfishers, and other swanlike creatures were floating in the foam-crested waters scant feet away from the top of the dike. Tugboats and heavy freighters of every make and model were plowing the waters just outside the vulnerable polders—way below the sea level on the other side. It was with a sense of wonder and relief that we landed on the other side in the heart of North Holland.

Many little houses with red-tiled roofs were hugging the age-old dikes, and little pathways would be leading from each individual house to the top of the ever-watchful and protecting crown of the dike. It was unbelievable that these small areas could support a fairly heavy traffic of cars and even trucks. The age-old structures had been pressed into the dual service of roadways and protectors from the ever-threatening North Sea. On the other hand, the modern traffic had outdated many old harbors and left them all but defenseless against the pressures of modern society.

The old cheese market in Alkmaar and other cities are still on display as a tourist attraction complete with cheese handlers with their colorful clothing, carrying the golden-yellow cheeses on flat-bottomed stretchers. Women in the age-old dress code of the forgotten fisher world are standing in the stores and stalls all along the center of the city. Pure white bonnets are contrasting in colorful harmony with the golden cheeses and an abundance of other old housewares in display in the same small stores and stalls.

The music of a street organ is overruling all the other noises of that colorful crowd in the age-old city of Alkmaar. All this activity is pulsating and swirling around the center that is culminating in the overpowering church and mint (market) structures around the market area with the cobblestone street. The streets are so narrow that all traffic is banned from this area, and cars are standing on either side of the road in the neighboring streets. Hopscotch on both sides of the road, and some are facing the wrong direction while others are parked on the sidewalk. It is a picture of organized confusion, something that would never work in the spacious country of Canada, but it seemed to work for the Dutch—somehow!

Total bedlam may be the rule of the day, but a certain order seems to prevail once a person comes in closer contact with the impossible heavy traffic all over the small Dutch road system. Our trip would not be complete if we did not see the harbor of the Zaan with the windmills and the old fishermen's dwellings, all restored in one area with a detail to the former romantic attraction. Little bridges over small waterways lead to the reproduction of fishermen's world of days gone by.

We could tell more about these appealing reproductions, but we have a long way to go, and the paper is not as cheap as it used to be. We better continue and go to the city of Amsterdam. The city of Amsterdam is a nuthouse, I think. Not without charm, mind you. It is unbelievable but true that the city of Amsterdam is built on poles or post pounded in the soft subsoil of the waterlogged and soggy landscape of this polder land. The pounding of post goes on day after day to support one of the fastest-growing cities of Europe. Anyone who has made the famous canal tour will have to agree that many old buildings are overhanging the canals in a way that seems to guarantee the early demise of these same brick structures. The individual houses are leaning like eternal drunks, seeking the protection and support of each other as the canal water keeps nibbling at those footings in an age-old pattern. And yet the buildings endure and stand the test of time!

When you travel by boat, you come to a place where a person can have a view through six or eight different brick bridges all built in the same half-circle pattern—bridges built long before the advent of the modern reinforced concrete. They endure and endure! On the other hand, we were not impressed with the cleanness of the canals. A lot of old housewares, rusty bicycle frames, tubs and old tires, paper and other residue were laying in the canals. It all made an unappetizing sight. It sure was no advertisement for the proverbial cleanness of the average Dutchman. We also went past the place where Rembrandt is supposed to have painted his famous *Night Watch*.

The city of Rotterdam was the next stop. The mighty harbor works in that city are next to none in the entire world. Mighty ocean liners are in dry dock as the earsplitting noise of the riveter and the welder reverberate day and night accompanied by the movement of the mighty cranes and draglines. They are loading and unloading ship after ship in never-ending rhythm of the thrifty Dutch harbor worker.

A great steel monument at the waterside of the harbor reminded us of the wanton destruction of the German air force during World War II. The war effort was all but forgotten, and the average dock worker seemed to have eyes and ears only for the work at hand. Containers of unbelievable proportions were moved all over the place in a cacophony of sight and sound—Rotterdam at work!

But we will leave them and go to a high house of three or four stories to find a place to sleep. A cousin of my wife had made room for us, and we were invited to climb at least three or four narrow stairways to get to the place of residence. The stairs were so narrow that we had to wonder what would happen if a person became so sick that he or she had to be carried out of the house; the stairways were that narrow. None of the furniture could be brought in along those winding stairwells. Great windows in the front of those apartments could be opened, and all the furniture had to be hoisted to the place of destiny. We were so high that we looked down on the crown of some hundred-year-old chestnut trees. It scared the living daylights out of us when we woke up in the morning.

Several Turkish people were also living under the same roof as my wife's cousin. It seems that these people could live on a shoestring. The beds in those apartments were never empty. One person would leave the bed and go to work, and another person would take his place in the just-vacated bed, an ideal arrangement for the other livestock in that same bed. Excuse me! I was trying to be funny. I did not mean that these folks were not clean in their lifestyle, but they were surely thrifty.

The other occupants of the apartment did not completely trust these folks with their strange customs. It was for that reason that I had to sleep on the bottom of the stairs in some kind of cubbyhole next to the public stairway. I had to be the sacrificial lamb in case something happened in the middle of the night. I was promoted to the job of watchdog, and I did a good job. Everything went well. We could return home the next day. All in good order.

A short visit to the Rijksmuseum was the next thing on the program. This was a little bit of a disappointment. The *Night Watch* was in restoration. A deranged person had taken exception to this famous painting and cut it up with a knife. We could see it from a distance, that's all. The other paintings were as interesting, but we did not have much time left, and the visit was much too short to my way of thinking.

I remember a visit to an old castle turned into an exposition with the fitting name of Golden Hands. Numerous displays were divided all over the old castle rooms. There were too many to mention. There was also a display of East Indian art that was exceptional in form and quality. Another room had a display of all the dolls of Princess Beatrice. This was enough to fill half the day.

Next, we came to the display of a young priest. This piece of art was more touching than anything we had seen in the whole building. He was making objects and forms of animals and humans out of candle wax. People seemed to come to life in a realistic way, and it was a pity that we could not come closer. He had a wax figure of the suffering Savior that was so realistic that I could not forget it for a long, long time. It shook me to the core of my being.

There was another display that upset me in a way different manner. This was about the afterlife. Many case histories were displayed about experiences of people who had been dead and came back to life. Most of them had seen a great light. They also had a feeling of complete peace in the life hereafter. It was suggested that many of these people had been of a non-Christian background. This is what made it so disturbing.

"No one shall come to the Father but by Me," said our Lord Jesus.

These words do not leave any doubt on this matter. There is no other way than through Him. This whole display had all the earmarks of the greatest deception of all time. The devil is only too well equipped for the final deception that seems to come to us from behind the grave. I was fully convinced then that this would be one of the most powerful tools of the Antichrist. Even Hollywood has jumped on the bandwagon of that deception.

We could tell many more stories about that first visit. However, I am a little worried about the situation on the home front, and so we will return home. All things were in excellent shape. Thank you! The children had done a very good job looking after the farm and all the livestock.

Our twenty-five-year wedding anniversary was coming up that fall, and the kids had given us the possibility of that trip as a present for the upcoming celebration. It was a nice gesture that was surely appreciated and long overdue.

We will go to this celebration after a visit to the past of the Christian school. This is also part of this memoir.

A desire for a Christian school had lived among us from the very first days in Canada. Some members in the church in Rocky were just as convinced that this was the way to go. I did not share that feeling initially, and I did not even want to support this movement—not wholeheartedly. It was my feeling that the start of a Christian school would take all the money I could scrape together. This would destroy all possibilities for a farm of my own. It was that simple!

Who can describe my amazement when I was reading the sales contract of my house in Tin Pan Alley! This was many years later. I had completely forgotten how that contract was made up. But I had made the condition that the unpaid balance owing would have to be paid to the Christian school if the school would start in the next five years. This did not happen, but the clause was in that contract. I did not remember this until I looked at the old papers of years ago. Most interesting!

It was in the early sixties that a proposal was made to start a school in the basement of a local church. I could not see that this was the right approach. The school would stay in that basement, and the possibilities of growth would be next to nothing. I thought that the supporters of the school were just a little too eager, while the desire was outpacing the wisdom at that junction of time. A few more people shared that opinion, and the proposal was outvoted in a public meeting. This was the beginning of an exodus of people who had their mind set on the start of that school in basement and nowhere else.

The minister of that day and three or four other families left the district of Rocky within the space of a few months. The school board had to start all again. A period of patient rebuilding had begun.

The school did start about five years later under much better conditions. The next proposal was forwarded in a most interesting meeting. There must have been about thirty-some voting members at that meeting. About two-thirds of the members could not see the feasibility, but the school was voted into being. This was a demonstration of faith like I have not seen very often. It was something like the beginning days of the church.

I was one member on the financial committee. A school for all children, whether rich or poor, was the aim of that little group. The tuition had to be held at a level that even the less fortunate could have their children attend Christian education. It was for that reason that our budget did not balance. We were about three or four thousand dollars short in that meeting of the finance committee.

It was at that same meeting that one member suggested that we should have enough faith to start with an unbalanced budget. The missing money would be provided in one form or another. Three or four thousand was an awful lot of money in those days! And yet the Lord provided. The oil in the lamp never did run out!

As for my hopes of a farm operation? It came to pass sooner than I had expected! The Lord was good indeed!

It is with thankfulness and some semblance of pride that I think back to that Gideon band who voted for the beginning of that school, about thirty members, and it appeared that almost three-quarters of them did not really believe that they could afford such an outlay of capital on top of their dues owing to the church.

It was with a certain amount of surprise and relief that we could observe the growth of the local church, almost immediately, after the beginning of Rocky Christian School. Several teachers had to be hired, and they became members of the CRC locally. This has changed in some respect because some teachers are hired from outside the CRC in the present school, and that's all for the better. Maybe?

But I was referring to the beginning days of the school, and that's where the influx of new church members was very noticeable. I am also very thankful for another aspect of church history that I was involved in. The recalling of all these happenings might be a little boring for the reader, but they are part of my memoirs nevertheless. It is with this in mind that I write the following memories of our involvement in this church action.

It was toward the end of 1972 that the synod of the CRC launched a new program called Key seventy-three. It was a program of goal setting. The idea was to reach every household in North America and Canada! All the individual churches were expected to reach out to the community with the message of hope and renewal: the proclamation of the saving graces of Jesus our Lord and Master.

Classis of North Alberta appointed the minister of our church as the coordinator of this program. He would be responsible for North Alberta. His task demanded that he would spend much time traveling from one church to the other, trying to clarify the aid and hopes of this project. More than a few eyebrows were raised over this enterprise. It was the feeling of many that the minister should work in his own parsonage rather than travel all over the neighborhood at the expense of his pastoral work. The result was to prove that the driving force had to come from the bottom up—that is, the average lay members of the church.

The church had to be divided into several districts and study groups with the aim that each group should come forward with suggestions for a more effective outreach into the community. The suggestions from each group were brought together in the end of the study period with the following results—as far as I can remember! (You will have to keep in mind that this is a one-man witness and a one-man interpretation of the ultimate conclusions. It is well to keep this in mind as you read this report.)

A suggestion was made for district study groups for the education and upbuilding of the church community. This was implemented, and it resulted in a better understanding of the scriptures and, last but not least, a better understanding of the sharing and caring power of the communion of saints. Members who had lived on the fringes of church life came to closer connections and a better understanding of the same comforting living relationships of our community.

There was another suggestion that had great implications for the future of our church and our community. The suggestion was brought forward that we should open our homes and our hearts for single parents or for young women looking for support and comfort. The idea was that we should ask people over for a weekend in our individual homes. This idea was also accepted, and the deacons were charged with the task of organizing these weekend outings for the people involved. I was head deacon at that time, so I know what I am talking about.

The deacons contacted the head nurse of the Red Deer Health Unit, Ms. Velma Day. She informed us that the government was starting a movement to take the handicapped people out of the institutions and into the community. Our efforts would be better directed if we invited some handicapped people over in our homes for as many weekends as we could handle. The Provincial Training School in Red Deer reacted favorably to our request and appointed a coordinator to bring the different organizations together. About fifteen or twenty families joined in this project, and they opened their homes and their hearts to the mentally handicapped people of the PTS in Red Deer. It was in this manner that we set weekends apart for the handicapped people in a program that lasted about ten years.

A remarkable thing happened when we started those relationships with many of those children. We were not helping them so much as they were helping us. We started to realize that these people had a lot to give for the benefit of us all. Not only that, but we also started to fall in love with those children. I know that this is a strange way of putting this, but it might be the best way to explain the interaction that developed between the children and us. We were looking forward to these visits almost as much as the patients themselves! We—my wife and I—had a young girl who had been in an accident. Both her parents had lost their lives in that same accident, and she never recovered from that shock. She became a handicapped person. We loved that girl so much that we were thinking about adopting her—unsuccessfully. Another family adopted her before we had started any procedures in that direction, but we still have very fond memories of that little girl.

I am happy to say that this was just a forerunner of many programs undertaken by the different churches to the benefit of the handicapped. COOP is one of them, and Rehoboth is another one that is going strong. These programs had a positive influence. How do you think you would react if you were closed in an institution under the supervision and care of a centralized system? No matter how well meaning it might be? People need the positive interaction with others. We need this to grow and prosper. It is the same for them. I was happy to be of service in another aspect of our growing church.

The growth of the church membership and their children had put us in the position that we had to create more room for meetings and educational purposes. A decision was reached along the normal ways of painful discussions and haggling. How far should we go? How much money should we spend? These and many more questions came on the order. But everything was resolved in good time, and we started the building of the social hall. The idea was to use as much volunteer labor as possible. All the tradesmen of our church were pressed into service again—that included me also. I was asked to lay the blocks with the help of a Catholic block layer and some unskilled laborers.

The block layer was not a professional man, but he had picked up that trade in later days, and he was hoping to pick up a little experience with an accomplished tradesman. That was I! I realize that this sounds a little over blown, but it was true nevertheless. I did have the training that he was lacking.

We had some beautiful discussions about the different aspects of our individual belief—our faith life! I have always been very aware of the different approaches in our respective churches and was only too willing to explain our approach to questions of faith in our Lord Jesus. This man had a childlike faith, in the same manner that I professed my faith, and it was in this manner that we had a very good time together. I am reminded of that person every time I come in the social hall.

He has passed away not long ago, and we experienced another loss. A good friend had left. The world is an emptier place. It is getting more lonesome around me always. Many have left, but I endure. Until now!

I have already mentioned on former pages that I had quit the body shop and started farming full time. This is not completely correct. I was doing a little bodywork on the side just to supplement my income.

I had a friend who was a Friesian by birth. We will not hold that against him too much! But it did shine through at the least-expected moments. My brother-in-law was a baker, and he started a business in Rocky in earlier years. This man, "the Friesian," was also a baker. He felt very insecure and threatened when my brother-in-law Rick started a business in our town. He took advantage of the fact that Rick had started a store in the wrong place and he could not get a license for that location.

Jack went to the police and demanded that the police close the outlet of my brother-in-law Rick. The policeman was more humane and not all that eager to follow up on this somewhat unreasonable demand. It went against the feeling of goodwill, a feeling that wrote many rules of conduct in those early years.

Rick was unable to defend himself, and he was struggling to make ends meet. Closure of his store would mean the end of a profitable business. It is hard to believe, but old Jack kept pushing and pushing until the police had to give in to his demand, and Rick was practically out of business when his outlet was closed. He went broke. Jack had won! His fellow member in church was out of business.

Jack did not feel all that pleasant about this whole affair, and he wanted to make amends of some kind, and this is where things became really interesting. He sent his helper to the body shop and had him ask for an estimate on his car, something that I refused to give him. I did not want to deal with that man.

Jack's son followed within hours of this refusal. He asked me for an estimate on his dad's car. I flatly refused once again. Another helper came within hours of the last refusal and asked for an estimate on Jack's car, something that I flatly refused again. I did not want to work for this man. It was at the last refusal that Jack went to the main office and asked them what kind of man they had in the body shop—a man who refused to accept work offered to him. My main employer told him that Hank must have a good reason if he did not want to work on his car. That was the end of the story. But not quite!

We became the best of friends in later years, and he became also my first customer in the shop at my house. He was also more than pleased with the result and made a lot of good advertisements on my behalf. This did not wipe out the fact that I had not much heart for the bodywork anymore. I did several jobs later but could not find much pleasure in this occupation anymore.

The fact is that I never did like the whole auto repair business to start with. I had to do it until I could farm full time, and that was the main reason that I did that work. Bricklaying was a far more satisfying line of work. A paint job is very demanding and usually a source of critiques. It also starts to deteriorate when it hits the street.

Brickwork is here to stay. Many examples of my brick and rockwork are around all over the country and will be there for many years to come. My memory will fade away, but my cement work will be recalled for many years after I am gone. I am saying this as an explanation for my preference of that line of work. Not as a reason to boast. I am just thankful that I could do this, and it made me many friends.

My former employer approached me with a request for the building of a fireplace in his house not many years later. But I am getting ahead of myself again . . .

A well-known farmer in the neighborhood came and asked me to build a double fireplace for him, something that I agreed to do but very reluctantly. He gave me all the help I could ask for, and that made the work a lot easier, but it was still hard going. There is a story doing the rounds that this man and some other fellows in town, including a Chinaman, would be gambling with unbelievable stakes on the table. "Two or three thousand dollars were peanuts in the kind of games they were playing."

This has never been proven to me, but I consider this well possible. He was that kind of a guy.

They were a hospitable sort of people. Lunch was always ready in the afternoon—and a very good lunch, I may add. She had been the cook in a lumber camp, and she knew how to cook. I would sit at the table and quietly say my prayers just as if I was at home. Who will believe my amazement when they asked me to open in prayer aloud, since they wanted to be included in my prayers? I would open every meal with prayer from that moment on. The reason for that has never been clear to me, but the fact was there, and I did what came in my way—just faithful and obedient.

This man did me a great service in return for my work that was very satisfactory, so he told me!

My farming operation was becoming more complex as time went by, and my square baler could not do the job anymore. I would have to invest in a new baler and new hay shed. Square bales won't last for even a day when the rains come down on the freshly made bales. The bales have to be picked up as you go along or the rain might spoil them. I just did not have the resources to bale and pick up hay in the one operation. Another problem is the fact that square bales in a stack will spoil also if they are not covered right away. This was the problem that I was facing.

My friend the gambler told me by high and low that I should invest in a round baler.

"Your bales are secure the minute you have baled them," he told me. "Only the outer layer will catch a little rain, but that does not amount to anything. Buy the biggest baler you can get. You need a tractor anyway, and it does not make any difference to the tractor how big the bales are."

That's how I became the owner of a round baler. One of the first in the district! Some people declared that I was crazy at first, but most farmers followed our example in a matter of years. This is what I owed to the insight of this man—the gambler.

One doctor in town sent his carpenter to ask me if I would do some rockwork at his house. This was another job that I was not anxious to start. I just did not have that kind of background and experience. I should explain that masonry is a trade in its own right. It takes a lot of knowing how, and I was not equipped for that. I refused to consider the possibility. But he kept coming and coming. Perseverance won the day, and I was talked into doing this fireplace for the doctor. Rock splitting is a hard and demanding job, and very few people learn to do this in the right manner. I was one of the lucky ones who could read the rocks and how they split!

This was a job of giant proportions, and I had to do this all by myself. The doctor would come with his lunch bucket in the afternoon, and we would have lunch together. He enjoyed the experience to the hilt, and so did I. A remarkable companionship was prevailing between the doctor and me until the job was finished.

He told me several things about his profession, and I told him some stories of the war. This went on until I finished that job. A job well done, and the doctor and his wife were more than pleased when it was all over. He even gave me a bonus as a token of his satisfaction.

I have to correct an oversight at this point. Everything did not go without any trouble. After all, I am the guy who is paranoid about the intellectuals, and he was a confirmed intellectual. One and one are three. Right? Trouble was bound to happen.

A real expert built the fireplace—that had to be me. There was no other mason in the whole district. That's clear. I had everything under control, except the doctor. The work progressed as planned according to the explicit wishes of the same doctor, until I started laying the firebricks in the floor section of the fireplace. That's when the trouble started. He did not see the need for that, and I insisted that the floor should have firebricks to do the job according to specifications.

The argument became so entrenched that I was ready to walk off the job. Something had to give, and it was fortunate at this point that the carpenter interfered and started acting as the peacemaker in this war of words. He arbitrated the battle and quieted the waters with the suggestion that he would help me to chisel out the necessary cement and help me to bring the bricks even with the rest of the floor. The result was a split between the doctor's wishes and my demands. The firebricks were about one inch above the floor level when everything was finished. The doctor's pride was salvaged, and my conscience was put to rest so that I could live with the fact that the firebricks came in the right place. Under the fire!

I had another argument with this same guy in later years—much along the same lines, but I will let that slip into oblivion. It would only prove that I am a stubborn person! Right? He asked me over many years later, and I was surprised at the quality of workmanship of that same fireplace. I had done a better job than I realized when I wrote the final bill.

CHAPTER 14

FURTHER EDUCATION
BY OUR CHILDREN

THIS JOB MUST have taken more out of me than I realized. It was in the spring of that year that I had another brush with death.

The farming operation had demanded the same amount of care while I was building that fireplace beside all my other problems. The workload must have been too much. I became sick several months after the job was finished. It looked as if I was struck down by the flu. Bed rest seemed the cure all in this particular case—and, yes, indeed.

I started feeling better on a Saturday morning. The flu had run its course, and I was ready to go back to the barn. The milking was completed without any problems, and I had a good meal at lunchtime. I ate more than was good for me, as a matter of fact, and I had to go back to bed. An excruciating pain started while I was lying in bed. The chest pain was unbelievable, so much so that I was surely convinced that I would die if someone or something did not take the pain away.

Mom did not hesitate for a moment. She told my son Henry to get me to the hospital. Right now! I do remember that I threw up that precious meal while I was in the car on the way to the hospital. That's about all. The rest was pain. Excruciating pain! I am sure that the pain would have killed me if the heart attack had not done this beforehand.

A young doctor was on call that morning, and he took drastic measures. I had to lie flat on my back and was not even allowed the raise my hand about the level of my heart. This treatment continued for at least three days. I was not allowed to make even a single movement. A nurse was at my bedside day and night. Morphine was used to keep the pain down. I don't know what else they did because the little boy was out cold. I will tell you one thing. Morphine does strange things to a person as you will see in a moment.

A beautiful young nurse was sitting at my bedside when my condition started to improve. I remember that I assured her, very earnestly, that I was sexually inclined, but she had nothing to worry about. I was not going to do anything to her. Just imagine! Here I was, lying flat on my back, not able to lift my hand above my head, assuring this young woman that she did not have to worry about my sexual intentions! How stupid can you get?

It was also during that period that I was watching *Armageddon*. A great battle was fought in front of my eyes, and then suddenly the skin and the flesh started falling off thousands of people right in front of my eyes. It was as real as can be. Very scary! The strange thing is that I did not seem to worry all that much. I do not understand this, but it is strange. Is it not?

The pastor's wife came for a visit when I was on the road to recovery. She explained that her husband was on a trip to Holland. She was filling in for him.

"They have promised me the best of the CRC for a visit," I told her, "and then you are coming!"

The poor woman looked as if I had hit her. She did not realize that I was under the influence of morphine.

"I can leave again," she said, "if you think that I am not good enough."

It was at that point that the greatness of my character came through.

"You might as well stay," I told her. "After all, you went to the trouble to come over here!"

Was that not nice of me? I am a nice person, but nobody knows that yet. Now you know!

Morphine seems to take away the ability to discriminate between what should be said and what should not be said. A farmer came to my bedside. I told him about my life as a farmer and that I was going to run my farm on a different footing when I came out of the hospital. The man made a scoffing motion then told me that I would never be much of a farmer. We would be better to look at his son—that was a farmer! This was an impressive remark, and I had to chew on that bone for a while and replied,

"Your son has no farm. The farm has your son!"

This was true enough, since the bank owned most of that farm to start with. It was an answer that was very straightforward but anything but polite. I would never have said this if I had been normal.

The good-looking young nurse whom I mentioned before made a bet with me about the outcome of a hockey game. The bet was for a Kentucky Fried Chicken. I won the bet, and she brought me the chicken. It seems that I must have been on the road to recovery when she started feeding me Kentucky Fried Chicken. I would think so anyway. I seemed to be in the finger-licking business again, and that was a good sign.

My friend, the doctor of the fireplace, came to my bedside in the company of his two sons, both doctors, and in company of another doctor and the one that looked after me. Five doctors in all! I don't know what I did to receive this kind of treatment, but I was in the best of spirits—almost as if I did not have a worry in the world, kidding with the august assembly as if nothing had happened. I was among friends, and everything was well with this world of mine.

One doctor looked on in amazement and finally burst out in some kind of frustration, "Don't you know what has happened to you? You had a heart attack. A heart attack that was so severe that one out of three dies in the ambulance on the way to the hospital."

He just could not grasp that I was in such a lighthearted mood. Neither could I! I had no fear of death that time when I was in the hospital. My faith seemed to be so strong that I was assured of the outcome. It would be OK no matter what would happen.

It is very difficult to put on paper how this could be. I lived by faith. That was all there was to it—but what about my wife? She had a very difficult time, since she had lost me for the time being and the future was very insecure. She had to spend the nights alone with her worries. The boys were helping with the farmwork, and many people were inquiring about my condition, but that is not much comfort when the whole world seemed to have caved in around her. The phone kept ringing all the time after the rumor of my heart attack started doing the rounds. This got so bad that she left the phone off the hook—always the same questions and always the same answers.

We never realized that we had that many friends. The whole community was shocked. I had never been sick before, and then this. It was hard to accept the fact that a fifty-four-year-old man could be felled down by a heart attack in the space of minutes. Offers of help started pouring in from all sides, but this changed when I came back from the hospital. I could have done with a little more help in the form of hay or other commodities. But that's another story . . .

It was during one of those difficult nights that my wife received a vision that everything would be all right with me. I would come back home. She always had a powerful prayer life, and now she received the confirmation that all would be well. Peace and quiet returned to her after she had heard this voice in the middle of the night.

"Do not worry. Hank will come home again."

Life became a little easier after that message from above, and she started looking forward to the time that I would return home. The head nurse came to my bedside at the end of about three weeks. She assured me that I should live a life as normal as possible.

"Don't think of yourself as mentally crippled. You will become one if you do," she said. "Many others have heart troubles. Life can be near normal if you take certain precautions!"

I was released from the hospital with these words of caution and of warning. My wife received a lecture from the young doctor who was taking care of me. It takes a special treatment to deal with a person in my condition, and she had a lot of training in that respect!—I am just kidding!

What I mean is that a heart patient needs special treatment in respect to mood swings and other kind of problems that develop after an experience like that. I could get more exact but will refrain from doing that—with great dignity, I may add. After all, I am a man of sterling character.

There is one-plus in this whole experience. We made many new friends, including the doctor who took care of me when I came to the hospital on that first day. He was to stay on as my doctor and as my friend. I will go into that a little further later in the story. Something else is on the program before we go into that.

The doctor gave me permission for a trip to my brother in BC. This seemed like a good idea, since I could do nothing at home for the time being, and it would be safe enough if we were careful about stress and exertion.

My brother was quite shocked when he met me on the first time—an experience like that makes a person weak beyond compare. It was a very weak person who was greeting brother Bert on that fateful day in the beautiful country of BC. Even so! I was alive and ready for some brotherly treatment! A little teasing never hurt anyone. Bert and his wife were well prepared to look after that end of the business.

They took us along for a visit to my sister, who lived nearby in a Spanish-looking dwelling somewhere near Abbotsford. She handed me a get-well card the minute we came in the door.

"I was going to send you this," she said. "You might as well take it along now. I won't have to send it anymore."

The procedure was more than a little unusual and a little disheartening, but the rest of the evening was full of fun and companionship, and that made up for that tactless remark. We were invited for a meal around a well-prepared table.

Johanna was eating some kind of tuna fish at that time. That's what she thought anyway. It was with a cry of dismay that my sister came to the discovery that her cat food was missing. One woman had put this can on the table by accident. Johanna was nibbling away on the food. She seemed to enjoy it; in fact, all phone calls would start with a meow after that little tidbit. The company was very sorry at first, but this turned into great hilarity when there were no ill effects by the looks of things. Except the meowing part, of course! It takes a loving sister to set a table like that!

What else could go wrong? I tell you what nearly went wrong. We went for a visit to the Elizabeth Park. This is a park built over an old dumping area. A person has to go in a deep hole to look at the whole panorama of beauty and breathtaking harmony of colors and flower patterns. I went down in that hole and forgot that I was not in shape to climb the stairs out of that hole. I would guess that these stairs have at least two hundred steps—two hundred or more! Hank was in the hole! Hank came close to staying in that hole! I had an awful time crawling back out of that hole and up the stairs to very welcome scenery on level ground.

The Butchart Gardens was the next attraction on the program. We had to go to the island for that occasion. This included a trip with the ferryboat. It was on this trip that we had the opportunity to watch a school of killer whales in action. They were weaving their way through the ocean waves—about two miles away from the ferry—an unusual sight according to the captain of the ship. It sure was exciting to watch as they went dipping and bobbing until these beautiful creatures disappeared behind the southern horizon. We had seen something that very few people on a ferry boat are privileged to watch.

A feeling of happiness and thankfulness came over me as I watched the ferry move over the ocean waves approaching the colorful shore of Vancouver Island. Little islands are scattered all over the surface of the ocean, and the scenery is ever vibrant and varied in myriads of different shapes and forms. The eye never grows tired of watching the multitude of birds of every color and plumage. The seagull and the many-colored ducks mingle with all other kinds of bird species. It was even more beautiful for me.

I had received another lease on life—a fact that I was well aware of in those days of beauty and relaxation.

The trip continued, and we went past the harbor of Victoria, filled with numerous ships of all shapes and sizes. Mighty ocean liners were plowing through the waves among a multitude of smaller fishing boats. The Parliament Building was as beautiful as anything we had ever seen with flowers in great numbers surrounding the well-kept lawns. All around the central city we went, including the wax museum and the aquarium along the ocean.

Everything was beautiful and breathtaking in its splendor and majesty. It was all too much for a man who was recovering from heart failure. This was not the end of the trip. The Butchart was waiting for our next visit—a feast for the eye and a balm for the weary heart that was hungering for rest.

There is a song in Dutch that has said it better than anyone else has: "The heart finds only rest when it rests in its God!"

I was reminded of this when we walked from beauty to beauty in never-ending variations. Words cannot express the fulfilling feeling of these days of rest and beauty. So I will not try.

All things must end, and this trip could not go on for long either. It was time to go back home and resume the task of everyday labor and caring for too many things to mention. Near-disastrous conditions were waiting for us when we arrived back home. The boys had done an excellent job of milking and caring for the milk cows, but they could not do everything, and I was well aware of that.

The trouble started when I had sold my number-one bull in the fall before the heart trouble. Another person had run into trouble with his cows, and he asked if he could buy our bull. We were not altogether ready for the sale of this animal, but I figured that it was my duty to help this man in his need. Fact is I had a small bull of good breeding as a standby, and this animal might carry us through in spite of his youth. It was only one and a half years old and too small to be any good. I did not know about the problem until it was too late. I would find this out soon enough to my great dismay.

It was only months before my heart attack that I noticed that my cows were not in calf. Something was wrong with the little bull, and I started breeding some of my cows with artificial insemination but not nearly enough. It was at that point that I ended in the hospital. That's when the difficulties started. The boys did not have time to check on this, and I came back to a herd of open cows. The boys had their own work also. The milk production was going down, and I was forced to buy about ten cows on the open market. I had to fulfill my quota or lose it. Disaster was staring me in the face.

None of the brethren in church was aware of my difficulties. The first emotional stages of my health failure were behind, and everybody had his or her own worries, so we were totally on our own as far as human help was concerned.

The Dutch Savings and Credit Union was a great help in those days of hardship. The manager of that financial institution sent money before I had signed any papers, most remarkable and heartwarming. But where was the help of the brothers of our church? We were in need and nobody noticed. I went to a farmer in the next county as a last resort. Nobody had cows for sale around that time. The quota was wide open, and the farmers could deliver to their hearts' content. The farmer in the next county had some cows for sale out of a herd of purebred cows. He was willing to help at a price. He would sell me four cows with payment due immediately for half the amount, and the rest within two months. It stands for reason that he did not sell his best cows, something that I could well understand.

Any farmer can tell you that it is almost impossible to train a cow to enter a strange milking parlor. I had to train half a dozen cows all simultaneously, and an immense struggle was ahead of me. You can believe me when I tell you that I came close to another heart attack in those trying days.

The haying had to be done beside all the other work, and I was facing most of the burdens all by myself. Not only that, but I also needed $4,000 of hay besides the hay that I could put up by myself. But miracles do happen! I ran into one in the form of a man of the Lutheran Church. He asked me to do a little brickwork in his basement.

I was at work there when I noticed a little plaque on the wall. It said, "For God so loved the world that He gave His only begotten Son, that whosoever believes in Him shall not perish but have everlasting life!"

I always feel happy when I meet a soul mate and fellow believer. This time was no exception. I could not help but marvel at those comforting words. It was heartwarming, but much more would be in store for me! He asked me if he could pay his bill with hay instead of money. This was more than welcome for me.

Then he asked me whether I was in need of more hay. He was selling his farm and wanted to sell his hay also. Of course, I was willing to buy, but I had no money, and I told him so.

"That's no problem," he said. "Pay when you can. Even if it takes five years!"

Four loads of hay were dumped in my yard two days after that discussion. It was manna from heaven! Nothing less. A Samaritan had seen my need and answered it. Just like the Samaritan in the parable that Jesus told in a time so long ago. This Lutheran believer had seen my need and reacted to it in an effective and a compassionate manner. I could pay him all but a thousand dollars at the time of delivery. The outstanding amount did not get paid until a year after the deal was agreed upon.

The modern-day Samaritan acted in the same compassionate way on that occasion. I met him and his wife in the store at that time. The unpaid balance was foremost in my mind when I ran into him that day. It was also the first thing I said when we started talking.

"I still owe you a thousand dollars on the hay that you delivered to me a year ago."

This was about the first thing I said on that occasion. It had bothered me more than I can tell that this had not been straightened out before this time of complete embarrassment on my part. He just smiled and asked after my health. This was a lot more important to him than the unpaid debt owing to him.

"Don't worry about that money," he said. "Your health I am concerned about. Not that little bit of money. Pay when you are ready for it. You don't have to pay any of it if you cannot afford it! Forget it. It is only money!"

This was not a statement made at the spur of the moment. He was absolutely sincere in what he said, and his wife was in complete agreement as she stood beside him, all smiles and every bit as concerned as he was. It is not hard to love people like that. It is a lot harder to think kindly about people who have done us wrong. That's the great challenge of God's children, and I am not good at it. The kindness of these people has touched me to the point that I will remember them until the day I die. These kinds of people helped me to get through those very difficult days!

I have known more folks from the Lutheran churches who have treated me every bit as well. It is strange that my relationship with our own church people is a hate-or-love relationship at the best of times. It may be that the people who love you hurt you the most. I found this to be true also in respect to my own children. A person is a lot more vulnerable in close relationships and love triangles. That's how it seems to be.

We are reminded of "The Parable of the Lost Son" when we think this through. A person is vulnerable if he allows him or herself to love another person. It's sad but true! We could tell a lot more about these kinds of relationships, but the farm will fall apart if we don't pay a little attention to that side of our life story.

We had done some brush cutting on one piece after the other so that most of the bush had been removed by the time that I ran in trouble with the heart. Most of the brush piles had been burned over for the first time, but that is only the beginning of a long process of land preparations. The unburned portions of the brush piles were still marking the greening fields, like scars of ugly fire—destruction of much beautiful but obsolete bush land. Obsolete in the sense that it was an obstruction to the budding farm operation that was starting to unfold over the former wild lands. Some might disagree with this statement, saying that it was a loss of bush land and a loss for the wild animals and birds. They would have a point in saying this, but a growing population can't be denied. Something has to give.

The early pioneer looked at these things from a different point of view. Most of my land was one big blueberry patch, and rabbits overran the rest. I have never seen so many rabbits in all my life. Rabbits here. Rabbits there. Rabbits, rabbits everywhere.

A lot of low pine tree growth was an excellent breeding ground for this kind of wild life. The rabbits brought on an overpopulation of coyotes. It is the cycle of nature where one species feeds on the other in a hard-to-understand rhythm of life and death.

On the other hand, it is not hard to understand that the low slough land was the perfect breeding ground for millions of mosquitoes and other insects of every description. It has been that way from time immortal until the human presence changed all that. Hank and Jo started intervening in the former order of things, and a farm was wrestled out of the virgin wild lands on the edge of Rocky town.

I remember how I used to plow some land of heavy gumbo soil. The clay was so heavy that a root system could not develop, and the grassroots did not reach any further than an inch or two. The grass sod would bunch up in front of the plow as if it was the skin of fresh boiled milk. This made for a situation that made it next to impossible to do any amount of plowing at all. It was absolutely backbreaking work to pull this heavy grass sod out of the plow frame. There was only one solution, and only a breaking plow could be of any help in this kind of situation.

I went to one Dutch neighbor with the request to loan a breaking plow. A flat denial was the answer. He could not help me out in this respect. He was afraid that his precious plow would get damaged. I have not forgotten that either. Bear in mind that a breaking plow is practically indestructible.

One Dutchman had refused to help me out, but that was not the end of the world. Hope was on the horizon . . . There was another Dutchman in the neighborhood. Not just a Dutchman! It was a Dutchman with a breaking plow that was better than the first one. Not only that, but he was also a member of our church. Things were coming up roses. This man would surely be able to help me out in my great need.

Alas! The poor man could not be bothered. He was unable to help me out. Since he was in desperate need of a lawn ornament, he painted that plow in a nice green color with yellow wheels. It looked really nice as it was sitting on his front lawn.

I drove past it every day on my way to work. Lovely thoughts of love and fellowship would fill my mind when I looked at that piece of art. This might sound as if I am bitter, but it was not that so much! The fact that a fellow Christian could be that way, that's what hurt!

Yow! I have to laugh at my own germinations; all this about a few men who did not trust me with their precious breaking plows. I am starting to get more childish in my old age. But even so! Many Christian businessmen will tell you that they would starve to death if they had to live off the mercies of their fellow church members. It is strange that it should be that way.

There is not much that can stop progress once it is on the move. The partnership of Hank and Jo would build a farm and bring up a family with the help of God if this was within His will.

I ran into an American oilman, and he told me that he had a breaking plow somewhere in the back of his farm. It was an old rusty thing, but I was welcome to it if I picked it up myself. He was not going to bring it, but this was no problem. My employer sent his son with the brand-new tow truck through a sea of mud. The mud was so thick that it ran on top of the wheels. This did not stop the young man. He was sent for a plow, and a plow he was going to bring to my place.

The oilman had never seen a church on the inside, and the employer's son very rarely. The oilman committed suicide later, and the employer's son died of alcohol abuse. It is a sad fact that I could not help either one, but it makes me feel guilty.

I had nothing to do with the death of either person, but the question keeps entering your mind: "How do we reach them?"

We had to rebuild that rusty old plow, and that solved part of the problem, but much more work had to be done before the farm would produce up to its potential. The brush piles had to be cleared, and the roots had to be picked. Root picking is one of the heaviest chores on the whole farm. It is not simply the matter of picking the roots off the ground. That's hard enough as it is! It is the moment that you pick a root, and half the world seems to be hanging on the other end. The unexpected weight can throw your back out in no time at all. It is those unexpected moments that can give you a crick in the back. I should know! It happened to me. It is an unending task to pick every root, and most little ones are left behind.

Someone asked our number-three son what we did with the root problem.

"We put them through the baler," he answered.

This sounded so funny that it became a catchword in the Dutch schoolchildren's little world. My boy was very close in his observation.

The baler picked up many roots. The old square baler would give a mighty "crunch" every time it hit one of those roots. The shear pin would break quite often, and the haying came to a standstill for some time. Roots were a problem with the square baler, but this problem was even worse with the round baler. The pickup would throw some small roots in front of the rollers, and the hay would be balling up before I was aware of the problem.

A bale like that has the weight of half a ton, and I had to turn back the heavy-loaded baler with the help of a pipe wrench. This was a job that was immensely heavy and even more time consuming. I am ashamed to say that I used some bad words occasionally. This is not hard to understand but very wrong nevertheless.

The time for haying was very limited. We had to milk in the morning and had to quit early in the evening to do the second milking. This did not help my peace of mind either, as you can well imagine. I never could have done it without the help of Jo! We would start at six in the morning, seven days a week. I would go to the milk house and start the sanitizer. This is the first cycle in the washing operation of the pipeline. Mom would go outside to round up the cows, while I was having a quick bite to eat. She would come back in the house to help the kids to school after that, and I would go milking.

It sounds so simple when I write this down. It was everything but that. It has happened on a winter morning when everything was dark outside that Mom would go in the big corral to line up the cows. One cow was in heat and jumped on everything insight, including Mom. This may sound funny, but it really was not funny at all.

It could be quite dangerous so early in the morning, especially with the bull running loose in the corral. Nobody will ever know trouble that my wife had to face in those early morning hours. Not even I understood the real extent of her courageous attitude.

I wonder at the marvel of it all. Is it a wonder that I love that woman with everything that is in me? She had a great love for the animals, and that made the main difference in our struggle to make ends meet. We made a go of it together, but not everything was going smoothly in the milking parlor by any means.

It happened one day that we had struggled to get an unwilling cow in front of the parlor doors. My wife popped up out of nowhere, just when this rebel cow was ready to go in, who was trying to be helpful, and said, "Kssssht." Just like that. "Kssssht!"

And the cow went Kssssht. She took off in the wild blue yonder or somewhere near that place. You have to know Mom to appreciate the humor of that moment. Although I must say that the humor of the incident was far from my mind when I started out to round up the cow, again!

This was only one difficulty that we had to cope with day after day. The effort to round up runaway cows is beyond description, but we got help from an unexpected source on the day that the cows broke out early in the morning. It was very misty that day, and the chance of a car driving into one of the cows on that misty road was very real indeed. I have to explain that our youngest daughter had a beautiful Arabian horse, a stallion. I will tell some more about that later!

As I was saying, the cows broke loose and stormed across the road. It was humanly impossible to round up those thirty head of milk cows—not in that heavy mist. Mom and I were absolutely defenseless, and disaster seemed imminent. It was at that critical moment that we heard a thundering sound of horse's hooves on the soggy ground.

Irene's horse came thundering out of the mist. He looked as big as a house against the misty background and twice as dangerous. He made a few circles around the herd of cows and drove the whole kit and caboodle back over the road. I would not have believed it if I had not seen this with my own two eyes.

It seems that others have experienced things like that, but it was new to Mom and me. We never had a horse like that again. He was almost human. It was a real pleasure to see Irene and that horse flying through the country. They were so united that they appeared to be one. You could not distinguish between the horse and the girl. Irene had that horse stabled in an English riding school in later days, but the owners of that stable did not appreciate her style of riding. She used to ride like an Indian, without saddle or stirrups, just a blanket. That's all she needed.

Irene was an excellent cowgirl. She could handle the cows better than any of the boys. I have seen her talking to some unwilling cows, and she would talk them right into the milking parlor. That's right! She talked them in the parlor. She could talk to animals. She could talk to humans also. She could talk to me, especially when I was angry.

It happened one day that I was extremely angry with one cow. Irene happened to come in at the moment that I was set to do something drastic. This was the grist for her mill, and it was an opportunity that she could not pass up. She went to the barn with a little board and came back with a board full of cow pie. A few pieces of straw were sticking out of the center.

It reminded me of the saying, "A soft answer turned away wrath."

She did it with a cow pie. I was not immune to this kind of peace offering, and the better side of my nature returned to take the upper hand. I have a better side stashed away somewhere, you know.

"This is for your information."

It was unbelievable. We seemed to roll from one crazy situation into another. The case of the rebel heifers was a case in point. We had two heifers that were absolutely useless. They would jump from one pasture into another, and it seemed that they were going on wings of a dove, so the song goes.

There was no help for it. The heifers were useless. They would have to go! All my boys and my son-in-law had showed up for the battle. Even the help of a good friend was welcomed in this battle of the giants—and a battle it was! One heifer was shot in the head but not good enough. It took off as if it really had sprouted a set of wings.

The whole army was in pursuit of this wayward beast. And, yes, it was finally standing still for a moment. My oldest son had her in the sights of his .32 rifle. He was about to pull the trigger when he noticed that the old man—"that is me!"—was straight in line with the speeding bullet. He drew back at the last moment and told the old man to get out of the way. The last thing he needed was an old guy on the other side of the gun— lining up the sights of his rifle. You will understand by now that I was the crazy old fellow who was trying to help in such a valiant way. Yeash!

The poor animal was run into the ground later that day. It was a pity. The meat is not very good after a strenuous chase like the one she just went through.

This took care of one heifer. Now the other one had to be brought to heel. The chase was on again over hill and dale. She was brought to a standstill in the muddy corner of the corral. Someone managed to get a rope on her head, and the battle seemed to be won—but not quite.

A young heifer has unknown resources. This one was no exception. She was to prove that in the next few minutes.

The boys managed to get a rope on her in a really muddy patch and in front of one boy. This guy was the proud owner of a set of eyeglasses.

He was standing there watching the proceedings as if he was not part of this adventure. He was to find out differently on short notice.

The heifer made a mighty jump in the air, at least five or six feet. Wayyyy up! Then she fell flat on her side in the mud puddle. All the brave warriors were covered with mud from head to toe, including the man with the glasses. Most of the guys could open their eyes after a while and continue the battle. Not the glass man. He could not see anything anymore. A couple of bright white spectrums looked out of that black muddy face after he removed his now useless glasses! Such were the times of our farming days. It was a long-drawn-out battle, but it did not bring in enough money to keep the family in vittles. I had to make some money on the side.

It was at that point that the young doctor of my days in the hospital came for a visit. He had told me in those days that I would lay rocks again.

"Just work a little less and charge a little more" was his advice at that time.

"I want you to make a fireplace for me."

I did not take him seriously then.

Just an encouragement, I was thinking at that time, and I respected him for it.

But . . . here he was. He wanted my opinion on some rockwork. He kept going to our fireplace and said, "This is not rockwork. This is artwork. I want you to build me a fireplace. It has to be a fireplace in the center of the house—in such a way that it can be seen from every room in the house."

I thought that he was kidding, but he was very serious as he continued.

"I have a friend in Calgary who is an architect. I am going to ask him to design a house that is exactly like that."

Oh sure! I was thinking. *We will see it when it happens.*

I had my doubts, but this is exactly what happened. He had the blueprints ready in a matter of months. Then he told me to start splitting rocks and building the foundation. Old Henry went to work in a passion on that fireplace, and it turned out to be one of the most imposing structures that I ever built. It was right in the center of the house, just like he said, and the house was built in such a way that every room had an outlook on that same chimney. Four flat, black-colored posts were supporting the whole center of the house, while the fireplace fit in there as snug as a bug in a rug.

We wanted a rough wooden beam out of the railroad bridge out of Nordegg for the mantelpiece, but this did not work out, and we had to settle for another piece of nice oak wood. A cement ridge was built around the firebox so that it did not interfere with the two door openings at the side of the structure. The whole thing was built out of split field rock with white mortar joints set off with dark trim and flat colored iron beams. I hate to brag, but I have to say it was a masterpiece of engineering and masonry work. I could not have done better myself. And that's a fact!

The doctor and I seemed to have some things in common by the way. We were attracted to each other. He was more than pleased with the job that I had done for him, but he was not so lucky with his carpenter.

"You were the only one who was really working," he told me later.

A fact that I did not want to confirm or deny! I had my own opinion about these affairs, and I did not want to get involved in a disagreement of that nature. Something else interested me a lot more. I was more interested in his thirst for knowledge about the after-death experiences. He had seen a lot of crippled and dying people when he worked as an intern in a large hospital in Edmonton. It was during that period that he started the study about the dying person.

He talked to me about this, and I bought a book for him named *Life after Death*.

This is a well-written book about the after-death experience. It shows in detail that our souls are eternal with an eternal destination and that our faith in the saving death of our Lord Jesus is the only basis for a complete and secure life. We had quite a few discussions about this, and he asked me once if I would go to a dying person. A nurse, who was studying the same subject, accompanied the young doctor to a dying patient of Christian background. This young man on his deathbed testified repeatedly about the saving grace of Jesus.

"It was most remarkable," the doctor said to me. "We asked him question after question, and he replied again and again with quotations out of the Bible."

I have never understood why the doctor wanted me to go there. There is no logical explanation for his behavior unless he was on his way to conversion and became a believer in later days. I will never know because he sold his house within the next two years and moved somewhere else to practice medicine.

But that was later. He invited Mom and me one evening for a dinner party with him and his young wife. This was a real eye-opener for me. I have never met a more likeable couple. They did not have a stitch of furniture in the whole house outside a table and the necessary chairs. Only their little daughter's bedroom was furnished.

Their own bedroom was absolutely bare of any luxury of any kind. They were sleeping in a sleeping bag right on the bare floor. This did not seem to bother them at all. They were the happiest people you can imagine. He told me in simple terms that he had a dream to build a house, and that's what he did. I had played a main part in that undertaking, and he was showing his appreciation in a lavish meal of pork chops with all the trimmings. He even had a supply of hard liquor for that occasion, and I came close to being drunk again—I said close but not completely.

It was a refreshing sight to see a young couple starting from the ground without a nickel to spare. This was a man after my own heart. Mom and I had started in the same way. He told me at that occasion that the fireplace could get so hot when he opened the outside air supply that the glass doors had been blown off more than once. This was not my fault, mind you!

It was on a nice summer day that he visited me in the hay field to say good-bye.

"I want you to know the reason that I am leaving," he said. "You are the one person that has a right for an explanation. That is the reason I come to visit with you now."

We sat there for three hours together on a bale of hay, and we discussed everything under the sun at that time. I told him that the doctors charged way too much for their services.

"No person should take more of society than that he puts in," I told him, and he agreed with me completely, but he said,

"It is so intoxicating when the money starts rolling in. A person can get hooked on that before he knows what is happening."

This was as honest an answer that I have heard in all my days. It was along those lines that we had a tremendous discussion. He told me that his house had been sold for one reason only—the fireplace. I will have to explain that this was in the beginning of the eighties, and nothing was moving in the real estate business. The doctor was a rare exception. One couple had been looking at the house, but they did not like the house in itself, but the woman fell in love with the fireplace.

"She kept going back to that fireplace and kept rubbing over the field rock surfaces. She would be at the door, ready to leave, and return to touch the rocks on that fireplace, since she could not get enough of that piece of work," the doctor said.

I would meet that woman later, and my life was never the same after that encounter—but that was later.

I had lost a good friend in the young doctor, but life goes on, and we have to move along with it.

It was in the fall of that year that all the op den Dries children were asked to come to Calgary for exploratory surgery. One of my younger brothers had lost his five-year-old daughter in a simple appendix operation. The two parents had brought the child to the hospital and were waiting for the results of the surgery. Then the doctor came in the waiting room white as a sheet. They had lost the child on the operating table.

She had gone into a high fever of uncontrollable proportions. Sudden death was the result of that unexplained fever reaction. I probably cannot explain the effects of that death on my brother and his wife. I will have to pass over that quietly.

The reaction was diagnosed as malignant hypothermia.

This allergy was under study at that time that we were called to the hospital. All the op den Dries children had to come in for that reason.

It was in early September that it was my turn to go under the knife. I went with a heavy heart, for this was one occasion that I was very afraid of dying. I was lying in the Foothills Hospital all by my lonesome self. Prayer did not seem to help. I was looking in one black void. Nothing was there but fear. Unadulterated fear! I was the most lonesome guy in the world at that moment. No comforting words from anyone.

"No soothing presence of men or spirit." I kept asking, "Where is my Lord?"

But no answer came—not then and not after the operation. It was in this manner that I was wheeled in a deep black void with nothing to look forward to. Everything to fear!

The first thing that I remembered was the presence of my wife and the voice of my daughter-in-law. But I was afraid. Oh so afraid! Not only was I afraid, but I was also almost choking. That made it even worse. I have no recollection of that surgery, but I was told that they nearly lost me on the operation table when the doctors were doing the surgery. This was bad, but it was not all! This was only the beginning. Much more was to come.

There was one doctor in charge of this program who was dedicated to the solution, or the cure, for this allergy that our family, and many other families, had problems with. He was seeking for a cure or a simple blood test to discover this problem in hereto unsuspecting people or families.

It was with this in mind that he jumped on one of my x-rays with more than normal enthusiasm. They had seen a shadow of a spot on one x-ray. I was told to report to the x-ray room again for more detailed x-rays. All to no avail; the x-rays did not prove anything, so I had to go under this machine four times in a row for a series of four or five x-rays at a time—the first time under the pretext that the machine was not thorough enough. The second time was with the excuse that the technician was not fully trained to do the job, and so on and so on. Something was in the wind! There was a smell downwind of the cheese factory in Denmark.

Old Hank was in for it. I had tested positive in my blood test, and the doctors wanted to follow through on this. That's how I have interpreted the following moves and dictates. I was told to come back after roughly three or four months. The doctors wanted to have a closer look at that suspicious spot on my lungs. That was that!

The old man had to return to the Foothills just before our thirtieth wedding anniversary. I remember clearly that I went to a doctor in the cancer wing about two weeks before the operation. This was a Christian by the sound of it. I told him that my trust was in the Lord and that I knew where I would be going in case that I would not pull through.

"That's right," he replied. "It is a beginning, and not the end."

These words were very helpful at the time. His advice was not! He told me that this exploratory surgery was a minor problem.

"Just a little cut in the top of your chest. That's all it will take."

"Let me tell you. It was anything but that!"

I had to report roughly four days before our anniversary for some preparatory tests and instructions. Then came the joker in the deck. The head surgeon visited me Friday night, a few days before the operation. This was a man of action by the looks of it. He sat down at my bedside and told me bluntly that it was ridiculous to have an operation for a spot on the lung that was all but invisible.

"But," he said, "we have a meeting tonight. I will let you know how we are making out. You should go home in my opinion and have an x-ray taken every half year. This is a very heavy operation, and it is foolishness to go through a heavy operation on such scant evidence."

He left me with these words, and I stayed where I was, completely flabbergasted! What a mess I was in this time! It was not at all pleasant! Not even one little bit.

I was informed later that the surgery would proceed as scheduled, November 30, 1981, right on our anniversary, and it was almost the last anniversary for Mom and me, since it was a very close call—too close! My wife and family were waiting for my release from the operating room, and one hour went by! Then two hours. Then some more time until one doctor came over to tell them that they wanted to keep me under close observation. They had nearly lost me again.

Nobody seems to know what went wrong, but I had a runaway fever, and I ended on a bed of ice with fans blowing over me. I had gone through a reaction. There was no doubt about that at all. The anesthesia! "A little fellow" told me later that he had never been so scared in his life. The trouble with runaway fever is that your brain can be destroyed and lose its ability to function properly. I was lying in that bed of ice for the better part of the day, according to my wife and children. I don't remember this myself. I do remember the pain. Do I ever remember that! The doctors had to spread my ribs apart and cut a half circle, the size of a dollar, out of one rib. This and a cut from the breastbone to the backbone made for a very unpleasant sensation. It was a long cry from the little cut in the top of my chest, such as was advocated by the doctor in the cancer ward.

The pain was unbelievable—one long nightmare of pain! No letup for days on end.

I can clearly remember that Friday evening when two young nurses had to look after me. They were in hurry and wanted to go to a party or something. This was important for those girls and did not leave much room for pussyfooting around with a little old Dutchman out of the sticks somewhere.

They told me to shove myself higher up in the bed, something I could not possibly do. The two girls grabbed me under the armpits and dragged me uphill without any further ado. Just imagine!—almost two hundred pounds of dead meat!

I was still hurting when a couple of other girls followed through not all that much later. I had to cough up flumes that time whether I had any or not. Those girls sat behind me on the bed and squeezed my chest, trying to have me cough up flumes. It hurt like crazy, and I grumbled like a porcupine in labor, since I must have a low threshold of pain. This did not make any difference for those girls, and they did not have much pity on me either. The flumes had to come, and I had to cough. I could not do either of the two. Some relief came when an older nurse arrived at the scene. She managed to bring on the desired effect with much less pain on my part. I must say that the girls were really sincere in their efforts. They did not have the right material to work with, that is all.

It is a good thing that I had not been smoking for many years. It is hard to say what would have happened if I still had been smoking at that time. So much for the girls!

My brother John was next in line. He came for a friendly visit and almost killed me.

He looked at me and said, "So they finally have you where they want you!"

This was accompanied by that infectious laugh of his—with the result that I had to laugh whether I wanted to or not. This was pure agony! Try it sometime when you have a pair of bruised ribs. You will like it! I am sure you will!

I must have been in that hospital close to three weeks, and the weather turned cold. Christmas was near, and the nurses wanted as many patients out of the hospital as possible. This is not hard to understand. The way they did it was a lot harder to follow. The head nurse came to my bed at eight in the morning.

She said without any warning beforehand, "You will have to leave at eleven o'clock this morning. Your bed will be taken away by then."

I was completely flabbergasted. I had no prior notice. It was twenty below outside, and it would take at least three hours to get someone from Rocky to Calgary. This is what I told them, but there was no help for it. I had to be out of there by eleven in the morning. I phoned home and explained the situation, but no one could come out on that short notice. About six in the evening was the best that could be expected.

Here was Mother's number-three son standing in the hallway of the hospital with nowhere to go.

My bed had been taken away. I have never seen anything so callous and coldhearted. The nuns in Germany in the war were kinder than these folks in Calgary.

It was my cousin who lived in Calgary who picked me up later after my cry for help. They looked after me until the evening, when my boys arrived and trundled me over the rough winter roads of wintertime Alberta. I could feel every dip and puddle in the road from Calgary all the way to my own doorstep. It is a miracle that I did not end up with a case of pneumonia when I was walking from the hospital to the parking lot of the Foothills Hospital in twenty-below weather.

You may think that I was exaggerating when I told you this story. It is absolutely true, every word of it. You may think that I was a complainer. This is your right, but don't say too much until you have walked around with a thirty-inch cut over your stomach and a pair of bruised ribs to cool you down—all this in twenty-below weather. By the way, this was twenty below Fahrenheit, not Celsius.

But everything was OK now. I was back in the arms of my beloved Johanna. Even that went sour. She did not want me to snuggle up to her. She was afraid that I would die in bed.

I owe much to the girls of Arie de Bryun. They did the milking for me at a reasonable price, never complaining. Art Terpsma and his brothers set out hay for me at a nominal fee. They would have done it for nothing, but that was not necessary. I had a little income at that time. This is how we struggled along for the next two or three months until spring came in the land and joy came through my soul. We were still allowed a little more time together, Johanna and I. Everything was coming up roses again.

It is an amazing thing, but I put up my own hay that summer, and I returned to my full workload in a matter of months; but even so, nobody can understand the pain when you try to get up in the morning when you are sporting a pair of bruised ribs. I have talked to people in that condition, and none of them were shouting for joy. Neither was I. Believe me. Too much complaining, hey? Let's go on with the show.

The summer went by normally enough. It was the fall that brought some surprises. It was on one fall day that a carpenter stopped by at our place. He asked me if I would consider building a fireplace out of split rock. He was building a house, and these people wanted me to build a fireplace for them. I gave him a flat refusal—not interested. I had enough on my plate without adding the complications of another fireplace. His face fell a few notches, and he went away with a hung-down look, while I went back to what I was doing—nothing.

That's not true! I always had something to do. But I figured that I should not take on more than I could handle. A day went by, and the carpenter was back. Would I reconsider? The lady had seen some of my work, and she did not want anyone else but me. That was easy enough; I was the only mason around in those days. Whatever—I refused again. There was nobody who could talk me into doing more rockwork—not in that point of my life.

The man came back again and again, up to six times in a row. It was at that point that I promised to have a talk with the lady in question—my first mistake. I should not have gone there, but I was stupid enough to do this. It turned out to be the same lady who had looked at the doctor's house. She would not be denied.

It was one of those occasions that two people hit it off just like that. She told me that I would build that fireplace for her no matter what the cost.

I said, "That is going to cost you a bundle."

She had a grin from ear to ear and replied, "Name your price. I will write out a check, right here and now."

That was it. I was hooked. Not a chance to get out of that anymore. She was reeling me in hook, line and sinker. I could have named my price and walked away without any conditions attached, just like that—this is not how it works, of course. I did not want any money before I had lifted a shovel of mud, but I did make the condition that I would not be rushed. I was recovering from a heart attack and some heavy surgery.

I would not accept any pressure in any shape or form. They could rest assured that I would walk off the job no matter how much had been done or how much had to be done. I was not kidding. I have done exactly that in other places, and I would do it again. I did come very close to doing the same thing here. This happened as follows.

The husband had a basement with two long windows, about eight feet apart. I was to build one fireplace in the basement and a second one exactly on top of the first one upstairs. I warned him that this could not be done, but he insisted.

HANK OPDENDRIES

The lines were drawn, while the battle raged on for more than a day. I absolutely refused to build those fireplaces under this condition, and I had my tools packed and was ready to go when the lady of the house came on the scene. This was the clincher. I had a weak spot for that woman, and I accepted a compromise.

Let me add that the bottom fireplace did smoke—just as I had predicted, but the onus was on them this time. I could not be blamed. They had been warned.

This job turned out to be one of the most peculiar assignments that I have ever undertaken. I am fairly sure that the other workers in that house thought that this lady and I were nuts at times. She could do the strangest things and get away with it. Her husband was an Irish man, and the Irish have the so-called Green Day in the spring. Every Irishman is supposed to wear green on the particular day. This was beautiful, and the lady got right in the spirit of the day. She caught her husband's hunting dog and painted the animal bright green. I thought that the Irishman was going to kill her, but for me, it was funny. "Unbelievably funny!"

The lady had received a set amount of money to build the house, and it was with this in mind that she came to me one day and said, "Come on, Hank, give me your final billing account. I am almost out of money, and I want to be sure that you get paid before the money runs out. The others can wait for the money!"

It was a lot of fun, but the job was not the healthiest I have done. The whole chimney had to be built outside in the middle of the winter. The carpenter had built a cage of plastic around the south side of the house, and we put a propane heater in that structure. It is not hard to understand that this was hard on the system. I had to inhale the propane fumes all day long, and not only that, but my cows also had to be milked in the morning and in the evening. That left between four and five hours to do the rockwork from day to day, except Sundays; I would not work on Sundays. We had agreed on that right initially, and they never argued that point. They never argued about anything in fact. I never heard one complaint in all those two months that it took me to complete that job, and that's no wonder. It was the nicest piece of work that I ever did.

This woman had a real knack of sprucing up the place in a very tasteful manner. She had a kitchen that was almost as big as my house.

All full of cupboards. Neither money nor efforts had been spared on the inside the house. It was a palace of taste and beauty, and the fireplace was the center of everything. She had ordered a marble-colored mantelpiece for the front of the fireplace, and this added in a meaningful way to enhance the beauty of the many-colored rocks.

"It is the most photographed fireplace in the country," she told me the other day. "People come from far and wide to have their picture taken in front of that piece of rockwork. Many a wedding party has been immortalized around that place, and I have received no end of compliments on my house and mostly on the living room."

I must say that I walked out of there with a slightly swollen head, but I do take these compliments with a grain of salt. A small grain, mind you! Fact is that it is a tactful way of using the opportunities. That's what makes the difference, and I know that only too well.

She also told me that this fireplace is burning every winter day—no exception. That is a switch! I have heard time and again from other customers that these masonry fireplaces take so much air out of the house.

"Just as if that is my fault."

Every fireplace has got a damper. There is no need for that. The chimney can be closed airtight. We have good memories of the Irish lady and her husband. Some of the nicest people to work for if you did an honest day's work and could cater to their wishes. It seems that we did rather well in this latest respect.

It was in one day when this guy visited me on the scaffold that I had some insight in the working of this man's brains. He was one of the smartest people that I ever laid eyes on. It was at that occasion that he told me about his decision to sell all but two of his Caterpillar tractors. Those machines had been bought for at least $100,000 or more. It was inconceivable that he would let these machines go for half price or less, but that is exactly what he did. He sold it all. He told me that the bottom would drop out of the oilfield business within the next year—a recovery was next to impossible in the foreseeable future. I looked at him in amazement and asked him whether he was sure of that.

"Yes," he said. "You can count on it!"

The records show that he was exactly right in his prediction. It would take years for the oil patch to recover.

CHAPTER 15

THE TWILIGHT YEARS

ALL THIS WAS of little value for me, since I was in the dairy business. I had to carry on as best as I knew how so that the next three years went by in relative peace and quiet. The kids were growing up, and one after the other wrecked one of my cars. I am thankful to say that none of them got into serious trouble or hurt anyone else in the process, but that is as far as it went.

I had a little Volkswagen when I left for a trip to the Old Country. It was not a first-rate car but good enough for the work I had to do with it, a prized possession you could call it. The top of the little car was cut off with a cutting torch when I came back after four weeks of relaxation in the Old Country. The boys developed a craving for a dune buggy. The Volkswagen was sitting there staring them in the eye. It became so bothersome that they had to do something about that. They learned how to handle a cutting torch! They also learned to drive a dune buggy.

Neither has been any good to them, and I was out of a favored means of locomotion. I could feel my hair turn gray when I looked at this sorry sight. What does a man do in a situation like that? I owed them for the work in the barn and with the cows during our vacation in Holland.

"I will tell you a secret!" I cut my hair short to cover up the gray hair while I cried in my pillow during the night. That is what I did.

Mom was not much help in that respect. She does not understand the relationship between a man and his Volkswagen. Very few people do!

My boys had a real calling for wrecking things. I had a nice old Chevy truck, dark green in color and well put together. It was stacked better than a sixteen-year-old girl. Her lines were beautiful and a feast for the eye, while her power was unsurpassed and she would purr along like a kitten—that is, until the boys got a hold of her! They tied a set of buffalo horns to the hood and made some alterations to that once beautiful body. The doors were ripped off, and the rest spruced up. Moving some unmovable objects had reshaped her body, and the truck came out as the loser in most of these exercises.

Her once desirable body became dull and unappetizing. A trip over the brush piles was the final indignity. She fell apart in one formless heap of misery and despair. It takes a lot to take a Dutchman down. We would not admit defeat. Not by a long shot. A trip to the auto wreckers was the next opportunity for some more punishment at the hands of my lover boys.

I picked up a nice little rolled over Datsun car. Two weeks of hard work and a little paint made for a very comfortable means of transportation, until one of my sons got his grimy little hands on her. He took it to cow town and started reshaping that society for years to come. I have never heard the full extent of that adventure, but I do know that it was more than a little debatable. The once beautiful little love bug came back as oil-guzzling old hag. There was no beauty left in that tired little body of hers. There was only one thing left to do! Pass it on to the next needy character. This friendly giant was only too well prepared to finish her off. He put a fence post through her eyeglasses. Her beauty was gone and her usefulness. She ended her days next to the hapless little Volkswagen in the tall grass of my pastureland.

Never mind! Little things like that don't get in the way of progress. There was still some life in the old Dutchman. He bought a wrecked Toyota car. This car had to succumb to the expertise and know-how of the former body man. It became a masterpiece of workmanship and a showpiece of a painter's know-how. It sat there green as grass. Let me explain that yellow and blue produce a nerve-racking green. This was used as a cover color, and it looked like a caterpillar of great magnitude. This heartrending love bug was placed in the hands of another future Einstein. He trundled along over all creation in a dream world of unsurpassed beauty.

The result? He planted it in a ditch, six feet deep with steep sides. He had made a flying leap of about ten feet trying to get her in the right position. Can you beat that?

HANK OPDENDRIES

Never mind! There was still life in the old boy! He bought a nice Chevy car with rear-end damage. This too had to succumb to the workmanship of the past master of auto body repair. It traveled all over the country all the way to BC and beyond, but not for long! It would be a pity to leave it that way. I donated this one to another one of my bright-eyed boys, with the result that I had to rescue this boy time and again when he ran out of gas and resources. It too was turned into an oil-guzzling giant. It was also turned into an oil refinery with reversed qualities. It was burning the oil instead of producing it. It landed on the trash heap also.

I won't mention the car with Coca-Cola in the brake system—this was supposed to be a cheaper form of brake fluid. Neither will I recall the Plymouth car that sat in front of my brother Gerrit's house. One wheel was missing. Even my boys could not run a car on three wheels—but they came close. They have done almost everything else.

It would not be right for me to mention that the boys made a Molotov cocktail and almost put the house on fire. All these things are things of the past. It should be forgotten. I used to have a forty-five-gallon drum full of gas. It was cheaper to buy gas in bulk than by the gallon in those days of long ago.

My boys thought that this was very unfitting, and they emptied the barrel time and again. They could not stand the thought that this gas was sitting there idly. It should be put to use. They even invented ways to alleviate the problem. They poured out a long trail of gasoline from the house to the road.

A woman out of the neighborhood had the misfortune of passing by my place when the boys ignited that trail of gasoline. The flames walked from the house to the road in less time than you can say "applesauce." Was that not nice of those boys?

This woman did not even need the headlights anymore. The road was as bright as day. I was not supposed the mention this. Forget that you read this. Or better yet! Don't read it at all!

The fact that they put the Volkswagen of an unpopular counselor into the social hall of church has no more importance than the fact that they put whiskey in the minister's glass—the glass on the pulpit, I mean! The good man needed that as much as a hole in the head. The boys did not know this. They were trying to do the man a favor.

I am really proud of my children when I think of moments like these. They were good all right. There is another evil under the sun. The young people had a novel idea. One of them had a car with a wide wheelbase. It fitted exactly over the railroad irons. The rails made an ideal place to drive the car—especially if you let most of the air out of the tires.

Nobody would have to be behind the steering wheel in that ideal situation, and it took only a dozen young people to fill that car. That was something that they managed to do that quite nicely. Thank you! This happened on an abandoned branch line of the CPR. A trip like that on the main line might have run into the complication of meeting a full-size train. That would not do! No, that would not do at all.

It was in the middle of those joy-filled days that Mom and I had to break out for a little while. We went for another trip to Holland. My oldest brother was still working then so that we had to fill our days with visits and the odd trip with brother Jan.

We went to the great polders of the former South Sea. It was as flat as the prairies but not so windy. Rich green grass and produce of every shape and substance were filling the fields in an ever-changing spectrum of beauty and abundance. The war years were all but forgotten, and Holland was as prosperous as ever, some long ways from the hungry years of the early forties. It was hard to believe, and I felt almost sorry that we had left this country of abundance—but not really!

It was during our travels that we landed on a place that looked like a hill—right in the middle of all that flatland. An age-old church was in the center of that hill, while several smaller buildings surrounded that church in an irregular fashion, just as if a giant hand had scattered them over the surface of that curious little island in the middle of that flat polder land, and this is just what it was—an island wrestled out of the middle of the Zuider Sea.

Numerous reminders of its former functions had been preserved and set aside for future generations. Old rusty buoys were lying in a circle around the small area. So were anchors of every size and description; some with and some without chains recalling the past of a once-thriving fishery. A light tower had served the fishermen as a guide and beacon for untold years until the thrifty Dutch had stopped that lucrative trade. Farmland was more precious than saltwater. The tradeoff was too much in favor of the farmer of future generations. The sea had to go. This was all that remained.

Nostalgia and the spirits of untold generations seemed to fill this place with longing for days gone by. Another curiosity was some sandstone caskets that were standing around in a number of places. They looked like coffins of unclear descriptions, and the question rose in my mind on what the meaning of these strange kinds of objects might be. My curiosity would soon be satisfied. A plaque on one of the objects pointed out that these were sandstone coffins used in desperation when the sea dike was breaking down. The dikes were only miles away where land and sea had wrestled in age-old battle for the possession of the land. The desperate dike workers had used these stone coffins as a last resort to strengthen the crumbling dikes. It was in those desperate moments that even the dead had to give up their rest in the age-old battle of man against the sea.

The church had been turned into a museum with many reminders of the past. Fossils were displayed under glass cages. Fossils and fossilized forms of land and sea animals, millions of years old, according to the version of some unknown brain. I have always regarded these statements with some apprehension. No human was there when these creatures roamed the earth.

The Bible seems to give a different version of the timetable of untold centuries. The Lord will make it clear to us someday. I like to believe the Bible as it was written. It has never let me down, and I am sure that it never will!

My mother had a saying from many generations ago: "With understanding it won't work. Believe it, without understanding."

It is as simple as that. Believe it, without understanding. Faith life is just what it implies—faith!

It was with this in mind that I looked at these relics but also at the evidence of life and disaster of a much more recent date. Some reminders of the last war had been thrown all over the sea bottom. Some planes had been found almost hidden under the slick surface of the ever-shifting sea bottom. Quite a number of planes could be reconstructed. The families and loved ones could be notified after these many years. It must have been a real comfort for many of those who lost sons or husbands overseas.

It is always better to know a little than to know nothing about the last resting-place of a loved one—no matter how remote or how far from home. It was along these lines that the sea gave up some of her secrets in that later date.

It was with a feeling of awe that we drove over that sea bottom with so many untold secrets and mysteries. Many fishermen have lost their lives in this abundantly rich fishing water of not so long ago. The Zuider Sea was the richest fishing ground of Europe before the industrious Dutch turned it into very productive farmland. Trees and scrubs had sprung up all over the country almost overnight, so it seemed to our astonished eyes. It was usual to see whole sections of full-grown trees all over the countryside.

It sure was all a long cry from the seashore of my childhood days, and I had to marvel at the progress of this war-torn country of our immigrant days of the late 1940 when we left on our journey of unknown destiny—Canada.

The mighty Delta works at the North Sea shore are even more impressive if that is possible! The Dutch decided to build some mighty dike works across the Schelde and some more great waterways along the west coast. The sea had destroyed hundreds of human lives. The destruction of life and livestock was beyond measure in those hectic days of the great flood. Hundreds upon hundreds of farms were wiped off the earth in that tempest of wind and water. The misery and suffering of the hard-hit population resounded through the whole Western world. It was so loud that even the Dutch government had to sit up and take notice. Billions of dollars were allocated for the building of a dike system that would block out the sea forever. The Lord willing!

We had the opportunity to have a look at those awesome products of human ingenuity. Awesome blocks of concrete were placed on a bed of gravel and basalt blocks right on the bottom of the sea. These unwieldy blocks of concrete were put in place within a margin of centimeters, and all this was done in the ever-watchful and harmful power of the great North Sea. Great sluices were put in place to regulate the ebb and flow of the mighty North Sea waters. We have seen cement blocks as high as sky scrapers set aside as spares in case the need might arise for further corrective measures against the might of wind and sea.

A person can spend days walking from one project to the other—one more impressive than the other, all according to human wisdom and know-how. But the Lord on high is the ruler yet! He will dictate the pathway of the stars and galaxies, also the ways of wind and water. He will dictate if these works will stand or fall. He will allow these things to stand by His grace and His grace only. I believe that the Dutch are well aware of this. At least some of them!

Holland is a showcase of old and new. Modern Holland is impressive but can hardly compare with its long and proud history. Many monuments are left as a reminder of the golden Middle Ages of Western Europe and of Holland in particular. Many beautiful churches are left as a testimony to the faith of our forefathers.

Especially the southern part of Holland is rich in church history. The *beeldenstorm* (destruction of Roman Catholic images in the Roman churches) has destroyed many beautiful sculptures erected by the faithful in former years. History has recorded that Holland fought for eighty years against the Roman Catholic nation of Spain. This was during the 1400s and 1500s. One of the Spanish Dukes had sworn to his king that he would send a stream of gold as thick as his wrist out of the rich Dutch country, back to Spain. The Spanish inquisition brought many Protestants to death in those days—burned on the stake or garroted with a noose after horrendous torture in the Spanish prisons. This was all done in the name of God and the Mother Mary. The so-called heretics were forced by fire and sword to return to the only true church—the Catholic Church.

It is small wonder that the ordinary Dutch population hit back and destroyed many once beautiful Catholic churches in Northern Holland. There are still many Protestant churches in the north with niches for the long-departed saints of the Catholic area. The niches are there, but the saints are gone.

I must add that the Dutch have always been some very tolerant people. This is the reason that there are many Catholic churches left in the southern provinces of the overall Protestant Dutch nation. And many Catholics live side by side to Protestant people in the best of harmony. I have always had a great love for the pomp and power of the former Catholic Church. Sightseeing in the age-old churches of years gone by is one of my greatest pleasures.

The Lange Jan Church in 's-Hertogenbosch is a prime example of the devotion of the former faithful of years gone by. It would take at least fifteen minutes to walk around that church from one end to the other. The inside is absolutely breathtaking in beauty and versatility. Every wing has its own altar, dedicated by the different tradesman or guilds, the plumber and the carpenter, the farmer and the goldsmith.

The leather worker and all the other tradesmen are represented in the brightly decorated niches of the guardian saints of all the different trades. Hundreds or maybe thousands of little candles are burning in front of many of these altars and in the side wings of the numerous portals and conclaves of this majestic building.

The Catholic faith has reached beyond the grave into the afterlife of the believers of all ages. Great gravestones with the inscriptions of the notables and rich of former days or years cover the floor of the church. The Dutch have an expression about the very rich. They call them "rich stinkers." This expression comes from the fact that the rich were buried inside the church, and it would take a long time before the body smell had disappeared out of the insides of this magnificent building. I did not know this, but it was explained to me at the time of our visit in the church of the Lange Jan.

I had a good reminder that the average person in Holland is anything but rich. A woman was selling postcards and other knickknacks in the center of the church, right under the eye of God. This is an eye painted in the ceiling about fifty feet or more above the ground level of the church. I wanted to buy some cards and pay with a hundred-dollar bill.

"Be careful, sir!" said this woman as she looked around the church in a very anxious manner. "Never pay with big money in a public place. Someone is likely to see you and follow you in a dark corner. You will be knocked cold, if you are lucky, and your money taken. It happens all the time!"

It was a good reminder that a person is never safe. Not even in a church. The son of Derk and Geertje had a lot to learn.

All this could have happened right under the eyes of the saintly Adolf. That's right! Even brother Adolf had his own saint in that church. I am just kidding! There was a sculpture dedicated to the saintly Adolf, but I don't think that it was referring to my brother. He has a little to go yet before that happens.

There was a pipe organ in that church of unbelievable proportions. It was all built out of rosewood, and it was eighty meters long when it was laid out on the church floor. That's what the church dictionary was saying anyway.

The willingness to give in the interest of the church and its message was clearly demonstrated repeatedly when you followed through the different stages of this most beautiful church. This was the overall impression I had from all those altars and pictures—one more beautiful than the other.

The church of the Middle Ages later was the greatest beneficiary of the artful masters of those early years. Many an altarpiece has been donated with the understanding that some highborn lady was immortalized in one of the paintings of the life of Jesus. It was along these lines that the artist of the early years eked out an existence. Rembrandt died as a poor man. His famous *Night Watch* was commissioned by a group of people who refused payment when the painting did not show their important personalities in their proper respect.

The temple of Jesus's day was turned into a house of dealing and wheeling by the profit-conscious priest and temple servants. The Middle Age church was dealing in souls and after-death securities in much the same manner. So many candles and so many masses for a departed person; it was in this way that those many early and devotedly believing common men erected buildings to immortalize the money-conscious servants of the man in Galilee who was born in a stable and lived the lowly life of a carpenter.

Do not think that I am judging this matter. No. I am thankful that so much beauty has been preserved in this manner. However, it is a fact that our salvation cannot be bought and paid for. This was so clearly demonstrated by the struggle of Martin Luther and Calvin, Huss, and so many others who gave it all for the clear proclamation of the saving grace of our Lord Jesus.

The outside of that church was almost as impressive as the inside. Hundreds of sculptures were standing in their respective niches, staring into all eternity with nothing else to do. The roof of the building and the tower were the most impressive. Many a colorful figure was depicted on the eves of the sloping church roof where one little plumber was hanging on desperately onto the side of the roof. His scornful wife chased him out of his house as the story goes. He could not live up to her expectations and was banned to the roof for time immortal. I think that he would get a lot of company if this practice were still in vogue presently. He might have to shove over and make room for me also.

The tower had saints of every size and descriptions. Level after level as the tower reached higher and higher to the low-hanging clouds of the mournful low country sky, ogres and werewolves were guarding the higher elevations of the old tower. It seems that the early church had a smattering of werewolves to scare away the evil spirits as they were spouting rainwater over the weathered green-colored roof. Even our Parliament buildings seem to have the protection of the same ogres. That's understandable! They need all the help that they can get! Yuk! Yuk!

We saw much the same thing on a trip to the age-old city of Aachen in Germany. This city goes back in origin to the time before the Crusades in the years of 1000 and later. There is a museum with old golden relics of the time of Karel the Great. He was one of the greatest rulers of the early years. It was by the might of his sword that he forced many a heathen into a form of Christianity. One has to wonder about that manner of persuasion by the early ruler of Christianity. Many of his golden trophies are still locked up in the vaults of the Aachen city hall.

We have seen many of those as we descended into the lower reaches of these darkened vaults. The light is very dim in there. This is done on purpose in an effort to preserve the objects from the ravages of time and war.

It was on the Great Market Square that I made one of the greatest mistakes of that trip. This square was covered with hippies of every form and description. There were good-looking specimens and also some who seemed to be the scum of the earth. It was in that square that my friend decided to change some money in the bank nearby, and I was foolish enough to pull my wallet out of my pocket at the same moment. Hundreds of eyes were following our every move in that sunlit square. It did not take long before we had a following from a couple of these husky boys. There is no doubt in my mind that they would have finished us off at the first opportunity. All that they were waiting for was the second mistake—a moment that we would be separated in some secluded area of that square. It seemed like the better part of valor to get out of there as fast as our car would travel. Live and learn, they say. I have a lot to learn, and that's a fact of life.

My friend Dick was not impressed.

He hit the steering wheel with both fists and exclaimed, "Those krauts. They stink. You can smell them a mile away!"

I was somewhat surprised at that explosion of that otherwise quiet and composed person. He was a very bitter person indeed. But who can blame him? He had held one of his friends falling apart in his arms as the result of the German atrocities in the Second World War. Things like that go a little further than skin deep. Believe me!

It was in a somewhat somber mood that we continued on our way home. Many memories came clouding our memories as a result of our latest experiences. But life goes on. It was time to go back to our home in Canada. New adventures were waiting for us. It had been a good time of relaxation, but our own task was waiting for us in that faraway Canada. Some task it was! Believe me!

It was around that time that we ran into trouble again in our church life. We had a new minister with some liberal ideas in the worship services. I am afraid that he was about ten years ahead of his time in that respect.

"It is no use bothering with the people over fifty years of age," he said on one occasion. "They are too set in their ways. There is no way of turning them around. We have to work with the younger generation from now on!"

There might have been a lot of truth in that remark, but it was not the wisest thing to say at that point in time. It is a fact that we are afraid of change. We like to keep things the way they are. This is not wise. Even so! It is also a fact that there is no future that is not grounded in the past. You cannot shove the past aside as immaterial and of no consequence, and that is what has been happening, even now! No tree can live without its roots, and no church will prosper if it does not honor the elderly. I am not saying this, but the Bible states this very clearly.

A mighty struggle developed after his efforts for evangelism along his way of thinking. A lot of sinning was done on both sides of the argument. It is the same way now. We have another minister with much the same way of thinking. We are hit time and again with the message that we are not evangelizing enough. The church would be full to overflowing if we would change the worship services and adapt to the ways of the world around us. I will honestly admit that I am completely mixed up.

We lived a life of separation in the Old Country. Don't touch and don't mix—that was the message of the church leaders of that day. Mom and I were not allowed to date because we did not belong to the same denomination. We had sermons of one hour and a half and services of two hours or more. And how is it now? We are required to shorten the sermons and fill the services with participation and entertainment. Is it any wonder that we need a little time to adapt to that new version of worship?

I can't help but think that the Pentecostal churches should have been full to overflowing if that was all there was to it. This is not the case. Our CRC is one of the most faithful churches in the way of giving. We were trained that way. It was our calling. At least that is what we were told again and again. And the irony of it all is the fact that it is just the same faithfulness that is our downfall in respect to change. We can't let go of the securities of the past.

It seems to be the same struggle that the Jews had in Jesus's day. They too had been taught to be faithful to the letter of the law. They too had trouble adapting to the new ways. Does this mean that we were not evangelizing in the way that we should have? I don't know. All of us fall short in our serving of our Lord and Master. It is not for lack of trying that we could not follow these ministers in their endeavor for change.

It is with a troubled mind that we see the sermons lose their meaning, and the Word is watered down in the effort to make it more palatable to the man on the street. The local church is losing members, but no new converts enter into the church—one watches and wonders. All this might have been of no significance if it had not been for the fact that the changes had been forced upon us in a roundabout way. The pastor would bypass his consistory instead of working within that august body of believers.

Worship committees and liturgical committees were set up with exactly that in mind. These committees are the tools of the ruling hierarchy. The pastors are trying to force the consistory's hand in every way possible. All this might have been good from the minister's viewpoint. But it was hardly conducive for the unity of the church. A spirit of division has taken over where a spirit of cooperation and love was ruling in days gone by.

I am not judging the actions of this body of believers. I just fail to understand the meaning of it all. The pastor has showered us with a great number of sermons in the last month or two, with the intent to burden us with a guilt complex of great proportions. He has succeeded very well in that. A spirit of uncertainty is prevailing, and the faithful

HANK OPDENDRIES

givers of yesterday are losing heart. It seems as if nothing is good enough any way you look at it.

It becomes harder and harder to balance the budget of the church. Small wonder! Is there a way back? I think so! There is a way as long as we are willing to give on both sides of the dispute. The building of the spiritual church should prevail, and we should try for a better understanding on both sides.

Well! I have covered the problems of today and yesterday—in church anyway! We are back to the same point as when we were in the dying days of that former ministry of about ten years ago—I was the bulletin reporter at that time. I wrote a number of suggestions at that time in an effort to stem the tide of discontent. It seems that our congregation has to go over the same suggestions all over again if they want to keep this church together. It is a shame that we are losing so much time in the effort of sorting things out in a peaceful manner. But enough of that!

It was around that time in 1985 that I ran into heart trouble once again. One of my sons had to bring me to the hospital with extreme chest pains. It looked as if I had another heart attack. The world was caving in around my ears once again. The pain was so extreme that I was near fainting. A nitroglycerin tablet under the tongue brought almost instant relief this time, but the doctor kept me in the hospital for closer observation with the net result that I had to go to Edmonton to a heart specialist.

A cardiogram was taken and a close-up of my heart in the TV camera. The whole procedure was quite interesting, for I could see this instrument poking around inside of my heart just like a coat hanger puttering around a Christmas tree. A tin wire was inserted in one of the main arteries in the lower inside of my hip. It was a remarkable experience, especially when one of the nurses was forcing down on that artery with her full weight in order to stop the bleeding of this main artery. I can't say that I was afraid. Just curious, that's all.

An incident in the recovery room was a lot more unsettling. I had to lie down without moving for the next four hours. The artery needed time to resettle and close over the cut made by the attending doctors.

There were two rooms adjacent to each other. Each room had about six beds with heart patients. It was in the latest hour of my recovery period that a number of men came running out of the next room, scared out of their wits by the looks of their faces. None of them could say anything, but they kept pointing to the room behind them. Something was seriously wrong, and I ran back to the room where they came from.

It was a scary sight all right that met my eyes. One of the heart patients had a convulsion of some kind. He was bouncing up and down in bed for a height of at least one foot at a time. It did not take an expert to see that he was in serious trouble, and it was my turn to run to the nursing station where the attending nurse hit the red alert button.

A great bedlam of explosive motion broke loose almost immediately. Nurses with medicine and stretchers came running from every direction, and the patient was attended to at once—with satisfactory results. The man lived through the ordeal after the prompt reaction of the medical staff.

The first nurse came past my bed with a conspiratorial smile as if to say, "We did all right that time! Didn't we?"

I had the same kind of feeling. I do not know why the others ran away from that critical moment in this man's life. I only know that we had every reason to be thankful in this battle with the Grim Reaper, a battle that was won this time.

These kinds of experience don't add to the peace of mind of a heart patient, and it was with a subdued mind that I traveled back to my beloved Johanna and the seven wonders of our world. The doctor told me that I had to quit working altogether from that time forth. He even wanted me to sell the farm and move to town. Any exertion or upsetting emotion was to be banned out of my life from that point in time.

I quit working, just like the doctor ordered, but I did not sell the farm. Too many memories were surrounding our existence on the farm. My working days were over, but that did not mean that my children should be banned from the countryside. I decided to stay put. "And what about your Johanna?" you may ask. You guessed it! She was with me all the way. She loved country life even more than I did, and it would have real punishment to move her to town. We made the decision to stay on the farm in spite of the fact that we had to quit milking.

I would like to tell the story that led up to this crisis in our lives. This had a lot to do with the treatment of the Alpha Milk Company and its employers. The milk hauler was a case in point. This scrawny little fellow kept pushing me and pushing me until I could not handle it anymore. My bulk tank was a very slow-cooling machine. It would take at least two hours to cool the milk to an acceptable level. He would arrive at our doorstep at eight o'clock or earlier, and it does not take a brain to figure that my days became earlier and earlier every time he came earlier. It came to the point that I had to start at five o'clock in the morning to keep ahead of this little runt.

I explained my problem to him, and things would change for a few days, and everything turned back to the situation as before. It was so bad that it has happened that I kept milking, and he was sitting in front of the milk house waiting with the patience of an elephant. It did not matter how long it would take! He would sit there and wait. He kept it up no matter what I said or did. I told him that he was pushing me into another heart attack if he kept this up. He was all sympathy—but he kept coming right on the dot.

Let me explain that our milk was graded on bacteria count. The count would rise with the temperature of the milk. He would put milk in his sample almost straight from the cow's udder. It was *udderly* ridiculous, and that's a fact! This was going on day after day—seven days a week—with no letup in sight until we reached the breaking point, and I had to put my herd of cows up for sale. It was hard to believe, but this same company hauled their sample box out of my milk house before the last milking was done.

This hurt me more than anything did—a deed so callous and unfeeling that it shook me to the core of my being. I had first-class milk for more than five years and the scrolls to prove it, but all to no avail. There was no sympathy from that quarter. None. None. None. None!

I sold my quota and the cows for a reasonable price, and that helped me through the years to come, but the future was grim indeed. We had no income for the next two years, but thankfully miracles still happen. I kept up my payments to the church and some to the school. I am not saying this because I feel so good about that. Just thankful the sale of quota and cows allowed us to put some money in the bank, and that was more than necessary.

The government took the first bite in income tax, and I paid close to twenty dollars in income tax in that year when I sold my quota out. Beside that I had no income outside of the interest. I had no income outside of the interest of my bank account, and that bank account was slowly but surely diminished and dwindled to below acceptable levels.

It was in desperation that I approached my doctor and asked him if there was a possibility for a handicapped pension. This was a serious mistake! I should have gone back to work in spite of what the doctor told me. But never mind!

The doctor put me in touch with the program of AISH—that means Assured Income for the Severely Handicapped. My first application was denied, believe it or not. I had to try once again. It looks as if the medical board had turned my application down. I would not be a bit surprised if some of my former friends, the doctors, had been on that board, but that is purely speculation on my part. Fortunately, we could reapply and launch an appeal to the decision of that board, and that's what we did.

We had to appear before a board of the municipality. The director of social services and a number of ordinary farm folk were on that particular board. I was lucky in a roundabout way, since the director had the same malignant hypothermia in his family as that we had, and he inquired about this situation.

So I told him that they nearly lost me at the operating table in Calgary. But that was beside the point. The overall impression was one of sympathy, and they encouraged me to go on with my life in the best way possible. They had decided to go with my house doctor's diagnosis and allowed a small pension of $720 a month. It was not much, but it made all the difference in the world for us.

I was walking on air when I went home to tell Mom the good news. We had a total income of about one thousand a month around that time. We were rich beyond measure! Even so, it had one limitation. All my other income had to be reported from that point on. This was the stinger. I was not afraid to do a little work, but I was afraid of the paperwork to reapply if I lost this allocation. It was safer to do nothing from that time on.

I would have liked to have done some work in the disaster areas in other countries but was afraid to do this, in case I ran into trouble with my overseers. Does this ring a bell? Are not all the welfare cases in the same boat? It was along those lines that our bank account kept dwindling, and our life was on hold for the foreseeable future. I would have liked to do the brickwork on the new church but had to cancel out on that too for the simple reason that I could not draw out of a disability pension and do brickwork at the same time. We were boxed in a corner,

HANK OPDENDRIES

and I was to meet that same deadlock every turn of the road in later days. A disabled person has to watch his step all the time.

I mentioned the new church . . . This came about in the following manner. We had a lot of trouble with the minister and a group of people in the church of the early eighties. This minister and his group wanted to reform the worship services in a manner that the rest could not follow. Quite a struggle developed, and it all came to a head when the matter was brought before the classis of North Alberta and the minister was repealed in that august body of learned fellows of the cloth. I won't go further in that matter.

It was during the term of that minister that we invited a couple of ministers from Home Missions into our church community. They would make out a mini map of possibilities and difficulties in our church. This report started out with the statement that they had never been in a church that was as united as the Rocky church. Looks can be deceiving. The whole church was divided beyond reconciliation in a matter of months after that, but that's a story in itself. We won't go into that either.

The church had outgrown all the available space at the time of this visit. The consistory had made plans again and again to correct that situation, and the congregation turned it down every time just as promptly. This had happened to the plans for an extension onto the building for several years already. Home Missions came with the suggestion that the consistory should show some leadership and force the issue.

This was a new approach. Their idea was that a small church would be more expensive but better for the outreach in the neighborhood. A smaller group might attract outside members a lot faster. Consistory followed through on that suggestion and came forward with plans for a second church. The pastor was much in favor of this new proposal, and the consistory supported him on this, and so it was decided that the vote had to be seventy-five in favor for starting a second church. The new church would be started if that vote passed.

The minister and his little group were all in favor of this proposal, but it was voted down by close to half of the congregation. Then the little group of the minister and his followers demanded a carrying vote of fifty-plus-one. An even greater majority voted this down. It was then that the consistory came with a last proposal of building a completely new church. This was a good plan, but this did not fit in at all with the plans of the minister and his splinter group.

My younger brother was chairman at that congregational meeting, and he was standing on the platform in the front of church like Daniel in the lion's den—all by his lonesome self. I felt really sorry for him.

The fact that his own minister was attacking his own consistory from the floor was more than I could handle, and I was really upset over this unusual action. Common practice is that a consistory member will speak his mind in a closed meeting, but consistory will close ranks when a proposal is brought forward in a congregational meeting. Proposal of consistory was that the carrying vote should be fifty-plus-one—the same as the previous vote on a second church. The minister and his little group were arguing from the floor that an important proposal like that should have 80 percent of the vote or more. It sure was not nice the way they attacked their own consistory.

This was one of those moments that I spoke up in anger and attacked that little group as follows. I was addressing the minister with the words.

"We have been beating around the bush long enough. Consistory has come with proposal after proposal, and you know very well that Home Missions has told us in consistory that it is not right to let 25 percent of the congregation have the deciding vote. We have done it the other way in respect to the vote on a second church. Fifty-plus-one was good enough. Now you turn around and demand eighty or more in that way, giving the final decision to 20 percent of the congregation. Our leaders have come forward time and again with proposals on other matters in the past, and we followed in faith. This happened when we built the first church, also with the addition of the social hall."

"Once again, when we started the Christian school in the same manner, here you come with demands for a vote of eighty-plus in favor in this matter. You are wrong." A spontaneous applause burst loose all through the church, and the vote for building a new church carried with close to 90 percent of the members present. A decision was made to take up pledges in the near future and follow through on these results. It turned out that the support was more than enough to carry on with the building plans.

The pastor was in full opposition in spite of all that, and he left the mother church with a half-dozen families as followers. They split. It was that simple. He left Rocky altogether after a span of about one to one and a half years. The church was built on a loan over the time of twenty years, and that was ten years ago. The building is more than half paid for by now. It has seen much use in a great number of functions. (The question arises) Where we right in our decision to build?

Here are the facts. The pastor did start his little second church according to his own vision, and it never did much better in respect to evangelism than the mother church. Their little group had to attract members out of other churches to see any growth at all. Other members went to other denominations with much the same result. Does that mean that they were a failure? I don't think so. But we would have been better off with their support.

We are facing the same problems all over again at the time that I write this. It is my hope that the charismatic group will show patience as well as the conservative group. A great deal of love and understanding will be required from here on in. I belong to the conservative section but realize full well that we cannot stand still. It is for that reason that I spoke once again in a congregational meeting during the fall of '95. I have warned that it was time to seek unity rather than division. It cannot all come from one side. Both sides will have to show restraint, and it is my feeling that the end result will fall in favor of the charismatic movement. Will it be an improvement? I don't know. Only time will tell.

I do know that the love of many is put to a severe test, and so is our faith life. I hope that the Lord will give us the ability and the love to keep building His church.

This then was the story of the new church building of the CRC in Rocky. I was privileged to lay some more bricks for the road sign at the side of number eleven. It is there where I met the new minister for the first time. I noticed in that first meeting that he had his mind made up in what direction he would move this church in spite of any opposition. He has followed through on this without any second thoughts. I wish him well, but I am afraid that he has been a pastor for a small group of like-minded people only. The rest was ignored and left like sheep in the wilderness. Too bad!

Moses thought that he had trouble when he walked through the desert with half a million Jews. He should have been there with half a million Dutchmen. Then he would have known what trouble was! I do not envy the pastor in his position.

It was our privilege that we could participate in another project not all that much later. The Christian school built a so-called schoolhouse with volunteer labor a year before last. I did some brickwork on that project also. Brother Gerrit was helping with the labor on that project, and we did our share in that respect once again. It would be nice if I could carry on for a few years longer in the same direction. I have also done a few projects with the understanding that a donation should be made in behalf of the Christian school. It is in that way that I might have been of some help in the struggle for Christian education. It was just a small thing, and many young women have put in a lot more time at Christian school, and we can never be thankful enough for that. It is through the sacrifice and faithfulness of many that this work has been carried on since the year 1970.

It was in the fall of 1986 that I had a most remarkable reunion. I was building a chimney for a member of our church at that time when the high school principal of the public high school came driving into the yard of the place where I was working. He called me down the ladder and asked me if I had done any underground work during the war. He would be interested in my experiences. I told him truthfully enough that I had never been in the underground movement.

"Did you drive a milk wagon during the war?" he asked me.

I did that all right.

"And did you help an Allied flyer at some point in time?" he asked.

This was true enough. I had helped a flyer in the fall of 1943, but that was so long ago that I had almost forgotten that affair. Nobody would have believed my story any way. Why bother with it after all those years?

It turned out that this principal was there on behalf of Bob Kellow. This was the Australian airman who had slept with me in the chicken coop way back in the hinterlands of Haarle, Holland. Bob had been back in Holland three or four times. He had been trying to discover the route of his escape in those eventful years. Information had been requested in the newspapers but with no results. It was at the last moment of his third visit that, just before he entered the plane in 1986, a person came walking through the border guards and told him that a farm family had assisted him in Haarle. The person who taught him the key words "Enkele reis Tilburg" was living in Canada, right in Rocky Mountain House—the same place as his old buddy Fred Sutherland.

Bob had been looking high and low all over Holland for this particular person, and he was right under his nose in Canada all the time. This was very interesting for me. It did not take long for me, and I was at the place of Fred to get some more additional information, and sure enough, I was to meet up with the stranger in the night from way back in 1943. His name was Kellow, and he was very interested in an interview with the guy who had taught him a few words in Dutch. He was going to come over from Winnipeg where he was residing with his wife of forty-some years. It was the most amazing coincidence that his airplane buddy had been living in the same town all those years. He never said anything, and neither did I.

Bob was at Fred's place before the week was out, and we had a tremendous reunion.

"Enkele reis Tilburg" was the first thing he was saying when I met him and his wife. "Did I learn my lesson right?"

These were the first words he said when I met him in Fred's place. He had never forgotten the famous words that had set him on his way to freedom at the time of his greatest need. He told us how he remembered the old farmer and his wife who had helped him with milk and honey, in a manner of speaking.

Let me explain that old farmer John and his wife were the first people he contacted in that lonesome journey that had lasted for three days already. Bob had not dared to contact anybody before that time in the fear that he would be turned in to the Germans. He was sincerely thankful for the welcome he received from these old people. He had been trying to relocate them on three previous trips to Holland, but no success, and that was not surprising, since the farm of old farmer John had burned down.

It was a real treat for all of us to relive the escape of danger of those fearful days of German occupation. They told us all about that fateful flight over war-torn Holland and the last moments leading up to the crash of the big Lancaster airplane. Bob was the last man out of that plane and also the last man to speak to the pilot Les Knight who was killed moments after Bob had left the plane. They told us all about the famous Dam Busters who had destroyed the big dams in the end of the Ruhr district—the heartland of the German war effort.

Fred was not all that eager about those memories. He had seen too many people trying to get away from that avalanche of water when the dams burst under the explosions of the skipping bombs. The scenes of the desperate people running away in vain returned back to him again and again in ever-recurring dreams.

Bob did not seem to have these inhibited memories. He was a different person altogether. I asked him whether he was scared on that eventful trip leading up to his escape to England three months after our little tête-à-tête in the underground chicken coop. He explained that he was quite scared until the moment that he made first contact with the farmer and his wife.

"I actually started enjoying the experience after you had helped me with the map reading and the lesson in Dutch!"

He had a big grin on his face and told his captivated audience about his trip along the railroad to Zutphen and buying his ticket to Tilburg, just as I had instructed him in that day so long ago. He walked through the middle of war-torn Holland in an Australian flyer uniform right past some German soldiers in different sections of his escape route all the way to Belgium, where he met up with the underground who helped him on his way for the rest of the journey.

Bob was a flashy kind of a guy, a little overbearing perhaps, but that did not take away the fact that he had done something remarkable, and he had reason to be proud of that fact. He had one of the most interesting escapes of his day with a minimum of danger to the folks who helped him on his way.

Bob and Fred treated us to a dinner at one of the swanky restaurants in Rocky. This was their way of saying thanks for the help they had received in those days long ago. Mom and I had one of the heydays of our lifetime. This was something out of a fairy tale—a dinner party with friends after all those years of forgetfulness. Some good had come out of that war after all!

We had an exchange of letters after Bob went back to Winnipeg. I reminded Bob on one occasion that he must have had an angel on each shoulder as he made his way back to freedom, and I was thankful that he gave all honors to our Heavenly Father in his book *Pathway to Freedom*. This is a well-written book—a book worth reading.

We had plans for a visit in the spring of 1987 to the fair city of Winnipeg, where Bob was going to show us around the city and give us a good time while he was at it. Sorry to say, but it never came to pass. Bob died on the operating table not all that much later. He had an enlarged heart and slipped away in an unexpected moment.

We did see his wife, Pall, in the spring of that year. She was a very nice lady, and she reminded me in many ways of my own wife, the same kindness and patience with their wayward men.

Bob's family gave us a good welcome that time, and we had a chance to visit one of our former ministers while we were in that fair city of Winnipeg.

Pall (Bob's wife) has also passed away since. She had some kidney problems and had to go for new blood once or twice a week. This could not go on indefinitely. She followed her husband not all that much later.

Fred Sutherland is the only surviving member of that Lancaster crew of the late 1943 flight to the Dortmund-Ems Canal in Germany. It is getting lonesome around the old boy, although he is in good health, and his wife is every bit as good as he is. I meet Fred once in a while. We always have some word exchange as we go on in years.

And now this is the end of the story of Big Wild Bob Kellow of Winnipeg. You can read his book *Pathway to Freedom* if you want to know more about this man of many wonders. It is sold at the air plane museum in Winnipeg, Manitoba.

There is one subject that I have avoided in this memoir. That is the passing away of one of my grandchildren, Daren, the youngest son of Swanney and Gerald. It is a little too hard to mention.

All I can say is "The Lord has given and He has taken away. Praised be the name of the Lord."

I do not understand, but I do believe that what He does is always right. I like to leave it at that.

This brings me to the time that I had another close call. It happened on May 10, 1991, when I attended a wedding in the Catholic Church. A friend of Irene's was getting married. I did not want to miss this joyful event, and Mom and I went there in the afternoon. I did not feel all that good but blamed that on a game of golf in the hot sun of that beautiful May morning. I might have a little bit of sunstroke. That's what I thought at that time.

I was lying on the couch without moving for most of the afternoon, while Mom was very angry with me. She figured that I was very antisocial in my behavior, and she did not say a word until I had to go to the bathroom. A lot of blood was mixed in the water that I was passing, so I told Mom that I had blood in my water.

She scoffed that off and said, "You had red beets for dinner yesterday. There is nothing wrong with you!"

She was not giving me the benefit of the doubt. I was not convinced even so and phoned my daughter-in-law Judy. She was not all that sure but told me to phone the hospital at once. It might be something serious.

This is what I did, and that doctor did not fool around at all. He told me to come in at once and hold my water if at all possible— something that was easier said than done.

My son Karl jumped in the car with me, and I gave him the ride of his life. I bypassed everything on the road. This was the one time that I broke all speed limits and drove right through a red stop light. Even my son Karl was a little white around the nose by the time that we arrived at the hospital. The doctor was not impressed with the situation either, and he told me to pass some blood in a bottle down in the washroom— something that was easier said than done.

A heavy blood clot had formed inside of my urine channel, and it took a lot of pain and pressure before the blood exploded all over the bathroom wall. I felt bad enough as it was, and this made it even worse, so I asked for some cleaning material to clean up the mess, but the nurse would not hear about it. She told me to get back inside, and she would look after the bathroom. I had little say in the matter, but I was very ashamed that this woman had to look after the mess I had made out of things.

These girls deserve a medal for the work they are doing. She escorted me back to emergency, and the doctor locked me up for the night right there in the hospital. He even made an appointment with the main hospital in Red Deer before I left that room.

Things did not look good, and I traveled to Red Deer the first thing on that Sunday morning. A person would think that there was no shortage of beds judging by the speed that everything was moving.

I was lying in bed by ten o'clock, and testing began almost immediately. They sent me from one room to the other in the next three days, and I must say that the trip to the operating room for the testing of the bladder and other organs was the most painful. It was there that the doctor referred to me as one of the famous op den Dries clan—the people with hypothermia. Everyone was walking on eggs by the time they finished with me.

I don't think that they put me under heavy sedation, for the procedure was extremely painful—a lot worse than the following test. I had to go through an x-ray machine in the shape of a tunnel, and that was absolutely painless. Several more tests followed, but it was not until the third day that the final test was made.

An older nurse took some kind of sound-sensitive test of my kidneys, and she gave me a funny look when she let me go—something like "poor soul."

Well, the poor soul was informed on the evening of the third day that he had cancer in the left kidney. The doctor and the head nurse came to my bedside and informed me that I had cancer and that the kidney had to come out. The doctor told me that they would inject the cancerous kidney with pure alcohol, and that would kill the kidney. The dead organ would be left in the body for approximately ten days after that. This would set up a reaction of the body against the dead tissue and consequently against all foreign materials, including the cancer. Some people hardly noticed the difference, while others had to suffer a lot. I was in the latter group of patients.

I asked the doctor what my chances would be, and he said that he could not give me much hope still. There is hope where there is life, and he encouraged me to face the ordeal with courage and faith. The strange thing is that I was not all that afraid.

The situation was very serious indeed, but I told the doctor that I was well prepared to meet the future.

"Do whatever you have to do," I told him. "My life is in God's hand. I know where I will be going if it does not work out right."

The head nurse looked at me with some optimism and said, "That is going to make all the difference in the world, if you can believe like that!"

I will never know why I was so calm and collected. They might have given me some tranquilizers beforehand. I don't know. Fact is that my brother Adolf was with me when I received the bad news, and neither one of us went overboard with emotions.

It was at that moment that Karl and Dick walked in the door, and I told them the sad news. I remember that I told them to bring the family together so that we could discuss Mom's future and the rest of my inheritance. These lover boys took it all in stride.

"There is time enough for that!" said one of the boys. "It is not over yet. We will see what happens from here on in."

That was that. I was put in place once again.

Adolf provided the comical note in all that misery. He had brought his video camera and had planned to take some video pictures of the old man in the hospital.

"I might as well forget about the pictures now!" he said. This sounded comical enough but not nearly as comical as the scene that followed. We assured him that this was as good a time as any to try out his new camera. This was corn on his mill.

Adolf was all business from that point on. He started demonstrating his progress with his brand-new toy, but something went wrong, and he pushed the wrong button. The whole camera folded open like a cauliflower in full bloom. It was the last thing that he had expected, and his face fell down to the top button of his coat. This looked so comical that we all burst out laughing in spite of the pain that was gnawing in the pit of my stomach.

It is no picnic when you walk around with the knowledge of a cancerous kidney. You can rest assured of that.

The injection followed within hours of the announcement, and I turned into a very sick boy. Much of the following days have gone out of my memory forever, but some things remain.

I had a very difficult neighbor on the one side of me. This man had been run over by a couple of his heifers. His whole lower back was damaged, and he did a lot of complaining, although he took a breather when he heard that I was in worse shape than he was.

I remember one night that I had an awful lot of pain, and he blamed it on the chicken that I had been eating that evening. Several other people in neighboring wards had the same symptoms after they had eaten of the chicken. It might be true. Maybe.

I had a number of very nice nurses. One was married to a relation of my brother. She went out of her way to make life bearable for me. I asked her for the window-side bed after the noisy neighbor was discharged and went home. I lived to regret that move.

The air conditioning was blowing full tilt over that new location, and I nearly froze to death right there in my own bed, and this cold stream of air chilled me to the marrow of my bones. This young nurse noticed that I was in trouble and wrapped me in some heated blankets right out of some kind of heater. It was like heaven on earth. I would never forget that girl for that reason alone.

I do remember one occasion in the middle of the night that two of the nurses were trying to measure the water level in my bladder. This had to be done by the means of an instrument that was inserted through the urinal channel.

Sad to say, but the two girls did not have much luck in that experiment. They just could not get through the narrow passageway of my fever-wracked body. The pain was beyond belief, and the girls were running out of patience and out of ideas, and so a male nurse was brought in as a last resort. He forced the instrument through, but do not ask me how.

It was on that occasion the one of the nurses said, "You must have a great will to live."

"No," I replied. "I believe!"

It was as simple as that.

The surgery followed not all that much later, and they almost lost me on the operation table once again.

The anesthesiologist visited me a day later and told me that they had been plenty worried. They had cooled me down once again with an ice bed and fans blowing away the overheated fever-ridden parts of my body, while old Henry was out cold and he does not remember all that much about that period.

I do remember the presence of an unbelievable power, "a full and peaceful force all around me." It was bigger than the entire world and so peaceful that nothing seemed to matter anymore.

I had some visitors at that time, but I was only interested in my brother Bert. I wanted to tell him about this beautiful feeling, but the others would not leave us alone. I am afraid that my behavior was not all that Christian at that particular moment. The effect of the morphine or other medicine must have dulled my sense of proportions once again. I do know that I hurt some people's feelings at that moment in time.

My brother Bert had the same experience when he was recovering from surgery. A person cannot be held accountable for his reactions in times like that.

It was with thanks in my heart that I left the hospital not that many days later. The Lord has given me a little more time with my wife and family, time of great thankfulness and enjoyment. I love my wife and family more than ever.

There is one thing that is hard to understand. You would think that a person would improve in his Christian lifestyle after so many close encounters with death. This does not seem to be the case. The same temptations and the same sins are following a person, day after day, as you carry on to the end of the road.

The love for my wife has grown ever deeper. We seem to become closer by the day. Pain and sorrow will do that to two people who have traveled together on life's pathway for almost forty-five years. It is absolutely uncanny the way Mom feels my moods and my needs after all these years. She will wake up in the dead of night and follow every movement I make. I think that she would wake up if a fly turned around on the wall, and that is a fact of life that is sometimes worrisome. It is real hard to be in control of all the livestock in our bedroom all day and all night, but it becomes real bad. But when Mom takes on the flies as well, nobody can keep track of all that.

I have redirected some kind of an earth stream or earth force. There is some kind of bad earth ray that seems to travel under her side of the bed. I can detect that with my dousing rod, and it is possible to move that ray over sideways. I realize that this sounds unbelievable, but it is true nevertheless. The human body seems to have possibilities of unknown dimensions. The physical abilities of humans are vastly underrated and not at all in conflict with our faith life—not in all cases. It is well to keep in mind that this is an area that deserves the greatest caution in all respects.

I have doused this ray in our waterbed on more than one occasion, but it always seems to come back. Mom has that head-splitting headaches at times. She has told me that it felt as if great balls of fire exploded inside of her head. It was last week that I used the divining rod more or less casually. A heavy ray was flowing right through her side of the bed. I moved this ray over and put a copper rod beside the place where it was flowing through the bed. All this was done without telling her about the precautions that I had taken. It was just by coincidence that she mentioned the fact that she had been without headaches ever since that day.

HANK OPDENDRIES

This seems like proof positive that there is something more to this than meets the eye. Like I said before, "It will not hurt and it might help." It is proof enough for me, and I will not hesitate to use this ability if it can be of service to anyone in need.

It was during the fall of 1991, after the cancer treatment, that Mom and I were blessed with the celebration of our fortieth anniversary—a great day for us if you take into consideration all the troubles and setbacks in forty years of marriage.

I will not deny that I became more and more nervous as the day of the celebration approached. My kids have done some crazy things in the past, and I was very apprehensive about the near future as the date of celebration approached. The girls had set up jar for a video camera fund on behalf of the old man—who was me. They also held a garage sale to help with the cost of the party that was sure to follow. And some party it turned out to be!

The whole op den Dries clan came out for the celebration—an open house in the afternoon and a banquet in the evening, and our children really made us proud. All things were done in good taste, and it turned out to be the best party in memory.

The grandchildren took a few swipes at old Opa and Oma. A few remarks that hit below the belt, but everything was done in style.

The brothers did equally well in that department. I got a few reminders of Mother and my shortcomings, and that set us right where we belonged—right at the bottom of the totem pole!

They played a bit of golf right on the stage, and brother Bert hit the golf ball so hard that it broke a few coffee cups. It was fortunate that he did not hit anything else. It could have proven to be costly, but we got past the brothers without too much damage to our alter ego. We have to be thankful for small blessings, right or not?

The performance of our children was the crowning moment of the evening. They had cut holes in some four-by-eight plywood and were standing in those holes from the knees up. Then they had tied some shoes to the kneecaps so that it looked as if they had no legs at all. Every last one had a mask in front of his or her face. Ugly faces and old faces. Long faces and short faces. Long teeth or no teeth at all. Some with beards and some without, all this followed a script of unbelievable imagination. All my brothers were remembered in mimicry of hilarious content. It was the funniest party that I ever attended. And all this was done in honor of Mother and me.

The boys said later on that they had thought that most of the material would have to come out of my life, but the surprising part was the role that Mom had played in our lives. She was a lot funnier than I was. I have always known that but did not bother to tell anyone. The best things in life are for free, so is Mom's humor, but we always kept that in the family.

The total dependence of our life on our Heavenly Father was absolutely not forgotten. This was the center of the whole celebration. Humor and solemn remembering are perfectly in harmony with each other if it is done in the right spirit—something that was really in evidence during the whole evening. We owe it all to our Father in Heaven, and we are well aware of that.

It was along those guidelines that we could sing joyful songs and close with the words, "I surrender all to Jesus. I surrender all."

It was a beautiful end to a beautiful day. It cost a little money, but what are friends for if you can't treat them to a celebration to have them share in our happiness as well as in our sorrow? I am a strong believer in this.

We are less than a year away from our forty-fifth anniversary at the time that I write this. Much more has happened, of course. I have turned over the better part of my farm to the children. We are living a good life, Mom and I, and I don't know how long it will be yet, but Mom and I have never been happier in our lives. Our greatest desire is that all our children and grandchildren and our great-grandchildren may follow Jesus.

Our life is not worth living if we do not follow the Lord. To know Him is to know riches beyond measure.

Mom and I hope and pray that all our children will follow that way—that is the only way to perfect happiness.

Rocky Mountain House

February 20, 1996

With all our love, Mom and Dad

It is too bad that Mom did not have more input in this story. It would have been altogether different and more interesting. But who knows? She might surprise us all yet. It would not be the first time!

ABOUT THE AUTHOR

CURRENTLY, HANK OP den Dries, at ninety years of age, continues to live at home on their farm with his wife of sixty-three years and the support of loving family. These memoirs have been written to capture the lives and faith of ordinary people who faced generations of change, turmoil, and suffering, and ever strengthening in peace, hope, and love.

Our writer with little education as a child in Holland has spent his lifetime continuing to gain knowledge, education, spiritual growth, and various skills in order to support his family. Hank is an accomplished bricklayer, auto body mechanic, dairy farmer, painter, and most of all husband and father.

His journey will take you from their homeland in Holland in a time of horse and buggy or bicycles to a world ravaged by World War II, bombs, and devastating losses. Canadian immigration with his parents and nine siblings saw Hank working in the sugar beets in Southern Alberta, along with many other immigrants, and finally settling in Central Alberta. These ordinary people took everything they had experienced and suffered, and put their hearts, faith, and hope into developing a foundation for homes, schools, and churches. Hank has injected some personal opinion on the different impacts and impressions from his lifetime. While doing so only proves his passion for creating a record of the ordinary immigrant as seen through one man's eyes and walking step forward at a time. No two footprints will ever leave the same impression, however; each man's footprint has its own story to tell in our journey of life.

HANK OPDENDRIES